The Principle of Integration in International Watercourse Cooperation Regimes

Legal Aspects of Sustainable Development

Series Editor

David Freestone

This series publishes work on all aspects of the international legal dimensions of the concept of sustainable development. Its aim is to publish important works of scholarship on a range of relevant issues including conservation of natural resources, climate change, biodiversity loss and the role of international agreements, international organizations and state practice.

VOLUME 29

The titles published in this series are listed at *brill.com/lasd*

The Principle of Integration in International Watercourse Cooperation Regimes

By

Pol Pallàs Secall

BRILL | NIJHOFF

LEIDEN | BOSTON

The Library of Congress Cataloging-in-Publication Data is available online at https://catalog.loc.gov
LC record available at https://lccn.loc.gov/2025936348

Typeface for the Latin, Greek, and Cyrillic scripts: "Brill". See and download: brill.com/brill-typeface.

ISSN 1875-0923
ISBN 978-90-04-73674-0 (hardback)
ISBN 978-90-04-73675-7 (e-book)
DOI 10.1163/9789004736757

This book is printed on acid-free paper and produced in a sustainable manner.

To Laura and Rita

Contents

PART 2
Mechanisms for the Legal Integration of the Economic, Social and Environmental Dimensions in International Watercourse Regimes

PART 3
Mechanisms of Institutional Integration of the Economic, Social and Environmental Dimensions in International Watercourses Regimes

Series Editor's Preface

I am pleased to include this work by Dr Pol Pallàs Secall as the twenty-ninth volume in the Brill/Nijhoff series on *Legal Aspects of Sustainable Development* published under my general editorship. The aim of this series is to publish works at the cutting edge of legal scholarship that address both the practical and the theoretical aspects of this important concept.

This work fits well into the general aims of the series as the concept of sustainable development has been categorized as resting on a "three-legged stool" with economic, social and environmental "legs". This volume, which started life as a doctoral dissertation at the University of Barcelona, examines the principle of the integration of the economic, social and environmental dimensions of sustainable development, within the field of international watercourses law.

First, it addresses the content and limits of the international obligation to integrate these economic, social and environmental dimensions. Then, to examine this in a novel way, it addresses international watercourse law as an area where the practice of integration can be studied in detail. International watercourse regulation is particularly susceptible to international regulatory conflicts involving economic, social and environmental interests. It presents itself, therefore, as a fruitful area for discussing the legal recognition, and application, of the principle of integration.

A particularly innovative and interesting aspect of the study is its examination of the application of the principle of integration in several international watercourse cooperation regimes. The case studies include nine international basins from different regions of the world that have highly developed cooperation regimes: the Danube River, the Dniester River, the International Joint Commission between Canada and the United States of America, the Lake Chad, the Mekong River, the Niger Basin, the Sava River, the Senegal River and the Volta River.

The conclusions drawn by the book will be of interest to scholars and practitioners from any area of international environmental law. The principle of integration is a norm of general application, so scholars in other specializations, such as biodiversity, climate change or renewable energy, will, I am sure, find it of great interest.

David Freestone
Washington DC

Acknowledgements

This book is a revised, abridged and updated version of my doctoral thesis, submitted in October 2023 and defended in December of the same year at the Faculty of Law of the University of Barcelona.

Writing this book would not have been possible without the dedication and guidance of my thesis supervisor, Mar Campins, who led me through the long process of writing a thesis and who made it a formidable learning experience. Thank you for being an example of academic rigour, of passion for environmental law and of commitment to the university.

During this adventure, I met researchers from various universities and institutions who in different ways contributed significantly to this book. The following are but a few of the most relevant individuals: Laura Movilla, Seline Trevisanut, Mara Tignino, Ángel Rodrigo, Francesco Sindico, Teresa Fajardo, Laurence Boisson de Chazournes, Komlan Sangbana and Lucia De Strasser. Thank you for your suggestions and your constructive criticism.

I would also like to thank all my colleagues in the Department of Public International Law and International Relations at the University of Barcelona who in one way or another have advised, guided or encouraged me at some point in the process: Xavier Pons, Andreu Olesti, Jordi Bonet, Laura Huici, Xavier Fernández, Rosana Alija, Ana Sánchez, Laura Salzano, Max Astorga, Marta Abegón, Elisenda Calvet, Marcia Rodrigues, Violeta Moreno-Lax, Gastón Medici, Anna Badia, Laura Planas and David Bondia.

Finally, I would like to thank my friends and family for their understanding, as I have been more absent than I would have liked to be in recent times. Above all, my heartfelt thanks go to Laura, who undertook her own doctorate at the same time as me, for your patience, support and understanding.

Acronyms

EIA	Environmental Impact Assessment
EPI	Environmental Policy Integration
EU	European Union
FAO	Food and Agriculture Organization
GEF	Global Environment Facility
GWP	Global Water Partnership
ICPDR	International Commission for the Protection of the Danube River
IEM	Integrated Environmental Management
US-Ca IJC	International Joint Commission between the United States of America and Canada
ILA	International Law Association
ILC	International Law Commission
INBO	International Network of Basin Organisations
IRBO	International River Basin Organisation
ISRBC	International Sava River Basin Commission
IWRM	Integrated Water Resources Management
LCBC	Lake Chad Basin Commission
MDGS	Millennium Development Goals
MRC	Mekong River Commission
NBA	Niger Basin Authority
NGO	Non-Governmental Organisation
OECD	Organisation for Economic Co-operation and Development
OMVS	Organisation pour la mise en valeur du fleuve Sénégal
OSCE	Organization for Security and Co-operation in Europe
PCSD	Policy coherence for sustainable development
SDGS	Sustainable Development Goals
SEA	Strategic Environmental Assessment
TFEU	Treaty on the Functioning of the European Union
UN	United Nations
UNEP	United Nations Environment Programme
UNGA	United Nations General Assembly
VBA	Volta Basin Authority
WEF nexus approach	water-energy-food nexus approach
WMO	World Meteorological Organisation
WTO	World Trade Organisation

General Introduction

1 The Challenge of Integration to Achieve Sustainable Development in International Law

Sustainable development has been a key concept for the international community since it was implicitly built into the narrative of the United Nations Declaration on the Human Environment, convened at the Stockholm Conference in 1972. Since then, it has served to structure important elements of international law. More than 40 years later, the United Nations (hereinafter, UN) summit for the adoption of the post-2015 development agenda[1] placed sustainable development at the heart of international policy, putting special emphasis on its essentially cross-cutting nature, to the extent that it is configured as a network of interconnected objectives that encompass the economic, social and environmental dimensions. The transversal nature of sustainable development demands mechanisms to channel interaction between the various sectors that make up these three dimensions in order to ensure that no one is prioritised over the other two.

In this context, international law has the potential to play a central role in the achievement of sustainable development and in addressing the challenges of integration that it poses. However, it should be noted that, at the same time, international law is undergoing a process of material and institutional specialisation, which the former president of the International Court of Justice's (hereinafter ICJ), Gilbert Guillaume,[2] identified with a phenomenon of legal fragmentation in 2001. The effective pursuit of sustainable development through international law is therefore confronted with the issue of fragmentation, in which the different areas to be harmonised are regulated by legal regimes that respond to different and often opposing State interests.[3]

1 United Nations summit for the adoption of the post-2015 development agenda, *Transforming our world: the 2030 Agenda for Sustainable Development*, A/RES/70/1 (21 October 2015), undocs.org/en/A/RES/70/1.

2 Judge Gilbert Guillaume, President of the International Court of Justice, *Speech to the General Assembly of the United Nations*, October 30, 2001, http://www.icj-cij.org/files/press-releases/5/2995.pdf.

3 Ellis, Jaye. 2010. "Sustainable Development and Fragmentation in International Society." In *Global Justice and Sustainable Development*, edited by Duncan French, 57–74. Leiden: Martinus Nijhoff Publishers. 59–60.

 | DOI:10.1163/9789004736757_002

While sustainable development is a broad objective that expresses an idea of intergenerational justice,[4] on a more practical level, it also implies the creation of linkages between sectors and regimes through concrete measures and instruments.[5] In this sense, it is not surprising that one of the widely accepted principles on which sustainable development is based is the principle of integration of the economic, social and environmental dimensions (hereinafter, 'principle of integration' and 'principle of integration of the economic, social and environmental dimensions' will be used interchangeably), understood as the international obligation to consider these three dimensions with the aim of making development-related activities sustainable. While this is usually deemed to be one of the most specific principles of international law for achieving sustainable development, it is often conflated with the notion of sustainable development itself.[6]

The challenge of integration posed by sustainable development is so manifest that enormous efforts have been made by the international community and other actors involved in sustainable development to design mechanisms through which it can be successfully achieved. Many of the instruments and measures put into practice by States specifically address the integration of economic, social and environmental dimensions. The sheer number of these instruments reflects a great dynamism in the practical materialisation of the principle of integration, although it also reveals the extent to which its boundaries are blurred. Therefore, this book reflects the desire to clarify the legal dimension of the practical implementation of sustainable development: the principle of integration of the economic, social and environmental dimensions.

The principle of integration is poorly conceptualised compared to its theoretical relevance and the magnitude of its practice. There is relatively little legal scientific literature on the subject, and, among those authors who have analysed it in greater depth, most have focused on its specific application in the context of European Union (hereinafter, EU) law.[7] It goes without saying

---

4 On this aspect of sustainable development see Weiss, Edith Brown. 1999. *Un Mundo Justo Para Las Futuras Generaciones: Derecho Internacional, Patrimonio Común y Equidad Intergeneracional*. Madrid: Mundi-Prensa.

5 Voigt, Christina. 2009. *Sustainable Development as a Principle of International Law*. Leiden: Martinus Nijhoff. 36.

6 See, for instance, Djeffal, Christian. 2011. "The Iron Rhine Case – A Treaty's Journey from Peace to Sustainable Development." *Heidelberg Journal of International Law* 71 (3): 569–86.

7 See, for instance, Dhondt, Nele. 2003. *Integration of Environmental Protection into Other EC Policies. Legal Theory and Practice*. Groningen: Europa Law Publishing; or Nollkaemper, André. 2002. "Three Conceptions of the Integration Principle in International Environmental Law." In *Environmental Policy Integration: Greening Sectoral Policies in Europe*, edited by A. Lenschow, 22–32. London: Earthscan.

that some studies have produced important conceptualisations of the principle in the framework of international law;[8] most notably, work in this area was conducted by the International Law on Sustainable Development Committee of the International Law Association (hereinafter, ILA) in 2006,[9] where it set out the main dimensions of the principle of integration. Although there seems to be a broad consensus in the legal doctrine on its paramount importance as a key element of sustainable development, analyses continue to focus primarily on its theoretical conceptualisation. As such, the relationship between the recognition of specific obligations deriving from the principle and its concrete application remains largely undetermined. While this may be due to the lack of a binding international legal instrument that establishes a clear definition and scope,[10] it might also reflect the technical difficulty that its application entails because of uncertainties deriving from the fragmentation of international law in the specific area under study.

On the one hand, international law provides a set of legal techniques for resolving situations of conflict between incompatible rules. A first glance reveals that some of these legal resources share important features with the tools that State practice, the doctrine and international case law have identified in order to apply the principle of integration in achieving sustainable development. On the other hand, it is possible to explore other instruments of an institutional nature, which States use with the same aim of addressing integration as a requirement for achieving sustainable development.[11]

However, these mechanisms, especially those of an institutional nature, have not yet been systematically analysed, nor have they been exhaustively

---

8 See in particular: Rodrigo Hernández, Ángel J. 2012. "El Principio de Integración de Los Aspectos Económicos, Sociales y Medioambientales Del Desarrollo Sostenible." *Revista Española de Derecho Internacional* 64 (2): 133–61; and Barral, Virginie, and Pierre-Marie Dupuy. 2016. "Principle 4: Sustainable Development through Integration." In *The Rio Declaration on Environment and Development: A Commentary*, edited by Jorge E. Viñuales, 157–79. Oxford: OUP.

9 ILA. Committee on International Law on Sustainable Development. 2006. "Report of the Toronto Conference." https://www.ila-hq.org/en_GB/documents/conference-report-toronto-2006-14.

10 It has been proposed, for instance, that a treaty on integration could provide the means for an integrated application of treaties. See Doelle, Meinhard. 2009. "Integration among Global Environmental Regimes: Lessons Learned from the Climate Change Mitigation." In *The Future of Ocean Regime-Buidling : Essays in Tribute to Douglas M. Johnston*, edited by Aldo Chircop, Ted McDorman, and Susan Rolston, 63–85. Leiden: Koninklijke Brill NV. 84–85.

11 Broude, Tomer. 2008. "Principles of Normative Integration and the Allocation of International Authority: The WTO, the Vienna Convention on the Law of Treaties, and the Rio Declaration." *Loyola University Chicago International Law Review* 6 (1): 173–207.

systematised. This is due in part to the large number of practices identified for the application of the principle of integration, but also to their diversity, which varies according to the legal sphere in which they are applied. It is therefore necessary to delimit the object of study to a specific area of international law. This is why this study focuses on the application of the principle of integration in the field of international watercourse law, an emerging international legal regime and a field of study of unquestionable and growing interest.

2 Integration in the Context of the Cooperation on International Watercourses: Object, Scope and Structure of the Book

In general terms, this book is situated in the debate on the application of the principle of integration in accordance with international law. It takes two key decisions regarding its scope. First, it does not address the issue of international responsibility for violation of the principle of integration as it focuses on its legal nature and content and its application. Second, the book focuses its analysis on the domain of international watercourse law. While the principle of integration is potentially applicable to many legal areas precisely because of the cross-cutting nature of sustainable development, the area of international watercourses is particularly susceptible to international regulatory conflicts involving economic, social and environmental interests for three reasons.

First, international watercourse law is a cross-cutting area of international law that cannot be generally identified with the protection of individual interests that is implicit in one of the dimensions of sustainable development. While legal areas such as international trade law, environmental protection or human rights could be easily classified in either the economic, the environmental or the social dimension, international watercourse law is at the crossroads of these interests. From one side, the interrelation of ecosystems and watercourses implies a close dependency of environmental protection on international watercourse law, which is translated into legal linkages between the international regimes regulating these issues. From other side, the dependent relationship between international watercourses and the life, health and wellbeing of the populations that live close to them put legal developmental interests at the core of international watercourse law.

Second, the relationships described above are particularly prone to conflict due to the scarcity of freshwater.[12] Only 2.5% of the world's water is

12 See in this regard some regional tendencies to withdraw a growing amount of fresh water as a proportion of total available freshwater resources: UN Secretary-General, *Progress*

freshwater, of which 0.4% is surface and atmospheric freshwater.[13] Despite their scarcity, these resources are not only necessary for a wide variety of uses but also vital and non-replaceable for human life and the provision of essential ecosystem services, as well as economic demands. In many international watercourses, the intensive use of water resources leads to competition between different uses which may sometimes be incompatible, thus increasing the risk of regulatory conflicts that can be framed in terms of sustainable development. Climate change and population growth can only add to the stress on freshwater resources.[14]

Third, the centrality of international watercourse law to the object of study of this book is clear in the case law of the ICJ[15] and in international arbitration,[16] which have clearly incorporated the concepts of sustainable development and, in particular, the integration of the economic, social and environmental dimensions into their rulings on international watercourses. It is safe to affirm that no other area of international law has served for so long and so intensively as the framework for managing the opposing interests in sustainable development as international watercourse law.

Therefore, since the law of international watercourses is such a fruitful legal area for discussing the recognition and application of the principle of integration, its analysis can provide valuable insight into the development of the principle and form the basis of conclusions on its role in international law relating to sustainable development.

The main research question that this book aims to answer is the following: *How the principle of integration is applied in current and potential practice in international watercourse cooperation frameworks?* The hypothesis is that general international law, as well as international watercourse law, incorporates the objective of sustainable development through the application of the

towards the Sustainable Development Goals Report, A/78/80-E/2023/64 (27 April 2023), undocs.org/en/E/2023/64. 95.

13 UNEP. 2007. *Global Environment Outlook 4 – GEO-4: environment for development*. Valleta: UNEP.

14 For an in-depth analysis of the global situation of the water crisis see Global Commission on the Economics of Water. 2023. *The What, Why and How of the World Water Crisis: Global Commission on the Economics of Water. Phase 1 Review and Findings*. Paris: OECD Environment Directorate.

15 See, in particular, Gabčikovo-Nagymaros Project (Hungary/Slovakia), Judgment, 1997 I.C.J. Rep. 7 (September 25); Pulp Mills on the River Uruguay (Argentina v. Uruguay), 2010 Judgment, I.C.J. Rep. 14 (April 20); Dispute over the status and use of the waters of the Silala (Chile v. Bolivia), Judgement, 2022 I.C.J. Rep. 614 (December 1).

16 See, in particular, Indus Waters Kishenganga Arbitration (Pakistan vs. India). Final award, 31 R.I.A.A (Perm. Ct. Arb. 2013).

principle of integration of the economic, social and environmental dimensions and that this, in turn, entails the implementation of specific legal and institutional integration mechanisms.

From this starting point, we can identify a set of questions that must be answered: A) What is the legal nature of the principle of integration? B) How does international watercourse law incorporate and apply the principle of integration? C) What mechanisms do States or international organisations adopt for the effective integration of the economic, social and environmental dimensions in the governance of international watercourses?

In order to make the analysis of international watercourse regimes more comparable, the research was limited to international watercourses that are totally or partially superficial and therefore excluded transboundary aquifers not connected to a surface watercourse. This is deemed necessary because, despite the growing importance of these water resources for human life, transboundary aquifers that do not form part of a surface watercourse are subject to a much more limited international regulation.

In addition, given that the research question addresses the recognition, incorporation and application of the principle of integration in international watercourse law, the regional systems that operate with significant autonomy from international law are also omitted from the book. This is particularly the case of EU law because it cannot be considered, in a strict sense, representative of the current state of the principle of integration in international watercourse law. EU law is a highly complex and comprehensive regime in which the principle of integration is enshrined in Article 11 of the Treaty on the Functioning of the European Union[17] (hereinafter, TFEU) and has developed in a specific manner according to the legal system of which it forms part.[18] Moreover, whether or not they cross national boundaries, watercourses located entirely in EU territory are regulated by Directive 2000/60/EC of the European Parliament and of the Council of 23 October 2000 establishing a framework for Community action in the field of water policy[19] (hereinafter, EU Water Framework Directive), which establishes a sophisticated regime for the governance of the EU's watercourses.[20]

17 Consolidated Version of the Treaty on the Functioning of the European Union, May 9, 2008, 2008 O.J. (C 115) 47.

18 On the development and application of the principle of Integration the framework of EU law see Dhondt, Nele. 2003. *Integration of Environmental Protection into Other EC Policies. Legal Theory and Practice*. Groningen: Europa Law Publishing.

19 Directive 2000/60/EC of the European Parliament and of the Council of 23 October 2000 establishing a framework for Community action in the field of water policy, 2000 O.J. (L 327) 1, 73. Article 11.

20 In relation to this directive see, for instance, Reichert, Götz. 2016. *Transboundary Water Cooperation in Europe. A Successful Multidimensional Regime?* Leiden: Brill.

The book is organised in three parts and 13 chapters. Part I focuses on international watercourse law to examine how the principle of integration fits into this legal sphere. This is done by determining firstly to what extent the principle of integration must govern cooperation on international watercourses and secondly whether the legal framework provided by international watercourse law is broad enough to allow the principle of integration to be applied.

As a preliminary step, however, Chapter 1 examines the emergence of the principle of integration and its legal configuration in international law. The chapter ends by examining the specific normative obligations arising from the principle of integration, which allows a preliminary outline to be drawn of the two dimensions of the principle of integration: *legal integration* and *institutional integration*, respectively. The practical application of each is further examined in Parts II and III of the book. Chapter 2 analyses how international watercourses and sustainable development as legal and political frameworks have been interpellated as they have evolved, and to what extent the law of international watercourses provides an appropriate cooperation framework for the application of the principle of integration.

Chapters 3 and 4 focus on the relationship between the principle of integration and the obligations laid down in international watercourse law. Specifically, Chapter 3 examines the relationship between the substantive obligations of equitable and reasonable use, the principle of not causing harm, and the principle of protection of the international watercourse; in other words, as an expression of the principle of integration as internal integration. Chapter 4 analyses the relationship between these substantive principles and with the procedural obligations between the riparian States, which can be seen as an expression of the principle of integration as an external integration.

Parts II and III focus on analysing the cooperation regimes of a set of international watercourses. Part II explores how legal integration is operationalised in the cooperation frameworks of these international watercourses. Chapter 5 analyses the legal integration techniques used by the States in the elaboration of water agreements. Chapter 6 looks at a different issue, the recognition of the principle of integration through the indirect application of other international agreements, even if it is not an explicit objective of the norm in question. Chapter 7 examines the incorporation of the principle of integration through norms that promote the consideration of sustainable development values in the application of international basin agreements. Finally, Chapter 8 focuses on the legal integration techniques used in the interpretation of these agreements by international jurisdictional bodies.

Part III addresses the issue of institutional integration. Taking up the theoretical definition of institutional integration given in Chapter 9, it analyses the practices and instruments that IRBOs undertake to operationalise this form of integration. To achieve a more precise analysis, a distinction is made between the practices and instruments of institutional integration and the different levels of action, building on the study of institutional integration from the general to the specific. Therefore, Chapter 10 focuses on the level of international basin policy. Chapter 11 analyses institutional integration at the level of international watercourse management. Finally, Chapter 12 analyses the practices and instruments applied in the planning of specific projects to ensure institutional integration.

The book ends with a chapter devoted to conclusions and final reflections.

3 Case Studies

The cooperation regimes on international watercourses detailed below are the main focus of the book. Nevertheless, it also examines certain aspects of other international watercourse cooperation regimes at various points, such as the Amazon River,[21] the Rhine,[22] the La Plata River,[23] the Pilcomayo River,[24] the Zambezi River[25] or the Okavango River.[26]

21 Peru, Bolívia, Ecuador, Colombia, Guyana, Suriname and Venezuela signed in 1978 the Treaty for Amazonian Cooperation (Treaty for Amazonian Cooperation, July 3, 1978, ECOLEX TRE-000515). In 1998, the Organización del Tratado de Cooperación Amazónica was established for its implementation, although it was not actually created until 2003, with a permanent Secretariat in Brasilia, Brazil.

22 In 1950, Germany, France, Luxemburg, the Netherlands and Switzerland created the International Commission for the Protection of the Rhine (ICPR), which was not given a Status until 1963 with the Convention on the international Commission for the Protection of the Rhine against Pollution. In 1999 the Convention on the Protection of the Rhine (Convention on the Protection of the Rhine, April 12, 1999, 289 O.J. 31.) was adopted. In 1974 the European Economic Community had become a Party of the ICPR and in 2001, following the recent adoption in 2000 of the EU Water Framework Directive, Switzerland as non-EU Member State agreed to support the catchment-wide coordination of the EU Member States in the ICPR on the basis of national laws.

23 El Tratado de la Cuenca del Plata [Treaty on the Rio de la Plata Basin], April 23, 1969, ECOLEX TRE-001020.

24 Shared by Argentina, Bolivia and Paraguay, the Pilcomayo River pertains to the La Plata system and its basin extends through 290.000 km2. The Comisión Trinacional para el Desarrollo de la Cuenca del Río Pilcomayo was established in 1995 (Acuerdo Constitutivo de la Comisión Trinacional para el Desarrollo de la Cuenca del Rio Pilcomayo [Agreement constituting the National Commission for the Development of the Riverbed Rio Pilcomayo], February 9, 1995, ECOLEX TRE-001235).

25 The international cooperation regime on the Zambezi River is established by the Agreement on the establishment of the Zambezi Watercourse Commission (Agreement on the establishment of the Zambezi Watercourse Commission, July 13, 2004, 3369 U.N.T.S.) and the SADC Protocol on Shared Watercourses (Revised Protocol on Shared Watercourses in the Southern African Development Community (SADC), August 7, 2000, 3370 U.N.T.S.).

26 In 1994, with the signature of the OKACOM Agreement (Agreement between the Governments of Angola, the Republic of Botswana and the Republic of Namibia on the

Danube River: Covering a total area of 801,463 km^2, the Danube basin extends through the territory of 19 countries, 14 of which (Germany, Austria, Czech Republic, Slovakia, Hungary, Slovenia, Croatia, Bosnia and Herzegovina, Serbia, Montenegro, Romania, Bulgaria, Moldova, Ukraine) signed the Convention on Cooperation for the Protection and Sustainable use of the Danube River[27] (hereinafter, Danube River Protection Convention) in 1994. The Convention arose from the need to regulate the uses of water and groundwater and to prevent hazards deriving from pollution and accidents. A large amount of treated water is spilled along the length of the river, ending in the Black Sea where it must be controlled. In 1998, the International Commission for the Protection of the Danube River (hereinafter, ICPDR) was created for the implementation of this treaty. It provides the framework for cooperation on conservation and the rational use of the Danube water resources, the application of preventive measures against floods, and measures to reduce pollution. Since 2000, the Convention has also governed the application of the transboundary dimension of the EU Water Framework Directive.[28] The ICPDR acts in parallel to the older Danube Commission, which was established in 1948 by the Convention regarding the regime of navigation on the Danube,[29] with the sole aim of enabling and developing free navigation along the river for commercial vessels.

Dniester River: The basin of the Dniester River extends mostly through Ukraine and Moldova. The total length of the river is 1,362 km, with a stretch of 220 km marking the border between the two countries. The regional economy includes heavily polluting industries, mainly located in the upper part of the basin, where around 70% of the water flowing through the river is collected. The water resources of the Dniester are also used for irrigation, municipal water supply and fisheries, while the riverbed alluvium is used for construction. The basin faces serious environmental threats deriving from pollution, biodiversity loss and climate change. In 1994, the Agreement between the Government of the Republic of Moldova and the Government of Ukraine on the Joint Use and Protection of Border Waters[30] was signed, which was to be

establishment of a Permanent Okavango River Basin Water Commission (OKACOM), September 15, 1995, LEX-FAOC017435) the Permanent Okavango River Basin Water Commission was created. However, the cooperation under this regime was stalled due to the Angolan civil war, not being able to resume its operation until 2002 with the signature of the peace agreement.

27 Convention on Cooperation for the Protection and Sustainable use of the Danube River. June 29, 1994, 342 O.J. 19.

28 EU Water Framework Directive, *supra* note 19.

29 Convention regarding the regime of navigation on the Danube, August 18, 1948, 33 U.N.T.S. 181.

30 Agreement between the Government of Ukraine and the Government of Moldova on joint boundary waters management and protection, November 23, 1994, LEX-FAOC065455.

governed by the Plenipotentiaries. This agreement only applied to the sections of the river marking the border between the two countries but established a regime for joint utilisation. In 2012, the countries signed the Treaty between the Government of the Republic of Moldova and the Cabinet of Ministers of Ukraine on Cooperation in the Field of Protection and Sustainable Development of the Dniester River Basin[31] (hereinafter, Dniester River Basin Treaty), which created the Commission on Sustainable Use and Protection of the Dniester River Basin.

International Joint Commission between Canada and the United States of America: The cooperation on international watercourses between Canada and the United States of America started in 1909 with the Treaty relating to the boundary waters and questions arising along the boundary between the United States and Canada[32] (hereinafter, Boundary Waters Treaty), which created the International Joint Commission (hereinafter, US-Ca IJC). The particularity of this regime is that it is not specific to one basin but instead applies to all of the watercourses shared by the two countries, which have a border of 8,891 km. However, specific boards were set up for each river (i.e. the International Columbia River Board of Control) or for particular parts of the watercourse (i.e. the International Kootenay Lake Board of Control). More recently, the Agreement between Canada and the United States of America on Great Lakes Water Quality[33] (hereinafter, Great Lakes Water Quality Agreement) of 2012 is particularly significant, as it is the most comprehensive cooperation agreement in the general US-Ca IJC framework. It regulates both the uses of the Great Lakes and the protection of their ecosystems and human health.

Lake Chad: The watershed feeding Lake Chad extends over 2,335,000 km^2 and includes portions of the territory of Cameroon, Niger, Nigeria, Chad, the Central African Republic, Algeria, Libya and Sudan. The lake is in an extremely fragile ecological situation due to the dramatic loss of water volume, which has decreased to 20% of the level recorded in the 1960s, mostly due to climate change and overuse of water for irrigation. Cooperation in the basin began in 1964 with the adoption of the Convention and Statutes Relating to the

31 Treaty between the Government of the Republic of Moldova and the Cabinet of Ministers of Ukraine on Cooperation in the Field of Protection and Sustainable Development of the Dniester River Basin, Moldova-Ukraine, November 29, 2012, ECOLEX TRE-160050.

32 Treaty relating to the boundary waters and questions arising along the boundary between the United States and Canada, United States of America-Canada, January 11, 1909, 36 U.S.T. 2448.

33 Protocol amending the Agreement between Canada and the United States of America on Great Lakes water quality, 1978 as amended on October 16, 1983 and November 18, 1987, June 7, 2012, 3125 U.N.T.S.

Development of the Chad Basin[34] by the four countries bordering the lake: Cameroon, Niger, Nigeria and Chad. This agreement established the Lake Chad Basin Commission (hereinafter, LCBC). The Central African Republic joined the organization in 1996 and Libya in 2008. In 2012, the Water Charter of the Lake Chad Basin[35] was adopted, which enshrines the right of access to water and adopts an integrated water resources approach.

Mekong River: The Mekong river has an estimated length of 4,909 km and its basin extends across the territory of China, Myanmar, Laos, Thailand, Cambodia and Vietnam. The Mekong is already heavily dammed for hydropower generation, especially in the sections belonging to China (18 dams), Laos (23), Vietnam (10) and Thailand (5), but some 74 new dams are planned for construction in the coming years. The cooperation framework has its origins in the creation in 1957 of the Committee for Coordination of Investigations on the Lower Mekong River Basin,[36] formed only by the four downstream countries: Laos, Thailand, Cambodia and Vietnam. In 1995, the same countries signed the Agreement on the Cooperation for the Sustainable Development of the Mekong River Basin[37] (hereinafter, Mekong Agreement), which established the Mekong River Commission (hereinafter, MRC). This agreement establishes a regime for the protection of the river as well as a framework for regulating its utilisation in a variety of areas including irrigation, hydro-power, navigation, flood control, fisheries, timber floating, recreation and tourism. The main governing body of the Commission is the Council, formed by ministry-level members, which has established the basin policies on issues such as maintenance of water flows, water quality, gender, flood management, fluvial transport, drought management, climate change adaptation and fisheries management.

Niger Basin: The Niger River is shared by Benin, Burkina Faso, Cameroon, Côte d'Ivoire, Guinea, Mali, Niger, Nigeria and Chad. Its basin covers an area of 2,117,700 km^2. Cooperation started in 1963 with an agreement on navigation and economic cooperation, which was replaced the following year by the Agreement concerning the Niger River Commission and the navigation and transport on the River Niger.[38] In 1980, the Niger Basin Authority

34 Convention and Statutes Relating to the Development of the Chad Basin, May 22, 1964, LEX-FAOC001076.

35 Water Charter of the Lake Chad Basin, January 1, 2011, FAOLEX LEX-FAOC203691.

36 Statute of the Committee for Co-ordination of Investigations of the Lower Mekong Basin, October 31, 1957, 12 U.N.L.S. 267.

37 Agreement on the Cooperation for the Sustainable Development of the Mekong River Basin. April 5, 1995, 2069 U.N.T.S. 3.

38 Agreement concerning the Niger River Commission and the navigation and transport on the River Niger, November 25, 1964, 587 U.N.T.S. 19.

(hereinafter, NBA) was created. In 2008, the Parties adopted The Niger Basin Water Charter,[39] which notably recognises the fundamental right of access to water of each person. Four appendixes complement the Charter in relation to the protection of the environment, prior notification of planned measures, cost and benefit-sharing from infrastructure of common interest, and the management of dams.

Sava River: The Sava River is a tributary to the Danube whose basin extends through the territory of Slovenia, Croatia, Bosnia and Herzegovina, Serbia, Montenegro and, to a lesser extent, Albania, covering a total area of 95,419 km^2. The basin contains several areas of protected habitat and species, including seven Ramsar sites. In 2002, Bosnia and Herzegovina, the Federal Republic of Yugoslavia (now the Republic of Serbia), the Republic of Croatia and the Republic of Slovenia concluded the Framework Agreement on the Sava River Basin,[40] which established the regime for the utilisation (including navigation), development, protection and management of the basin. The Framework Agreement also established the institutional mechanism for the implementation of this regime: the International Sava River Basin Commission (hereinafter, ISRBC). Four additional protocols have been formalised to regulate navigation, pollution prevention, flood protection and sediment management.

Senegal River: The 337,500 km^2 basin of the Senegal River extends through four countries: Mali, Guinea, Mauritania and Senegal. In 1972, Mali, Mauritania and Senegal signed an agreement declaring the Senegal an international river[41] and another establishing the Organisation pour la Mise en Valeur du fleuve Sénégal[42] (hereinafter, OMVS). In 1978 and 1982, several agreements were signed on the joint management and ownership of infrastructure of common interest, including provisions on its financing. In 2002, the Parties adopted the Charte des Eaux du Fleuve Sénégal[43] (hereinafter, Charter of Waters of the Senegal River), which, among other things, establishes the principles for the allocation of water resources, a regime for the approval of new projects, the forms of stakeholder participation in the decision-making process, and measures for the environmental protection of the basin. Guinea joined the OMVS in 2006.

39 La Charte de l'Eau du Bassin du Niger [The Niger Basin Water Charter], August 23, 2008, ECOLEX TRE-146761.

40 Framework Agreement on the Sava River Basin, December 3, 2002, 2366 U.N.T.S. 479.

41 Convention relative au Statut du fleuve Sénégal [Convention relating to the statute of the Senegal river], March 11, 1972, LEX-FAOC016004.

42 Convention creating organization for the development of the Senegal River, May 11, 1972, LEX-FAOC091150.

43 Charte des eaux du fleuve Sénégal [Charter of Waters of the Senegal River], May 28, 2002, ECOLEX TRE-153511.

Volta River: The Volta River basin extends across the territory of Burkina Faso, Ghana, Mali, Côte d'Ivoire, Togo and Benin and has a total area of 394,196 km^2. In 2007, the above countries signed the Convention on the Status of the Volta River and the establishment of the Volta Basin Authority[44] (hereinafter, VBA), which entered into force in 2009. As part of the Volta Basin Strategic Action Programme[45] (VSIP) – which is supported by the World Bank, the International Monetary Fund, the Global Environment Facility (hereinafter, GEF) and the International Cooperation on Rivers in Africa (CIWA) – the VBA developed the Water Charter for the Volta River Basin[46] (hereinafter, Draft Water Charter for the Volta River Basin), which was validated by the Council of Ministers in 2019. Inspired by the principles of IWRM, the Charter sets out comprehensive regulation for the environmental protection of the basin and for the sustainable utilisation of its water resources. This instrument is now pending adoption by the Summit of Heads of State and Government.

44 Convention portant Statut du fleuve Volta et création de l'Autorité du Bassin de la Volta [Convention establishing the Volta River Statute and the Volta Basin Authority], January 19, 2007, LEX-FAOC180705.

45 VBA. n.d. "VSIP Project." Accessed December 11, 2024. http://abv.int/en/vsip-project/.

46 VBA, *Water Charter for the Volta River Basin* (10 May 2019), https://abv.int/wp-content/uploads/2022/02/Water-Charter_VBA_Eng.pdf.

PART 1

The Principle of Integration of the Economic, Social and Environmental Dimensions and the Sustainable Governance of International Watercourses

Introduction

This first part of the book seeks to determine how the principle of integration has been incorporated into international watercourse law and how it operates according to the particularities of this specific branch of international law. Chapter 1 provides an examination of the legal nature and scope of the principle of integration within the broader context of international environmental law. Subsequently, the book delves into the application of this principle specifically within the legal framework governing international watercourses, necessitating analysis along two primary dimensions.

On the one hand, it is necessary to determine if and how international watercourse law provides for the adoption of the principle of integration. It is possible, for instance, that specific rules in this legal domain preclude the effective application of the principle of integration and its meaningful translation into cooperation on international watercourses. It is therefore important to examine the extent to which sustainable development and international watercourses law have influenced each other. Moreover, it may also be the case that the scope of application of international watercourse law is too narrow to encompass the interests covered by the principle of integration. These issues are addressed in Chapter 2.

On the other hand, it is also necessary to ascertain how the two dimensions of the principle of integration, legal integration and institutional integration, are translated into the legal framework of international watercourse law. The analysis takes as its starting point the hypothesis that this translation occurs through internal integration of the substantive principles of international watercourses and external integration of these principles with procedural principles. This is addressed in following two chapters.

Chapter 3 analyses the substantive principles of international watercourse law for two purposes: first, to assess how each principle itself incorporates the principle of integration; second, to consider the extent to which the relationship between these principles of international watercourse law reflects the application of the principle of integration. And provide an adequate legal framework for applying the principle of integration. Chapter 4 analyses the procedural norms of the general law of international watercourses. The objective is to assess to what extent these norms provide the legal tools to apply the principle of integration as an obligation in order to incorporate economic, social and environmental considerations into the decision-making process in international watercourse governance.

 | DOI:10.1163/9789004736757_003

CHAPTER 1

The Integration of the Economic, Social and Environmental Dimensions of Sustainable Development as a Norm

Integration of the economic, social and environmental dimensions is commonly regarded as an ancillary but central principle of sustainable development.[1] However, the content, normative nature and the obligations – if any – that it implies remain largely undefined in the doctrine. This Chapter aims to clarify these questions as an introduction to the analysis of the implementation of the principle of integration in the specific area of international watercourse law.

First, it is necessary to analyse the problem the principle of integration is intended to solve. This requires consideration of the legal context in which it has appeared. The point is made that the answer embodied in the principle of integration is provided against a major issue in current international law: the fragmentation of the international legal order. It is therefore of the utmost relevance to consider how the international community has tackled this issue through soft law instruments devoted to sustainable development.

The second Section continues analysing the legal nature of integration according to the sources of international law. The resulting insights are necessary to determine if the principle of integration has entered the realm of international law and, if so, in what quality (customary norm, conventional obligation, or both).

Finally, the third Section focuses on determining the normative content of the principle of integration. It is assumed from the outset that the normative implications of the principle of integration can be varied and that they can have an unequal level of enforceability. The Section is structured according to the two obligations emanating from the principle of integration: on the one hand, the normative content is presented as an obligation of applying international law inter-systemically, that is, by establishing linkages between the different legal domains of sustainable development; on the other, as an obligation of conducting an integrated decision-making process that ensures that the different values and interests of sustainable development are taken into account.

1 French, Duncan. 2005. *International Law and Policy of Sustainable Development*. New York: Juris Publisher. 54–57.

 | DOI:10.1163/9789004736757_004

1 The Emergence of a Notion of Integration of the Economic, Social and Environmental Dimensions of Sustainable Development

The fact that human societies are a subsystem that exists within nature, on which it depends, is now considered self-evident. However, the hegemonic economic system is based on the assumption of unlimited natural resources and their intensive use, despite the fact that we have long been aware of the implications of the ecological crisis.[2] In the legal sphere, this dissociation of the economic system from the environment is expressed in the fragmentation of international law to a great extent. The difficulties of accommodating the inconsistencies between distinct legal areas such as, for example, the regulation of international trade and the protection of the environment have been studied extensively.[3] The poor relationship between these areas of law is mainly due to the contrasting interests of the actors involved, among which the representatives of the economic sector enjoy incomparably greater power.[4]

The international community's multilateral response over the last half-century has been based on the notion of sustainable development. In this context of fragmentation, then, the challenge facing sustainable development is that of integration. This Section analyses the process through which sustainable development has emerged, in which integration has become the core element. First, Subsection i) focuses on placing sustainable development in the broader context of the fragmentation of international law. It is argued that the integrative thrust of sustainable development is meant to give a response to one dimension of this phenomenon. Next, Subsection ii) analyses how the international community has developed the notion of integration conceptually. Particular attention is paid to the work undertaken by international conferences and the United Nations General Assembly (hereinafter, UNGA), but also to the

2 As a benchmark study on this topic, see Meadows, Donella H, Dennis L Meadows, Jorgen Randers, and William W. Behrens III. 1972. *The Limits to Growth*. New York: Universe Books.

3 See, for instance: Petersmann, Ernst-Ulrich. 1995. *International and European Trade and Environmental Law after the Uruguay Round*. London: Kluwer Law International; Schoenbaum, Thomas J. 1992. "Free International Trade and Protection of the Environment: Irreconcilable Conflict?" *American Journal of International Law* 86 (4): 700–727; Elizalde Carranza, Miguel Ángel. 2006. "Las Medidas Comerciales Multilaterales Para La Protección Del Medio Ambiente y El Sistema Multilateral Del Comercio." Universitat Pompeu Fabra; and Fernández Pons, Xavier. 2021. "Conservation and Sustainable Use of Biodiversity in the International Regulation of Trade in Goods." In *Biological Diversity and International Law: Challenges for the Post 2020 Scenario*, edited by Mar Campins Eritja and Teresa Fajardo del Castillo, 79–99. Cham: Springer.

4 Benvenisti, Eyal, and George W. Downs. 2007. "The Empire's New Clothes: Political Economy and the Fragmentation of International Law." *Stanford Law Review* 60 (2): 595–631.

important contribution of the ILA to developing the legal dimension of the concept.

1.1 *Sustainable Development in the Context of a Fragmented International Legal Order*

Particularly during the 1990s and the 2000s, the fragmentation of international law became a central topic of legal scholarship. The interest was triggered by the expansion of international law to regulate other areas, such as human rights, environmental protection, disarmament and international cooperation.[5] Largely as a result of this process, specialised tribunals proliferated (e.g. the International Criminal Tribunal for the former Yugoslavia or the International Tribunal for the Law of the Sea), ousting the ICJ from its preeminent position in international justice and leading to fears of the appearance of self-contained legal regimes of international law that would eventually overlap and compete.[6]

Some doctrinal positions on the topic are particularly negative, especially when considering the underlying causes of fragmentation. Dupuy warned that the creation of new jurisdictions could imply "the illusion of completely autonomous sub-systems"[7] that would not need to apply general international law.

Nevertheless, after the initial fears over the fragmentation of international law, several authors have developed a more tempered view, referring to the issue in neutral terms such as 'regime interaction'[8] and 'legal pluralism,'[9] or adopted a more positive approach, considering fragmentation a 'refinement of international law' and that "it is time to bury the f-word."[10] Indeed, the

---

5 Casanovas y la Rosa, Oriol. 2011. "Aproximación a Una Teoría de Los Regímenes En Derecho Internacional Público." In *Unidad y pluralismo en el Derecho Internacional Público y en la Comunidad Internacional*, edited by Ángel J. Rodrigo and Caterina García, 41–60. Tecnos. 42.

6 Peters, Anne. 2017. "The Refinement of International Law: From Fragmentation to Regime Interaction and Politicization." *International Journal of Constitutional Law* 15 (3): 671–704.

7 Dupuy, Pierre-Marie. 1999. "The Danger of Fragmentation or Unification of the International Legal System and the International Court of Justice." *New York University Journal of International Law* 31: 791. 796.

8 Trevisanut, Seline, and Nikolaos Giannopoulos. 2018. "Investment Protection in Offshore Energy Production: Bright Sides of Regime Interaction." *Journal of World Investment and Trade* 19 (5–6): 789–827.

9 Burke-White, William W. 2004. "International Legal Pluralism." *Michigan Journal of International Law* 25 (4): 963–79.

10 Peters, Anne. 2017. "The Refinement of International Law: From Fragmentation to Regime Interaction and Politicization." *International Journal of Constitutional Law* 15 (3): 671–704. 672.

phenomenon has even been described as a sign of maturity.[11] Concerns over the issue led to action by the International Law Commission (hereinafter, ILC), which in 2006 issued a report on the results of the study group on the fragmentation of international law, finalised by Martii Koskenniemi.[12]

The aim of the study was to analyse to what extent the instruments for conflict resolutions provided by international law were sufficient to tackle the major threats posed by fragmentation. The study group assumed that it was the task of legal reasoning to build systemic relationships in a legal context in which international norms are not created in a centralised legislative purposive manner, but rather out of conflicting motives and objectives.[13] In such an environment, "legal reasoning will either have to seek to harmonize the apparently conflicting standards through interpretation or, if that seems implausible, to establish definite relationships of priority between them."[14] The final conclusions of the ILC are fairly reassuring in considering that traditional legal mechanisms to tackle normative conflicts in international law provide satisfactory resources to address the issue of fragmentation.[15]

Arguably, there are two main approaches to dealing with the fragmentation of international law. The dominant approach until now has consisted of the interpretation and application of treaties. This inspired the ILC's work on fragmentation, which focused on "the splitting up of the law into highly specialized "boxes" that claim relative autonomy from each other and from the general law."[16] The other approach to addressing the risks of fragmentation has been the establishment of institutional mechanisms, which have been used "to manage conflict between environmental regimes, but also to maximise the very real benefits that can be derived from conflated and overlapping mandates."[17]

11 Remiro Brotons, Antonio. 2011. "La Noción de Regímenes Internacionales En El Derecho Internacional Público." In *Unidad y pluralismo en el Derecho Internacional Público y en la Comunidad Internacional*, edited by Ángel J Rodrigo Hernández and Caterina García, 167–76. Tecnos. 170.

12 ILC, *Fragmentation of International Law: Difficulties Arising from the Diversification and Expansion of International Law, Report of the Study Group of the International Law Commission. Finalized by Martti Koskenniemi*, A/CN.4/L.682 (2006), undocs.org/A/CN.4/L.682

13 Ibid. Paras. 34–35.

14 Ibid. Para. 36.

15 Report finalized by Martti Koskenniemi, *supra* note 12, Para. 492.

16 Ibid. Para. 13.

17 Scott, Karen N. 2011. "International Environmental: Managing Fragmentation Through Institutional Connection." *Melbourne Journal of International Law* 12: 177–216. 182.

Regardless of the causes of the fragmentation of international law or whether this phenomenon is seen as a problem, there seems to be a consensus that measures must be implemented to address it. In this context, the concept of 'sustainable development' comes naturally to mind. It encompasses, among other things, the integration of environmental, economic and social dimensions. In this regard, Voigt affirms that:

> [t]he most important aspect of sustainable development is integration. Integration in its legal sense means the simultaneous consideration of social, economic, and environmental aspects of a subject in a 'normative continuum', i.e. in the negotiation process, the provisions of the final treaty texts, their implementation and eventually in the decisions of international courts and tribunals.[18]

Sustainable development did not emerge in response to the fragmentation of international law; rather, it is rooted in evidence of the negative impact of human activities on the environment.[19] However, in the legal domain, sustainable development is faced with a fragmentation problem that requires integration between the bodies of environmental, economic and human rights law. Since sustainable development is aimed precisely at overcoming this problem, it has been described as "*un concept intersystémique par nature.*"[20] As expressed by Schrijver, "[h]ow should the various and quite different lines of evolution in international law in the relevant areas (development, environment, and human rights) be linked to each other, adjusted to each other and formed into a coherent whole in the pursuit of sustainable development?."[21] On this basis, it can be presumed that the integrationist aim of sustainable development can profit from some of the tools offered by international law to tackle fragmentation. The following Subection will analyse what is proposed by the international community to achieve this.

---

18 Voigt, *Sustainable Development as a Principle of International Law*, 374.

19 Barral, Virginie. 2018. "The Principle of Sustainable Development." In *Principles of Environmental Law*, edited by Ludwig Krämer and Emanuela Orlando, 103–14. Edward Elgar. 103–104.

20 Dubin, Laurence. 2009. "Fonction Intersystémique Du Concept de Développement Durable." In *La Circulation Des Concepts Juridiques : Le Droit International de l'environnement Entre Mondialisation et Fragmentation*, edited by Hélène Ruiz Fabri and Lorenzo Gradoni, 175–98. Paris: Société de législation comparée. 178.

21 Schrijver, N. J. 2007. "The Evolution of Sustainable Development." *Collected Courses of the Hague Academy of International Law* 329: 217–412. 378.

1.2 *The Evolution of Sustainable Development as an Integration Challenge*

Certainly, the concept of sustainable development has developed alongside the notion of integration of the economic, social and environmental dimensions (hereinafter, 'integration' and 'integration of the economic, social and environmental dimensions' will be used interchangeably) from its inception. International conferences convened by the UN have played a leading role in advancing the concept and agenda of sustainable development over the last 50 years and, hence the process must be analysed with a specific focus on those events and their outcome documents. The doctrine has also been important in the understanding of the principle of integration, in particular the work of the ILA.

The international community's work on sustainable development can be traced back to 1972 with the United Nations Declaration on Human Environment convened at the Stockholm Conference[22] (hereinafter, Stockholm Declaration). The Stockholm Conference was held largely in response to the increasing concern among States about the effects on the quality of human life of unlimited economic growth and the acknowledgement that natural resources are exhaustible.[23] This growing environmental awareness was also apparent in the publication of *The Limits to Growth* by the Club of Rome in the same year.[24] The environmentalist approach at the origin of the Conference was viewed with suspicion by many developing countries that had recently gained independence from former colonial powers, fearing that environmental measures would harm their economic aspirations.[25]

One important outcome of the Stockholm Conference was the creation of the United Nations Environment Programme[26] (hereinafter, UNEP). More important for the purpose for this study, however, was the elaboration of the

22 United Nations Conference on the Human Environment, *Declaration of the United Nations Conference on the Human Environment,* in Report of the United Nations Conference on the Human Environment, A/CONF.48/14/Rev.1. (5–16 June 1972), undocs.org/en/A/CONF.48/14/Rev.1.

23 Fitzmaurice, Malgosia. 2001. "International Protection of the Environment." *Collected Courses of the Hague Academy of International Law* 293: 9–488. 33–35.

24 Meadows, Donella H, Dennis L Meadows, Jorgen Randers, and William W. Behrens III. 1972. *The Limits to Growth.* New York: Universe Books.

25 In relation to the 1972 Stockholm Conference see generally Schrijver, "The Evolution of Sustainable Development," 244–247.

26 UN General Assembly, Resolution 2997 (XXVII), *Institutional and financial arrangements for international environmental cooperation,* A/RES/2997(XXVII) (15 December 1972), undocs.org/A/RES/2997(XXVII).

Stockholm Declaration,[27] which is commonly considered a foundation of international environmental law[28] and the basis for the evolution of the principle of integration into its current form. The Declaration contains 26 principles,[29] which establish some basic notions of sustainable development, albeit without specific reference to the concept as such,[30] and place a strong focus on redressing the discrimination instituted under colonialism.[31]

Principle 4 establishes the idea that the environment should be taken into account in the planning of economic development: "Man has a special responsibility to safeguard and wisely manage the heritage of wildlife and its habitat, which are now gravely imperilled by a combination of adverse factors. Nature conservation, including wildlife, must therefore receive importance in planning for economic development."[32] The principle is written in vague terms, but the relationship between economic development and the retreat of wildlife is clearly stated, together with the idea that humans have the duty to do something about it.[33] This formulation advances a notion of integration, although only considering environmental and economic concerns.

Principle 11 raises the issue of potential negative effects of environmental policies on the economic development of developing countries and the equality of those effects for the industrialised ones.[34] This principle expresses the concerns of developing countries that environmental standards could result in a protectionist policy for international trade with industrialised countries.[35]

---

27 Stockholm Declaration, *supra* note 22.

28 Pallemaerts, Marc. 1992. "International Environmental Law from Stockholm to Rio: Back to the Future?" *Review of European Community & International Environmental Law* 1 (3): 254–66. 255.

29 On the adequacy of the term principle to refer to the dispositions included in the Stockholm Declaration see Prieur, Michel. 2022. "Revisión de Los Cincuenta Años Del Derecho Internacional Ambiental: La Definición de Los Principios." *Revista Catalana de Dret Ambiental* 13 (2): 1–10.

30 See, for instance, Principle 2, which set the idea of preserving the environment for the next generations. In Stockholm Declaration, *supra* note 22.

31 See, for instance, Principle 1. In Ibid.

32 In Ibid. Principle 4.

33 On this principle see Sohn, Louis B. 1973. "Stockholm Declaration on the Human Environment." *Harvard International Law Journal* 14 (3): 422–515. 459–460.

34 "The environmental policies of all States should enhance and not adversely affect the present or future development potential of developing countries, nor should they hamper the attainment of better living conditions for all, and appropriate steps should be taken by States and International organizations with a view to reaching agreement on meeting the possible national and international economic consequences resulting from the application of environmental measures." In Stockholm Declaration, *supra* note 22, Principle 11.

35 On this principle see Sohn, "Stockholm Declaration," 411.

Certainly, provisions of this kind significantly limited the ambition of environmental law and policy in the name of economic progress.

A clear notion of integration might be deemed to be enshrined in Principle 13, which introduces a sense of compatibility between economic development and the environment:

> In order to achieve a more rational management of resources and thus to improve the environment, States should adopt an integrated and coordinated approach to their development planning so as to ensure that development is compatible with the need to protect and improve environment for the benefit of their population.[36]

Note that such compatibility should be achieved by the States through an "integrated and coordinated approach to their development planning". In fact, the importance of 'planning' in order to achieve the objectives of the Declaration is mentioned on several occasions and is particularly relevant in Principle 14, which stresses the importance of rational planning as a means to reconcile economic development and environment.[37] Both principles state the need for the integration of environmental protection concerns at the planning stage of development activities, opening the door to the deployment of more specific ways to operationalise this objective. However, as noted by Sohn, while Principle 13 is written in more general terms, the drafters avoided the phrase 'States should' in Principle 14, which, although more specific, is not formulated as a mandate.[38]

In 1987, the United Nations World Commission on Environment and Development issued a milestone report under the title *Our Common Future*, which offered a clear characterisation of sustainable development. This document, also known as the Brundtland Report[39] by the leadership of Gro Harlem Brundtland, former Norwegian Prime Minister, was drafted at the request of the UNGA with the ambitious objective "to propose long-term environmental strategies for achieving sustainable development by the year 2000 and beyond."[40]

---

36 Stockholm Declaration, *supra* note 22, Principle 13.

37 "Rational planning constitutes an essential tool for reconciling any conflict between the needs of development and the need to protect and improve the environment." Ibid. Principle 14.

38 Sohn, "Stockholm Declaration," 411.

39 World Commission on Environment and Development, *Report of the World Commission on Environment and Development: "Our Common Future"*, A/42/427 (4 August 1987), undocs.org/en/A/42/427.

40 Ibid. Foreword.

Sustainable development was defined as "development that meets the needs of the present without compromising the ability of future generations to meet their own needs."[41] According to this well-known definition, development is understood not only as economic growth *per se* but as the fulfilment of the basic and aspirational needs of the whole population. At the same time, the sustainability of economic development requires that basic standards be maintained in the long term, working as a conditional requirement to justify economic growth. It is within this overarching concept of sustainable development that a more specific role may be envisioned for integration.

According to the Brundtland Report, environmental concerns are to be integrated in economic development activities in the same way that they are embedded in the real world. Indeed, this constituted the essential element of the Report: "[t]he common theme throughout this strategy for sustainable development is the need to integrate economic and ecological considerations in decision making."[42] Therefore, the 'take into account' mandate is not limited to the planning process, but extends to decision-making more generally.

In response to the recommendation of the United Nations World Commission on Environment and Development on the translation of the conclusions of the Brundtland Report into a Programme of Action on Sustainable Development,[43] in 1989 the UNGA approved the organisation of the United Nations Conference on Environment and Development (hereinafter, UNCED) to renew the international commitment.[44] It was finally set to be held in 1992 in Rio de Janeiro.[45]

The UNCED led to a Declaration and the action plan Agenda 21, which has been described as 'permeated' by integration.[46] The Rio Declaration on

41 World Commission on Environment and Development, *Report of the World Commission on Environment and Development: "Our Common Future"*, A/42/427 (4 August 1987), undocs.org/en/A/42/427. Chapter II. Para. 1.

42 Ibid. Chapter II, para. 72.

43 Ibid. Para. 124.

44 UN General Assembly, Resolution 44/228, *United Nations Conference on Environment and Development*, A/RES/44/228/E (22 December 1989), undocs.org/en/A/RES/44/228.

45 On the UNCED see, generally: Juste Ruiz, José, and Mireya Castillo Daudí. 2014. *La Protección Del Medio Ambiente En El Ámbito Internacional y En La Unión Europea*. Valencia: Tirant lo Blanch. 22–24; Timoshenko, Alexandre S. 1995. "From Stockholm to Rio: The Institutionalization of Sustainable Development." In *Sustainable Development and Interantional Law*, edited by Winfried Lang, 143–60. London: Graham & Trotman / Martinus Nihjoff; Birnie, P, A Boyle, and C Redgwell. 2009. *International Law and the Environment*. 3rd ed. Oxford: OUP. 50–52.

46 Birnie, Boyle a Redgwell affirm that "[i]ntegration permeates the Rio instruments, as well as Agenda 21". In Birnie, Boyle and Redgwell, *International Law and the Environment*, 116–117.

Environment and Development[47] (hereinafter, Rio Declaration) has become a primary authoritative instrument in international environmental law.[48] It comprises a set of 27 principles, of which Principle 4 clearly expresses an idea of integration of economic, social and environmental dimensions: "In order to achieve sustainable development, environmental protection shall constitute an integral part of the development process and cannot be considered in isolation from it."[49] The wording hints at a broader understanding the principle of integration, applicable to the overall process of development. It can, however, be argued that the vagueness of the formulation is a hindrance to enforcement: stating merely that something is to form 'part of' a process is a rather soft statement that does not need to lead to any concrete result.

Moreover, Principle 4 of the Rio Declaration has been criticised for merging environmental law and the law related to economic and social development, suggesting that there is no conflict between them. It might introduce a dangerous ambiguity that allows for environmental policies to be subordinated to economic interests.[50] However, if we examine the proposals made by States in the preparatory work of the Rio Declaration that the content of Principle 4 was not easily agreed upon.[51] The final formulation coincides with the proposal of the Group of 77, a coalition within the UNGA of developing countries and China. Nevertheless, this version was the result of a prior proposal made by the same countries that clearly conditioned environmental concerns to developmental ones: "States and international organizations shall address environmental issues in the process of development by integrating environmental concerns

47 United Nations Conference on Environment and Development, *Rio Declaration on Environment and Development*, in Report of the United Nations Conference on Environment and Development, A/CONF.151/26 (Vol. 1) (12 August 1992), undocs.org/en/A/CONF.151/26 /Rev.1(vol. I).

48 According to Boyle, "the 1992 Rio Declaration on Environment and Development [...] has become the most authoritative general statement of the core rules and principles of International environmental law, comparable in its legal status to the 1948 Universal Declaration of Human Rights." In Boyle, Alan. 2022. "International Lawmaking in an Environmental Context." *Collected Courses of the Hague Academy of International Law* 427: 51–108. 72.

49 Ibid. Principle 4.

50 Pallemaerts, Marc. 1992. "International Environmental Law from Stockholm to Rio: Back to the Future?" *Review of European Community & International Environmental Law* 1 (3): 254–66.

51 For a complete analysis of the evolution of this principle in the preparatory works of the UNCED, see Barral and Dupuy, "Principle 4: Sustainable Development through Integration."

with the imperatives of economic growth and development."[52] Since other countries such as Portugal, Denmark, Iceland, Norway, Sweden, the United States, Australia and Japan had tried to give a more central role to the principle of integration, placing it first and providing a more balanced formulation,[53] the final draft might be deemed to reflect a middle ground between two strongly opposing positions.

While declarations emanating from international conferences are unlikely to be drastically against the dominant economic system, Article 4 should be read together with Agenda 21[54] – the programmatic document resulting from the UNCED – as comprising the whole cycle of policies, both at the planning and the implementation stage. Of the more than 300 pages of Agenda 21, the integration of environmental and development concerns receives particular attention in chapters 8, 38 and 39, which are closely related. Chapter 8, titled 'Integrating environment and development in decision-making', presents integration of the economic, social and environmental dimensions as the outcome of a decision-making process and outlines the means to ensure that it is achieved.

Of the four sections of the chapter, the first is the most relevant to this study.[55] It makes a general call for a reshaping of national decision-making processes, placing the environment at the centre of economic and political decision-making to achieve "a full integration of these factors."[56] The following specific objectives are established: conducting a national review of all sectoral policies, strategies and plans to ensure the integration of environmental and developmental issues; strengthening institutional structures to allow the integration of environmental concerns across all levels of decision-making; and

52 Preparatory Committee for the United Nations Conference on Environment and Development, *Report of the Fourth session celebrated in New York 2 March-3 April*, A/CONF.151/PC/WG.III/L.34 (1 April 1992), undocs.org/ A/CONF.151/PC/WG.III/L.34. 8.

53 See in this regard the proposal of Denmark, Iceland, Norway and Sweden: "Environmental protection and economic and social development ultimately cannot be achieved at the expense of each other. Environment and development goals should be pursued simultaneously, in an integrated fashion." In Ibid. 33.

54 United Nations Conference on Environment and Development, *Agenda 21*, in *Report of the United Nations Conference on Environment and Development*, A/CONF.151/26 (Vol. I) (12 August 1992), undocs.org/en/A/CONF.151/26/Rev.1(vol. I).

55 Chapter 8 is divided in four sections: a. Integrating environment and development at the policy, planning and management levels; b. Providing an effective legal and regulatory framework; c. Making effective use of economic instruments and market and other incentives; d. Establishing systems for integrated environmental and economic accounting. In Ibid. Chapter 8.

56 Ibid. Para. 8.2.

the adaptation of mechanisms for the involvement of individuals, groups and organisations in decision-making.

The first group of activities are directly concerned with the integration of environment and development in the decision-making process.[57] They can be characterised by a general focus on cross-sectoral integration, which must be reflected in vertical and horizontal intra-governmental collaboration; the importance of monitoring and assessment in obtaining the necessary information for decision-making; and the role of the public, which should have access to the relevant information and the means for effective participation.

The remaining activities focus on the adaptation of planning and management systems for an integrated decision-making process. They comprise the systematic use of economic, social and environmental data and information for integrated planning and management; the detection of synergies between sectors; impact assessments at project, policy and programme levels; integrative area approaches focusing at, for instance, watershed level; the adoption of integrated management systems and approaches; and the involvement of local communities regarding environmental accidents and local hazards.[58] Although the list of activities is somewhat confusing and repetitive in places, it provides a comprehensive view of the practical mechanisms required to ensure integrated decision-making in the context of sustainable development.

In September 2000, the Millennium Summit adopted the Millennium Development Goals[59] (hereinafter, MDGs), which were further developed with an implementation plan the following year.[60] The MDGs are an expression of the preoccupations of the international community in the late 1990s, when hunger was a primary concern (particularly in Africa), the HIV/AIDS pandemic was spreading, and the economic crisis of Latin America, the Asian financial crisis and the economic demise of post-Soviet countries were more pressing realities than they are today.[61] This may explain why the plan focuses mainly on economic and social development cooperation and makes relatively little provision for environmental concerns.

57 Ibid. Para. 8.4.

58 Ibid. Para. 8.5.

59 UN General Assembly, Resolution 55/2, *United Nations Millennium Declaration*, A/RES/55/2 (18 September 2000), undocs.org/A/RES/55/2.

60 UN Secretary-General, *Road map towards the implementation of the United Nations Millennium Declaration. Report of the Secretary-General*, A/56/326 (6 September 2001), undocs.org/en/A/56/326.

61 McArthur, John W. 2014. "The Origins of the Millennium Development Goals." *SAIS Review of International Affairs* 34 (5): 5–24.

Of the eight Goals in which the MDGs were structured, environmental protection is the focus of only one of them.[62] The new commitment marked a deviation from the approach adopted eight years earlier at the Rio Conference. In the MDGs, much more emphasis was placed on economic development as a means of eradicating poverty than on sustainability. Moreover, the MDGs did not appear to be clearly interlinked, although there is a clear interdependence between some of the Goals. In fact, the MDGs have been criticised as making rather limited provision for integration, approaching the sustainability challenge merely as an obligation to add the environment to the other Goals already in place.[63] It has been pointed out that this reflects the problems governments encounter in implementing the sustainable development concept in actual policies.[64] Since there is no systematic interrelation between the Goals, the kind of action they promote keeps being piecemeal and is unlikely to have far-reaching impact.

The 2002 World Summit on Sustainable Development in Johannesburg led to the adoption by the conference of a resolution (hereinafter, Johannesburg Declaration) and an implementation plan.[65] The main purpose of this summit was to further implement the Rio Declaration, the Goals of Agenda 21 and the MDGs, placing a special focus on regional cooperation and defining the roles of the actors involved, in particular the UN. No major addition was made to the concept of sustainable development, nor to the principle of integration, but the resolution was notable for its description of three pillars of sustainable development: economic development, social development and environmental protection. The idea had already been put forward in earlier documents, but this was the first time that the concept had been synthesised in this specific formula.

In 2012, another resolution on sustainable development was adopted as an outcome of the United Nations Conference on Sustainable Development

62 Ibid.

63 World Resources Institute, United Nations Development Programme, United Nations Environment Programme, and World Bank. 2005. *World Resources 2005: The Wealth of the Poor – Managing Ecosystems to Fight Poverty. World Resources 2005*. Washington, DC: WRI. 154.

64 "Many believe that environmental issues have in fact lost ground in international development circles in the past decade or so, precisely because of the difficulty in pinning down the concept of environmental sustainability in a way that governments can understand and put to use in decision-making. In its current construction, MDG-7 only exacerbates this dilemma". Ibid. 154.

65 World Summit on Sustainable Development, *Johannesburg Declaration on Sustainable Development*, in Report of the World Summit on Sustainable Development, A/CONF.199/20 (26 August-4 September 2002), undocs.org/en/A/CONF.199/20.

(hereinafter, Rio+20 Declaration) held in Rio de Janeiro.[66] The concept of integration of the three pillars of sustainable development remained unchanged, but the outcome document stressed the lack of progress in its application and the setbacks suffered in the last years due to several events, such as the financial crisis of 2008. The 2012 Rio+20 Declaration envisaged an institutional framework and a programme for action. In both cases, it is especially relevant to note the emphasis on addressing the complexity of issues related to sustainable development in a systemic and integrated manner. The document proposes to strengthen the institutional framework for sustainable development in order to:

> (a) Promote the balanced integration of the three dimensions of sustainable development; (b) Be based on an action- and result-oriented approach giving due regard to all relevant cross-cutting issues with the aim to contribute to the implementation of sustainable development; (c) Underscore the importance of interlinkages among key issues and challenges and the need for a systematic approach to them at all relevant levels; (d) Enhance coherence, reduce fragmentation and overlap and increase effectiveness, efficiency and transparency, while reinforcing coordination and cooperation.[67]

In its programmatic section, the Rio+20 Declaration stresses that goals should be set in such a way that their interrelatedness is fully accounted for. That is, addressing and incorporating all three dimensions of sustainable development and their interlinkages.[68]

In 2015 took place the United Nations Summit on Sustainable Development, the outcome of which was the document *Transforming our world: the 2030 Agenda for Sustainable Development*[69] (hereinafter, Agenda 2030). This document was adopted subsequently by the UNGA, thus endorsing the objectives contained in it. From a discursive point of view, the Sustainable

66 United Nations Conference on Sustainable Development, *The future we want*, A/RES/66/288 (11 September 2012), undocs.org/en/A/RES/66/288.

67 United Nations Conference on Sustainable Development, *The future we want*, A/RES/66/288 (11 September 2012), undocs.org/en/A/RES/66/288. 14.

68 Ibid. Para. 246.

69 United Nations summit for the adoption of the post-2015 development agenda, *Transforming our world: the 2030 Agenda for Sustainable Development*, A/RES/70/1 (21 October 2015), undocs.org/en/A/RES/70/1.

Development Goals (hereinafter, SDGs)[70] set out a highly integrated approach between economic, environmental and social interests if compared to the MDGs.[71] This is probably due to the different context in which the two programmes were devised and the different problems they are intended to tackle. The MDGs focused mainly on critical problems such as poverty or health and were the product of a North-to-South action intended to engage developing countries in tackling global problems. The SDGs, by contrast, aim to include the whole spectrum of human interactions with the environment and channel them in a sustainable way.

From an institutional point of view, the SDGs are also more conducive to integration of the economic, social and environmental dimensions than previous attempts. The High-Level Political Forum has greater authority than previous UN institutions of its type to coordinate, interlink, mobilize resources for implementation, and monitor progress, which should allow for a better integration of the three dimensions of sustainable development. Nevertheless, States remain the primary implementers of the SDGs, hence the integration of Targets, strategies and plans for implementation at the national level will be a key aspect in applying the interlinked structure of the SDGs.[72]

In the context of this research, the most relevant feature of SDGs is the deeper sense of integration of the economic, social and environmental dimensions as an indivisible and interlinked whole. This approach specifically resolves one of the problems that hampered progress towards the MDGs: the non-acknowledgement of the complex interlinkeage between issues on the agenda.[73] As put by Huck, "the integratedness of SDGs is one of the outstanding core messages of the Agenda 2030, which is to be understood as a whole and not as a random collection of isolated goals that can be picked up and

70 For a complete analysis of the SDGs from a legal point of view, see Fernández Liesa, Carlos R., and Ana Manero Salvador, eds. 2017. *Análisis y Comentarios de Los Objetivos de Desarrollo Sostenible de Las Nacionaes Unidas*. Cizur Menor: Aranzadi Thomson Reuters; or Huck, Winfried. 2022. *Sustainable Development Goals. Article-by-Article Commentary*. Baden-Baden, Germany: Nomos.

71 Jong, Eileen de, and Marjanneke J. Vijge. 2021. "From Millennium to Sustainable Development Goals: Evolving Discourses and Their Reflection in Policy Coherence for Development." *Earth System Governance* 7 (100087): 1–12.

72 Stafford-Smith, Mark, David Griggs, Owen Gaffney, Farooq Ullah, Belinda Reyers, Norichika Kanie, Bjorn Stigson, Paul Shrivastava, Melissa Leach, and Deborah O'Connell. 2017. "Integration: The Key to Implementing the Sustainable Development Goals." *Sustainability Science* 12 (6): 911–19.

73 Haas, Peter M., and Casey Stevens. 2017. "Ideas, Beliefs, and Policy Linkages." In *Governing through Goals. Sustainable Development Goals as a Governance Innovation*, edited by Norichika Kanie and Frank Biermann. MIT. 138.

instrumentalised individually."[74] They have a network structure in which all Goals are mutually connected by shared Targets and, more importantly, each Goal is connected to at least one Target of each of the three dimensions of sustainable development.[75] Some of the SDG Targets are conflicting while others are mutually reinforcing, which is not surprising considering that the SDGs reflect the nature of sustainable development itself. They allow for policymakers to consider issues linked to a given policy that can be more effectively addressed together than if they are tackled in isolation.

The SDGs, with their clearly measurable set of Targets, are an innovative approach to sustainable development. However, they have been criticised for being toothless and not providing sufficient guarantees for the accomplishment of their objectives. The essential problem is the disconnect between the Targets and the causes, making it unlikely that any major change will be achieved without questioning the foundations of global social metabolism. In this regard, Cardesa-Saltzmann and Pigrau conclude that the SDGs "reflejan [...] una falta de transcendencia constitucional del concepto normativo de desarrollo sostenible en el ordenamiento jurídico internacional, que le impide vertebrar un equilibrio real entre las dimensiones económica, social y ambiental de la gobernanza global."[76] This analysis is in line with other more general critical views on sustainable development.[77]

Moreover, studies have found that the SDGs are widely used as a conceptual framework by some international organisations, but that they have failed to foster policy integration. The process is rather the opposite. In those organisations where policy integration is already in place, the SDGs are used to reframe existing policies.[78]

---

74 Huck, Winfried. 2022. *Sustainable Development Goals. Article-by-Article Commentary*. Baden-Baden, Germany: Nomos. In fact, this author considers the "integrated nature of SDGs" as one of the internal principles of SDGs.

75 O'Connor, David, James Mackie, Daphne van Esveld, Hoseok Kim, Imme Scholz, and Nina Weitz. 2016. "Universality, Integration, and Policy Coherence for Sustainable Development: Early SDG Implementation in Selected OECD Countries." *Working Paper*. World Resources Institute.

76 Cardesa-Saltzmann, Antonio, and Antoni Pigrau Soler. 2017. "La Agenda 2030 y Los Objetivos Para El Desarrollo Sostenible. Una Mirada Crítica Sobre Su Aportación a La Gobernanza Global En Términos de Justicia Distributiva y Sostenibilidad Ambiental." *Revista Española de Derecho Internacional* 69 (1): 279–85. 283.

77 For critical views of sustainable development see, for instance, Viñuales, Jorge E. 2013. "The Rise and Fall of Sustainable Development." *Review of European, Comparative and International Environmental Law* 22 (1): 3–13; or Jaria-Manzano, Jordi. 2020. *La Constitución Del Antropoceno*. Valencia: Tirant Humanidades. 244–272.

78 Bogers, Maya, Frank Biermann, Agni Kalfagianni, and Rakhyun E Kim. 2022. "Sustainable Development Goals Fail to Advance Policy Integration: A Large-n Text Analysis of 159 International Organizations." *Environmental Science and Policy* 138 (October): 134–45.

The contribution of the doctrine to the development of the principle of integration has been particularly valuable. Although an academic association such as the ILA does not create international law as such, its doctrinal work in the area of sustainable development and the principle of integration has made a significant contribution to its understanding. In the 2002 New Delhi Conference, the ILA's Committee on the Legal Aspects of Sustainable Development had established a set of seven principles on sustainable development. They were enshrined in the New Delhi Declaration of Principles of International Law Relating to Sustainable Development[79] (hereinafter, ILA New Delhi Declaration), which was addressed to the Secretary-General of the United Nations to be circulated as a document of the World Summit on Sustainable Development in Johannesburg in July of the same year. As can be understood from the title and from the conference report,[80] the Declaration is intended not to set out general principles of sustainable development but to identify the principles of international law that support it, deriving either from general international law or from international environmental law.[81] Indeed, the seventh principle is "The principle of integration and interrelationship, in particular in relation to human rights and social, economic and environmental objectives",[82] which is taken from general international law and described as the very backbone of the concept of sustainable development.[83]

The principle of integration and interrelationship expressed in the ILA New Delhi Declaration is characterised by five dimensions. The first is possibly the most innovative in respect of the developments seen above: "The principle of integration reflects the interdependence of social, economic, financial, environmental and human rights aspects of principles and rules of international law relating to sustainable development as well as of the interdependence of the needs of current and future generations of humankind."[84] Therefore, integration extends to the principles and rules that regulate the different dimensions

79 ILA. Committee on Legal Aspects of Sustainable Development. 2002. "Resolution 3/2002. New Delhi Declaration of Principles of International Law Relating to Sustainable Development." https://www.ila-hq.org/en_GB/documents/conference-resolution-english-new-delhi-2002-3.

80 Ibid.

81 The seven principles contained are: sustainable use of natural resources; equity and the eradication of poverty; common but differentiated responsibilities; precautionary approach; public participation and access to information and justice; good governance; and integration and interrelationship. In ILA New Delhi Declaration, *supra* note 79.

82 Ibid. Principle 7.

83 Ibid.

84 Ibid. Principle 7.1.

of sustainable development. This implies a clear normative approach to the issue of integration, which was lacking in prior definitions of integration.

The second dimension is the interdependence of the needs of current and future generations.[85] This is less easily defined, as it is sometimes considered another dimension of sustainable development along with the sustainable use of natural resources or the principle of integration itself.[86] The third dimension is the reliance on all levels of governance for the implementation of the principle of integration together with all sectors of society,[87] establishing an institutional dimension of integration both vertically and horizontally. The fourth is the resolution of conflicts between competing economic, financial, social and environmental considerations through existing or new institutions.[88] This is an implicit call to address traditionally confronted interests. Finally, the fifth dimension is the interrelationship in terms of application and interpretation between the principles of sustainable development set out in the declaration,[89] establishing a form of internal integration.

The ILA New Delhi Declaration does not seem to have transcended to the Johannesburg Declaration, but it is telling of the growing recognition of the principle of integration as a central element of sustainable development, at least in academia. It is also a relevant attempt to develop the content of the principle. In fact, the work of the ILA's Committee on International Law on Sustainable Development at the 2006 Toronto Conference was devoted precisely to conceptualising the principle of integration from a legal perspective. The Committee aimed to move beyond the practicalities of integration to establish a 'framework of integration', based on the assumption that integration could not be limited to the definition given in Principle 4 of the Rio Declaration and was in fact much more complex.[90] Therefore, it suggested for analytical purposes a structure of three pillars: systemic integration, institutional integration and normative integration.

85 Ibid.

86 See, for instance, Sands, Philippe, Jacqueline Peel, Adriana Fabra Aguilar, and Ruth MacKenzie. 2012. *Principles of International Environmental Law*. 3rd ed. Cambridge: Cambridge University Press. 206–216.

87 ILA New Delhi Declaration, *supra* note 79, Principle 7.2.

88 Ibid. Principle 7.3.

89 Ibid. Principle 7.4.

90 See, generally, ILA. Committee on International Law on Sustainable Development. 2006. "Report of the Toronto Conference." https://www.ila-hq.org/en_GB/documents/conference-report-toronto-2006-14. 3–4.

The first pillar is defined as the "imperative that sustainable development must be achieved without, in any way, undermining any of the three pillars."[91] In the discussions undertaken by the Committee, it was acknowledged that such an idea is idealistic and that more practical forms of implementation are required. The second pillar, institutional integration, is considered the most obvious and the most closely aligned with Principle 4 of the Rio Declaration. It would operate through mechanisms to ensure that sustainable development concerns are included in the decision-making process. On the one hand, it implies an integrated decision-making process, both internally in each institution (intra-institutional integration) and between institutions in vertical and horizontal relations (inter-institutional integration). On the other hand, integration should operate at the level of projects, policies and programmes and at organisational level.[92]

Finally, the pillar of legal integration focuses on the interrelationship between norms, which entails normative integration and integration as a tool of judicial reasoning. Normative integration can be applied in three ways: between treaties regulating different aspects of sustainable development (intra-treaty integration); between different bodies of law that have developed in isolation to some extent (inter-disciplinary integration); and the incorporation of an integrated approach for sustainable development into existing laws (intra-disciplinary). Legal integration as a judicial reasoning tool, meanwhile, focuses on "the use of integrative techniques as part of the judicial reasoning-process,"[93] which can derive from the integrative nature of the norms to be applied when these norms incorporate sustainable development considerations, but may also be mandated unilaterally by the tribunal.[94]

2 The Legal Nature of the Principle of Integration

Once it has been determined the process through which the principle of integration has developed as a principle of international environmental law, it is necessary to analyse what normativity it has in this legal domain. The aim here is to conduct a systematic analysis of the legal basis of the principle of integration to determine its customary or conventional character. The following two sections should allow to determine the extent to which the principle of

91 Ibid. 5.
92 Ibid. 7–12.
93 Ibid. 13.
94 Ibid. 12–22.

integration is reflected in norms emanating from these two sources of international law.

2.1 *The Principle of Integration as a Customary Norm*

It must be now considered if the principle of integration has acquired the character of a customary norm, as some authors have sustained.[95] Ascertaining the customary nature of the principle of integration would imply that it is generally applicable to all States, – except for those that had expressly and persistently objected to it while the rule was in the process of formation, and regardless of the legal nature of other concurring norms of international law.[96]

The customary nature of a norm can only be ascertained if it complies with two conditions. On the one hand, the acts carried out under the alleged norm must amount to an extensive and uniform practice;[97] on the other hand, "they must also be such, or be carried out in such a way, as to be evidence of a belief that this practice is rendered obligatory by the existence of a rule of law requiring it."[98] In other words, in addition to the extensive and uniform character of a given practice, it must comply with the requirement of the *opinio iuris sive necessitates.*[99] Due to the uncertainty over the conditions required for the formation of customary norms, the ILC studied the matter and, in 2018, adopted the Draft conclusions on identification of customary international law,[100] which were in turn supported by the UNGA for their consideration by the States.[101]

---

95 See for instance: Rodrigo, "El Principio de Integración"; Barral and Dupuy, "Principle 4: Sustainable Development through Integration," 157–180.

96 See, for instance, Monaco, Riccardo. 1968. "Cours Général de Droit International Public." *Collected Courses of the Hague Academy of International Law* 125 (III): 93–335. 139–140; Visscher, Paul De. 1972. "Cours Général de Droit International Public." *Collected Courses of the Hague Academy of International Law* 136: 7–202. 61–77; Díez de Velasco Vallejo, Manuel. 2013. *Instituciones de Derecho Internacional Público.* 18th ed. Madrid: Tecnos, 140.

97 North Sea Continental Shelf (Federal Republic of Germany/Denmark; Federal Republic of Germany/Netherlands), Judgment, 1969 I.C.J. Rep. 3 (February 20). Para. 74.

98 Ibid. Para. 77.

99 For doctrinal analysis of the formation of customary law, see Virally, Michel. 1983. "Cours Générale de Droit International Public." *Collected Courses of the Hague Academy of International Law* 183 (V): 9–382. 184–186.

100 ILC, *Draft conclusions on identification of customary international law*, A/CN.4/SER.A/2018/Add.1 (Part 2), at 65–66 (2018), https://legal.un.org/ilc/publications/yearbooks/english/ilc_2018_v2_p2.pdf.

101 UN General Assembly, Resolution 73/203, *Identification of customary international law*, A/RES/73/203 (11 January 2019), undocs.org/en/A/RES/73/203.

The practice that is relevant in order to consider the existence of a customary norm is essentially that of the States,[102] although the ILC recognises that in certain circumstances the practices of international organisations might contribute to the formation of customary norms.[103] One of the most common practices carried out by States is the adoption of national plans for sustainable development based on the principle of integration. This had been a trend over the last decades,[104] but since 2015 it has become a general practice as an application of Agenda 2030.[105] It is rare to find any recent national strategy on sustainable development that does not claim to be an implementation of Agenda 2030. This can easily be observed through the Voluntary National Reviews delivered by the States to the High-level Political Forum on Sustainable Development,[106] in which almost all UN member States have described their efforts to pursue the SDGs through the adoption of a national plan, among other measures. These national plans might be deemed to be an application of the principle of integration since, as seen above, the network structure of SDGs adopted by Agenda 2030 is itself a clear expression of integration for sustainable development.

Another widespread practice is the performance of Environmental Impact Assessment (hereinafter, EIAs) for projects with potentially harmful effects on the environment, as they are one of the most important tools for the application of the principle of integration.[107] EIAs will be analysed more in depth in Chapter 4, but it is necessary to acknowledge their widespread practice here. This can be seen in the adoption of national laws to introduce such a

102 The ILC provides a non-exhaustive and non-hierarchical list of acts that might be considered forms of State practice: "diplomatic acts and correspondence; conduct in connection with resolutions adopted by an international organization or at an intergovernmental conference; conduct in connection with treaties; executive conduct, including operational conduct "on the ground"; legislative and administrative acts; and decisions of national courts." (Draft conclusions on identification of customary international law, *supra* note 100, Conclusion 6.2.).

103 This can only happen when the States have transferred exclusive competences to those organisations and their practices might be equated to those of the States (Draft conclusions on identification of customary international law, *supra note* 100, Conclusion 4, Commentary (6)).

104 Rodrigo Hernández, Ángel J. 2015. *El Desafío Del Desarrollo Sostenible*. Madrid: Marcial Pons. 167.

105 Agenda 2030 establishes that the introduction of the SDGs in national planning as one of the commitments of States. In Agenda 2030, *supra* note 69, Para. 55.

106 High-level Political Forum on Sustainable Development. "Voluntary National Reviews | High-Level Political Forum." Accessed December 11, 2024. https://hlpf.un.org/vnrs.

107 ILA Report of the Toronto Conference, *supra* note 90, 10–11; Rodrigo, *El Desafío Del Desarrollo Sostenible*. 154.

mechanism into the national legal system.[108] At the international level, EIAs are also a general practice in the context of projects which might have transboundary effects.[109] In fact, the obligation to conduct an EIA in such cases has been recognised as a general principle of international law,[110] so while their application is now common, it will become more widely so in the future.

State practice in applying the principle of integration can also be assessed through the implementation of integration obligations set out in international treaties, what would coincide with the 'conduct in connection to treaties' referred to by the ILC.[111] In this regard, conventions with wide international adherence have the potential to be more relevant as their implementation might be deemed representative of international practice.[112] Action taken in accordance with the Convention on Biological Diversity[113] (hereinafter, CBD) is possibly one of the most relevant examples, both because it has been ratified by most of the countries[114] and because it provides this type of provision for integration.[115] But the application of other environmental treaties is also important in this regard. See for instance the implementation of the United Nations Convention to Combat Desertification in Those Countries Experiencing Serious Drought and/or Desertification, Particularly in Africa[116] (hereinafter, Convention to Combat Desertification) or some important regional

108 Already in 1996, a study found more than 100 countries with EIA legislation (Sadler, Barry. 1996. *Environmental Assessment in a Changing World: Evaluating Practice to Improve Performance.* Ottawa: Canadian Environmental Assessment Agency. 25).

109 Conducting an EIA is one of the contentious points in some cases brought to the ICJ. See, for instance, Gabčikovo-Nagymaros Project (Hungary/Slovakia), Judgment, 1997 I.C.J. Rep. 7 (September 25); or Certain Activities Carried Out by Nicaragua in the Border Area (Costa Rica v. Nicaragua) and Construction of a Road in Costa Rica along the San Juan River (Nicaragua v. Costa Rica), Judgment, 2015 I.C.J. Rep. 665 (December 15).

110 Pulp Mills on the River Uruguay (Argentina v. Uruguay), 2010 Judgment, I.C.J. Rep. 14 (April 20). Para. 204. This matter will be analysed in more depth in Chapter 4.

111 Draft conclusions on identification of customary international law, *supra note* 100, Conclusion 6.2.

112 On the custom generated by the application of treaties see Dinstein, Yoram. 2006. "Customary International Law and Treaties." *Collected Courses of the Hague Academy of International Law* 322: 423–27. 376–379.

113 Convention on Biological Diversity, June 5, 1992, 1760 U.N.T.S. 79.

114 Up to 196 States have become members of the CBD by the 3 of March 2023.

115 See CBD, *supra* note 113, Article 6(b).

116 United Nations Convention to Combat Desertification in those Countries Experiencing Serious Drought and/or Desertification, Particularly in Africa, October 14, 1994, 1954 U.N.T.S. 3. See UNCCD Evaluation Office. "Evaluation of the Drought Initiative: Final Report," 2022. https://www.unccd.int/sites/default/files/inline-files/Drought Initiative evaluation final report.pdf.

treaties, such as the TFEU through its article 11,[117] the Barcelona Convention for the Protection of the Marine Environment and the Coastal Region of the Mediterranean.[118]

An overview of the practices described so far shows that they have the sufficient generality required for the formation of customary law. The ILC's Draft Conclusions on Identification of Customary International Law state that "[t]he relevant practice must be general, meaning that it must be sufficiently widespread and representative, as well as consistent."[119] Since the practices examined derive from conventions that are universal and widely ratified, they might be deemed to be widespread and representative. While it is true that none of these practices is undertaken by all existing States, universality of practice is not a condition for the formation of customary law,[120] nor is it necessary that such practice be identical. Indeed, as stated by the ICJ: "The Court does not consider that, for a rule to be established as customary, the corresponding practice must be in absolutely rigorous conformity with the rule."[121] Therefore, practice in the application of different treaties might provide the basis for the appearance of a single customary norm so long as it is consistent, as it is the case here.

As stated by the ILC, the second constituent element of customary law, the *opinio iuris*, might be proved through several forms of evidence.[122] Some of these are especially relevant in the case of integration of the economic, social and environmental dimensions. To begin with, all soft law instruments analysed in the first Section of this Chapter can be considered signs of the existence of an *opinio iuris* relating to the principle of integration,[123] since they

---

117 This provision requires that the environmental impacts of any sectoral policy forwarded by the EU be duly assessed, which is a clear example of the adoption of the principle of integration in a constitutive treaty such as the TFEU.

118 Convention for the Protection of the Marine Environment and the Coastal Region of the Mediterranean, February 16, 1995, 1102 U.N.T.S. 27. See UNEP, and Mediterranean Action Plan and Plan Bleu. 2020. *State of the Environment and Development in the Mediterranean.* Nairobi: UNEP.

119 Draft conclusions on identification of customary international law, *supra* note 100, Conclusion 8.1.

120 Dinstein, "Customary International Law and Treaties," 218–226.

121 Military and Paramilitary Activities in and against Nicaragua (Nicaragua v. United States of America), Judgment, 1986 I.C.J. Rep. 14 (June 27). Para. 186.

122 "[P]ublic statements made on behalf of States; official publications; government legal opinions; diplomatic correspondence; decisions of national courts; treaty provisions; and conduct in connection with resolutions adopted by an international organization or at an intergovernmental conference." (Draft conclusions on identification of customary international law, *supra* note 100, Conclusion 10.2.)

123 In relation to this argument see Rodrigo, *El Desafío Del Desarrollo Sostenible*. 167.

were negotiated by the delegations of States in international conferences and, therefore, are an indirect expression of the views of States.[124]

This understanding of the role of resolutions emanating from international organisations and international conferences has a basis in the ICJ resolution on *Military and Paramilitary Activities in and against Nicaragua* (*Nicaragua v. United States of America*), which recognised it in "the attitude of the Parties and the attitude of States towards certain General Assembly resolutions, and particularly resolution 2625 (XXV)"[125] and to the "United States acceptance of the principle of the prohibition of the use of force which is contained in the declaration on principles governing the mutual relations of States participating in the Conference on Security and Co-operation in Europe".[126]

For the purpose of this Chapter, it is of outmost relevance that the resolutions of international conferences viewed earlier in Section a) were voted by most of the States, but also the actual adoption by the UNGA of the outcome document emanating from the United Nations summit for the adoption of the post-2015 development agenda *Transforming our world: the 2030 Agenda for Sustainable Development*.[127] Particularly of this last resolution it has been recognised its capacity to overcome its formal recommendatory character and have legal consequences.[128] In this regard, if the 2030 Agenda is seen as the latest step in a series of international conferences supporting sustainable development with increasing legal character, it is not unreasonable to recognise in this process the expression of an *opinio iuris*.

Treaties might also play a role in the creation of customary law.[129] The ILC identifies three ways in which this relationship operates, of which one is

---

124 As explained by the ILC, "Draft conclusion 12 concerns the role that resolutions adopted by international organizations or at intergovernmental conferences may play in the determination of rules of customary international law. It provides that, while such resolutions, of themselves, can neither constitute rules of customary international law nor serve as conclusive evidence of their existence and content, they may have value in providing evidence of existing or emerging law and may contribute to the development of a rule of customary international law" (Draft conclusions on identification of customary international law, *supra* note 100, 107).

125 Military and Paramilitary Activities in and against Nicaragua (Nicaragua v. United States of America), Judgment, 1986 I.C.J. Rep. 14 (June 27). Para. 188.

126 Ibid. Para. 189.

127 Agenda 2030, *supra* note 69.

128 Díaz-Galán, Elena. 2022. "The 2030 Agenda for Sustainable Development's Legal Value: A New Regulatory Trend?" *Iberoamerican Journal of Development Studies* 11 (2): 30–52. 47–48.

129 On this topic see, generally, Mendelson, Maurice H. 1998. "Formation of Customary International Law." *Collected Courses of the Hague Academy of International Law* 272: 155–410. 294–346.

relevant here: "A rule set forth in a treaty may reflect a rule of customary international law if it is established that the treaty rule [...] has given rise to a general practice that is accepted as law (opinio juris), thus generating a new rule of customary international law."[130] As will be shown in the next Section, there are several treaties that contain provisions on integration. On the basis of the corresponding *travaux préparatoires*, an evolution can be observed in the consideration given to integration, which might show the emergence of the *opinio iuris* regarding the consuetudinary character of the principle of integration.

The negotiations of the so-called 'Rio conventions' – of which only the United Nations Framework Convention on Climate Change (hereinafter, UNFCCC)[131] refers to integration as a principle – show that, in the early 1990s, the principle of integration was too recent a development to be considered a customary law. It was enshrined in all three conventions with differing formulations and forms. However, the adoption thirty years later of the Agreement under the United Nations Convention on the Law of the Sea on the Conservation and Sustainable Use of Marine Biological Diversity of Areas beyond National Jurisdiction[132] (hereinafter, BBNJ Convention) draws an evolution in this regard. The draft contains "[a]n integrated approach to ocean management" in Article 5 on 'General principles and approaches',[133] marking a shift away from the conventions discussed above. In this case, the 'integrated approach' is a generally applicable mandate of the BBNJ Convention rather than an implementing obligation. Moreover, it must be taken into account that despite the many proposals to make changes to Article 7 of the BBNJ Convention, the inclusion of the 'integration approach' was not disputed by any delegation during the negotiations. Considering that the inclusion of the principle of integration in the 'Rio conventions' was less straightforward, this might be indicative of the consolidation of an *opinio iuris* regarding the consuetudinary character of the principle of integration.

Clear evidence of the principle of integration operating as a customary norm might also be found in the positions maintained by States before international courts. This is apparent in all of those cases in which one of the interests at stake is an activity that might be considered 'developmental' and which may enter into conflict with environmental concerns. If seen from this perspective,

130 Draft conclusions on identification of customary international law, *supra* note 100, Conclusion 11.1(c).

131 United Nations Framework Convention on Climate Change, May 9, 1992, 1771 U.N.T.S. 107. Article 3.4.

132 Agreement under the United Nations Convention on the Law of the Sea on the Conservation and Sustainable Use of Marine Biological Diversity of Areas beyond National Jurisdiction, June 19, 2023, N/A U.N.T.S.

133 Ibid. Article 7(g).

in most of the cases brought to the ICJ the Parties accepted that their rights should be balanced in some way with environmental standards.

As established in Article 38.1.d. of the Statute of the ICJ,[134] the judicial recognition of customary norms is a subsidiary means of recognition of international law. However, due to the difficulties of identifying customary norms, the opinions of international courts are particularly relevant.[135] The ILC explicitly accepts this form of recognition and notes that: "Decisions of international courts and tribunals, in particular of the International Court of Justice, concerning the existence and content of rules of customary international law are a subsidiary means for the determination of such rules."[136]

The clearest recognition of the principle of integration was expressed in the *Arbitration Regarding the Iron Rhine (IJzeren Rijn") Railway (Belgium/Netherlands)*.[137] The explicit recognition of an international obligation is made with respect to the duty to prevent and mitigate significant harm.[138] However, the argument is based on the explicit assumption that integration between economic and environmental concerns must be operationalised by linking their corresponding areas of law. In addition, the fact that the arbitral tribunal recalls Principle 4 of the Rio Declaration in support of its argument[139] implies that the customary character of the principle of integration extends to both the legal relationship between the environment and development and to the decision-making process itself. In other words, both the normative and institutional dimensions of the principle of integration are part of the principle of integration as a customary norm of international law.

Also relevant is the arbitral award on *Indus Waters Kishenganga Arbitration (Pakistan vs. India)*, which explicitly recognises the "customary international requirements of [...] reconciling economic development with the protection of the environment."[140] The arbitral tribunal argued that Pakistan could not

134 United Nations, Statute of the International Court of Justice, October 24, 1945, N/A. U.N.T.S.

135 Dinstein, "Customary International Law and Treaties," 315–320.

136 Draft conclusions on identification of customary international law, *supra* note 100, Conclusion 13.1.

137 Arbitration Regarding the Iron Rhine ("Ijzeren Rijn") Railway (Belgium/Netherlands), 27 R.I.A.A (Perm. Ct. Arb. 2005). Para 59.

138 This obligation will be analysed in depth in the next Chapter, but it has an extensive recognition in international jurisprudence. See Trail smelter case (United States/Canada), 3 R.I.A.A (Perm. Ct. Arb. 1941); Corfu Channel case (United Kingdom v. Albania), Judgment, 1949 I.C.J. Rep. 4 (April 9); Legality of the Threat or Use of Nuclear Weapons, Advisory Opinion, 1996 I.C.J. Rep. 226. Para. 29; Pulp Mills on the River Uruguay (Argentina v. Uruguay), 2010 Judgment, I.C.J. Rep. 14 (April 20). Para. 101.

139 Arbitration Regarding the Iron Rhine ("Ijzeren Rijn") Railway (Belgium/Netherlands), 27 R.I.A.A (Perm. Ct. Arb. 2005). Para 59.

140 Indus Waters Kishenganga Arbitration (Pakistan vs. India). Final award, 31 R.I.A.A (Perm. Ct. Arb. 2013). Para. 87.

be deprived of enough water to operate the Neelum-Jhelum Hydro-Electric Project according to Paragraph 15(iii) of Annexure D of the 1960 Indus Waters Treaty, as long as this water would not deprive India of the sufficient water to fulfil its rights according to this same agreement.[141] The tribunal also recognised, however, that the amount of water that India would be entitled to divert would also be limited by "customary international principles for the protection of the environment in force today."[142] Since this obligation of 'reconciling' is translated into an obligation to weigh developmental and environmental norms without precluding a specific outcome in terms of sustainability, it must be considered that the arbitral tribunal is invoking the principle of integration.

2.2 *The Principle of Integration in Conventional Environmental Law*

This Subsection analyses the conventional nature of the principle of integration. Since the principle of integration is a principle of international environmental law and its application as a customary norm can only be defined loosely in terms of its obligational content, conventional expressions may provide more specific insights of its materialisation in particular regimes.

The recognition of the principle of integration can be found mainly in conventional environmental law. As pointed out by Sands,[143] it is particularly present in the conventions deriving from the UNCED. Nevertheless, the forms in which such integration is meant to take place differ significantly in the scope and the level of action required from the States. In the field of biodiversity, for instance, integration appears in some of the main conventions. Section b) of Article 6 of the CBD[144] provides that: "Each Contracting Party shall, in accordance with its particular conditions and capabilities: [...] (b) Integrate, as far as possible and as appropriate, the conservation and sustainable use of biological diversity into relevant sectoral or cross-sectoral plans, programmes and policies." Similarly, several conventions refer to the integration of natural conservation into other sectoral plans, programmes or policies. The ASEAN Agreement on the Conservation of Nature and Natural Resources, for instance, states in relation to land use and planning that the Parties:

> shall endeavour to take the necessary measures to ensure the integration of natural resource conservation into the land use planning process and shall, in the preparation and implementation of specific land use plans

---

141 Ibid.

142 Ibid. Para. 85.

143 Sands, Philippe. 1994. "International Law in the Field of Sustainable Development." *British Yearbook of International Law* 65 (1): 303–381. 338–339.

144 CBD, *supra* note 113.

> at all levels, give as full consideration as possible to ecological factors as to economic and social ones.[145]

The UNESCO Convention for the protection of the world cultural and natural heritage, instead, provides that the Parties shall: "adopt a general policy which aims to give the cultural and natural heritage a function in the life of the community and to integrate the protection of that heritage into comprehensive planning programmes."[146] In those cases, it is the general nature of the plan, programme or policy in question that makes it possible to consider the three dimensions of sustainable development and for the resulting norm to be an expression of the principle of integration.

Some treaties have a more restricted focus, limited to the management of certain areas of environmental interest. The Convention for the Protection of the Marine Environment and the Coastal Region of the Mediterranean,[147] for instance, states the following: "the Contracting Parties shall: [...] commit themselves to promote the integrated management of the coastal zones, taking into account the protection of areas of ecological and landscape interest and the rational use of natural resources."[148]

Other examples are the Protocol on Integrated Coastal Zone Management in the Mediterranean[149] under the above-mentioned convention; the Protocol concerning Specially Protected Areas and Biological Diversity in the Mediterranean;[150] the Convention to Combat Desertification;[151] or the Kuwait regional convention for cooperation on the protection of the marine

145 ASEAN Agreement on the Conservation of Nature and Natural Resources, July 9, 1985, 67 ASEAN Legal Instruments. Article 12.

146 Convention for the protection of the world cultural and natural heritage, November 16, 1972, 1037 U.N.T.S. 151. Article 5.

147 Convention for the Protection of the Marine Environment and the Coastal Region of the Mediterranean, February 16, 1995, 1102 U.N.T.S. 27.

148 Ibid. Article 4.3.e).

149 Protocol on Integrated Coastal Zone Management (ICZM) in the Mediterranean, January 21, 2008, 2742 U.N.T.S. In relation to this treaty, see Campins Eritja, Mar. 2011. "Un Nuevo Paso En La Dirección Correcta: La Gestión Integrada de Las Zonas Costeras Mediterráneas." *Revista General de Derecho Europeo* 24.

150 "General obligations [...] Each Party shall take the necessary measures to: The Parties shall adopt strategies, plans and programmes for the conservation of biological diversity and the sustainable use of marine and coastal biological resources and shall integrate them into their relevant sectoral and intersectoral policies." In Protocol concerning Specially Protected Areas and Biological Diversity in the Mediterranean, June 10, 1995, 2102 U.N.T.S. 181. Article 3.4.

151 United Nations Convention to Combat Desertification in those Countries Experiencing Serious Drought and/or Desertification, Particularly in Africa, October 14, 1994, 1954 U.N.T.S. 3. Article 4, Section 2, first paragraph.

environment from pollution, although in that case integrated management is only mentioned in the preamble.[152]

There are also instruments that provide for the integration of a specific domain of nature conservation into the broader scope of economic and social development or the decision-making processes of the State in more general terms. An example of this formulation is Section a) of Article 10 of the CBD, which states that "Each Contracting Party shall, as far as possible and as appropriate: (a) Integrate consideration of the conservation and sustainable use of biological resources into national decision-making."[153]

Another formulation is provided by Article 7(g) of the BBNJ Convention, which refers to the "integrated approach to ocean management."[154] Here, integration is formulated not as a principle but as an approach. However, while the article is titled "General principles and approaches", some of the elements it lists cannot be qualified as principles or as approaches,[155] indicates a lack of relevance of the name. The substance of this article is that the elements listed are to guide the Parties in achieving the objectives of the convention. Since there are no other elements delimiting this clause, an integrated approach to management (in this case in relation to the ocean) should be understood as considering a wide range of factors, including social and environmental ones.[156]

The conventions on climate change also include an 'integration' clause. In the case of the UNFCCC,[157] this can be found in Article 3, where the clause is expressed in a very similar sense to Article 6 of the CBD, pledging to include climate change in national development programmes: "Policies and measures to protect the climate system [...] should be appropriate for the specific conditions of each Party and should be integrated with national development programmes."[158] In the same vein, Article 4 refers to the inclusion of climate change considerations in each social, economic and environmental policy.[159]

---

152 In its preamble, it recognises the "need to develop an integrated management approach to the use of the marine environment and the coastal areas which will allow the achievement of environmental and development goals in a harmonious manner". In Kuwait Regional Convention for co-operation on the protection of the marine environment from pollution, April 24, 1978, 1140 U.N.T.S. 133. Preamble, sixth paragraph.

153 CBD, *supra* note 113, Article 10.

154 BBNJ Convention, *supra* note 132, Article 7(g).

155 See paragraphs (c), (h), (k), (m) and (n). In Ibid.

156 An example of what is commonly understood by 'integrated approach to management' can be found in the concept of Integrated Water Resources Management, which will be analysed in depth in Chapter 4.

157 UNFCCC, *supra* note 131.

158 Ibid. Article 3, section 4.

159 "Take climate change considerations into account, to the extent feasible, in their relevant social, economic and environmental policies and actions". Ibid. Article 4, Section 1, para. f).

A more clearly worded integration clause is also present in the Paris Agreement:

> "Parties recognize the importance of integrated, holistic and balanced non-market approaches being available to Parties to assist in the implementation of their nationally determined contributions, in the context of sustainable development and poverty eradication, in a coordinated and effective manner, including through, inter alia, mitigation, adaptation, finance, technology transfer and capacity building, as appropriate.[160]

The above examples illustrate the general and explicit inclusion of the principle of integration in treaties in the area of international environmental law – although in a few cases the integrative clause has been added in the preamble to avoid including it in the body of the treaty.[161] However, it is increasingly common to find linkages between the economic, social and environmental dimensions in treaties from other branches of international law, even if integration is not referred to specifically.[162] As noted by Sands,[163] there is a growing tendency to cross-link between treaties in different legal domains compared to the rather hermetic treaties of the 1950s and 1960s such as the General Agreement on Tariffs and Trade[164] of 1947 or the constituent treaty of the International Monetary Fund.[165] One example is the Preamble of the Agreement establishing the World Trade Organisation,[166] which explicitly mentions sustainable development and recognises the need to pursue social interests, such

160 Paris Agreement, December 15, 2015, 3156 U.N.T.S. Article 6, Section 8.

161 See, for instance, Kuwait Regional Convention for co-operation on the protection of the marine environment from pollution, April 24, 1978, 1140 U.N.T.S. 133. Preamble, sixth paragraph.

162 Cordonier and Khalfan propose a gradient of integration of social, economic and environmental considerations in treaties. They distinguish between 'separate spheres', 'parallel yet interdependent spheres', 'partially integrated spheres' and 'highly integrated new regimes'. In Cordonier Segger, Marie-Claire, and Ashfaq Khalfan. 2004. *Sustainable Development Law: Principles, Practices, & Prospects*. New York: OUP.

163 Sands, Philippe. 1999. "Sustainable Development: Treaty, Custom, and the Cross-Fertilization of International Law." In *International Law and Sustainable Development. Past Achievements and Future Challanges*, edited by A. Boyle and D. Freestone, 39–60. Oxford: OUP. 43.

164 General Agreement on Tariffs and Trade, October 30, 1947, 64 U.N.T.S. 187.

165 Articles of Agreement of the International Monetary Fund, December 27, 1945, 2 U.N.T.S. 39.

166 Agreement establishing the World Trade Organization, April 15, 1995, 1867 U.N.T.S.

as the attainment of full employment, and the preservation of the environment in the realisation of economic development activities.[167]

Similar linkages are apparent in Article 4 of the Montreal Protocol on Substances that Deplete the Ozone Layer,[168] which contains several provisions for the prohibition of trade with substances that deplete the ozone layer. In particular, it prohibits the exportation and importation of substances which deplete the ozone layer with third Parties to the Protocol.[169] It also prohibits State subsidies, aid, credits, guarantees or insurance programs to such exports and of technology that can facilitate its production.[170]

3 The Normative Content of the Principle of Integration

Having determined the origin of the principle of integration, its conceptual development and its insertion in international law, it remains to consider what is implied by the application of the principle. Specifically, it must be defined the normative content of the principle of integration and, by extension, what normative performance might be expected from it. Initially, the normative content can be divided into two streams.

On the one hand, the principle of integration may involve the establishment of normative linkages between different regimes of international law. This is related to the unifying effect of the integration of the economic, social and environmental dimensions in the context of the fragmentation of international law referred to earlier in Chapter 1. In cases where developmental and environmental interests are affected simultaneously, the principle of integration should provide the mechanisms to apply norms from both domains to a certain extent. Such analysis will feed into Part III of the book.

On the other hand, the principle of integration may be translated into an obligation for decision-makers to conduct an integrated decision-making process. That is, a process allowing for the full spectrum of sustainable development values to be taken into account, which will have a certain bearing on the outcome. This, in turn, might require the use of certain tools and institutional mechanisms to provide decision-makers with all the necessary elements for integration. In other words, integration might give ground to procedural

---

167 In Ibid. Preamble, first paragraph.

168 Montreal Protocol on Substances that Deplete the Ozone Layer, September 16, 1987, 1522 U.N.T.S. 3.

169 Ibid. Article 4. Paras. 1–2.

170 Ibid. Article 4. Para. 6.

obligations. This is largely consistent with the concept of integration that derives from Article 4 of the Rio Declaration, which will be the focus of Part IV of the book.

3.1 *The Principle of Integration as an Obligation of Inter-Systemic Application of International Law*

One main purpose of the principle of integration is to produce the legal inter-systemic linkages between the various areas of law that have a bearing on sustainable development. The principle of integration in this sense must be understood as aimed at link different normative spaces so that each incorporates the values of the other. In this sense, it would have an 'intersystemic' function, aimed at coordinating the heterogeneity of normative systems based on different values.[171] The ILA also identified this consequence of the principle of integration, which was stated in the 2002 New Delhi Declaration to reflect "the interdependence of social, economic, financial, environmental and human rights aspects of principles and rules of international law relating to sustainable development as well as of the interdependence of the needs of current and future generations of humankind."[172]

This dimension of the principle of integration can operate in two ways depending on the subject responsible for its application. On the one hand, it operates in the norm-creating stage by providing norms that form the legal basis for integration. Most obviously, this means to create normative *passerelles* between the regimes regulating the different domains of sustainable development; it also comprises the use of other legal techniques to consider under one regime the interests of other regimes. This is a mandate directed to those subjects with the capacity to create binding international norms; namely, States and international organisations in certain cases. More specifically, understood in this sense, the principle of integration would apply to the negotiators of treaties, who should ensure that the resulting text provides a legal basis for the integration of economic, social and environmental concerns. As explained by Rodrigo, "[l]a implementación del principio de integración exige, en primer lugar, que sea incorporado en los tratados internacionales con el objetivo de ayudar a la integración normativa de forma intencional ya sea intratratado o bien entre tratados del miso o diferente régimen."[173]

---

171 Dubin, "Fonction Intersystémique Du Concept de Développement Durable", 175–98. Paris: Société de législation comparée. 175–176. This author is referring to the concept of sustainable development, but the inter-systemic function attributed to it can be considered to coincide with the content of the principle of integration.

172 ILA New Delhi Declaration, *supra* note 79, Principle 7.1.

173 Rodrigo, *El Desafío Del Desarrollo Sostenible*. 171.

This purpose of integration was already identified in Agenda 21. In Chapter 39 of this instrument dedicated to international legal instruments and mechanisms, the States recognised "[t]he need to clarify and strengthen the relationship between existing international instruments or agreements in the field of environment and relevant social and economic agreements or instruments"[174] and accordingly established the objective to review and develop international environmental law to "promote the integration of environment and development policies through effective international agreements or instruments taking into account both universal principles and the particular and differentiated needs and concerns of all countries."[175] This purpose of the principle of integration can be pursued by the treaty negotiators through a variety of normative techniques that allow for the consideration under one regime of the values of other regimes,[176] as this research will explain in Chapter 7.

However, although the subjects responsible for applying the principle of integration through the inter-systemic implementation of international law are easily identified and the overall objective is clear, the matter of enforceability is less straightforward. The normative character of this dimension of the principle of integration is only generally established, such that there is no scope for deriving a specific obligation for subjects of international law that could eventually be the object of litigation. This is particularly so as it affects a central competency in the sovereignty of States: the capacity to negotiate and adopt international agreements. It most closely aligns with the sense of a directing principle envisioned by De Sadeleer, as it channels a normative policy.[177]

However, the political thrust of the principle of integration must not be underestimated. In this regard, Nollkaemper has observed the following: "Arguments of policy provide reasons for legislative bodies to develop the law in order to further the objective. As such, we can assume that the integration principle as a policy has co-inspired more particular legal rules."[178] Therefore,

---

174 Agenda 21, *supra* note 54, Para. 39.1.b.

175 Ibid. Para. 39.2.

176 For an analysis of legal techniques operating inter-systemic linkages see Gradoni, Lorenzo. 2009. "Systèmes Juridiques Internationaux : Une Esquisse." In *La Circulation Des Concepts Juridiques : Le Droit International de l'environnement Entre Mondialisation et Fragmentation*, edited by Hélène Ruiz Fabri and Lorenzo Gradoni, 27–52. Paris: Société de législation comparée.

177 Sadeleer, Nicolas De. 2002. *Environmental Principles: From Political Slogans to Legal Rules*. Oxford: OUP. 269–270.

178 Nollkaemper, André. 2002. "Three Conceptions of the Integration Principle in International Environmental Law." In *Environmental Policy Integration: Greening Sectoral Policies in Europe*, edited by A. Lenschow, 22–32. London: Earthscan. 25.

the principle of integration as a guide for the norm-creation stage might exert a strong political influence; indeed, the analysis of conventional law presented in the previous Section shows that it has certainly done so.

On the other hand, the inter-systemic linkages between the different regimes can take place through the application and interpretation of norms by international courts in the context of a dispute. This expression of the principle of integration is what the ILA has called 'integration as a judicial reasoning tool'.[179] The principle of integration enables international judges to apply and interpret applicable law in such a way that it integrates other dimensions of sustainable development regulated in norms that are not directly applicable in a given case.[180]

The principle of integration as a judicial reasoning tool operates through three interpretative techniques, which are not exclusive of the principle of integration, but that might be put into practice for its operationalisation. The first of these techniques is the teleological interpretation of norms or concepts.[181] The second is the systemic interpretation of international norms,[182] as provided in Article 31.3.c) of the Statute of the Vienna Convention on the Law of the Treaties,[183] especially through the interpretation of evolutionary concepts.[184] The third technique is the interpretation of open-textured obligations.[185] These techniques of interpretation and their capacity to operationalise the principle of integration are the focus of Chapter 10.

The principle of integration in the sense explained in this Chapter – that is, operating as a principle that guides the creation of norms and their

179 ILA Report of the Toronto Conference, *supra* note 90, 18–22.

180 Rodrigo, *El Desafío Del Desarrollo Sostenible*. 158.

181 On this topic see, for instance, Zarbiev, Fouad. 2009. "L'interprétation Téléologique Des Traités." In *La Circulation Des Concepts Juridiques : Le Droit International de l'environnement Entre Mondialisation et Fragmentation*, edited by Hélène Ruiz Fabri and Lorenzo Gradoni, 199–242. Paris: Société de législation comparée.

182 On this topic see, generally, Cazala, Julien. 2009. "Le Rôle de l'interprétation Des Traités à La Lumière de Toute Autre « règle Pertinente de Droit International Applicable Entre Les Parties » En Tant Que « passerelle » Jetée Entre Systèmes Juridiques Différents." In *La Circulation Des Concepts Juridiques : Le Droit International de l'environnement Entre Mondialisation et Fragmentation*, edited by Hélène Ruiz Fabri and Lorenzo Gradoni, 95–136. Paris: Société de législation comparée.

183 Vienna Convention on the Law of the Treaties, May 23, 1969, 1155 U.N.T.S. 331. Article 31.3.c).

184 On this topic see, for instance, Alland, Denis. 2012. "L'interprétation Du Droit International Public." *Collected Courses of the Hague Academy of International Law* 362: 41–394. 207–215.

185 On this topic see, for instance, Kearns, Thomas R. 1972. "Open Texture and Judicial Law-Making." *Social Theory and Practice* 2 (2): 177–87.

interpretation – would fit with what Lowe has named 'interstitial norms'.[186] Under his definition, the principle of integration would be "a meta-principle, acting upon other legal rules and principles – a legal concept exercising a kind of interstitial normativity, pushing and pulling the boundaries of true primary norms when they threaten to overlap or conflict with each other."[187] Interstitial norms do not regulate behaviour by themselves. Their normative content is to be found in the norms to which they refer, which do have prescriptive content. In other words, the content of the integrating norm is the integration of two or more external norms.

Again, the vagueness of the principle of integration understood as a principle of interpretation prevents it having a binding nature. However, it can certainly guide interpretation. Indeed, it has been recognised that "as a goal or policy it is perfectly adequate to offer some guidance to judges in their approach to establishing priorities and accommodations between conflicting primary norms."[188] But despite the lack of bindingness for the courts, there are several examples in international case law of judgements applying the principle of integration in this interstitial manner.

For instance, the arbitral tribunal in *Indus Waters Kishenganga Arbitration* (*Pakistan vs. India*)[189] established that India's right to use the international watercourse was limited by Paragraph 15(iii) of Annexure D of the 1960 Indus Waters Treaty and by the principles of international environmental law. Those two norms would constitute the integrated norms, while the obligation to implement normative integration would also derive from customary law: the Tribunal's duty to take into consideration both norms derives from the "customary international law requirements of [...] reconciling economic development with the protection of the environment."[190]

186 Lowe, "Sustainable Development and Unsustainable Arguments". As examples of such kind of norms, Rodrigo mentions the principle of coherence and, precisely, the principle of integration of the economic, social and environmental aspects of sustainable development (In Rodrigo Hernández, Ángel J. 2011. "La Integración Normativa y La Unidad Del Derecho Internacional Público." In *Unidad y Pluralismo En El Derecho Internacional Público y En La Comunidad Internacional*, edited by Ángel J Rodrigo Hernández and Caterina García, 321–55. Madrid: Tecnos. 333–336).

187 Lowe, "Sustainable Development and Unsustainable Arguments", 31.

188 Lowe, Vaughan. 1999. "Sustainable Development and Unsustainable Arguments." In *International Law and Sustainable Development. Past Achievements and Future Challanges*, edited by A. Boyle and D. Freestone, 19–37. Oxford: OUP. 34. In this Chapter, Lowe discusses sustainable development, but in a sense that allows considering his analysis applicable to the principle of integration as used in this study.

189 Indus Waters Kishenganga Arbitration (Pakistan vs. India). Final award, 31 R.I.A.A (Perm. Ct. Arb. 2013).

190 Ibid. Para. 87.

3.2 *The Principle of Integration as an Obligation to Conduct a Decision-Making Process that Considers Economic, Social and Environmental Concerns*

The second obligation concerns the manner in which decisions pertaining to sustainable development are made. As seen above, integrated decision-making is the approach most closely aligned with Principle 4 of the 1992 Rio Declaration, which establishes that "environmental protection shall constitute an integral part of the development process and cannot be considered in isolation from it."[191] The general character of this formulation requires further examination of what integration means in this context. Dernbach offers the following definition:

> Integrated decisionmaking is a direct response to the tendency of governments, corporations, and other decisionmakers to treat the environmental or social aspects of a project or program separately from its other development aspects. [...] Thus, integrated decisionmaking is a response to the fragmented decisionmaking process that causes unsustainable development, and its centrality to sustainable development is expressly and implicitly supported by the Rio texts.[192]

Therefore, integration can be understood as the requirement to make the decision-making process much more complex; or, in other words, to acknowledge the complexity of the consequences that a decision might entail. The content of this obligation, therefore, can be summarised as 'to conduct the decision-making process in a way that ensures that economic, social and environmental aspects are taken into account. This is, of course, a very general obligation, in line with its 'principled character', as analysed above. How this is translated into specific actions will depend to a great extent on the policy or management domain in relation to which the decisions are made. This is the focus of Part III of the book, which analyses the specific tools through which an integrated decision-making process is operationalised.

Another question is to whom the obligation applies. Although the extent of its applicability is a matter for discussion, for the purpose of this research it is sufficient to recognise that it is applicable to all decision-makers as subjects of international law. This can be derived from the recognition of the customary

191 Rio Declaration, *supra* note 47, Principle 4.

192 Dernbach, John C. 2003. "Achieving Sustainable Development: The Centrality and Multiple Facets of Integrated Decisionmaking." *Indiana Journal of Global Legal Studies* 10 (1): 247–85. 251–257.

character of this obligation notwithstanding its particular expressions in conventional law. Thus, the subjects would be generally the States, but also those international organisations with the competences to make decisions in areas affecting sustainable development. This is the case of International River Basin Organisations (hereinafter, IRBOs), whose activities are the focus of Part III. Since they are usually in charge of defining the joint policy on an international watercourse or managing a particular aspect or element (e.g. a hydropower regime; the protection of a given ecosystem), they are usually responsible for decisions pertaining to the environmental impact of development actions (or indeed the impact on development of environmental measures).

Having defined the content and the subjects of the obligation to conduct integrated decision-making deriving from the principle of integration, we must answer a further question: is it an obligation of result or an obligation of conduct?

This question seems to have been settled by the international case law. In *Gabčikovo-Nagymaros Project (Hungary/Slovakia)*, having acknowledged that the "need to reconcile economic development with protection of the environment is aptly expressed in the concept of sustainable development,"[193] the ICJ derived an obligation for the parties to cooperate in order to find a solution. However, the Court declared itself incompetent to determine the outcome of these negotiations, thereby avoiding having to establish a concrete obligation of result and only specifying the manner in which a result should be sought: "It is for the Parties themselves to find an agreed solution that takes account of the objectives of the Treaty, which must be pursued in a joint and integrated way, as well as the norms of international environmental law and the principles of the law of international watercourses."[194] In other words, what is being mandated by the Court is not an obligation of result in terms of sustainability but rather an obligation of conduct. Integration, understood as the establishment of a decision-making process that allows social and economic factors to be considered alongside environmental factors, would be consistent with this approach.[195]

In *Arbitration Regarding the Iron Rhine (IJzeren Rijn") Railway (Belgium/Netherlands)*, the arbitral tribunal ruled on the obligations of the Parties regarding the protection of the environment in applying the Iron Rhine Treaty. As in the

193 Gabčikovo-Nagymaros Project (Hungary/Slovakia), Judgment, 1997 I.C.J. Rep. 7 (September 25). Para. 140.

194 Ibid. Para. 141.

195 For a reading of the judgment on this sense see Dubin, "Fonction Intersystémique Du Concept de Développement Durable", 182.

above case, the arbitral tribunal found that new developments in international (and EU) law "require the integration of appropriate environmental measures in the design and implementation of economic development activities."[196] Again, the arbitral tribunal does not derive an obligation of result from this acknowledgement of the development of environmental law, but rather an obligation to 'take into account' the new standards in the decision-making process. In fact, the arbitral tribunal explicitly cites Principle 4 of the Rio Declaration as a reflection of this new obligation under international law.[197]

It follows from international case law that when environmental interests conflict with developmental interests an obligation of conduct is triggered. There is no obligation that an integrated decision-making process must effectively lead to a sustainable outcome. At this point, the maximum interrelation between the two interests lies in the 'promotional' character of integration. As put by Birnie, Boyle and Redgewell, "although international law may not require development to be sustainable, it does require development decisions to be the outcome of a process which promotes sustainable development."[198] Voigt expresses a similar idea, although apparently considering integration as a dimension of sustainable development,[199] while Barral and Dupuy criticise that this obligations remains merely an obligation of conduct and note that:

> A purely formal process of integration whereby environmental considerations are simply 'taken into account' within the development decision-making process with no actual impact on the decision outcome may well fall short of being considered a sufficient effort in striving to achieve sustainable development. Surely, if the principle of integration were to have solely a procedural content, the status quo may be forever perpetuated and progress towards sustainable development never be achieved. In fact, the principle could altogether be meaningless as States could formally 'take into account' say environmental considerations, but then discard them as irrelevant or not sufficiently relevant to modify the development decision. States could thus continue with their business as usual, continue ignoring the intimate interdependence between socio-economic

196 Arbitration Regarding the Iron Rhine ("Ijzeren Rijn") Railway (Belgium/Netherlands), 27 R.I.A.A (Perm. Ct. Arb. 2005). Para. 59.

197 Ibid.

198 Birnie, Boyle and Redgwell, *International Law and the Environment*, 126–127.

199 Voigt, *Sustainable Development as a Principle of International Law*, 332–333.

> development and environmental protection and frustrate the attainment of the objective of sustainable development.[200]

While their analysis is undoubtedly accurate, the conclusions these authors draw do not seem to be supported by the case law of the ICJ or by international arbitral law. However, between a formal 'taking into account' that allows the environmental or the developmental interests to be dropped at any time with no consequences for the decision-maker and an obligation of result, a middle ground can be found in the notion of 'due diligence'. Although the "[d]iligence of the process does not necessarily ensure sustainability of the outcome,"[201] in a given case it can be ascertained if the decision-maker has conducted the process in such a way that the different interests in question are duly considered and the final decision reflects this effort. The practice reveals a wide variety of instruments through which diligence can be channelled, which are analysed in Part IV.

---

200 Barral and Dupuy, "Principle 4: Sustainable Development through Integration," 8–9.

201 Voigt, *Sustainable Development as a Principle of International Law*, 332–333.

CHAPTER 2

The Principle of Integration and International Watercourse Cooperation Frameworks

This Chapter analyses how international watercourses – as an element of the physical environment that is fundamental to the lives of many people – and sustainable development – as a global legal and political framework – have been interpellated as they have evolved. The first Section of which focuses on the dialogue between sustainable development and transboundary water resources. For this purpose, the general discourse on sustainable development – which is the context in which the principle of integration is born – is examined to assess the extent to which it has incorporated sustainable water management concerns and transboundary water resources. Next, it is examined how the general law on international watercourses has adopted sustainable development as an objective in its own right. This should make it possible to assess the extent to which international watercourse law has become a friendly legal environment for the principle of integration, allowing it to influence cooperation on international watercourses.

The second Section analyses the feasibility of applying the principle of integration in the law of international watercourses. The analysis focuses primarily on the definition of international watercourse as this is the legal concept that delimits the scope of application of this domain of international law and, hence, the legal domain in which the application of the principle of integration is the object of this study. However, an analysis is also offered of the material scope of international watercourse law, based on the assumption that the greater the number of activities regulated by this regime, the more feasible it is to consider the interests entailed by the principle of integration.

Finally, the principle of cooperation and the emergence of an obligation to institutionalise cooperation in international watercourses is discussed in the third Section.

1 International Watercourses and Sustainable Development: Issues of Mutual Concern

International watercourse law has evolved over the last decades largely in parallel with the spreading of sustainable development and the associated

 | DOI:10.1163/9789004736757_005

requirement to implement the principle of integration. In turn, sustainable development as an area of legal relevance owes its rapid development in large part to the practices of States relating to international watercourses. Thus, important mutual influences can be observed between these two fields. It is paradigmatic that several of the ICJ judgments and international arbitral awards that have contributed significantly to sustainable development are also key decisions in the field of international watercourse law.[1] This two-way process of influence is analysed here.

1.1 *The Progressive Inclusion of International Watercourses in the Sustainable Development Discourse*

The debate around sustainable development has included water resources as an issue of concern from its inception, albeit usually in a very general way. International watercourses are encompassed in the definitions of water resources, freshwater resources, and other similar concepts. This is even clearer when considering that the relevance of discussions on sustainable development at the international level – at the UN, for example – lies in the potential for coordinated action on shared interests, such as international watercourses. As discussed in the next Subection, international law has developed its own concept of international watercourses, which is generally understood to include not only the main stream, but also the related elements extending to the whole of the basin and including the groundwater connected to it.[2] In the first part of this Section, however, the focus is placed on the general inclusion of water concerns in sustainable development discourse, in the understanding that this necessarily encompasses international watercourses.

Amongst the soft law instruments, the protection of water resources was recognised in the Stockholm Declaration of 1972, whose principle 2 of which recognises the need to preserve water, among other natural resources, for future generations, stating that "[t]he natural resources of the earth, including the air, water, land, flora and fauna and especially representative samples of

1 See, in particular, Gabčikovo-Nagymaros Project (Hungary/Slovakia), Judgment, 1997 I.C.J. Rep. 7 (September 25); and Pulp Mills on the River Uruguay (Argentina v. Uruguay), 2010 Judgment, I.C.J. Rep. 14 (April 20). For an analysis of those judgements in relation to sustainable development see Szabó, Marcel. 2017. "Sustainable Development in the Judgments of the International Court of Justice." In *Sustainable Development Principles in the Decisions of International Courts and Tribunals: 1992–2012*, edited by Marie Claire Cordonier Segger and C. G. Weeramantry, 266–80. Abingdon: Routledge.

2 For a general explanation on the concept of international watercourse under international law see, for instance: McCaffrey, Stephen C. 2019. *The Law of International Watercourses*. 3d ed. Oxford: OUP. 28–60.

natural ecosystems, must be safeguarded for the benefit of present and future generations through careful planning or management, as appropriate."[3]

The Brundtland Report also underlined the close relationship between sustainable development and the preservation of water. In its definition of sustainable development, it points to the diversion of watercourses as a developmental human action affecting the environment which can pose a threat to life-support systems.[4]

The Rio declaration[5] did not make any specific reference to water or watercourses. However, the action plan accompanying the Rio Declaration, Agenda 21,[6] expresses a clear awareness of the importance of water for sustainable development. Water is associated with the satisfaction of human needs[7] and highlighted as important for health and sanitation, especially in relation to human settlements,[8] but it also has a major importance in the Chapter devoted to environmental protection: water resources are considered vulnerable to atmospheric changes, air pollution, and loss and degradation of forests.[9]

However, the most relevant part of Agenda 21 in relation to water is Chapter 18, which is devoted entirely to freshwater resources. The Chapter stresses the central role of water in achieving sustainable development, recognising the multi-sectoral nature of water resource development and its economic and social value, as well as emphasising its environmental importance.[10]

---

3 United Nations Conference on the Human Environment, *Declaration of the United Nations Conference on the Human Environment*, in Report of the United Nations Conference on the Human Environment, A/CONF.48/14/Rev.1. (5–16 June 1972), undocs.org/en/A/CONF.48/14/Rev.1. Principle 2.

4 World Commission on Environment and Development, *Report of the World Commission on Environment and Development: "Our Common Future"*, A/42/427 (4 August 1987), undocs.org/en/A/42/427.

5 United Nations Conference on Environment and Development, *Rio Declaration on Environment and Development*, in Report of the United Nations Conference on Environment and Development, A/CONF.151/26 (Vol. I) (12 August 1992), undocs.org/en/A/CONF.151/26/Rev.1(vol. I).

6 United Nations Conference on Environment and Development, *Agenda 21*, in *Report of the United Nations Conference on Environment and Development*, A/CONF.151/26 (Vol. I) (12 August 1992), undocs.org/en/A/CONF.151/26/Rev.1(vol. I).

7 Ibid. See, for instance, paras. 3.8(p), 5.23.

8 Ibid. See, for instance, paras. 6.3, 7.5(d), 7.35

9 See paras. 9.19, 9.25 and 11.10 in Ibid. On this topic see IPCC. 2008. *Climate Change and Water. Technical Paper of the Intergovernmental Panel on Climate Change.* Geneva: IPCC Secretariat; and Stefano, Lucia de, James Duncan, Shlomi Dinar, Kerstin Stahl, Kenneth M. Strzepek, and Aaron T. Wolf. 2012. "Climate Change and the Institutional Resilience of International River Basins." *Journal of Peace Research* 49 (1): 193–209.

10 Agenda 21, *supra* note 54. Para. 18.2.

It also acknowledges the importance of 'transboundary water resources' for the States and the need to cooperate in this area.[11] To achieve these objectives, this instrument establishes seven programme areas,[12] the first of which is 'integrated water resources development and management'.

The definition of integrated water resources development and management as a programme area of Agenda 21 was largely inspired by the Dublin Statement on Water and Sustainable Development[13] (hereinafter, Dublin Statement), a document arising from a preparatory event of the UNCED held a few months earlier. The Statement was based on four guiding principles, the first of which also encompassed the notion of integration of the economic, social and environmental dimensions: "[s]ince water sustains life, effective management of water resources demands a holistic approach, linking social and economic development with protection of natural ecosystems. Effective management links land and water uses across the whole of a catchment area or groundwater aquifer."[14]

This approach is latter developed in Agenda 21, where integrated management of water resources is based on four objectives, which have to be implemented at the level of catchment basin:

a. To promote a dynamic, interactive, iterative and multisectoral approach to water resources management, including the identification and protection of potential sources of freshwater supply, that integrates technological, socio-economic, environmental and human health considerations;
b. To plan for the sustainable and rational utilization, protection, conservation and management of water resources based on community needs and priorities within the framework of national economic development policy;
c. To design, implement and evaluate projects and programmes that are both economically efficient and socially appropriate within clearly defined strategies, based on an approach of full public participation,

11 Ibid. Para. 18.4.

12 Integrated water resources development and management; Water resources assessment; Protection of water resources, water quality and aquatic ecosystems; Drinking-water supply and sanitation; Water and sustainable urban development; Water for sustainable food production and rural development; and Impacts of climate change on water resources. In Agenda 21, *supra* note 54, Para. 18.5.

13 International Conference on Water and the Environment, *Dublin Statement on Water and Sustainable Development*, 37.819/H/D/M1SC (1992), https://wedocs.unep.org/20.500.11822/30961.

14 Ibid. Principle 1.

including that of women, youth, indigenous people and local communities in water management policy-making and decision-making;

d. To identify and strengthen or develop, as required, in particular in developing countries, the appropriate institutional, legal and financial mechanisms to ensure that water policy and its implementation are a catalyst for sustainable social progress and economic growth.[15]

According to Agenda 21, these objectives are also to be pursued in relation to transboundary waters, for which harmonisation of strategies and action programmes is recommended.[16] In any case, it should be noted that integration in relation to water resources is envisioned as a management principle in both the Dublin Statement and Agenda 21 and is also to be applied to the management of international watercourses. As summed up by Wouters, these two instruments directly linked to UNCED share the idea that sustainable development requires an integrated water resource management strategy.[17]

The subsequent resolutions on sustainable development adopted by international conferences or the UNGA reiterate the importance of water to the fulfilment of human needs and to the environment.[18] Especially relevant in this regard is the resolution adopted more than twenty years later establishing Agenda 2030,[19] which places a stronger focus on the interrelationship between sectors. SDG 6 is devoted specifically to water under the title "Ensure availability and sustainable management of water and sanitation for all" and is subdivided into six targets, of which the fifth is especially relevant for this research. As explained in the first Chapter, the interrelated structure of SDGs embodies the very nature of integration of the economic, social and environmental

15 Agenda 21, *supra* note 54, Para. 18.9.

16 Ibid. Para. 18.10.

17 Wouters, Patricia K., and Alistair S. Rieu-Clarke. 2001. "The Role of International Water Law in Promoting Sustainable Development." *Journal of Water Law* 12 (5): 281–83.

18 The Millenium Declaration mentions water both in relation to poverty eradication and in relation to the protection of the environment, as it does its Road map (UN General Assembly, Resolution 55/2, *United Nations Millennium Declaration*, A/RES/55/2 (18 September 2000), undocs.org/A/RES/55/2; and UN Secretary-General, *Road map towards the implementation of the United Nations Millennium Declaration. Report of the Secretary-General*, A/56/326 (6 September 2001), undocs.org/en/A/56/326). The Johannesburg Declaration and its implementation plan also profusely integrate water as a key element of sustainable development (World Summit on Sustainable Development, *Plan of implementation of the World Summit on Sustainable Development*, in *Report of the World Summit on Sustainable Development*, A/CONF.199/20 (26 August-4 September 2002), undocs.org/en/A/CONF.199/20).

19 United Nations summit for the adoption of the post-2015 development agenda, *Transforming our world: the 2030 Agenda for Sustainable Development*, A/RES/70/1 (21 October 2015), undocs.org/en/A/RES/70/1.

dimensions,[20] but Target 6.5 specifically mentions the implementation of integrated water resources management.[21] Sindico has analysed the key role of integrated water resources management in Agenda 2030, and he has highlighted its essential role in order to achieve the other Targets of SDG 6, so it has an internal function in the SDG itself. He has also pointed its external function, as it is also necessary to achieve Targets of several other SDGs.[22]

In addition, Target 6.5 states that integrated water resources management should be implemented at the transboundary level.[23] Transboundary water cooperation is necessary to implement integrated water resources management as established in Target 6.5, but also to achieve Targets from other SDGs. The indicators to monitor Target 6.5 are set accordingly to this two-fold aim: "6.5.1 Degree of integrated water resources management implementation (0–100)" and "6.5.2 Proportion of transboundary basin area with an operational arrangement for water cooperation."[24] This means, on the one hand, that in the current international agenda on sustainable development, international cooperation on international watercourses is recognised as necessary to achieve sustainable development. On the other hand, the relevance of watercourses for sustainable development is considered in two senses: quantitatively, as, according to indicator 6.5.2, it is assumed that the existence of a transboundary operation arrangement for water cooperation is a good sign in itself and is worth considering; and qualitatively, as, according to indicator 6.5.1, such cooperation should adopt an integrated water resources management approach.

This analysis shows that water resources have been part of sustainable development since the debate first arose and have gradually become a central concern. Proof of this is the inclusion of water as the focus of a specific SDG.

---

20 See International Council for Science. 2017. *A Guide to SDG Interactions: From Science to Implementation.* Edited by D.J. Griggs, M. Nilsson, A. Stevance, and D. McCollum. Paris: International Council for Science.

21 Agenda 2030, *supra* note 19, Target 6.5.

22 Such as Target 13.2 (on the integration of climate change measures into national policies, strategies and planning), 15.5 (on the degradation of natural habitats, loss of biodiversity protection and prevention of the extinction of threatened species) and 16.1 (on the reduction of violence and related death rates). Sindico, Francesco. 2016. *Transboundary Water Cooperation and the Sustainable Development Goals.* Paris: UNESCO. 21–26.

23 Agenda 2030, *supra* note 19, Target 6.5.

24 According to paragraph 75 of Agenda 2030, all goals and targets must be monitored by a set of global indicators, in addition to national and regional indicators. The global indicators had to be developed at UN level and where finally agreed in 2017 (UN General Assembly, Resolution 71/313, *Work of the Statistical Commission pertaining to the 2030 Agenda for Sustainable Development,* A/RES/71/313 (6 July 2017), undocs.org/A/RES/71/313).

In this context, and as a specific area within the wider field of water resources, international watercourses are also increasingly recognised as an essential element in sustainable development, largely due to the enormous quantitative importance of this resource. As a result, consensus has grown in the international community around the need for international cooperation on international watercourses with a view to ensuring their sustainable development. Even more importantly for this study, the idea that cooperation on international watercourses should also entail an integrated approach has been consolidated. The specific relevance lies in the fact that this is the background against which international watercourse law has developed over the last decades, both regionally and globally. The following Subsection looks at the question of how this background has been reflected in international watercourse law.

1.2 *Sustainable Development as an Issue of Concern in International Watercourse Law: the Integrative Response*

The law on international watercourses has ancient origins, having traditionally focused on the delimitation of borders and navigation and not addressing other uses until much later.[25] Sustainable development, by contrast, is a relatively new concept, as is the principle of integration. However, sustainable development has had a significant influence on international watercourse law in the last decades, having been incorporated into global international watercourses law conventions and many international basin agreements,[26] while the principle of integration has also affected this area of international law. This Section reviews the main instruments of international watercourse law to determine, on the one hand, the extent to which sustainable development has become an objective of international watercourse law and, on the other hand, to what extent the principle of integration has been adopted as an element to achieve it.

The first instrument to consider is the Convention on the Protection and Use of Transboundary Watercourses and International Lakes (hereinafter, UNECE Water Convention),[27] as it was the first multilateral agreement to regulate

25 For a general explanation on the evolution of international watercourses law and more specifically on the law of watercourses as border delimitations and the law of international watercourses for navigation see, for instance: McCaffrey, *Law of International Watercourses*, 63–196.

26 See Fitzmaurice, Malgosia, and Virginie Barral. 2021. "The Relationship between the Law of International Watercourses and Sustainable Development." In *Research Handbook on International Environmental Law*, edited by Malgosia Fitzmaurice, Marcel Brus, and Panos Merkouris, 413–40. Cheltenham: Edward Elgar.

27 Convention on the Protection and Use of Transboundary Watercourses and International Lakes, March 17, 1992, 1936 U.N.T.S. 269.

international watercourses. It was originally adopted in 1992 as a regional agreement in the framework of the UNECE. However, in 2003 the Parties to the Convention opened it to non-UNECE members,[28] which is why there are currently two global conventions on international watercourses (the other one being the Convention on the Law of the Non-Navigational Uses of International Watercourses).[29]

The UNECE Water Convention[30] is a framework convention whose main aim is the prevention, control and reduction of transboundary impact.[31] It applies to all international waters, defined as "surface or ground waters which mark, cross or are located on boundaries between two or more States; wherever transboundary waters flow directly into the sea, these transboundary waters end at a straight line across their respective mouths between points on the low-water line of their banks."[32] It is structured in three parts. In Part I, Article 2 establishes the general provisions regarding the main obligations for the States and the principles that must guide them.[33] This article also defines the catchment area as the framework for cooperation between the Parties.[34] The rest of Part I establishes rules for the prevention, control and reduction of transboundary impact; the monitoring of transboundary waters; the implementation of common research programmes; the exchange of information;

---

28 Amendments to Articles 25 and 26 of the Convention on the Protection and Use of Transboundary Watercourses and International Lakes, November 28, 2003, 2897 U.N.T.S.

29 On the compatibility and complementarity between the two conventions, see: Tanzi, Attila. 2019. "The Global Water Treaties and Their Relationship." In *Research Handbook on International Water Law*, edited by Stephen C. McAffrey and Riley T. Denoon, 44–58. Cheltenham: Edward Elgar; Lammers, Johan G. 2018. "The Interplay between the UN Watercourses Convention and the UNECE Convention on the Protection and Use of Transboundary Watercourses and International Lakes." In *The UN Convention on the Law of the Non-Navigational Uses of International Watercourses: A Commentary*, edited by Laurence Boisson de Chazournes, Makane Moïse Mbengue, Mara Tignino, Komlan Sangbana, and Jason Rudall, 409–27. Oxford: OUP.

30 In relation to this Convention see, generally: Torres Cazorla, María Isabel. 2000. "Otra Vuelta de Tuerca Del Derecho Internacional Para Regular Los Cursos de Agua Internacionales: El Convenio de Helsinki de 17 de Marzo de 1992." *Anuario Español de Derecho Internacional* XVI: 225–62; UNECE. 2013. *Guide to Implementing The Water Convention*. New York and Geneva: United Nations; Tanzi, Attila, Owen McIntyre, Alexandros Kolliopoulos, Alistair Rieu-Clarke, and Rémy Kinna, eds. 2015. *The UNECE Convention on the Protection and Use of Transboundary Watercourses and International Lakes*. Leiden, The Netherlands: Brill Nijhoff.

31 UNECE Water Convention, *supra* note 27, Article 1.2 and 2.6.

32 Ibid. Article 1.1.

33 Ibid. Article 2.1, 2.2 and 2.5.

34 Ibid. Article 2.6.

international responsibility, and the protection of information.[35] Part II establishes more specific rules to be implemented by the riparian Parties through the adoption of bilateral or multilateral agreements.[36] Finally, Part III regulates the institutional framework of the Convention, which encompasses a Meeting of the Parties, a Secretariat and a mechanism for the settlement of disputes.[37]

This Convention refers to sustainability twice in its preamble[38] but only once in its operative part, where it describes "sustainable water-resources management"[39] as one of the objectives to be pursued by the States when adopting legal, administrative, economic, financial and technical measures to prevent, control and reduce transboundary impact.[40] As noted by Rieu-Clarke, the most concerted effort to implement this mandate can be seen in the activities related to ecosystems.[41] On this point, it is relevant to recall the draft of the 1993 Guidelines on the Ecosystem Approach in Water Management, which made the general recommendation that "Integrated policies and strategies should be developed and implemented in order to resolve the complex and interrelated conservation and management problems of aquatic ecosystems, and to overcome the management of water resources in isolation from other ecosystem components.[42]

Although not explicitly, the principle is also clearly enshrined in Article 2 as follows: "[w]ater resources shall be managed so that the needs of the present generation are met without compromising the ability of future generations to meet their own needs."[43] This Convention was adopted in March 1992, a few months before the Rio Declaration[44] and, as such, before sustainable development became a mainstream concept. The fact that sustainable development

35 Ibid. Articles 3 to 8.

36 Ibid. Articles 9 to 16. On this specific issue see Nikiforova, Nataliya. 2017. "Strengthening the Implementation of Transboundary Water Agreements: Insights from the UNECE Water Convention Implementation Committee." In *Routledge Handbook of Water Law and Policy*, edited by Alistair Rieu-Clarke, Andrew Allan, and Sarah Hendry, 275–86. Abingdon: Routledge.

37 UNECE Water Convention, *supra* note 27, Articles 17, 19 and 22.

38 Ibid. Preamble, paras. 3 and 5.

39 Ibid. Article 3.1(i).

40 Ibid. Article 3.1(i).

41 Rieu-Clarke, Alistair. 2015. "The Sustainability Principle." In *The UNECE Convention on the Protection and Use of Transboundary Watercourses and International Lakes*, edited by Attila Tanzi, Owen McIntyre, Alexandros Kolliopoulos, Alistair Rieu-Clarke, and Rémy Kinna, 195–210. Leiden: Brill Nijhoff. 204–207.

42 UNECE, *Guidelines on the Ecosystem Approach in Water Management*, ECE/ENVWA/31 (November 1993), https://unece.org/DAM/env/water/publications/documents/Library/Old_documents_found_library/ECE_ENVWA_31_eng.pdf. 1.

43 UNECE Water Convention, *supra* note 27, Article 2.5(c).

44 Rio Declaration, *supra* note 5.

was so clearly included in the final draft of the UNECE Water Convention may reflect what Rieu-Clarke considers "an evolution and consolidation of shared understanding amongst UNECE States on transboundary water challenges and the principles that should be applied in order to foster equitable and sustainable cooperation."[45] Nonetheless, due to the doubts expressed by several delegations about the legal status of sustainable development, together with the polluter-pays principle and the principle of precaution, the bindingness of Article 2(5) was diluted.[46] Following the proposal of the United States, the final draft stated that States should 'be guided' by these three principles, rather than expressing them in the form of an obligation.[47]

If sustainable development as an objective is not given a central place in the UNECE Water Convention, the principle of integration seems to receive even less attention, as no explicit reference is made to it or to any related concepts, such as inter-sectoral integration or integrated management. This said, the principle might be considered implicit for two reasons. On the one hand, the strong focus of the UNECE Water Convention on the prevention of transboundary impact on the environment and on preventing pollution in particular, is aimed at limiting the effects of development activities. Not surprisingly, industrial activities are particularly targeted as sources of polluting substances.[48] On the other hand, the UNECE Water Convention foresees certain tools or approaches that provide for the implementation of integration of the economic, social and environmental dimensions, such as the obligation to conduct an EIA[49] or the application of the ecosystem approach.[50]

The Convention on the Law of the Non-Navigational Uses of International Watercourses[51] (hereinafter, UN Watercourses Convention) also integrates the concept of sustainability, both in its preamble[52] and in its operative part.

---

45 Rieu-Clarke, Alistair, 2019. "Remarks on the Drafting history of the convention." In *The UNECE Convention on the Protection and Use of Transboundary Watercourses and International Lakes*, edited by Attila Tanzi, Owen McIntyre, Alexandros Kolliopoulos, Alistair Rieu-Clarke, and Rémy Kinna, 3–14. Leiden: Brill Nijhoff.

46 Ibid.

47 UNECE, Working Party on Water Problems, *Report of Fifth Special Session as adopted by the Working Party on 18 October 1991*, ENVWA/WP.3/18 (8 November 1991), undocs.org/ENVWA/WP.3/18. Para 8.

48 See, UNECE Water Convention, *supra* note 27, Articles 3.2 and 9.2(f).

49 Ibid. Article 3.1(h).

50 Ibid. Article 3.1(i).

51 Convention on the Law of the Non-Navigational Uses of International Watercourses, May 21, 1997, 2999 U.N.T.S.

52 The fifth paragraph states that the Parties to the convention express the conviction that a framework convention will ensure, among other things, the "promotion of the optimal

The Convention was adopted in 1997 by the UNGA,[53] twenty-seven years after it asked the ILC to initiate a study on the law of international watercourses.[54] The ratification process was slow and sufficient ratifications for its entry into force were not received until 17 August 2014.

The Convention contains thirty-three articles and is structured in seven parts. The scope of application is set out in Article 1, which extends to the "uses of international watercourses and of their waters for purposes other than navigation and to measures of protection, preservation and management related to the uses of those watercourses and their waters"[55] and specifically excludes navigation.[56] Part II contains the general principles deemed customary law: the equitable and reasonable utilisation, the obligation not to cause significant harm, and the general obligation to cooperate and regular exchange of information.[57] Part III establishes rules in relation to planned measures, such as the exchange of information on planned measures, the notification process, and consultation.[58] Part IV sets norms regarding the protection and preservation of ecosystems and the prevention, reduction and control of pollution, among others.[59] Part V is devoted to provisions on prevention and mitigation of harmful conditions and emergency situations.[60] Finally, Part VI is titled "Miscellaneous provisions", key among which is the establishment of a process for the settlement of disputes.[61]

---

and sustainable utilization thereof for present and future generations". In Ibid. Preamble, para. 5.

53 As general doctrinal analysis of the UN Watercourses Convention see, among others: Boisson de Chazournes, Laurence, Makane Moïse Mbengue, Mara Tignino, Komlan Sangbana, and Jason Rudall, eds. 2018. *The UN Convention on the Law of the Non-Navigational Uses of International Watercourses: A Commentary*. Oxford: OUP; Rieu-Clarke, Alistair, Ruby Moynihan, and Bjørn-Oliver Magsig. 2012. *UN Watercourses Convention: User's Guide*. Dundee: IHP-HELP Centre for Water Law, Policy and Science; Tanzi, Attila, and Maurizio Arcari. 2001. *The United Nations Convention on the Law of International Watercourses*. The Hague: Kluwer Law International; Ponte Iglesias, María Teresa. 2012. "El Derecho de Los Usos de Los Cursos de Agua Internacionales Para Fines Distintos de La Navegación." In *La Politica Comunitaria de Aguas: Marco de La Acción Estatal y Autonómica*, edited by Adela M. Aura y Larios de Medrano, 218–33. Madrid: Dykinson.

54 UN General Assembly, Resolution 2669 (XXV), *Progressive development and codification of the rules of international law relating to international watercourses*, A/RES/2669(XXV) (8 December 1970), undocs.org/en/A/RES/2669(XXV).

55 UN Watercourses Convention, *supra* note 51, Article 1.1.

56 Ibid. Article 1.2.

57 Ibid. Articles 5, 7, 8 and 9.

58 Ibid. Articles 11 to 19.

59 Ibid. Articles 20–26.

60 Ibid. Articles 27 and 28.

61 Ibid. Articles 29–33.

Sustainable development was introduced in the UN Watercourses Convention in relation to the principle of equitable and reasonable utilisation, which is based on the limitation of sovereign rights of States to use international watercourses and the notion of 'equitable participation' in this use. Therefore, it can be understood as the right of riparian States to use and benefit from the international watercourse in a manner that takes into account all the factors and circumstances present in the case, rejecting approaches based on equal apportionment or unlimited use.[62] This principle is analysed in depth in Chapter 3. What is relevant to note here is that Article 5 of the UN Watercourses Convention states that in order to observe the principle of equitable and reasonable utilisation, a watercourse should be used "with a view to attaining optimal and sustainable utilization thereof and benefits therefrom, taking into account the interests of the watercourse States concerned, consistent with adequate protection of the watercourse."[63] In this way, the UN Watercourses Convention links the general principle of sustainable development to a core principle of international watercourse law.

The formulation of the principle of equitable and reasonable utilisation was not a straightforward process in the drafting of the ILC. Tomuschat proposed replacing the term 'optimal' with 'sustainable', arguing that the first term may induce error since it "appeared to impose an obligation on States to work to achieve optimal utilization with a view to squeezing the last drop of use out of a watercourse,"[64] while the latest "included the notion of long-term utilization."[65] Special Rapporteur Rosenstock countered this proposal, arguing that such a change "would create an imbalance to the detriment of the economic development of watercourses."[66] Yankov, meanwhile, contended that the concept of 'sustainable development' reflected much better the new approach adopted by States in the UNCED,[67] and Calero Rodrigues noted the non-settled status, warning that it could stop being used in the future despite being widely used in the present.[68] It was also pointed out that accepting Tomuschat's proposal

62 For a thorough analysis of this principle as enshrined in the UN Watercourses Convention, see Caflisch, Lucius. 2018. "Equitable and Reasonable Utilization and Factors Relevant to Determining Such Utilization (Articles 5 and 6)." In *The UN Convention on the Law of the Non-Navigational Uses of International Watercourses: A Commentary*, edited by Laurence Boisson de Chazournes, Makane Moïse Mbengue, Mara Tignino, Komlan Sangbana, and Jason Rudall, 77–94. Oxford: OUP.

63 UN Watercourses Convention, *supra* note 51. Article 5.1.

64 ILC, *Summary record of the 2354th meeting*, A/CN.4/SR.2354 (1994), https://legal.un.org/ilc/documentation/english/summary_records/a_cn4_sr2354.pdf. Para. 24.

65 Ibid.

66 Ibid. Para. 25.

67 Ibid. Para. 26.

68 Ibid. Para. 27.

would put at risk the consensus on Article 5 in the UNGA.[69] It was Idris who proposed to add 'and sustainable' to the term 'optimal',[70] an option that was not accepted at this meeting, but which would be the formulation finally adopted in 1997 by the UNGA according to the proposal of the Working Group of the Whole.[71]

Only four months after the adoption of the UN Watercourses Convention, the ICJ referred to this instrument in the resolution on *Gabčikovo-Nagymaros Project (Hungary/Slovakia)*.[72] The Court expressed the need for the new customary norms regarding the protection of the environment to be taken into account in interpreting the basin agreement under discussion.[73] In this regard, it is significant that the judgement of 1997 endorses the "concept of sustainable development". The ICJ refers to sustainable development as a concept that expresses a general interest of humanity but stops short of affording it specific legal status by stating that:

> Throughout the ages, mankind has, for economic and other reasons, constantly interfered with nature. In the past, this was often done without consideration of the effects upon the environment. [...] This need to reconcile economic development with protection of the environment is aptly expressed in the concept of sustainable development.[74]

As noted by Rodrigo, in *Gabčikovo-Nagymaros Project (Hungary/Slovakia)* the Court was extremely prudent in its definition of the legal status of environmental principles. This may have been due to the inclusion of principles with no hard definition, such as that of sustainable development, but it came at the detriment of other environmental principles of a more clearly procedural nature.[75] The well-known separate opinion by Judge Weeramantry was motivated precisely by the excessive caution exercised by the Court in refusing to

69 Ibid. Para. 31.

70 Ibid. Para. 32.

71 UN General Assembly, Resolution 51/229, *Convention on the law of the non-navigational uses of international watercourses*, A/RES/51/229 (8 July 1997), undocs.org/A/RES/51/229.

72 Although at that time it had not yet entered into force, as it had only been signed by three states: South Africa, Syria and Venezuela.

73 Gabčikovo-Nagymaros Project (Hungary/Slovakia), Judgment, 1997 I.C.J. Rep. 7 (September 25). Para. 112.

74 Ibid. Para. 140.

75 Rodrigo Hernández, Ángel J. 1998. "La Aportación Del Asunto Gabcikovo-Nagymaros Al Derecho Internacional Del Medio Ambiente." *Anuario Español de Derecho Internacional* XIV (August): 769–807. 800–801.

confer legal status on sustainable development. The judge argued that sustainable development is in fact a principle of modern international law and underlines the important role it has to play both in this specific case and in future cases.[76] This separate opinion is especially relevant as a sign of the changing common understanding of sustainable development in international justice.[77]

However, the Court derives legal consequences from the concept of sustainable development since it compels the Parties to seek an integrated solution to the controversy based on a balance between developmental interests and environmental interests.[78] The application of the principle of integration is even clearer in light of the Court's definition of its intertemporal dimension, since it notes that: "Such new norms have to be taken into consideration, and such new standards given proper weight, not only when States contemplate new activities but also when continuing with activities begun in the past."[79] Therefore, the ICJ establishes that integration is not a mere norm to be applied from that point on, but a principle to be generally considered in law in those cases where it is deemed applicable according to the legal interests in question.

Sustainable development has been invoked by the ICJ in other cases concerning international watercourses. In the previous Chapter, the use of this concept in *Pulp Mills on the River Uruguay (Argentina v. Uruguay)* was mentioned in relation to the substantive character of the principle of integration. The Court went a step further than in *Gabčikovo-Nagymaros Project (Hungary/ Slovakia)*, finding that Article 27 of the Statute establishing the Administrative Commission of the River Uruguay (CARU) reflected the concept of sustainable development.[80] Such an affirmation implies a clear acceptance of sustainable

---

76 Gabčikovo-Nagymaros Project (Hungary/Slovakia), Judgment, 1997 I.C.J. Rep. 7 (September 25) (Weeramantry, C.G., separate opinion). 86.

77 In relation to *Gabčikovo-Nagymaros Project (Hungary/Slovakia)* see also: Bourne, Charles B. 1997. "The Case Concerning the Gabčíkovo-Nagymaros Project: An Important Milestone in International Water Law." *Yearbook of International Environmental Law* 8 (1): 6–12; or Hey, Ellen. 2000. "International Water Law Placed in a Contemporary Environmental Context: The Gabcikovo-Nagymaros Case." *Physics and Chemistry of the Earth, Part B: Hydrology, Oceans and Atmosphere* 25 (3): 303–8.

78 "It is for the Parties themselves to find an agreed solution that takes account of the objectives of the Treaty, which must be pursued in a joint and integrated way, as well as the norms of international environmental law and the principles of the law of international watercourses." Gabčikovo-Nagymaros Project (Hungary/Slovakia), Judgment, 1997 I.C.J. Rep. 7 (September 25). Para. 141.

79 Ibid. Para. 140.

80 "Regarding Article 27, it is the view of the Court that its formulation reflects not only the need to reconcile the varied interests of riparian States in a transboundary context and in particular in the use of a shared natural resource, but also the need to strike a balance between the use of the waters and the protection of the river consistent with the

development as part of customary international water law. Article 27 of the Statute does not mention sustainable development explicitly, but it is an agreement adopted in 1975, when the concept was still comparatively undeveloped.

The use of the concept of sustainable development and the application of the principle of integration to solve disputes regarding international watercourses can also be appreciated in international arbitral jurisdiction. The *Indus Waters Kishenganga Arbitration* (*Pakistan vs. India*), already discussed in Chapter 1, is a crucial example. The arbitral tribunal based its opinion on India's duty to ensure that a minimum flow reach Pakistan as enshrined in customary international environmental law,[81] which included the application of sustainability criteria.[82] In addition, as argued in the previous Chapter, the acknowledgement of sustainable development by this arbitral tribunal implied the application of the principle of integration. Therefore, it must be stressed that both sustainable development and the principle of integration are part of this area of international law.

The reception of the principle of integration by international watercourse law has also been recognised by the ILA. In 2004, the Committee on Water Resources Law of the ILA revised its 1966 Helsinki Rules on the Uses of the Waters of International Rivers[83] (hereinafter, Helsinki Rules) in the understanding that customary law regarding international watercourses had changed significantly in the previous 38 years, which in the Committee's view was highly relevant given the slow pace of ratification of the UN Watercourses Convention.[84] The ILA 2004 Berlin Conference[85] is notable for the addition of two articles. Article 6 is devoted to integrated management, establishing that "States shall use their best efforts to integrate appropriately the management of waters with the management of other resources". Commentary on this Article recognises that it represents the inclusion of the principle of integration, which had been considered previously by the ILA in the New Delhi

objective of sustainable development." In Pulp Mills on the River Uruguay (Argentina v. Uruguay), 2010 Judgment, I.C.J. Rep. 14 (April 20). Para. 177.

81 Indus Waters Kishenganga Arbitration (Pakistan vs. India). Final award, 31 R.I.A.A (Perm. Ct. Arb. 2013). Para. 85.

82 Ibid. Para. 86.

83 ILA. 1967 "Helsinki Rules on the Uses of the Waters of International Rivers." https://unece.org/fileadmin/DAM/env/water/meetings/legal_board/2010/annexes_groundwater_paper/Annex_II_Helsinki_Rules_ILA.pdf.

84 ILA. Committee on Water Resources Law 2004. "Report of the Berlin Conference." https://www.ila-hq.org/en_GB/documents/conference-report-berlin-2004-5.

85 Ibid.

Declaration,[86] as essential for the sustainable use of waters and other resources.[87] Article 7 is titled "Sustainability" and provides that "States shall take all appropriate measures to manage waters sustainably." In relation to this Article, the committee affirms that sustainability regarding the management of water resources has become a customary norm.[88]

As a final remark, it may be noted that global conventional watercourse law does not enshrine the principle of integration in any explicit manner. Nonetheless, it can be considered implicit in the general references to 'sustainable development' or 'sustainable management'. Interestingly, it is through international jurisprudence in the form of ICJ rulings and arbitral cases that sustainable development has become established as an objective of international watercourse law and integration as an instrumental principle for its application. The work undertaken by scholars and academic associations might have also had an influence on this process. However, the analysis presented in this Subsection also shows that the application of sustainable development and its integrative thrust in cooperation on international watercourses is strongly conditioned by the nature of the shared natural resource and the specific legal framework in which it operates. The following chapters examine how the principle of integration fits in this cooperative framework and with the legal principles specific to international watercourses law.

2 Drivers of the Application of the Principle of Integration in International Watercourse Law

The cooperation framework established by the riparian countries and the general international law affecting the relations in this framework condition the application of the principle of integration in the governance of international watercourses. As such, the scope of this legal framework – international watercourse law – will largely determine the real possibilities of integrating the economic, social and environmental dimensions. First and foremost, the physical scope of this legal regime must be delimited. Therefore, it is necessary to start by defining the components that make up the concept of international

86 ILA. Committee on Legal Aspects of Sustainable Development. 2002. "Report of the New Delhi Conference." https://www.ila-hq.org/en_GB/documents/conference-report-new-delhi-2002-8.

87 ILA. Committee on International Law on Sustainable Development. 2004. "Report of the Berlin Conference." https://www.ila-hq.org/en_GB/documents/conference-report-berlin-2004-13. 14.

88 Ibid. 15.

watercourse, which is the element where the relations regulated by international watercourse law take place. This question is addressed in the first part of this Section.

The second element conditioning the application of the principle of integration is the regulation of the uses of international watercourses. The utilisation of international watercourses has varied over the years, with some uses gaining relevance and others becoming secondary. Since each of these uses reflects different economic or social interests and can have environmental impact, their regulation is a key aspect from the point of view of the principle of integration. In relation to this issue, both global conventions on international watercourses and international basin regimes are analysed.

2.1 *The Concept of International Watercourse*

A key question regarding the application of the principle of integration in relation to international watercourse law is which waters are regulated. To answer this, it is necessary to determine the scope of the concept of 'international watercourse', which leads to two further questions. First is the central issue of what is to be understood as a 'watercourse' according to international law; second is the issue of when that watercourse is considered to be 'international'. These two questions are analysed first in relation to the UN Watercourses Convention and second in relation to the UNECE Water Convention.

Traditionally, international agreements regarding shared freshwater only took into account surface water, where rivers were understood as pipelines unrelated to the environment surrounding them. The 1815 Vienna Convention, for instance, defined a river in the following terms: "[l]es Puissances dont les États sont séparés ou traversés par une même rivière navigable."[89] At that time, watercourses were seen as clear lines that could cross or delimit a border, disregarding tributaries, groundwater and other related elements. It is a comparatively recent trend to understand watercourses as systems that include surface water and groundwater.[90] In Article 2(a), the UN Watercourses Convention defines a watercourse as a "system of surface waters and groundwaters constituting by virtue of their physical relationship a unitary whole and normally flowing into a common terminus."[91] This was the consensus definition reached by the governments that negotiated the Convention.

89 Acte du Congrès de Vienne, June 9, 1815, Bibliothèque nationale de France ark:/12148/bpt6k91227n. Article 108.

90 For a description of this evolution, see McCaffrey, *Law of International Watercourses*, 88–91.

91 UN Watercourses Convention, *supra* note 51, Article 2(a).

However, the definition of watercourses quickly became a controversial topic. The first Sub-Committee on the Law of the Non-Navigational Uses of International Watercourses, chaired by Mr. Richard D. Kearney, revealed disagreements between the States when they were asked about the appropriate scope of the definition of an international watercourse. Although the Sub-Committee noted that 'river basin', 'drainage basin' or 'catchment basin' were the concepts used in the most recent cooperation agreements on the matter,[92] from the outset the representatives of some States found these terms to be too broad and pushed for the consideration of a concept that, although hydrologically inaccurate, would in their view be a more appropriate basis for study of the legal aspects pertaining to an international watercourse. Brazil, Ecuador, Spain, Poland and Austria agreed with the much narrower definition proposed by Colombia of "a river which traverses or separates the territories of two or more States."[93]

In 1980 the ILC adopted, as a working hypothesis, the concept of 'international watercourse system' put forward by the Special Rapporteur Stephen Schwebel, which was defined in the following terms:

> A watercourse system is formed of hydrographic components such as rivers, lakes, canals, glaciers and groundwater constituting by virtue of their physical relationship a unitary whole; thus, any use affecting waters in one part of the system may affect waters in another part.
>
> An "international watercourse system" is a watercourse system, components of which are situated in two or more States.[94]

However, the lack of consensus made the ILC defer this question to later discussion.[95] The matter was not reviewed until the forty-third session of 1991, in which the Special Rapporteur Stephen McCaffrey found sufficient consensus

92 ILC, *Report of the International Law Commission on the work of its sixty-third session, 3 May–23 July 1976*, A/31/10 (1976), https://legal.un.org/ilc/documentation/english/reports/a_31_10.pdf. Paras. 116–117.

93 ILC, *First report on the law of the non-navigational uses of international watercourses by Mr. Richard D. Kearney, Special Rapporteur*, A/CN.4/295 (1976), https://legal.un.org/ilc/documentation/english/a_cn4_295.pdf. Paras. 6–9.

94 ILC, *Report of the International Law Commission on the work of its thirty-second session, 5 May–25 July 1980*, A/35/10 (1980), https://legal.un.org/ilc/documentation/english/reports/a_35_10.pdf. Para. 90.

95 ILC, *Report of the International Law Commission on the work of its thirty-eighth session, 5 May–11 July 1986*, A/41/10 (1986), https://legal.un.org/ilc/documentation/english/reports/a_41_10.pdf. Para. 236.

between the members to maintain the concept of 'system' as a defining dimension of international watercourse.[96]

The idea would not change substantially until the adoption of the UN Watercourses Convention. In the form that appears in the final text, the definition as a 'system' implies, according to the ILC, that a watercourse includes "rivers, lakes, aquifers, glaciers, reservoirs and canals. So long as these components are interrelated with one another, they form part of the watercourse."[97] The definition is broad enough to encompass the area covered by the drainage basin, hence the two concepts are now generally considered to have the same meaning.[98] As a result, the Convention applies to activities taking place in the basin as long as they affect the protection, preservation and management of the watercourse.

Two other – albeit related – issues in relation to the material scope of the Convention were also discussed at length during the above discussions: the inclusion of groundwater and the inter-basin links due to artificial infrastructures. On the first issue, two opposing positions emerged during the course of the negotiations.[99] On the one hand, some members argued that groundwater should be excluded from the definition of international watercourse.[100] Being mostly upstream countries, their main concern was that adopting as broad a concept as the basin would extend regulation to areas of the national territory that in their opinion should not be included.[101] In short, they saw this concept as diminishing their sovereignty.

---

96 ILC, *Report of the International Law Commission on the work of its forty-third session, 29 April–19 July 1991*, A/46/10 (1991), https://legal.un.org/ilc/documentation/english/reports/a_46_10.pdf. Para. 54.

97 ILC, *Report of the International Law Commission on the work of its forty-sixth session, 2 May–22 July 1994*, A/49/10 (1994), https://legal.un.org/ilc/documentation/english/reports/a_49_10.pdf.

98 Tanzi and Arcari, *United Nations Convention on the Law of International Watercourses*, 56–63.

99 On the discussions in the ILC on this topic see Sindico, Francesco, and Laura Movilla. 2018. "The Interplay between the UN Watercourses Convention and the Law on Transboundary Aquifers (Article 2)." In *The UN Convention on the Law of the Non-Navigational Uses of International Watercourses: A Commentary*, edited by Laurence Boisson de Chazournes, Makane Moise Mbengue, Mara Tignino, Komlan Sangbana, and Jason Rudall, 383–408. Oxford: OUP; Movilla Pateiro, Laura. 2014. *El Derecho Internacional Del Agua: Los Acuíferos Transfronterizos*. Barcelona: J.M. Bosch. 186–225.

100 ILC, *Report of the International Law Commission on the work of its forty-third session, 29 April–19 July 1991*, A/46/10 (1991), https://legal.un.org/ilc/documentation/english/reports/a_46_10.pdf. Para. 49.

101 ILC, *First report on the law of the non-navigational uses of international watercourses by Mr. Stephen Schwebel, Special Rapporteur*, A/CN.4/320 and Corr.1. (1979), https://legal.un.org/ilc/documentation/english/a_cn4_320.pdf. Paras 43–44.

The other position would be represented by the Special Rapporteur Robert Rosenstock, who proposed that the Draft Articles should refer to all groundwater, including types not connected to the surface watercourse. The proposal was rejected by many members of the Commission as an unrelated body of water would not match the definition of watercourse in which the various waters form a unitary whole "by virtue of their physical relationship", but also because they considered the principles of international watercourse law to be hardly applicable to these traditionally unregulated types of water resource.[102]

This stance was not amply shared among the members, hence the current Article 2(a) of the UN Watercourses Convention is applicable to groundwater connected to the watercourse, although it also makes clear that it does not apply to groundwater not connected to surface water, even if an aquifer of this kind extends across the boundaries of two countries.[103] This might be regarded as a middle ground. The exclusion of confined aquifers may reflect the fact that the ILC did not consider this kind of aquifer during the long process of the draft article, which it was under pressure to complete.[104] However, the importance in many regions of transboundary groundwater unrelated to a watercourse forced the ILC to adopt a resolution on confined international watercourses in which it recommended that the States be guided by the principles of the UN Watercourses Convention in regulating confined aquifers and encouraged them to enter into agreements for their regulation.[105]

In relation to the other point of disagreement, the inter-basin limits due to artificial structures, it must be taken into account that Article 2(1) of the UN Watercourses Convention defines watercourses as "normally flowing into a common terminus". *A priori*, this definition precludes the possibility of one watercourse splitting at some point into two streams that discharge in different places. The States were divided between those in favour of keeping the 'common terminus' concept and those that considered the concept to be outdated. The first group saw in the sentence a geographical limit on the scope of the

---

102 ILC, *Report of the International Law Commission on the work of its forty-fifth session, 3 May–23 July 1993*, A/48/10 (1993), https://legal.un.org/ilc/documentation/english/reports/a_48_10.pdf. Paras. 368–369.

103 On this topic, see Sindico, Francesco. 2020. *International Law and Transboundary Aquifers*. Cheltenham: Edward Elgar, 34–40; Eckstein, Yoram, and Gabriel E Eckstein. 2005. "Transboundary Aquifers: Conceptual Models for Development of International Law." *Groundwater* 43 (5): 679–90. 686; and Movilla, *El Derecho Internacional Del Agua*, 183–184.

104 McCaffrey, *Law of International Watercourses*, 44.

105 ILC, *Report of the International Law Commission on the work of its forty-sixth session, 2 May–22 July 1994*, A/49/10 (1994), https://legal.un.org/ilc/documentation/english/reports/a_49_10.pdf. 135.

Convention. Their main fear was that the connection between watercourses through canals would create an artificial unity between naturally independent watercourses.[106] The opposing group considered the idea to be hydrologically inaccurate and misleading, while it could leave important bodies of water out of the scope of the convention.[107]

The Special Rapporteur Stephen McCaffrey was in favour of deleting the "common terminus" phrasing, but his proposal met with opposition.[108] The addition of the word 'normally' appears to be the result of a compromise between those two groups to reflect the current hydrologic knowledge according to which many rivers "flow to the sea in whole or in part via groundwater, a series of distributaries which may be as much as 300 kilometres removed from each other (deltas) or empty at certain times of the year into lakes and at other times into the sea."[109] The "common terminus" phrase is problematic and certainly unnecessary. If the possibility exists that two watercourses not leading to the same terminus interact, the requirement of a common terminus could leave outside the scope of the Convention non-international watercourses, which are connected through a canal with an international watercourse. In practice, each case will have to be analysed separately. Nevertheless, the question of connected watercourse systems is likely to grow in importance since, as water becomes scarcer, transfers of this resource are expected to become increasingly frequent.[110]

Once a stream of water matches the concept of 'watercourse' under international law, it is also necessary for it to be deemed 'international' in order to fall within this legal domain. This is the second issue noted at the beginning of this Section, which, although key, is also much simpler. The UN Watercourses Convention states the requirement that "parts of [it] are situated in different States."[111] This provision rules out the traditional distinction between contiguous and successive rivers, the first being those rivers that create a border and the second those rivers that cross the territory of two or more States. This is, in fact, a natural consequence of considering watercourses as systems instead of lines crossing or demarcating a border, the legal implications of which are

106 International Law Commission. 1993. Report of the Commission to the General Assembly on the Work of Its Forty-Fifth Session. Vol. II, 87–88.

107 Report of the ILC on the work of its 46th session, *supra* note 105, 90.

108 ILC, *Report of the International Law Commission on the work of its forty-fifth session, 3 May–23 July 1993*, A/48/10 (1993), https://legal.un.org/ilc/documentation/english/reports/a_48_10.pdf. Para. 365.

109 Report of the ILC on the work of its 46th session, *supra* note 105, 91.

110 McCaffrey, *Law of International Watercourses*, 46.

111 UN Watercourses Convention, *supra* note 51, Article 2(b).

notable: the same principles and norms are applicable to the whole of the international watercourse.[112]

In addition to the UN Watercourses Convention, it is important to consider the particularities of the definition given in the UNECE Water Convention, which uses the concept of 'transboundary waters', defined as "any surface or ground waters which mark, cross or are located on boundaries between two or more States; wherever transboundary waters flow directly into the sea, these transboundary waters end at a straight line across their respective mouths between points on the low-water line of their banks."[113] The definition gives this Convention a wider scope than the UN Watercourses Convention, since it includes groundwater not necessarily connected to surface water. Article 2(6), in reference to the scope of the cooperation between riparian States, states that cooperation will extend to the "catchment area", which can also be understood in the sense of a "drainage basin". This inclusive concept implies that as long as they interact with the transboundary waters, elements such as air, fauna, climate or historical monuments fall within the scope of the Convention.[114]

As can be inferred from the wording of Article 1(1), the UNECE Water Convention includes any transboundary groundwater irrespective of its connection to surface water or its termination in a desert sink or an enclosed lake.[115] As such, even confined aquifers would fall within the scope of this Convention as long as they cross an international boundary. Article 2(6) corroborates this, as cooperation focusing on 'catchment areas' may be applicable also to transboundary water not connected to the sea.[116]

This analysis of the two global conventions on international water law show that when they are applicable, their regulatory scope extends to the basin as a whole. The UNECE Water Convention is more explicit on this point, but the same conclusion can be drawn from the UN Watercourses Convention. The two conventions exclude sea waters by virtue of their definitions of a 'system of waters' or 'transboundary waters'. However, both conventions also foresee the impact that some activities can have on the marine environment throughout

---

112 Aura y Larios de Medrano, Adela M. 2008. *La Regulación Internacional Del Agua Dulce. Practica Española.* Navarra: Editorial Aranzadi. 83–85.

113 UNECE Water Convention, *supra* note 27, Article 1(1).

114 Fitzmaurice, Malgosia, and Panos Merkouris. 2015. "Scope of the UNECE Water Convention." In *The UNECE Convention on the Protection and Use of Transboundary Watercourses and International Lakes*, edited by Attila Tanzi, Owen McIntyre, Alexandros Kolliopoulos, Alistair Rieu-Clarke, and Rémy Kinna, 103–15. Leiden: Brill Nijhoff. 106.

115 UNECE. 2013. *Guide to Implementing The Water Convention.* New York and Geneva: United Nations. 14.

116 On this topic see Sindico, *International Law and Transboundary Aquifers*, 51–55.

an international watercourse. On this point, Article 23 of the UN Watercourses Convention provides that States must cooperate to take measures on a watercourse if this is necessary to protect the environment, including estuaries.[117] Seemingly, Article 2(6) of the UNECE Water Convention adds protection of the marine environment as an objective of the general obligation to cooperate for the prevention, control and reduction of transboundary impact.[118]

The practice of States in adopting the basin as their framework for cooperation is somewhat variable, but it is clearly associated to the most developed regimes. Unsurprisingly, most of the regimes analysed in this study encompass the whole of the basin, including groundwater.[119] The main obstacle to the basin-wide application of basin agreements is therefore the existence of non-Parties whose territory includes part of the basin. The MRC is a paradigmatic case, as a large part of the Mekong basin is in Chinese territory, and China is not a Party to the cooperation agreement.[120]

Although the basin is adopted as the geographical basis for the application of the two global conventions on international watercourses and in many cooperation agreements for specific international watercourses, it remains to be examined how the concept is dealt with in customary law. International case law has not shed much light on the issue. In *Lac Lanoux (Espagne/France)*, the arbitral tribunal seemed to partially reject the basin as the criteria to apply international law as it stated that "[t]he unity of a basin is sanctioned at the juridical level only to the extent that it corresponds to human realities."[121]

The much more recent *Dispute over the status and use of the waters of the Silala*, on the other hand, is a lost opportunity for the ICJ to settle this question. Regarding Chile's request for the Court to recognise the Silala River as an international watercourse to which customary international law applies, the Court merely acknowledged that the Parties had converged in the course of the proceedings and was therefore not called to give a decision. However, this acceptance did not amount to an assumption of the basin approach by the two Parties in dispute, as Bolivia did not consider Article 2 of the UN Watercourses

117 UN Watercourses Convention, *supra* note 51, Article 23.

118 UNECE Water Convention, *supra* note 27, Article 6(2).

119 See, for instance: Article 3(1) in relation to Article 1(b) of the Danube River Protection Convention; Article 3 of the Charter of Waters of the Senegal River; Article 2.1 of the Dniester River Basin Treaty; or Article 5 in relation to Article 1 of the Water Charter of the Lake Chad Basin.

120 Currently, the Parties to the Mekong Agreement are the Kingdom of Cambodia, the Lao People's Democratic Republic, the Kingdom of Thailand and the Socialist Republic of Vietnam.

121 Lac Lanoux (Espagne/France), 12 R.I.A.A (Perm. Ct. Arb. 1957). 304.

Convention to reflect customary law.[122] The only matter clarified by the Court was that "modifications that increase the surface flow of a watercourse have no bearing on its characterization as an international watercourse."[123]

The difficulties encountered by the ILC in establishing consensus on this issue suggest that it was not a well-established and uncontested norm of customary law at the time the negotiations took place. This disagreement was also clear when the States issued their comments on the Draft articles. While some criticised the concept of 'international watercourse' for being too wide and including groundwater,[124] others considered it too narrow.[125] Similar opposing opinions were expressed on the day the Draft articles were adopted by the UNGA.[126] Moreover, as Aura y Larios de Medrano points out, according to the interventions of ILC members, there was no intention to codify customary law at any point in the drafting of Article 2. It was always understood as a conventional rule. This author concludes from her analysis that "no existe, hoy por hoy, una noción consuetudinaria universal de lo que se ha de considerar aguas dulces internacionales en el ámbito universal."[127]

2.2 *The Water Uses Regulated by International Watercourse Law*

The principle of integration requires that many different interests be considered in the decision-making process. As seen above, the geographical scope and the extent to which the hydrological cycle is included in such process are key factors. However, given that international watercourses can be affected by a multiplicity of human activities, the extent of the regime in terms of regulated uses will determine the possibility of effective application of the principle of integration. Again, the broader the scope of the regime, the better.[128] In international watercourse law, in order to establish what interests are included in the basin regime it must be answered the question of what uses are regulated. This Section analyses the scope of international watercourse law in this regard.

122 Dispute over the status and use of the waters of the Silala (Chile v. Bolivia), Judgement, 2022 I.C.J. Rep. 614 (December 1). Paras. 50–59.

123 Ibid. Para. 93.

124 See the comments by Colombia, Ethiopia and Turkey. In UN Secretary-General, *Draft articles on the law of the non-navigational uses of international watercourses and resolution on confined transboundary groundwater, Report of the Secretary-General*, A/51/275 (6 August 1996), undocs.org/A/51/275. 21–22, 24.

125 See the comments by Hungary and Portugal, in Ibid 23–24.

126 See Turkey, Pakistan and Rwanda. In UN GAOR, 51st Sess., 99th plen. mtg., U.N. Doc A/51/PV.99 (21 May 1997), undocs.org/en/A/51/PV.99. 4–5 and 12.

127 Aura y Larios de Medrano, *La Regulación Internacional Del Agua Dulce*, 114.

128 Dernbach, "Achieving Sustainable Development," 266.

The freedom of navigation of international watercourses was regulated much earlier than other uses. The 1919 Treaty of Versailles and the 1921 Convention and Statute on Freedom of Transit (Barcelona Statute) signalled the peak of the liberalisation of fluvial navigation, which had grown in importance since the Napoleonic Wars.[129] However, the internationalisation of international watercourses experienced a regression, especially during the post-Second World War period and as decolonisation progressed. The Barcelona Statute had been ratified by few countries and the new international order was less amenable to freedom of navigation, which was perceived as favouring the interests of old colonial powers. Both the Soviet Union and the new post-colonial States rejected the universalising stance of the US in this regard. Therefore, there is currently no general rule on freedom of navigation in international watercourses. Customary law only guarantees a right of navigation to riparian countries, although this is conditional on regional regimes.[130]

It was not until well into the 20th century that other uses of international watercourses became much more relevant and therefore needed regulation. The UN Watercourses Convention was drafted in a context where navigation was already highly regulated, so it explicitly excludes this use.[131] In fact, the ILC did not discuss the suitability of excluding navigation from the Draft Articles as the mandate given by the UNGA was already on non-navigational uses, but it certainly discussed which uses should be included in the notion of 'non-navigational uses'. In this regard, the Sub-Committee on the Law of the Non-Navigational Uses of International Watercourses recognised that it was not only impossible but also unnecessary to create an exhaustive list.[132]

---

129 Boisson de Chazournes, Laurence, and S. M.A. Salman, eds. 2005. *Water Resources and International Law/Les Ressources En Eau et Le Droit International.* Leiden: Martinus Nijhoff Publishers. 14–17.

130 Movilla, *El Derecho Internacional Del Agua*, 63–65.

131 UN General Assembly, Resolution 2669 (XXV), *Progressive development and codification of the rules of international law relating to international watercourses*, A/RES/2669(XXV) (8 December 1970), undocs.org/en/A/RES/2669(XXV).

132 Nevertheless, the Sub-Committee proposed to ask the States if the work of the ILC should be based on the following outline of fresh water uses: "1. Agricultural uses (a) Irrigation (b) Drainage (c) Waste disposal (d) Aquatic food production 2. Economic and commercial uses (a) Energy production (hydroelectric, nuclear and mechanical) (b) Manufacturing (c) Construction (d) Transportation other than navigation (e) Timber floating (f) Waste disposal (g) Extractive (mining, oil production, etc.) 3. Domestic and social (a) Consumptive (drinking, cooling, washing, laundry, etc.) (b) Waste disposal (c) Recreational (swimming, sport, fishing, boating, etc.)." (ILC, *Report of the Sub-Committee on the Law of Non-Navigational Uses of International Watercourses*, A/CN.4/283 (1974), https://legal.un.org/ilc/documentation/english/a_cn4_283.pdf. Para. 30.).

The question was forwarded to the States, most of which considered this outline acceptable. Some of them proposed the addition of other uses,[133] while some States also formulated caveats to the effect that the list did not establish an order of priority or hierarchy between the uses and that it did not aim to be exhaustive.[134] The version that was finally adopted by the UNGA is coherent with these comments, as Article 1.1 of the UN Watercourses Convention restricts the scope of the Convention to regulate the "uses of international watercourses and of their waters for purposes other than navigation and to measures of protection, preservation and management related to the uses of those watercourses and their waters."[135] Also in line with these early responses of the States, Article 10.1 establishes the non-existence of any inherent priority among the possible uses of an international watercourse,[136] with the residual provision that in case of conflict a "special regard" must be given to vital human needs.[137]

It is inferred from Article 1.1 that the concept of 'non-navigational uses' must be understood in a very broad sense. First, because the Convention applies not only to 'uses of international watercourses', but also to the uses of 'their waters'. As noted by Tanzi and Arcari, this is relevant as water resources deriving from an international watercourse remain within the scope of the Convention even after their diversion.[138] Second, because it regulates the uses of international watercourses, but also any measures for their protection, preservation and management. Finally, because according to Article 1.2, even some navigation would fall within the scope of the Convention in the event that it affects the other uses: "The uses of international watercourses for navigation is not within the scope of the present Convention except insofar as other uses affect navigation or are affected by navigation."[139] In fact, it is difficult to imagine which uses apart from navigation could not be included in such a formulation. The ILC commented on this article accordingly, stating that: "on any watercourse

133 See the replies of Netherlands, Nicaragua and Philippines in: ILC, *Replies of Governments to the Commission's questionnaire*, A/CN.4/294 and Add.1 (1976), https://legal.un.org/ilc/documentation/english/a_cn4_294.pdf. 170–171.

134 See in this regard Brazil, Poland and Spain. In Ibid. 168 and 171.

135 UN Watercourses Convention, *supra* note 51, Article 1.1.

136 Ibid. Article 10.1.

137 Ibid. Article 10.2. This article also states that conflicts between uses must be resolved according to Articles 5 and 7, which enshrines the principles of equitable and reasonable utilisation and the principle of no harm. These elements are the object of the following sections.

138 Tanzi and Arcari, *United Nations Convention on the Law of International Watercourses*, 49.

139 UN Watercourses Convention, *supra* note 51, Article 1.2.

where navigation takes place or is to be instituted, navigational requirements and effects and the requirements and effects of other water projects cannot be separated by the engineers and administrators charged with development of the watercourse."[140]

The UNECE Water Convention might be deemed to be even more open regarding the type of uses included in its scope. In fact, this derives from the fact that it does not refer to 'uses' as such, but to the wider concept of 'transboundary impact'. This concept, which is a central element of the Convention, as the next Section shows, is defined as "any significant adverse effect on the environment resulting from a change in the conditions of transboundary waters caused by a human activity, the physical origin of which is situated wholly or in part within an area under the jurisdiction of a Party, within an area under the jurisdiction of another Party."[141] From the plain reading of the text, all uses can be considered to be included in the concept of 'human activity'. Even navigation, which is explicitly excluded from the UN Watercourses Convention, is a human activity that might fall within the scope of the UNECE Water Convention as long as it does so *ratione materiae*.[142]

The regional regulation of international watercourses is marked by the diversity of uses considered. Among the international basin agreements analysed in this research, the only use that is always regulated to some extent is that of the environmental needs of the watercourse. Some agreements refer to environmental protection,[143] while others may refer to the water needs for the protection of ecosystems,[144] habitats[145] or biodiversity.[146] Water resources for basic human needs[147] and navigation[148] are also commonly regulated in international basin agreements.

140 Report of the ILC on the work of its 46th session, *supra* note 105, 89–90.

141 UNECE Water Convention, *supra* note 27, Article 1.2.

142 See, in this regard, Fitzmaurice, "Scope of the UNECE Water Convention," 106–109.

143 See, for instance: Mekong Agreement, Article 3; Article 2, paragraph 6 of The Niger Basin Water Charter.

144 See, for instance: Article 3(1)(d) of the Danube River Protection Convention; and Article 1 of the Water Charter of the Lake Chad Basin.

145 See Convention on the Protection of the Rhine. Article 3.1(d).

146 See, in this regard: Article 4.2 of the Great Lakes Water Quality Agreement; Article 2(1) of the Danube River Protection Convention; Article 2.d) of the Convention on the Protection of the Rhine; and Article 2.b) of the Dniester River Basin Treaty.

147 See: Article 3.2 of the Convention on the Protection of the Rhine; Article 14 of The Niger Basin Water Charter; Article 8 of the Charter of Waters of the Senegal River; and Article 3.1(a)(i) of the Great Lakes Water Quality Agreement.

148 See Article 2.1(a) of the Framework Agreement on the Sava River Basin; Article 14 of The Niger Basin Water Charter; Chapter 7 of the Water Charter of the Lake Chad Basin; Article 8 of the Charter of Waters of the Senegal River; Article 1 of the Mekong Agreement.

Other uses are less generally regulated and regional tendencies can be identified. While pollution control is more relevant in heavily industrialised regions, references to the use of the international watercourse for agriculture, fishing or livestock rearing are more common in basins in the Global South.[149] Specific to European regimes is the regulation of preventive measures against floods, droughts, and ice hazards.[150] Other uses are less commonly regulated and less regionally specific, such as health, water for hydropower generation, tourism, recreational purposes, timber floating, forestry, and mining. In most of these regimes, the regulated uses establish a closed framework for cooperation, but some explicitly state that the uses enumerated are not meant to be an exhaustive list.[151]

3 The Principle of Cooperation and Its Institutionalisation

The cooperation principle in international watercourse law is a specific application of the general obligation in international law to cooperate in good faith.[152] In the context of international watercourse law, there is no doubt that the application of the substantive obligations already presented cannot be operationalised without international cooperation.[153] Moreover, cooperation between States has been identified from an early stage as a key element for the

149 See, in this regard: Article 1 of the Mekong Agreement; Article 14 of The Niger Basin Water Charter; Section 3 of the Water Charter of the Lake Chad Basin; and Article 8 of the Charter of Waters of the Senegal River.

150 See, in this regard: Article 8.1.c) of the Dniester River Basin Treaty; Article 3.4 of the Convention on the Protection of the Rhine; Article 3(1)(b) of the Danube River Protection Convention; and Article 2.1(c) of the Framework Agreement on the Sava River Basin.

151 See: Article 14 of The Niger Basin Water Charter; Article 1 of the Mekong Agreement.

152 For an analysis of the general principle of cooperation in international law see: Šahović, Milan. 1972. "Codification Des Principes Du Droit International Des Relations Amicales et de La Coopération Entre Les Etats." *Collected Courses of the Hague Academy of International Law* 137: 243–310. See also Sands et al. *Principles of International Environmental Law,* 203–205; Friedmann, W. 1969. "General Course in Public International Law." *Collected Courses of the Hague Academy of International Law* 127: 39–246. For a complete analysis of the principle of cooperation in relation to international watercourses law, see Leb, *Cooperation in the Law of Transboundary Water Resources.* See also: Caflisch, Lucius. 1989. "Règles Générales Du Droit Des Cours d'eau Internationaux." *Collected Courses of the Hague Academy of International Law* 219 (VII): 9–225. 186–187; Farrajota, M. M. 2005. "Notification and Consultation in the Law Applicable to International Law". In *Les Ressources En Eau et Le Droit International = Water Resources and International Law,* edited by Laurence Boisson de Chazournes and Salman M.A. Salman, 281–339. Leiden: Martinus Nijhoff. 283–284.

153 Leb, *Cooperation in the Law of Transboundary Water Resources,* 73–106.

achievement of sustainable development.[154] Mention has already been made of the relevance given in Agenda 2030 to cooperation between States on water resources, and the two specific indicators to measure such cooperation (the 'Degree of integrated water resources management implementation' and the 'Proportion of transboundary basin area with an operational arrangement for water cooperation'). This dimension of sustainable development was generally underlined in the Stockholm Declaration[155] and in the Rio Declaration,[156] and was specifically applied to shared water resources in Agenda 21.[157] The law of international watercourses has developed accordingly and, today, the inclusion of sustainable development as a specific objective of this body of law is closely related to the principle of cooperation.[158]

The arbitral tribunal in *Lac Lanoux* (*Espagne/France*) case did not mention the principle of cooperation explicitly but assumed it to be applicable.[159] Years later, the ICJ determined in *Gabčikovo-Nagymaros Project* (*Hungary/Slovakia*) that for Hungary and Slovakia to repair the consequences of their unilateral acts, they had to restore cooperation under the regime on shared water resources, which in turn would reflect the concept of common utilisation of the watercourse in accordance with Article 5.2 of the UN Watercourses Convention.[160] In *Pulp Mills on the River Uruguay* (*Argentina v. Uruguay*), the Court reinstated the need for cooperation to achieve equitable and reasonable utilisation of the watercourse, especially through the application of procedural obligations. It stated that:

> The Court considers that the procedural obligations of informing, notifying and negotiating constitute an appropriate means, accepted by the Parties, of achieving the objective which they set themselves in Article 1 of the 1975 Statute [the optimum and rational utilization]. These obligations are all the more vital when a shared resource is at issue, as in the case of the River Uruguay, which can only be protected through close and continuous co-operation between the riparian States.[161]

154 Schrijver, "The Evolution of Sustainable Development," 334–336.
155 Stockholm Declaration, *supra* note 3, Principle 24.
156 Rio Declaration, *supra* note 5.
157 Agenda 21, *supra* note 54, Section 18 (in general).
158 Weiss, "Evolution of International Water Law," 209–210.
159 Lac Lanoux (Espagne/France), 12 R.I.A.A (Perm. Ct. Arb. 1957). 308.
160 Gabčikovo-Nagymaros Project (Hungary/Slovakia), Judgment, 1997 I.C.J. Rep. 7 (September 25). Para. 147.
161 Pulp Mills on the River Uruguay (Argentina v. Uruguay), 2010 Judgment, I.C.J. Rep. 14 (April 20). Para. 81.

As a general principle deriving from customary international watercourse law, the cooperation principle has in turn been adopted by the two global conventions in this field.[162] In Article 8(1) of the UN Watercourses Convention, the duty to cooperate is expressed in the following broad terms: "Watercourse States shall cooperate on the basis of sovereign equality, territorial integrity, mutual benefit and good faith in order to attain optimal utilization and adequate protection of an international watercourse." For its part, the UNECE Water Convention also lays down the general duty to cooperate in Article 2(6), while further detailing the objectives of cooperation and establishing the catchment area as the geographical area in which this cooperation is to take place.

As mentioned above, the UNECE Water Convention also enshrines the general obligation to cooperate, although with some variations that derive from the difference in overall objectives between this and the UN Watercourses Convention. Article 9(1) starts by specifying that cooperation must take the form of bilateral or multilateral agreements, while stating that such cooperation must serve to "define their mutual relations and conduct regarding the prevention, control and reduction of transboundary impact". By contrast, the UN Watercourses Convention is less specific in defining how cooperation must be made effective and establishes that the purpose of cooperation is not only the avoidance of harm (or 'impact', as stated in the Convention) but also optimal utilisation.

The difference between the two Conventions is also apparent in the degree of cooperation that they promote. Thus, Wouters and Leb note that "[t]he objective to tie Parties closely together through institutionalized cooperation and joint action runs as a *fil rouge* in the [UNECE Water] Convention"[163] through a variety of obligations. The general obligation to cooperate, either in the UN Watercourses Convention or the UNECE Water Convention must be translated into specific obligations and measures to be effective.

In *Pulp Mills on the River Uruguay (Argentina v. Uruguay)*, the ICJ applies this criterion in relation to the obligation to cooperate established in the agreement between Argentina and Uruguay noting that "It is the opinion of the Court that compliance with this obligation cannot be expected to come through the individual action of either Party, acting on its own. Its implementation requires

162 Wouters, Patricia, and Christina Leb. 2015. "The Duty to Cooperation in International Water Law – Examining the Contribution of the UN Water Conventions to Facilitating Transboundary Water Cooperation." In *The UNECE Convention on the Protection and Use of Transboundary Watercourses and International Lakes*, edited by Attila Tanzi, Owen McIntyre, Alexandros Kolliopoulos, Alistair Rieu-Clarke, and Rémy Kinna, 285–295. Leiden: Brill Nijhoff. 290.

163 Wouters, "The Duty to Cooperation in International Water Law," 292–293.

co-ordination through the Commission."[164] Given the broad terms used to define the obligation to cooperate in this particular bilateral agreement, the Court's position may be deemed relevant as it can be assumed that a similar stance would be adopted if applied, for instance, to Article 8 of the UN Watercourses Convention.

Customary law regarding international watercourses and the two global conventions provide several of those obligations. Among the rights and obligations directly deriving from the general principle of cooperation, Leb distinguishes those that are of behaviour and those that seek a specific outcome. The first one are generally referred as 'procedural obligations' and include the obligations to exchange data and information or the obligation of prior notification. These procedural obligations are key to prevent transboundary harm. The second ones would be the cooperation mechanisms with the purposes of attaining joint monitoring and assessment obligations, or setting early warning systems. These aspects are relevant to comply with both the principle of protection of the watercourse, the prevention of transboundary harm and the attainment of optimal utilization.[165]

The international State practice reveals that most of international watercourses have some form of institutional structure for cooperative action.[166] The functions and attributions of these joint mechanisms and their role in applying the principle of integration in the governance of international watercourses are dealt with in Chapters 9 to 12 and not described in detail here. However, it is necessary to consider their relationship with the principle of cooperation.[167] The river commissions established to regulate navigation, mainly during the second half of the 19th century, can be regarded as the predecessors of modern international organisations.[168] According to Díez de

---

164 Pulp Mills on the River Uruguay (Argentina v. Uruguay), 2010 Judgment, I.C.J. Rep. 14 (April 20). Para. 184.

165 Leb, Christina. 2019. "Implementation of the General Duty to Cooperate." In *Research Handbook on International Water Law*, edited by Stephen C. McAffrey and Riley T. Denoon, 95–108. Cheltenham: Edward Elgar.

166 A comprehensive study carried out by Susanne Schmeier listed 119 River Basin Organisations. In Schmeier, Susanne. 2013. *Governing International Watercourses: River Basin Organizations and the Sustainable Governance of Internationally Shared Rivers and Lakes.* Abingdon: Routledge.

167 On this topic, see generally Boisson de Chazournes, Laurence. 2013. "Organismes et Commissions de Bassin: Aspect de Cooperation Régionale et de Règlement de Différends." In *Liber Amicorum Raymond Ranjeva : L'Afrique et Le Droit International : Variations Sur l'organisation Internationale = Africa and International Law : Reflections on the International Organization*, 435–44. Paris: Editions A. Pedone.

168 Amerasinghe, C. F. 2005. *Principles of the Institutional Law of International Organizations.* 2nd ed. Cambridge: Cambridge University Press. 4.

Velasco, fluvial commissions would have been the first permanent institutional structures, which are a necessary component of international organisations.[169] They have not only increased dramatically in number[170] but have also evolved significantly in terms of structure and competences.[171] Such organisations are usually complex institutions with international subjectivity and the capacity to adopt legally binding acts.[172]

In the literature on the theory of international watercourse regimes, these institutions are referred to as IRBOs. All the regimes on international watercourses analysed in this research have IRBOs, which play a key role when reinforced cooperation is sought in the governance of a watercourse.[173] The ICJ itself has recognised that the establishment of this type of organisation serves to provide a more stable system for cooperation than simply holding bilateral negotiations.[174] Nevertheless, the need to create these joint mechanisms is not strongly expressed in the law of international watercourses. Article 8.2 of the UN Watercourses Convention states that: "watercourse States may consider the establishment of joint mechanisms or commissions, as deemed necessary

169 Díez de Velasco Vallejo, Manuel. 2010. *Las Organizaciones Internacionales*. 16th ed. Madrid: Tecnos. 40.

170 See Oregon State University. n.d. "International River Basin Organization Database." Accessed December 11, 2024. https://transboundarywaters.ceoas.oregonstate.edu/international-river-basin-organization-database.

171 See in this regard a classic categorisation provided by Colliard between fluvial commissions, which would include technical commission, technical-administrative commissions and commissions with normative or jurisdictional functions; and operation organisms, which include permanent commissions and international societies. In Colliard, "Régime Des Fleuves Internationaux," 419–439.

172 According to Schemeier, an IRBO is an "institution that provides a set of institutionalized principles, norms, rules and river basin governance mechanisms around which actors' expectations converge in the issue-area of water resources governance. [...] In addition, the definition of an RBO implies some degree of bindingness, robustness and institutionalization of the institution". Schmeier, *Governing International Watercourses*, 23. See also, the analysis of the ICJ of the CARU, which would be an IRBO, regarding its nature and role. In Pulp Mills on the River Uruguay (Argentina v. Uruguay), 2010 Judgment, I.C.J. Rep. 14 (April 20). Paras. 84–92.

173 See, for instance, Article 11 of the Mekong Agreement, which establishes the Mekong River Commission (MRC); Article 15 of the Framework Agreement on the Sava River Basin obliging the Parties to create the International Sava River Basin Commission; or the Organisation pour la Mise en Valeur du Fleuve Sénégal, which was created by the 1972 Convention creating organization for the development of the Senegal River (Convention creating organization for the development of the Senegal River, May 11, 1972, LEX-FAOC091150) and currently in charge of applying the Charter of Waters of the Senegal River.

174 Pulp Mills on the River Uruguay (Argentina v. Uruguay), 2010 Judgment, I.C.J. Rep. 14 (April 20). Para. 90.

by them, to facilitate cooperation on relevant measures and procedures".[175] The phrasing 'may consider the establishment' clearly indicates that the text is setting out a guideline rather than laying down an obligation. Article 24 of the Convention also mentions the possibility of establishing such joint bodies for the specific case of consultations regarding the management of an international watercourse.[176] Again, this is presented as a guideline and not as an obligation.[177] In the UN Watercourses Convention, therefore, there is no obligation for States to establish IRBOs.[178]

IRBOs play a more central role in the UNECE Water Convention. Article 9(2) clearly lays down an obligation to create joint organisms in order to meet the various cooperation obligations set out in the Convention. The functions of these basin organisations are listed in detail, though not exhaustively.[179] This list is also relevant inasmuch as it gives substance to Article 8(2) of the UN

---

175 UN Watercourses Convention, *supra* note 51, Article 8(2).

176 "Watercourse States shall, at the request of any of them, enter into consultations concerning the management of an international watercourse, which may include the establishment of a joint management mechanism." UN Watercourses Convention (*supra* note 51), Article 24(1).

177 Ziganshina, Dinara R. 2018. "Protection, Preservation, and Management, Ch. 11 Management (Article 24)." In *The UN Convention on the Law of the Non-Navigational Uses of International Watercourses: A Commentary*, edited by Laurence Boisson De Chazournes, Makane Moïse Mbengue, Mara Tignino, Komlan Sangbana, and Jason Rudall, 214–37. Oxford: OUP. 226.

178 McIntyre, Owen. 2020. "The Legal Role and Context of River Basin Organizations." In *River Basin Organizations in Water Diplomacy*, edited by Anoulak Kittikhoun and Susanne Schmeier, 25–48. Abingdon: Routledge. 28.

179 "(a) To collect, compile and evaluate data in order to identify pollution sources likely to cause transboundary impact; (b) To elaborate joint monitoring programmes concerning water quality and quantity; (c) To draw up inventories and exchange information on the pollution sources mentioned in paragraph 2 (a) of this article; (d) To elaborate emission limits for waste water and evaluate the effectiveness of control programmes; (e) To elaborate joint water-quality objectives and criteria having regard to the provisions of article 3, paragraph 3 of this Convention, and to propose relevant measures for maintaining and, where necessary, improving the existing water quality; (f) To develop concerted action programmes for the reduction of pollution loads from both point sources (e.g. municipal and industrial sources) and diffuse sources (particularly from agriculture); (g) To establish warning and alarm procedures; (h) To serve as a forum for the exchange of information on existing and planned uses of water and related installations that are likely to cause transboundary impact; (i) To promote cooperation and exchange of information on the best available technology in accordance with the provisions of article 13 of this Convention, as well as to encourage cooperation in scientific research programmes; (j) To participate in the implementation of environmental impact assessments relating to transboundary waters, in accordance with appropriate international regulations." UNECE Water Convention, *supra* note 27, Article 9.2(d).

Watercourses Convention.[180] Finally, as mentioned above, these organisations are given particular importance in the UNECE Water Convention, Article 10 of which establishes that all consultations aimed at cooperation within the scope of the Convention must be conducted through a joint body.

The potential for effective cooperation between riparian States without a joint body is a matter for discussion. Evidently, the existence of such an organism would make it dramatically easier to meet the various procedural obligations referred to above. The ICJ makes this point in *Pulp Mills on the River Uruguay* (*Argentina v. Uruguay*), stating that by creating the CARU, the IRBO, and investing it with the necessary operational capacities, "the Parties have sought to provide the best possible guarantees of stability, continuity and effectiveness for their desire to co-operate in ensuring 'the optimum and rational utilization of the River Uruguay'."[181]

It is possibly the need to enter into consultations to maintain a fair balance between the uses of a watercourse and its protection that has led so many countries to establish joint bodies.[182] Tanzi and Arcari argue that although a general customary obligation to establish joint bodies cannot be assessed since there is no *opinio iuris* in that sense, "[t]he consistent practice to that effect can be ascertained to be based at least on a consistent *opinio necessitates.*"[183] In fact, the international practice reveals that river basin organisations play an increasingly important role in the protection of international watercourses, with functions ranging from the creation to the application of norms.[184]

---

180 Tanzi and Arcari, *United Nations Convention on the Law of International Watercourses*, 189.

181 In Pulp Mills on the River Uruguay (Argentina v. Uruguay), 2010 Judgment, I.C.J. Rep. 14 (April 20). Para. 90.

182 McCaffrey, *Law of International Watercourses*, 539.

183 Tanzi and Arcari, *United Nations Convention on the Law of International Watercourses*, 191.

184 In the specific aspect of protection of watercourses from pollution, see Sangbana, Komlan. 2017. *La Protection Des Eaux Douces Transfrontières Contre La Pollution: Dimensions Normatives et Institutionnelles*. Geneva: Schulthess. 157–280.

CHAPTER 3

The Principle of Integration and the Substantive Obligations of International Watercourses Law

International watercourses are regulated by both substantive and procedural norms,[1] a legal domain where many disputes arising have concerned the relationship between them.[2] The relevance of substantive obligations of international watercourse law is paramount in relation to the principle of integration as each obligation represents different interests, such as the rights of one State to utilise the watercourse, the rights of other States to not be harmed by this use, and the protection of the shared watercourse. Initially, a certain overlap can be identified between the dimensions covered by the principle of integration and the interests protected by these obligations of international watercourse law. This Chapter analysis each of these obligations, considering whether, and to what extent, their relationship embodies the principle of integration.

1 The Substantive Obligations

The substantive obligations of international watercourse law determine the conduct of riparian States when their activities affect the international watercourse or their co-riparians throughout it. Well-established substantive obligations in this area of international law are the obligation of equitable and reasonable utilisation and the obligation of no harm, while the protection of international watercourses and their ecosystems can be considered an

1 As distinguished by Brunée, "[s]ubstantive rules set out standards that must be met through States' actions or conduct, such as harm prevention goals or emissions targets. Procedural obligations, in turn, include the duties to notify, warn, inform, or consult States potentially affected by transboundary impacts, and to undertake (transboundary) environmental impact assessments." Brunnée, Jutta. 2019. "Procedure and Substance in International Environmental Law." *Collected Courses of the Hague Academy of International Law* 405: 75–240. 100.

2 In the cases resolved by the ICJ concerning international watercourses the dispute never concerned the substantive or procedural nature of the alleged breached norm, but rather the relationship between different norms. See Pulp Mills on the River Uruguay (Argentina v. Uruguay), 2010 Judgment, I.C.J. Rep. 14 (April 20). Paras. 169–266; Certain Activities Carried Out by Nicaragua in the Border Area (Costa Rica v. Nicaragua) and Construction of a Road in Costa Rica along the San Juan River (Nicaragua v. Costa Rica), Judgment, 2015 I.C.J. Rep. 665 (December 15). Paras. 113–120.

 | DOI:10.1163/9789004736757_006

emerging substantive obligation.[3] This section will analyse these three in order to compare them with the principle of integration.

1.1 *Equitable and Reasonable Utilisation*

The obligation of equitable and reasonable utilisation is a central element in the law of international watercourses that has evolved significantly during the last century.[4] The filtration of sustainable development as a core element of this obligation is a driving factor of this evolution.[5] The discussion on equitable and reasonable utilisation has its origin in federal cases of the United States[6] and is based on the classic principle of *sic utere tuo.*[7] In *Nebraska v. Wyoming*, the Supreme Court of the United States found in 1945 that the water claims of the two states were incompatible as they surpassed the available water in the North Platte River. Wyoming asked the Court to make an equitable allocation of water resources, while Nebraska based its claim to rights on its past use of the river's water resources. The Court accepted that the priority of appropriation was to be the guiding principle, but also found that a just and equitable allocation required considering other factors that could limit those previous appropriations.[8] The Court also rejected an allocation logic based on equality. Equitability, instead, requires that water allocation be determined according to a number of elements that could lead to differences in the amount of water to which each state is entitled.[9]

The obligation progressively gained centrality in international law and there is no doubt of its customary nature today. The ICJ expressed itself clearly in this regard in *Dispute over the status and use of the waters of the Silala*:

---

3 See in this regard, Movilla Pateiro, Laura. 2022. "La Progresiva Ecologización Del Derecho Internacional de Los Cursos de Agua. Manifestaciones Convencionales, Jurisprudenciales y Consuetudinarias." *Revista Catalana de Dret Ambiental* XIII (2): 1–42.

4 See, generally, McCaffrey, *Law of International Watercourses*, 444–466; Aura y Larios de Medrano, *La Regulación Internacional Del Agua Dulce,* 109–166.

5 See, on this topic, Fitzmaurice and Barral, "The Relationship between the Law of International Watercourses and Sustainable Development"; and Fuentes, Ximena. 1999. "Sustainable Development and the Equitable Utilization of International Watercourses." *British Yearbook of International Law* 69 (1): 119–200.

6 See, for instance, New jersey v. new York, US Supreme Court 1931; Nebraska v. Wyoming. US Supreme Court 1945.

7 Caflisch, "Règles Générales Du Droit Des Cours d'eau Internationaux," 141.

8 The Court argued: In Nebraska v. Wyoming. US Supreme Court 1945 589, 618.

9 On this topic see McIntyre, Owen. 2013. "Utilization of Shared International Freshwater Resources – the Meaning and Role of 'Equity' in International Water Law." *Water International* 38 (2): 112–29.

> Under customary international law, every riparian State has a basic right to an equitable and reasonable sharing of the resources of an international watercourse. [...] In the present case, under customary international law, the Parties are both entitled to an equitable and reasonable use of the waters of the Silala as an international watercourse and obliged, in utilizing the international watercourse, to take all appropriate measures to prevent the causing of significant harm to the other Party.[10]

The ILA's Helsinki Rules of 1966 already included reasonable and equitable use as its fourth rule, establishing a conditionality on the use that riparian States can make of the international watercourse.[11] They may use it as long as they do so in a reasonable and equitable manner. On the one hand, as the ILA's comments on this obligation make clear, equitable utilisation implies a rejection of the absolute territorial sovereignty position.[12] On the other hand, this condition creates the need to determine when a use is reasonable and when it is equitable on a case-by-case basis. That is why Article V enumerates a set of parameters with which to carry out this determination, including, among others: the hydrology, climate, prior and current uses of the watercourse, and the economic and social needs of the basin population.[13]

A new element in the ILA's formulation is the 'reasonability' requirement, which must be differentiated from equitability. Caflisch considered this concept in relation to other terms used in conventional law such as "rational", "optimal" or "best possible", and also with paragraph i) of Article 5 of the Helsinki Rules, which provides the factor "avoidance of unnecessary waste in the utilization of waters of the basin."[14] According to this view, reasonableness would be related to a sense of efficiency and good management that should contribute to the availability of water for the States. However, the content of this obligation was still to be developed, especially with the adoption of the UN Watercourses Convention and the jurisprudence of the ICJ on the matter.[15]

---

10 See its recognition in Dispute over the status and use of the waters of the Silala (Chile v. Bolivia), Judgement, 2022 I.C.J. Rep. 614 (December 1). Para. 97.

11 ILA. 1967 "Helsinki Rules on the Uses of the Waters of International Rivers." https://unece.org/fileadmin/DAM/env/water/meetings/legal_board/2010/annexes_groundwater_paper/Annex_II_Helsinki_Rules_ILA.pdf. Article IV.

12 Ibid.

13 Ibid. Article V.2.

14 Caflisch, "Règles Générales Du Droit Des Cours d'eau Internationaux," 150.

15 On the relationship between the Helsinki Rules and the UN Watercourses Convention, see Bourne, C. B. 1997. "The Primacy of the Principle of Equitable Utilization in the 1997 Watercourses Convention." *Canadian Yearbook of International Law* 35: 215–32. 215–217.

Thirty years later, the UN Watercourses Convention adopted the formulation provided by the ILA in 1966, expressing it in similar terms. Article 5 reads as follows:

1. Watercourse States shall in their respective territories utilize an international watercourse in an equitable and reasonable manner. In particular, an international watercourse shall be used and developed by watercourse States with a view to attaining optimal and sustainable utilization thereof and benefits therefrom, taking into account the interests of the watercourse States concerned, consistent with adequate protection of the watercourse.
2. Watercourse States shall participate in the use, development and protection of an international watercourse in an equitable and reasonable manner. Such participation includes both the right to utilize the watercourse and the duty to cooperate in the protection and development thereof, as provided in the present Convention.[16]

As commented by the ILC, paragraph one contains the basic rule of equitable and reasonable utilisation by which riparian States have both a right to utilise the watercourse and an obligation to do so equitably and reasonably.[17] The ILC also provides a distinction between equitable and reasonable, largely resolving the doubt that the ILA failed to address with the Helsinki Rules. Where 'equitable' would refer to the satisfaction of each State's water necessities in qualitative and quantitative terms, 'reasonable' would be applicable in those cases where not all beneficial uses can be realised and a 'conflict of uses' arises. In such cases, preserving the equality of right requires adjustments and accommodations.[18]

The second phrase of the first paragraph establishes the objective of equitable and reasonable utilisation, which must seek to be optimal and sustainable. Regarding optimal utilisation, the ILC clarifies that it should not be understood as the achievement of maximum use or economic benefit, but rather as the attainment of "maximum possible benefits for all watercourse States and achieving the greatest possible satisfaction of all their needs, while

16 Convention on the Law of the Non-Navigational Uses of International Watercourses, May 21, 1997, 2999 U.N.T.S. Article 5.

17 ILC, *Draft articles on the law of the non-navigational uses of international watercourses and commentaries thereto and resolution on transboundary confined groundwater*, A/CN. 4/SER.A/1994/Add.l (Part 2) (1994) https://legal.un.org/ilc/texts/instruments/english/commentaries/8_3_1994.pdf. 97.

18 Ibid. 98; on this topic see also Rieu-Clarke, Moynihan and Magsig, *UN Watercourses Convention*, 107.

minimizing the detriment to, or unmet needs of, each."[19] Sustainable utilisation is defined by the ILC by literal reference to paragraph 18.16. of Agenda 21,[20] which states that "[w]ater resources development and management should be planned in an integrated manner [...], that is to say, they should incorporate environmental, economic and social considerations based on the principle of sustainability."[21]

Nevertheless, the ILC's explanations do not seem to have been assumed straightforwardly. Four months after the adoption of the UN Watercourse Convention and long before its entry into force in 2014, the obligation of equitable and reasonable utilisation was invoked as a fundamental norm by the ICJ in *Gabčikovo-Nagymaros Project (Hungary/Slovakia)* by reference to the Convention.[22] The Court refers to it twice when discussing whether Hungary had been deprived of its right to a reasonable and equitable utilisation of the watercourse by Czechoslovakia: first, to clarify its inalienability for Hungary;[23] and second, to affirm that it would have effectively been infringed by Czechoslovakia.[24] Although the Court acknowledges the UN Watercourses Convention as a modern development of international law, its reference to equitable utilisation was stated exclusively in terms of the rights of each State, instead of the obligation that it also contains. The importance of the invocation of equitable and reasonable utilisation in this case lies not in the effective insertion of its content into international law but rather in the relevance given to solving the dispute.[25]

In *Pulp Mills on the River Uruguay (Argentina v. Uruguay)*, when discussing if Uruguay may had breached Article 1 of the 1975 Statute establishing the

---

19 Ibid.

20 Ibid.

21 United Nations Conference on Environment and Development, *Agenda 21*, in *Report of the United Nations Conference on Environment and Development*, A/CONF.151/26 (Vol. I) (12 August 1992), undocs.org/en/A/CONF.151/26/Rev.1(vol. I). Para. 18.16.

22 Gabčikovo-Nagymaros Project (Hungary/Slovakia), Judgment, 1997 I.C.J. Rep. 7 (September 25).

23 Ibid. Para. 78.: "The suspension and withdrawal of that consent constituted a violation of Hungary's legal obligations, demonstrating, as it did, the refusal by Hungary of joint operation; but that cannot mean that Hungary forfeited its basic right to an equitable and reasonable sharing of the resources of an international watercourse".

24 Ibid. 56. Para. 85: "The Court considers that Czechoslovakia, by unilaterally assuming control of a shared resource, and thereby depriving Hungary of its right to an equitable and reasonable share of the natural resources of the Danube – with the continuing effects of the diversion of these waters on the ecology of the riparian area of the Szigetkoz – failed to respect the proportionality which is required by international law."

25 See in this regard, Aura y Larios de Medrano, *La Regulación Internacional Del Agua Dulce*, 154–162.

Administrative Commission of the River Uruguay (CARU), the Court clearly conditioned compliance with the obligation of equitable and reasonable utilisation on the pursuit of sustainable development.[26] This is even more relevant considering that neither of the two concepts was clearly included in the Statute. The two Parties in the conflict referred to both concepts in their pleadings.[27] In fact, Uruguay invokes sustainable development in terms of a right of each Party embedded into the equitable and reasonable utilisation obligation[28] or, to cite Article 1 of this instrument, the "optimum and rational utilization of the [r]iver". Also, Argentina defended the need for sustainable development to be considered an applicable principle, since Article 31.3(c) of the Vienna Convention on the Law of Treaties entailed interpreting the Statute in "the light of principles governing the law of international watercourses and principles of international law ensuring protection of the environment."[29] The final decision of the Court sanctioned that position, although Argentina and Uruguay used it with opposing consequences.[30]

Thus, the ICJ in *Pulp Mills on the River Uruguay (Argentina v. Uruguay)* determines that equitable and reasonable use is contingent on compliance with sustainable development.[31] Other authors have gone even further, proposing that equitable and reasonable utilisation has become the specific manner of implementing sustainable development in the specific context of cooperation on international watercourses.[32] However, the simple identification between

26 "[I]t is the opinion of the Court that Article 27 embodies this interconnectedness between equitable and reasonable utilization of a shared resource and the balance between economic development and environmental protection that is the essence of sustainable development." In Pulp Mills on the River Uruguay (Argentina v. Uruguay), 2010 Judgment, I.C.J. Rep. 14 (April 20). Para. 177.

27 McCaffrey points out that the fact that both Parties referred to equitable and reasonable utilisation "strengthens its status as a cornerstone of the customary international law governing the use of international watercourses". In McCaffrey, *Law of International Watercourses*, 222.

28 Pulp Mills on the River Uruguay (Argentina v. Uruguay), 2010 Judgment, I.C.J. Rep. 14 (April 20). Para. 152.

29 Ibid. Para. 55.

30 Ibid. Para. 177.

31 In Fitzmaurice and Barral's words, "[s]uch judicial pronouncement confirms that sustainable development has successfully coloured the interpretation of the principle of equitable and reasonable use which now incorporates environmental protection concerns, and that utilisation of a shared resource will only be equitable and reasonable if it is sustainable." (Fitzmaurice and Barral, "The Relationship between the Law of International Watercourses and Sustainable Development", 422).

32 See, for instnace, McIntyre, O. 2017. "Substantive Rules of International Water Law." In *Routledge Handbook of Water Law and Policy*, edited by A. Rieu-Clarke et al. Routledge. 240.

equitable and reasonable utilisation and sustainable development has to be rejected. As seen above, the obligation of equitable and reasonable utilisation pursues other objectives in addition to achieving sustainable development as it also expresses a right of equitable use. Taking this into account, although equitable and reasonable use must necessarily be sustainable, it is possible that a given sustainable use of an international watercourse may not be equitable and reasonable. It should not be forgotten, despite the mutual influence, the emergence of the obligation of equitable and reasonable use predates the concept of sustainable development and, arguably, the development of environmental law. Moreover, the obligation of not causing transboundary harm, which is analysed in the following Subsection, might also contribute to sustainable development.

The parallels between sustainable development and equitable and reasonable utilisation are also apparent in Article 6 of the UN Watercourses Convention. This article lists non-exhaustively the factors that must be taken into account in considering whether the uses of an international watercourse comply with the obligation of equitable and reasonable utilisation.[33] Paragraph 3 of this article establishes that the weight to be attributed to each factor is relative to the other factors and that all of them must be considered together.[34] This weighting process, which in the case of international watercourses requires cooperation between the riparian States, resembles the purpose of the principle of integration, especially so as the list includes economic, social and environmental factors. As such, a high degree of correspondence can be expected between the instruments applied to ensure a decision-making process consistent with the principle of integration and the weighting of the factors determining equitable and reasonable utilisation.

The limit to this correspondence will be the need to guarantee the right to equitable use of each riparian State. The ICJ in the *Dispute over the status and use of the waters of the Silala* underlined this dimension by stressing that equitable and reasonable utilisation was "not to be applied in an abstract or static

33 "(a) Geographic, hydrographic, hydrological, climatic, ecological and other factors of a natural character; (b) The social and economic needs of the watercourse States concerned; (c) The population dependent on the watercourse in each watercourse State; (d) The effects of the use or uses of the watercourses in one watercourse State on other watercourse States; (e) Existing and potential uses of the watercourse; (f) Conservation, protection, development and economy of use of the water resources of the watercourse and the costs of measures taken to that effect; (g) The availability of alternatives, of comparable value, to a particular planned or existing use." (UN Watercourses Convention, *supra* note 16, Article 6.1).

34 Ibid. Article 6.3.

way but by comparing the situations of States concerned and their utilization of the watercourse at a given time."[35] Therefore, the weighting between the factors listed in Article 6 must serve also this inter-State purpose.

The UNECE Water Convention also contains the obligation of equitable and reasonable utilisation. Paragraph (c) of Article 2 provides that the Parties will take the appropriate measures "[t]o ensure that transboundary waters are used in a reasonable and equitable way, taking into particular account their transboundary character, in the case of activities which cause or are likely to cause transboundary impact."[36] However, this provision is mentioned as one specific measure to comply with the main obligation of taking "all appropriate measures to prevent, control and reduce any transboundary impact."[37] It has been argued that this provision should not be understood as a downgrading of equitable and reasonable utilisation in favour of the prevention of significant transboundary harm,[38] while it is true that the Guide to Implementing The Water Convention affirms that those two obligations, together with the cooperation obligation, are the three-pillar normative cornerstone of the UNECE Water Convention.[39]

Nevertheless, from the plain reading of Article 2(c) it seems clear that the obligation of equitable and reasonable utilisation plays a minor role in this Convention. Movilla has suggested that the Guide's affirmation of the three-pillar cornerstone may be an attempt to reinforce the presence and relevance of equitable and reasonable utilisation, in line with the strategy of joint promotion and complementarity of the two global conventions.[40] It should be recalled that, despite its non-binding status, the Guide was adopted by the Parties.

As is to be expected given the very recent development of the obligation of equitable and reasonable utilisation, its regulation at regional level is highly variable. It can be found in the basin agreements adopted from the 1990s

---

35 Dispute over the status and use of the waters of the Silala (Chile v. Bolivia), Judgement, 2022 I.C.J. Rep. 614 (December 1). Para. 98.

36 Convention on the Protection and Use of Transboundary Watercourses and International Lakes, March 17, 1992, 1936 U.N.T.S. 269. Article 2(c).

37 Ibid. Article 2.1.

38 McIntyre, Owen. 2015. "The Principle of Equitable and Reasonable Utilisation." In *The UNECE Convention on the Protection and Use of Transboundary Watercourses and International Lakes*, edited by Tanzi, Attila, Owen McIntyre, Alexandros Kolliopoulos, Alistair Rieu-Clarke, and Rémy Kinna. Leiden, The Netherlands: Brill Nijhoff.

39 UNECE. 2013. *Guide to Implementing The Water Convention*. New York and Geneva: United Nations. 15.

40 Movilla Pateiro, Laura. 2021. *La Dimensión Normativa de La Gobernanza Internacional Del Agua Dulce*. Valencia: Tirant lo Blanch. 146.

onwards. In most cases, it is simply mentioned as a guiding principle or an objective of cooperation on international watercourses.[41] The Framework Agreement on the Sava River Basin, for example, states that equitable and reasonable utilisation will be determined according to the relevant factors established by international law.[42] Three of the most recent international basin agreements, however, also provide a list of factors: the Niger,[43] Chad Lake,[44] and Volta[45] basin agreements. The fact that these lists also contain the factors stated in Article 6 of the UN Watercourses Convention illustrates a clear influence of this Convention,[46] but there is also an appreciable adaptation to the particular necessities of the basin through supplementary factors. Thus, the Niger Basin Water Charter, the Water Charter of the Lake Chad Basin, and the Draft Water Charter for the Volta River all include a considerably longer list of factors than the UN Watercourses Convention.

1.2 *Not to Cause Significant Harm*

The obligation not to cause significant harm has its origin in the maxim *sic utere tuo ut alienum non laedas*, which can be translated as "so use your own as not harm that of another."[47] The arbitral tribunal in the 1941 *Trail smelter case* (*United States/Canada*)[48] famously applied this obligation as it found that

---

41 Dniester River Basin Treaty, Article 4.2.a); Agreement on the establishment of the Zambezi Watercourse Commission, Article 5; Charter of Waters of the Senegal River Article 4; SADC Protocol on Shared Watercourses, Article 2.b); Danube River Protection Convention, Article 2(1); Mekong Agreement, Article 5.

42 Framework Agreement on the Sava River Basin, Article 7.2).

43 The Niger Basin Water Charter. Article 4.

44 Water Charter of the Lake Chad Basin, Article 13.

45 Draft Water Charter for the Volta River Basin, Article 13.

46 On the extent of the general influence of the UN Watercourses Convention on international basin agreements, see Rieu-Clarke, Alistair. 2019. "From Treaty Practice to the UN Watercourses Convention." In *Research Handbook on International Water Law*, edited by Stephen C. McAffrey and Riley T. Denoon, 11–25. Edward Elgar.

47 On the the obligation not to cause significant harm in relation to international watercourses law, see generally: Colliard, Claude-Albert. 1968. "Régime Des Fleuves Internationaux." *Collected Courses of the Hague Academy of International Law* 125: 337–442. 378–397; Caflisch, "Règles Générales Du Droit Des Cours d'eau Internationaux," 135–140; Lammers, Johan G. 1984. *Pollution of International Watercourses: A Search for Substantive Rules and Principles of Law*. Boston: Martinus Nijhoff; McCaffrey, *Law of International Watercourses*, 467–506; and Salman, Salman M.A. 2018. "The Obligation Not to Cause Significant Harm (Article 7)." In *The UN Convention on the Law of the Non-Navigational Uses of International Watercourses: A Commentary*, edited by Laurence Boisson de Chazournes, Makane Moïse Mbengue, Mara Tignino, Komlan Sangbana, and Jason Rudall, 95–122. Oxford: OUP.

48 Trail smelter case (United States/Canada), 3 R.I.A.A (Perm. Ct. Arb. 1941).

"[u]nder the principles of international law [...] no State has the right to use or permit the use of its territory in such a manner as to cause injury by fumes in or to the territory of another or the properties or persons therein."[49] The obligation not to cause significant harm has been recognised as part of international law in other cases,[50] while in the case on the *Legality of the Threat or Use of Nuclear Weapons*[51] the ICJ left no doubt as to the customary nature of the obligation.[52]

From their inception, soft law instruments developing sustainable development discourse have integrated the obligation not to cause significant harm. The Stockholm Declaration clearly enshrines it in Principle 21, as a limit to the sovereign permanent right of States to exploit their own resources.[53] This was a point of controversy in the negotiation of the Declaration, as there was a significant divide between the countries in favour of subjecting permanent sovereignty over natural resources to considerations of environmental context and the countries opposed to placing any restriction on the exercise of their sovereign power.[54] The Rio Declaration also states the obligation not to cause significant harm in its Principle 2 by tacking Stockhom's Declaration version almost unchanged.[55]

---

49 Ibid. 1965.

50 Corfu Channel case (United Kingdom v. Albania), Judgment, 1949 I.C.J. Rep. 4 (April 9); Pulp Mills on the River Uruguay (Argentina v. Uruguay), 2010 Judgment, I.C.J. Rep. 14 (April 20), para. 101; Indus Waters Kishenganga Arbitration (Pakistan vs. India). Final award, 31 R.I.A.A (Perm. Ct. Arb. 2013), para. 449. On this issue see Tignino, Mara, and Christian Bréthaut. 2020. "The Role of International Case Law in Implementing the Obligation Not to Cause Significant Harm." *International Environmental Agreements: Politics, Law and Economics* 20 (4): 631–48.

51 Legality of the Threat or Use of Nuclear Weapons, Advisory Opinion, 1996 I.C.J. Rep. 226.

52 Ibid. Para. 29. Also cited in Gabčikovo-Nagymaros Project (Hungary/Slovakia), Judgment, 1997 I.C.J. Rep. 7 (September 25), para. 53.

53 United Nations Conference on the Human Environment, *Declaration of the United Nations Conference on the Human Environment*, in Report of the United Nations Conference on the Human Environment, A/CONF.48/14/Rev.1. (5–16 June 1972), undocs.org/en/A/CONF.48/14/Rev.1. Principle 21.

54 Preparatory Committee for the United Nations Conference on the Human Environment, *Report of the Intergovernmental Working Group on the Declaration on the Human Environment*, A/CONF.48/PC.12 (14 June 1971), undocs.org/en/A/CONF.48/PC.12. Paras. 16–19, 33–36, 58–64. For a complete analysis of those negotiations see Sohn, "Stockholm Declaration," 485–493.

55 "States have, in accordance with the Charter of the United Nations and the principles of international law, the sovereign right to exploit their own resources pursuant to their own environmental and developmental policies, and the responsibility to ensure that activities within their jurisdiction or control do not cause damage to the environment of other States or of areas beyond the limits of national jurisdiction." (United Nations Conference on Environment and Development, *Rio Declaration on Environment and Development*,

Moreover, the obligation not to cause significant harm has been enshrined in several environmental agreements, such as the United Nations Convention on the Law of the Sea[56] (hereinafter, UNCLOS), the CBD,[57] the UNFCCC,[58] and the 1979 Convention on Long-Range Transboundary Air Pollution, in which it can be considered implicit in the prohibition of 'long-range transboundary air pollution' as defined therein.[59]

However, these declarations and conventions use the obligation not to cause significant harm from an environmental point of view, rather than in a general sense, addressing only transboundary harm to the environment, however broad a concept this may be.[60] This creates a problem that is commonly encountered in the application of the obligation not to cause significant harm to international watercourse law: what is considered to be 'harm' in such a context and to what extent it includes harm to the environment of another State in addition to other harmed goods. In this regard, McCaffrey notes that harm may take several forms of which he provides a non-exhaustive list.[61] This enumeration can be understood in light of the UN Watercourses Convention if Article 7 is read together with Article 21, which focuses more specifically on prevention, reduction, and control of pollution.[62] Hence, harm can be caused by affecting the flow of water, but also its quality.

The obligation not to cause significant harm is clearly enshrined in Article 7 of the UN Watercourses Convention.[63] It is also a well-established substantive

---

in Report of the United Nations Conference on Environment and Development, A/CONF.151/26 (Vol. I) (12 August 1992), undocs.org/en/A/CONF.151/26/Rev.1(vol. I)).

56 United Nations Convention on the Law of the Sea, December 10, 1982, 1833 U.N.T.S. 3. Article 193 and 194(2).

57 Convention on Biological Diversity, June 5, 1992, 1760 U.N.T.S. 79. Article 3.

58 United Nations Framework Convention on Climate Change, May 9, 1992, 1771 U.N.T.S. 107. Preamble.

59 Convention on Long-range Transboundary Air Pollution, November 13, 1979, 1302 U.N.T.S. 217. Article 1(b).

60 McCaffrey, *Law of International Watercourses*, 485.

61 "[P]ollution, obstruction of fish migration, erosion of one bank of a contiguous watercourse caused by works on the opposite bank, increased siltation due to upstream deforestation, construction, or unsound grazing practices, interference with the flow regime, erosion of the riverbed resulting from channelling of the river upstream, negative impacts on the riverine ecosystem due to conduct in another riparian state, [or] the bursting of a dam." (McCaffrey, *Law of International Watercourses*, 470).

62 It reads: "For the purpose of this article, "pollution of an International watercourse" means any detrimental alteration in the composition or quality of the waters of an international watercourse which results directly or indirectly from human conduct." UN Watercourses Convention, *supra* note 16, Article 21.

63 "Watercourse States shall, in utilizing an international watercourse in their territories, take all appropriate measures to prevent the causing of significant harm to other watercourse States." (UN Watercourses Convention, *supra* note 16, Article 7.1).

obligation of customary watercourse law, as recently recognised by the ICJ in the *Dispute over the status and use of the waters of the Silala*.[64] The proposed draft by the ILC stated: "Watercourse States shall exercise due diligence to utilize an international watercourse in such a way as not to cause significant harm to other watercourse States."[65] Although this formulation was ultimately rejected, the plain reading of this article implies that it is to be understood as a due diligence obligation.[66] It is not a prohibition of causing significant harm, but rather an instruction to take 'appropriate measures' to prevent it.

The logical consequence is that significant harm may occur without constituting a breach of the obligation under Article 7(1), provided that appropriate measures had been taken for its prevention. Therefore, the norm will only be considered breached when "a watercourse State whose use causes significant harm can be deemed to have breached its obligation to exercise due diligence so as not to cause significant harm only when it has intentionally or negligently caused the event which had to be prevented."[67]

The due diligence character of the obligation not to cause significant harm was nonetheless a controversial topic in the ILC discussions. There is an appreciable shift from the 1991 version, in which Article 7 read as an obligation of result,[68] to the 1994 version finally put forward by the ILC, which was explicitly defined as a due diligence obligation.[69] The mitigation of the 1991 version of this obligation was the product of negotiations between supporters of the obligation of equitable and reasonable utilisation and proponents of the obligation not to cause significant harm, who perceived the two to be mutually exclusive.[70] The relationship between these two norms is specifically analysed later in this Chapter.

---

64 Dispute over the status and use of the waters of the Silala (Chile v. Bolivia), Judgement, 2022 I.C.J. Rep. 614 (December 1), para. 97. See also the comment to Article 16 of the ILA's Berlin Rules (ILA. Committee on Water Resources Law 2004. "Report of the Berlin Conference." https://www.ila-hq.org/en_GB/documents/conference-report-berlin-2004-5).

65 ILC, *Report of the International Law Commission on the work of its forty-sixth session, 2 May–22 July 1994*, A/49/10 (1994), https://legal.un.org/ilc/documentation/english/reports/a_49_10.pdf. 102.

66 Aura y Larios de Medrano affirms in this regard that it is just a difference in drafting. In Aura y Larios de Medrano, *La Regulación Internacional Del Agua Dulce*, 94.

67 Report of the ILC on the work of its 46th session, *supra* note 65, 103.

68 "Watercourse States shall utilize an international watercourse in such a way as not to cause appreciable harm to other watercourse States." ILC, *Report of the International Law Commission on the work of its forty-third session, 29 April–19 July 1991*, A/46/10 (1991), https://legal.un.org/ilc/documentation/english/reports/a_46_10.pdf. 67.

69 Report of the ILC on the work of its 46th session, *supra* note 65, 102.

70 Tanzi and Arcari, *United Nations Convention on the Law of International Watercourses*, 151–160.

As a customary rule of international watercourse law, the obligation not to cause significant harm has been established as an obligation of due diligence. In *Pulp Mills on the River Uruguay (Argentina v. Uruguay)*, the Court based the principle of prevention on the obligation not to cause significant harm, stating that "[a] State is thus obliged to use all the means at its disposal in order to avoid activities which take place in its territory, or in any area under its jurisdiction, causing significant damage to the environment of another State."[71] In a later case, the ICJ established that due diligence obligation of preventing transboundary harm includes the conduction of an EIA in certain cases.[72]

Acknowledging the due diligence character of this norm leads to the question of what harm is to be prevented; in other words, it is necessary to determine when a transboundary impact is deemed to have breached the obligation not to cause significant harm. The UN Watercourses Convention establishes that harm must be 'significant', introducing the notion of a threshold that must be reached in order for harm to be considered as such.[73] However, the extent of harm required in both quantitative and qualitative terms to qualify as 'significant' is not specified in Article 7 of the UN Watercourses Convention. The ILC specified that 'significant' was to be understood as more than 'trivial' and less than 'substantial'.[74]

Such an assertion does not provide a concrete definition for application in a specific case. Two elements help to determine the threshold. On the one hand, it must be taken into account that during the drafting of the UN Watercourses Convention, the concept of 'harm' was generally understood to mean any effect on the watercourse that could impair its use by the harmed State.[75] Consequently, the possibilities left by the planned or executed measure to the affected riparian State to utilise the watercourse in a manner that is equitable

71 Pulp Mills on the River Uruguay (Argentina v. Uruguay), 2010 Judgment, I.C.J. Rep. 14 (April 20). Para. 101.

72 Certain Activities Carried Out by Nicaragua in the Border Area (Costa Rica v. Nicaragua) and Construction of a Road in Costa Rica along the San Juan River (Nicaragua v. Costa Rica), Judgment, 2015 I.C.J. Rep. 665 (December 15). Para. 104.

73 In 1982, Special Rapporteur Stephen Schwebel proposed 'appreciable' although it was not the word finally adopted by the ILC. In ILC, *Third report on the law of the non-navigational uses of international watercourses, by Mr. Stephen M. Schwebel, Special Rapporteur*, A/CN.4/348 and Corr.1 (1982), https://legal.un.org/ilc/documentation/english/a_cn4_348.pdf. Para. 137.

74 ILC Draft articles on the law of international watercourses, *supra* note 17, 95, para. 15.

75 ILC, *Third report on the law of the non-navigational uses of international watercourses, by Mr. Stephen M. Schwebel, Special Rapporteur*, A/CN.4/348 and Corr.1 (1982), https://legal.un.org/ilc/documentation/english/a_cn4_348.pdf. 94.

and reasonable is a parameter to measure the significance of the expected or inflicted harm.

There is also a subjective element to consider. Given the vagueness of the concept of significant harm, Tanzi and Arcari argue that it is for the riparian States to determine the harm threshold according to their particular circumstances.[76] In other words, 'significant harm' is not an objective concept but rather a minimum standard to give ground to discussion between the riparian States on the acceptability of the potential or produced harm and, possibly, the measures to mitigate or compensate for it. As noted by the ILC,[77] this consequence can be derived from *Fisheries Jurisdiction (United Kingdom v. Iceland)*,[78] and it means that what is deemed significant harm in a one case may not have the same consideration in another, and vice versa, as the definition depends on the circumstances.[79] This configuration of the obligation not to cause significant harm gives a central role to the procedural rules of notification and consultation, as they are indispensable for its operationalisation. These procedural obligations are analysed further in next Chapter.

The UNECE Water Convention clearly has a more explicit focus than the UN Watercourses Convention on preventing transboundary harm, since it is mainly concerned with preventing pollution of the international watercourse.[80] This relevance of the obligation not to cause significant harm is immediately apparent, since it is stated at the very beginning of the Convention. Article 2.1 provides that "[t]he Parties shall take all appropriate measures to prevent, control and reduce any transboundary impact."[81]

76 Tanzi and Arcari, *United Nations Convention on the Law of International Watercourses*, 149–150.

77 ILC Draft articles on the law of international watercourses, *supra* note 17, 104, para. 13.

78 Fisheries Jurisdiction (United Kingdom v. Iceland), Judgment, 1974 I.C.J. Rep. 3 (25 July). Paras. 75 and 78.

79 McCaffrey, *Law of International Watercourses*, 494–496.

80 Unlike the UN Watercourses Convention, on which there is discussion on which of the two substantive obligations is privileged, there is broad unanimity in considering that the ECE Water Convention favours the no harm rule. See in this regard, Movilla, *La Dimensión Normativa de La Gobernanza Internacional Del Agua Dulce*, 154.

81 The UNECE Water Convention, defines 'transboundary impact as "any significant adverse effect on the environment resulting from a change in the conditions of transboundary waters caused by a human activity, the physical origin of which is situated wholly or in part within an area under the jurisdiction of a Party, within an area under the jurisdiction of another Party. Such effects on the environment include effects on human health and safety, flora, fauna, soil, air, water, climate, landscape and historical monuments or other physical structures or the interaction among these factors; they also include effects on the cultural heritage or socio-economic conditions resulting from alterations to those factors". UNECE Water Convention, *supra* note 36, Article 1(2).

On the one hand, as can be seen from this excerpt, the obligation to prevent transboundary harm in the UNECE Water Convention is linked to the concept of 'transboundary impact', which is defined in Article 1.2 as consisting of a "significant adverse effect on the environment". In this regard, it must be noted that this formulation of the obligation not to cause significant harm, which uses the terms 'significant adverse effect' instead of 'significant harm', establishes a higher standard than the UN Watercourses Convention.

On the other hand, the definition of 'transboundary impact' mentions a wide variety of elements on which the transboundary impact may be exerted, including, fauna, soil, air, and water. The scope of sectors in which riparian countries must cooperate in order to prevent harm is wider than that of the elements covered by the UN Watercourses Convention.[82]

The UNECE Water Convention also uses the term 'significant' in Article 2.1 in defining what is to be considered a transboundary impact. However, this Convention provides more elements to weigh impact than the UN Watercourses Convention does to weigh harm. Thus, the *Guide to Implementing The Water Convention* produced by the UNECE[83] notes that Article 2.1 of the UNECE Water Convention should be read in relation to Annex II on "best environmental practice" and Annex III on "water-quality objectives and criteria."[84] It is stressed that this "open[s] up the Convention to the evolving trends and practices in the field of water law, hence, incorporating them ex ante with special reference to the due diligence obligation under consideration."[85]

The relationship between the obligation not to cause significant harm and sustainable development differs significantly in the two global Conventions on international watercourse law. The sustainability mandate in the UNECE Water Convention is foreseen in paragraph 3 of Article 2.5 as one of the guiding principles for the Parties in applying Articles 1 and 2. In fact, sustainable development is not mentioned explicitly but defined in the statement to the effect that "[w]ater resources shall be managed so that the needs of the present generation are met without compromising the ability of future generations to meet their own needs."[86] In this regard, sustainability is clearly embedded in

82 Tanzi, Attila and Alexandros Kolliopoulos. 2015. "The No-Harm Rule". In *The UNECE Convention on the Protection and Use of Transboundary Watercourses and International Lakes*, edited by Attila Tanzi, Owen McIntyre, Alexandros Kolliopoulos, Alistair Rieu-Clarke, and Rémy Kinna, 133–145. Leiden: Brill Nijhoff. 134–135.

83 UNECE. 2013. *Guide to Implementing The Water Convention.* New York and Geneva: United Nations.

84 Ibid. 19.

85 Tanzi and Kolliopoulos, "The No-Harm Rule," 141.

86 UNECE Water Convention, *supra* note 36, Article 2(5), para. 3.

the no-harm rule as specifically formulated in the UNECE Water Convention. In the UN Watercourses Convention, however, sustainability is explicitly mentioned in Article 5 concerning the equitable and reasonable utilisation of the watercourse, but not in Article 7 in relation to the obligation not to cause significant harm.[87]

The international basin agreements analysed in this research differ in their approach to regulating the no-harm obligation and the importance it is afforded, but there is also a geographical divide. The international basin regimes in Global-North countries tend to prohibit transboundary impact in a manner consistent with the UNECE Water Convention, tending to place a stronger focus on the prevention, reduction, and/or elimination of pollution.[88] The Framework Agreement on the Sava River Basin is explicit in this regard as it establishes an obligation to regulate measures to eliminate and reduce transboundary impact, but it also contains the no-harm rule in a manner consistent with the UN Watercourses Convention.[89] Other agreements make no such explicit provision, although the obligation might be considered implicit as they regulate the prevention of pollution and harm is presumed as a trigger for the obligation to notify.[90]

By contrast, international basin agreements in Global-South countries tend to adopt a more classic formulation of the no-harm obligation, stressing its inter-State character.[91] The Water Charter of the Lake Chad Basin is particularly detailed in relation to this obligation as its fifth Chapter is entirely devoted to the "[b]an on significant harm to others" and contains the provisions on notification and on conduct of EIAs and Strategic Environmental Assessments (hereinafter, SEAs).[92]

---

87 Spijkers suggests that the SDGs provide the framework for a 'green evolution' of the no harm rule as formulated in the UN Watercourses Convention. It would allow to put the focus on the harm on the environment of the watercourse, rather than on the other riparian States. In Spijkers, Otto. 2016. "The Cross-Fertilization between the Sustainable Development Goals and International Water Law." *Review of European, Comparative and International Environmental Law* 25 (1): 39–49. 44–47.

88 See: Danube River Protection Convention, Articles 6 and 7; Dniester River Basin Treaty, Article 8.1.

89 Framework Agreement on the Sava River Basin, Article 8 and 9.

90 Convention on the Protection of the Rhine, Article 4(i) and 5.4(e); Great Lakes Water Quality Agreement, Article 6(c).

91 See The Niger Basin Water Charter, Article 5; Mekong Agreement, Articles 7 and 8; Agreement on the establishment of the Zambezi Watercourse Commission, Article 14.2; SADC Protocol on Shared Watercourses, Article 3.10.a); Charter of Waters of the Senegal River, Article 16.

92 Water Charter of the Lake Chad Basin, Articles 42–48.

1.3 *Protection of International Watercourses*

International watercourse law is increasingly influenced by international environmental law. As Boisson de Chazournes put it, the regimes established for the protection of international water basins "cannot be interpreted and applied in clinical isolation from other norms of international law, and in particular from international environmental law."[93] Consistently with this evolutionary reading of international watercourses law, environmental protection is both a parameter to weigh equitable and reasonable utilisation and a core element in the evaluation of transboundary harm. This is why protection of the environment and the ecosystems of international watercourses can be considered ancillary to equitable and reasonable utilisation and the no-harm obligation. In this regard, the doctrine has qualified it as an emerging customary rule among the other substantive obligations of international watercourse law.[94] This development was already observed in the resolution on *Gabčikovo-Nagymaros Project* (*Hungary/Slovakia*), where the ICJ determined that the new norms and standards deriving from environmental law had to be taken into consideration by the States in implementing new and existing activities that could affect an international watercourse.[95]

International watercourse law has integrated environmental protection concerns by setting two main obligations: on the one hand, the prevention, control and reduction of pollution; on the other, the protection and preservation of ecosystems, with specific provisions usually foreseen with regard to the introduction of alien or new species and the protection of the connected marine environment. Both elements are present in Articles 20, 21 and 22 of the UN Watercourses Convention. It has already been noted that the inclusion of these obligations in Part IV of the Convention, and therefore separately to the substantive obligations of Part II, indicates their emerging character as independent customary norms.[96]

In particular, Article 21.2 of the UN Watercourses Convention enshrines the general obligation to prevent, reduce, and control pollution in the following terms: "Watercourse States shall, individually and, where appropriate, jointly, prevent, reduce and control the pollution of an international watercourse that may cause significant harm to other watercourse States or to their environment,

---

93 Boisson de Chazournes, Laurence. 2021. *Fresh Water in International Law*. Second Edition. Oxford: OUP. 182.

94 Movilla "La Progresiva Ecologización Del Derecho Internacional de Los Cursos de Agua," 27.

95 Gabčikovo-Nagymaros Project (Hungary/Slovakia), Judgment, 1997 I.C.J. Rep. 7 (September 25). Para. 140.

96 Movilla, *La Dimensión Normativa de La Gobernanza Internacional Del Agua Dulce*. 175.

including harm to human health or safety, to the use of the waters for any beneficial purpose or to the living resources of the watercourse."[97] The ILC noted that Article 21.2 is a specific application of the two general obligations – the obligation of equitable and reasonable utilisation and the obligation not to cause significant harm – contained in Articles 5 and 7.[98] Since this article mentions harm but not equitability, McCaffrey concludes that it should be interpreted in the sense that pollution would be deemed inequitable as long as it would produce significant harm to other States.[99] As such, the obligation to prevent, reduce, and control the pollution of an international watercourse seems particularly contingent of the application of the no-harm obligation as established in Article 7. This is also consistent with the type of obligation emanating from Article 21.2. In the same way that the no-harm obligation has been defined as a due diligence obligation, the Working Group of the Whole that drafted the UN Watercourses Convention clarified that Article 21, together with articles 22 and 23, "impose a due diligence standard on watercourse States."[100]

Since the UNECE Water Convention is concerned primarily with avoiding transboundary impact through international watercourses, the prohibition of pollution occupies a more central place. In defining what measures must the Parties adopt in order to prevent, control, and reduce any transboundary impact, Article 2.2(a) states that they have to "prevent, control and reduce pollution of waters causing or likely to cause transboundary impact".[101] Moreover, Article 2.5(b) introduces the polluter-pays principle,[102] which is also contained in the same wording in the Protocol on Water and Health to the 1992 Convention on the Protection and Use of Transboundary Watercourses and international Lakes[103] (hereinafter, the UNECE Protocol on Water and Health). The inclusion of such a principle illustrates the greater weight given to the prevention of pollution in the UNECE Water Convention than in the UN Watercourses Convention, where it services as an effective provision to discourage pollution.[104]

97 UN Watercourses Convention, *supra* note 16, Article 21(2).

98 Report of the ILC on the work of its 46th session, *supra* note 65, 42, para. 3.

99 McCaffrey, *Law of International Watercourses*, 511.

100 UN General Assembly, *Report of the Sixth Committee convening as the Working Group of the Whole*, A/51/869 (11 April 1997), undocs.org/A/51/869. 5.

101 UNECE Water Convention, *supra* note 36, Article 2.2(a).

102 Ibid. Article 2.5(b).

103 Protocol on Water and Health to the 1992 Convention on the Protection and Use of Transboundary Watercourses and international Lakes, June 17, 1999, 2331 U.N.T.S. 202. Article 5(b).

104 It has been underlined the complementarity of this principle with the preventive aim of the UNECE Water Convention. See Duvic-Paoli, Leslie-Anne, and Pierre-Marie Dupuy. 2015. "The Polluter-Pays Principle in the 1992 UNECE Convention on the Protection and

The protection of ecosystems is the other main consideration in the protection of international watercourses. Agenda 21 links the sustainable utilisation of watercourses to the protection of ecosystems.[105] Seemingly, target 6 of SDG 6 aims to "protect and restore water-related ecosystems, including mountains, forests, wetlands, rivers, aquifers and lakes" by 2020.[106] There is only one associated indicator: "6.6.1 Change in the extent of water-related ecosystems over time."[107] However, this obligation has also an important basis in binding instruments such as the CBD[108] or the Convention on Wetlands of International Importance Especially as Waterfowl Habitat (hereinafter, Ramsar Convention).[109]

The UN Watercourses Convention opens Part IV on protection, preservation, and management with Article 20, which is titled "Protection and preservation of ecosystems Watercourse" and establishes a general obligation for the States to protect the ecosystems of international watercourses, either individually or jointly.[110] In the commentaries on this article, the ILC defined ecosystems as follows:

> [E]cological unit[s] consisting of living and non-living components that are interdependent and function as a community. 'In ecosystems,

Use of Transboundary Watercourses and International Lakes." In *The UNECE Convention on the Protection and Use of Transboundary Watercourses and International Lakes*, edited by Attila Tanzi, Owen McIntyre, Alexandros Kolliopoulos, Alistair Rieu-Clarke, and Rémy Kinna, 176–94. Leiden: Brill Nijhoff. 183–185.

105 United Nations Conference on Environment and Development, *Agenda 21*, in *Report of the United Nations Conference on Environment and Development*, A/CONF.151/26 (Vol. I) (12 August 1992), undocs.org/en/A/CONF.151/26/Rev.1(vol. I). Para. 18.2.

106 Agenda 2030, *supra* note 19. McCaffrey rightly notes that setting 2020 as the time limit for its achievement underscores its importance as it is unlikely that States could manage to achieve just after 5 years of the adoption of the *Agenda 2030*, while all others targets in SDG 6 set 2030 as the relevant year. In McCaffrey, *Law of International Watercourses*, 516.

107 UN General Assembly, Resolution 71/313, *Work of the Statistical Commission pertaining to the 2030 Agenda for Sustainable Development*, A/RES/71/313 (6 July 2017), undocs.org/A/RES/71/313. In line with McCaffrey's comment referred in the previous footnote, it is also significant the unspecific character of this indicator.

108 Article 1 of the CBD (*supra* note 57) read in relation to article 2 makes ecosystems the object of protection of this Convention, while paragraphs (d) and (f) of Article 8 establishes the obligation for the Parties to protect and restore ecosystems.

109 Convention on wetlands of international importance especially as waterfowl habitat, February 2, 1971, 996 U.N.T.S. 245.

110 "Watercourse States shall, individually and, where appropriate, jointly, protect and preserve the ecosystems of international watercourses." UN Watercourses Convention, *supra* note 16, Article 20.

> everything depends on everything else and nothing is really wasted.' Thus, '[a]n external impact affecting one component of an ecosystem causes reactions among other components and may disturb the equilibrium of the entire ecosystem'.[111]

This conceptualisation of ecosystems adds to the idea of interdependence between riparian States on which international watercourse cooperation is based, as the ecosystem of a watercourse forms a unit and therefore any impact on it produced in one country can potentially affect a co-riparian State.[112]

Similarly to the prevention, reduction, and control of pollution, the ILC commented that Article 20 was in fact a specific application of Article 5. Consequently, in order to be equitable and reasonable, the use of a watercourse must ensure adequate preservation of ecosystems.[113] Moreover, the ILC goes on to state that "[i]n essence, it requires that watercourse States shield the ecosystems of international watercourses from harm or damage. It thus includes the duty to protect those ecosystems from a significant threat of harm."[114] Thus expressed, under the UN Watercourses Convention, the protection of ecosystems is closely linked to the other two substantive obligations by precisely giving content to them. In other words, no application of the obligation of equitable and reasonable utilisation or the obligation not to cause significant harm is possible without considering the protection of ecosystems. On this point, McIntyre notes that "the extensive elaboration and detailed articulation of environmental rules and principles in recent years [...] significantly enhances the weight to be accorded to environmental considerations in the balancing of factors involved in the determination of an equitable regime for the utilization of an international watercourse."[115]

From the above discussion, however, it should not be concluded that the protection of ecosystems is not an autonomous obligation in the context of international watercourse law. A close analysis of Article 20 of the UN Watercourses Convention shows that, unlike Article 21, it does not require any

111 Report of the ILC on the work of its 46th session, *supra* note 65, 119, para. 2.

112 In this regard, McCaffrey points out that, since they form a 'system', the concept of community of interests is especially suitable in that case. In McCaffrey, *Law of International Watercourses*, 151–157.

113 ILC, *Report of the International Law Commission on the work of its forty-sixth session, 2 May–22 July 1994*, A/49/10 (1994), https://legal.un.org/ilc/documentation/english/reports/a_49_10.pdf. 119, para. 3.

114 Ibid.

115 McIntyre, Owen. 2007. *Environmental Protection of International Watercourses under International Law*. Aldershot: Ashgate, 315.

transboundary harm in order to be triggered. Therefore, according to this provision, the States are obliged to protect watercourse ecosystems from any hazardous activity regardless of its potential transboundary impact.[116] In addition, as also clarified by the ILC, this obligation is one of due diligence rather than an obligation of result.[117]

In a similar vein, the UNECE Water Convention provides that in order to prevent, control, and reduce transboundary impact the Parties must, among other obligations, "ensure that transboundary waters are used with the aim of ecologically sound and rational water management, conservation of water resources and environmental protection"[118] and that they must take the appropriate measures to conserve and restore the ecosystems.[119] This Convention goes to establish in Article 3 that ecosystems are a parameter to adopt stricter requirements for the prevention, control and reduction of transboundary impact, including prohibition in individual cases.[120] Paragraph (i) of this article states that the application of the ecosystem approach as a form of sustainable management of the watercourse is promoted.[121] As noted by McIntyre.[122] the early publication in 1993 of the *Guidelines on the ecosystem approach in water management*[123] for the effective application of the ecosystem approach, but also continued work on the topic, is proof of the importance of the ecosystem approach in the UNECE Water Convention.[124] The ecosystem approach as a particular manner to develop a joint policy of an international watercourse is further explored in Chapter 10.

The analysis of international basin agreements reveals that regional watercourse law tends to give a more central position to the protection of watercourses than the UN Watercourse Convention, adopting a more environmentalist approach to cooperation. All of the treaties considered here have

---

116 McCaffrey, *Law of International Watercourses*, 521–522.

117 Report of the ILC on the work of its 46th session, *supra* note 65, 122, para 4.

118 UNECE Water Convention, *supra* note 36, Article 2.2(b).

119 Ibid. Article 2.2(d).

120 Ibid.

121 Ibid. Article 3(i).

122 McIntyre, Owen. 2014. "The Protection of Freshwater Ecosystems Revisited: Towards a Common Understanding of the 'ecosystems Approach' to the Protection of Transboundary Water Resources." *Review of European, Comparative and International Environmental Law* 23 (1): 88–95. 89.

123 UNECE, *Guidelines on the Ecosystem Approach in Water Management*, ECE/ENVWA/31 (November 1993), https://unece.org/DAM/env/water/publications/documents/Library/Old_documents_found_library/ECE_ENVWA_31_eng.pdf

124 See, for instance, UNECE. 2007. *Recommendations on Payments for Ecosystem Services in Integrated Water Resources Management*. New York and Geneva: United Nations.

among their objectives the protection of the environment, which is afforded a varying degree of centrality.[125] In some cases, there is a clear focus on this objective, to the extent that the agreement can be considered primarily environmental in nature.[126] In two cases, however, environmental protection is not explicitly stated, although it can be considered implicit in the general objective of sustainable development, management, or similar formulations.[127]

Broadly speaking, regional tendencies can be identified between international basin agreements. African water charters, despite having a more environmentalist aim than the UN Watercourses Convention, seem clearly inspired by it. They usually regulate protection measures in a separate Chapter, alongside provisions on the use of the watercourse and other matters.[128] European agreements, by contrast, share the UNECE Water Convention's stronger focus on pollution and water quality.[129]

2 Internal Integration of Substantive Obligations as the Basis for Legal Integration

Up to this point, three obligations of international watercourse law have been analysed that are, *a priori*, closely related. Some of these interrelations have been referred to tangentially, but in this Section they will be analysed specifically. The aim of this analysis is to determine the extent to which the interrelationship between these obligations responds to, or contributes to, the application of the principle of integration in the context of international watercourses. Therefore, the relationship between the obligations of equitable and reasonable use and of not causing significant harm is analysed, as well as the relationship between these two and the protection of international watercourses.

---

125 Charter of Waters of the Senegal River, Article 2, para. 3; SADC Protocol on Shared Watercourses, Article 7.b); Mekong Agreement, Article 3; The Niger Basin Water Charter, Article 2, para. 6 and 7;

126 See, generally, the Convention on the Protection of the Rhine; Great Lakes Water Quality Agreement; Danube River Protection Convention; Dniester River Basin Treaty.

127 See, generally: Framework Agreement on the Sava River Basin; Agreement on the establishment of the Zambezi Watercourse Commission.

128 The Niger Basin Water Charter, Chapter III; Charter of Waters of the Senegal River, Titre 4; Water Charter of the Lake Chad Basin, Chapter 3.

129 In this regard, it is telling that several of the European basin agreements contain the polluter-pays principle. See the Convention on the Protection of the Rhine, Articles 4(d), 5.3–4, 5.6; Danube River Protection Convention, Articles 2(4) and 5–8; Dniester River Basin Treaty, Articles 4.2.d) and 8.

Whether the obligation of equitable and reasonable use has priority over the obligation not to cause significant harm or vice versa has been one of the most controversial questions in the regulation of international watercourses.[130] The controversy arises from the generally held opinion that the former obligation would benefit upstream riparian States while the latter would benefit downstream States.[131] The debate can also be considered in terms of the sustainability of the practices that the priority application of each obligation would promote. *A priori*, it may be considered that prioritising the right to an equitable and reasonable utilisation of the international watercourse would favour unsustainable practices, while prioritising the no-harm obligation would have the opposite effect, since States could more easily oppose a transboundary impact on the watercourse environment in their territory.

In this regard, it must be recalled that the second paragraph of Article 7 of the UN Watercourses Convention refers to Articles 5 and 6 on the obligation of equitable and reasonable utilisation as a parameter for negotiations between the Parties concerning the elimination or mitigation of harm already caused.[132] The no-harm obligation is therefore secondary to the obligation of equitable and reasonable utilisation since the causing of harm may not be unlawful provided that it falls in a margin of reasonableness.

In this respect, two different opinions may be identified. For some authors these two obligations "are in reality, two sides of the same coin"[133] in the sense that no unreasonable harm can be done without the utilisation of the watercourse becoming consequently inequitable; for others, however, each

130 Movilla, *La Dimensión Normativa de La Gobernanza Internacional Del Agua Dulce*. 151–152. On this topic, see also Utton, Albert E. 1996. "Which Rule Should Prevail in International Water Disputes: That of Reasonableness or That of No Harm?" *Natural Resources Journal* 36 (3): 635–41.

131 As demonstrated by Salman, this might not be necessary the case since upstream countries can also be harmed by prior uses of the watercourse by downstream countries and the claim of acquired rights by those. In Salman, Salman M.A. 2010. "Downstream Riparians Can Also Harm Upstream Riparians: The Concept of Foreclosure of Future Uses." *Water International* 35 (4): 350–64.

132 Where significant harm nevertheless is caused to another watercourse State, the States whose use causes such harm shall, in the absence of agreement to such use, take all appropriate measures, having due regard for the provisions of articles 5 and 6, in consultation with the affected State, to eliminate or mitigate such harm and, where appropriate, to discuss the question of compensation. (UN Watercourses Convention, *supra* note 16, Article 7).

133 See, for instance: Islam, Nahid. 2010. *The Law of Non-Navigational Uses of International Watercourses. Options for Regional Regime-Building in Asia*. Alphen aan den Rijn: Wolters Kluwer. 497.

obligation has a different weight.[134] In fact, this debate took place in the ILC drafting committee for the UN Watercourses Convention, where delegates defended different visions of the relationship between the two substantive obligations. Al-Khasawneh, for instance, argued that the wording of Article 7 in the version passed in the first reading of the forty-sixth session converted the no-harm rule into a due diligence obligation that weakened it *vis-à-vis* to the obligation of equitable and reasonable use.[135] Rao, by contrast, considered that Article 7 was dispensable after all because, in his opinion, the no-harm obligation was sufficiently embedded in the equitable and reasonable use obligation.[136]

Seemingly, when the Sixth Committee convening as the Working Group of the Whole revised the draft articles, discussion of this issue re-emerged.[137] Some countries like France[138] considered that the draft convention favoured downstream countries by prioritising the no-harm obligation, while Slovakia[139] and Ethiopia[140] claimed that it did not clearly establish the priority of the obligation of equitable and reasonable utilisation, which would threaten the likelihood that the instrument would be generally accepted. Egypt, meanwhile, read Articles 5, 6 and 7 in such a way that equitable and reasonable utilisation was conditional upon not causing harm, since the no-harm rule was an "established principle of customary international law."[141]

The final decision of the ILC seems to favour the predominance of the obligation of equitable and reasonable utilisation, and most of the doctrine seems based on the same conclusion.[142] However, as noted by Eckstein,[143] the case

---

134 Caflisch, for instance, defends that the principle of equitable and reasonable utilisation have priority over the no-harm principle. In Caflisch, "Règles Générales Du Droit Des Cours d'eau Internationaux," 161.

135 ILC, *Summary record of the 2355th meeting*, A/CN.4/SR.2355 (1994), https://legal.un.org/ilc/documentation/english/summary_records/a_cn4_sr2355.pdf. Para. 6.

136 Ibid. Para. 12.

137 UN GAOR, 51st Sess., 99th plen. mtg., U.N. Doc A/51/PV.99 (21 May 1997), undocs.org/en/A/51/PV.99.

138 The French delegation stated that "[t]he Convention that has just been adopted is, in fact, clearly weighted in favour of the interests of downstream States. Thus, it seems unfortunately ill-suited to reducing the existing tensions in various geographic zones between States with international rivers flowing through them." Ibid. 8.

139 Ibid. 7.

140 Ibid. 10.

141 Ibid. 11.

142 See: Bourne, "Primacy of the Principle of Equitable Utilization"; or Aura y Larios de Medrano, *La Regulación Internacional Del Agua Dulce*.

143 Eckstein, G. 2020. "The status of the UN Watercourses Convention: does it still hold water?" *International Journal of Water Resources Development* 36: 2–3. 429–461.

law of the CIJ has been contradictory in this regard. In *Gabčikovo-Nagymaros Project (Hungary/Slovakia)*, "the court never mentioned the principle of no significant harm, even though Hungary relied on it heavily in its pleadings,"[144] while in *Pulp Mills on the River Uruguay (Argentina v. Uruguay)* it hardly made reference to the obligation of equitable and reasonable utilisation. Instead, the Court stated that "[a] State is thus obliged to use all the means at its disposal in order to avoid activities which take place in its territory, or in any area under its jurisdiction, causing significant damage to the environment of another State."[145] And in referring to the advisory opinion on the *Legality of the Threat or Use of Nuclear Weapons*, it also affirmed that '[t]his Court has established that this obligation "is now part of the corpus of international law relating to the environment'."[146]

The prioritisation of one of the two substantive obligations over the other remains a matter of confusion. Tanzi and Arcari observe that the "wording of those provisions seems perfectly crafted in order to provide absolutely the same weight to both."[147] Indeed, Article 5.1 of the UN Watercourses Convention establishes optimal and sustainable utilisation as the objective of the obligation of equitable and reasonable utilisation, while Article 7 also aims to establish an equitable balance by defining the no-harm not as an obligation of result but as an obligation of due diligence, "and by stressing that harm may be caused by a diligent, possibly equitable, use, leaving the Parties involved to agree on how to balance the equities, distribute the benefits and/or redress the harm."[148] In the view of these authors, this intentional ambiguity is what makes the Convention a suitable framework for resolving actual or potential international law disputes.

The authors further argue that if Articles 5, 6 and 10[149] of the UN Watercourses Convention are read from a systemic point of view, no factor relevant to equitable utilisation is given priority. As such, the decision to place the

---

144 Ibid. 437. Also in this same sense, see McCaffrey, *Law of International Watercourses*, 485.

145 Pulp Mills on the River Uruguay (Argentina v. Uruguay), 2010 Judgment, I.C.J. Rep. 14 (April 20). Para. 101.

146 Ibid. Para. 101.

147 Tanzi and Arcari, *United Nations Convention on the Law of International Watercourses*, 178.

148 Ibid.

149 Article 10.1 of the Convention provides that no use of the watercourse is to have priority over another: "In the absence of agreement or custom to the contrary, no use of an international watercourse enjoys inherent priority over other uses". The only exception to this general rule is established by Article 10(2) in favour of vital human needs: "In the event of a conflict between uses of an international watercourse, it shall be resolved with reference to articles 5 to 7, with special regard being given to the requirements of vital human needs." In UN Watercourses Convention, *supra* note 16.

no-harm obligation in a separate article (Article 7) would give it a certain priority over the other factors, but not over the obligation of equitable and reasonable utilisation itself, while causing harm would not automatically imply that a certain use would be inequitable.[150] Whether on purpose or as a result of the transactions carried out within the ILC, this is a convincing conclusion. At the same time, this position is akin to claiming that the UN Watercourses Convention is founded in the objective to achieve sustainable development. If there is equality between these two substantive obligations, there is no way that developmental activities could be considered lawful according to this Convention if they are inequitable according to the parameters set in Article 6, or if they produce significant harm in the terms defined in Article 7.

The theory of the priority of the obligation of equitable and reasonable utilisation over the obligation not to cause significant harm due to customary law and the UN Watercourses Convention is further called into question by two recent developments. First and foremost, the increasing influence of the UNECE Water Convention reinforces the no-harm obligation due to its focus on the avoidance of transboundary impact. This renewed influence is due to the opening of the Convention to other countries beyond the UNECE Parties in 2013,[151] but also to the subsequent addition of new members as the UN Watercourses Convention has stagnated. While in 2023 only Gambia has ratified the UN Watercourses Convention,[152] five countries have ratified the UNECE Water Convention.[153]

The most recent case law of the ICJ, after the initial lack of clarity between the judgements on *Gabčikovo-Nagymaros Project (Hungary/Slovakia)* and *Pulp Mills on the River Uruguay (Argentina v. Uruguay)* cases, seems to put both obligations at the same level, at least in cases where the dispute concerns pollution

---

150 Tanzi and Arcari, *United Nations Convention on the Law of International Watercourses*, 179.

151 Amendments to Articles 25 and 26 of the Convention on the Protection and Use of Transboundary Watercourses and International Lakes, November 28, 2003, 2897 U.N.T.S.

152 Ghana was the last country to ratify the UN Watercourses Convention on the 22 of June 2020, day in which it also ratified the UNECE Water Convention (United Nations Treaty Collection. 2023. "5. Convention on the Protection and Use of Transboundary Watercourses and International Lakes." Accessed May 5, 2023. https://treaties.un.org/Pages/ViewDetails.aspx?src=IND&mtdsg_no=XXVII-5&chapter=27&clang=_en).

153 They were: Guinea-Bissau, 14 June 2021; Togo, 28 September 2021; Cameroon, 1 November 2022; Nigeria, 22 March 2023; and Iraq, 24 March 2023 (United Nations Treaty Collection. 2023. "5. Convention on the Protection and Use of Transboundary Watercourses and International Lakes." Accessed May 5, 2023. https://treaties.un.org/Pages/ViewDetails.aspx?src=IND&mtdsg_no=XXVII-5&chapter=27&clang=_en).

or environmental harm of some kind.[154] In the *Dispute over the status and use of the waters of the Silala*, in fact, the Court boldly establishes the concurrent applicability of the obligation of equitable and reasonable utilisation and the no-harm obligation. It notes that: "In the present case, under customary international law, the Parties are both entitled to an equitable and reasonable use of the waters of the Silala as an international watercourse and obliged, in utilizing the international watercourse, to take all appropriate measures to prevent the causing of significant harm to the other Party."[155] The arbitral award in *Indus Waters Kishenganga Arbitration* (*Pakistan vs. India*) also reinforces this idea, as the right of Pakistan to receive water is based both on the right to be able to use the water resources for hydropower purposes and India's duty to avoid transboundary harm.[156]

The second issue that had to be analysed in this Subsection was the interrelationship between the obligation of equitable and reasonable utilisation and the obligation not to cause significant harm, on the one hand, and the obligation of protection of watercourses, on the other. Analysis has already been made of the progressive 'environmentalisation' of equitable and reasonable utilisation and the no-harm obligations. The equitable and reasonable utilisation of the watercourse requires taking into consideration environmental concerns, while causing harm usually requires some form of damage to the environment of co-riparian countries. As summarised by McCaffrey, "causing significant harm to the ecosystems of international watercourse should be considered to be *per se* inequitable and unreasonable since that will harm the watercourse itself and ultimately other riparians."[157] Evidence has also been given in the prior Section of the growing autonomy of the obligation of protection of international watercourses.

This raises the question of which of these two developments, if any, would drive the application of the principle of integration in the context of international watercourse law. At this point the concept of internal integration is useful, understood here as the relation of dependency of substantive obligations between them on the one hand, and the procedural obligations between them on the other hand. External integration, which is discussed in the next

154 See, in this regard, Certain Activities Carried Out by Nicaragua in the Border Area (Costa Rica v. Nicaragua) and Construction of a Road in Costa Rica along the San Juan River (Nicaragua v. Costa Rica), Judgment, 2015 I.C.J. Rep. 665 (December 15). Para. 104.

155 Dispute over the status and use of the waters of the Silala (Chile v. Bolivia), Judgement, 2022 I.C.J. Rep. 614 (December 1). Para. 97.

156 Indus Waters Kishenganga Arbitration (Pakistan vs. India). Final award, 31 R.I.A.A (Perm. Ct. Arb. 2013). Paras. 446–454.

157 McCaffrey, *Law of International Watercourses*, 520.

Chapter, would be the relationship between substantive and procedural obligations.[158] The internal integration of the obligations of international watercourse law has yet to be completely settled by the international tribunals or in doctrine. However, there are strong reasons to believe that such a close dependency exists. Integration can be considered the trend internally between the procedural obligations,[159] and a similar statement could be made for the substantive ones.

The ICJ appears to have embraced this integrative approach in interpreting the Statute on the river Uruguay between Argentina and Uruguay when it notes that: "The Court considers that the attainment of optimum and rational utilization requires a balance between the Parties' rights and needs to use the river for economic and commercial activities on the one hand, and the obligation to protect it from any damage to the environment that may be caused by such activities, on the other."[160] Moreover, it is on this very point of reasoning that the Court argues that 'sustainable development' would be the synthesising concept for the integration of the substantive obligations of international watercourse law by pointing out that: "it is the opinion of the Court that Article 27 embodies this interconnectedness between equitable and reasonable utilization of a shared resource and the balance between economic development and environmental protection that is the essence of sustainable development."[161]

Therefore, it might be affirmed that the application of the principle of integration does not lie in the consideration of environmental factors for the equitable and reasonable utilisation of a watercourse or the prevention of transboundary harm. Ultimately, these two obligations are meant to protect the interests of the riparian States. Although several of the States' interests are

158 It is followed here the division made by McIntyre at McIntyre, Owen. 2013. "Procedural Rules and Protection of Transboundary Rivers." In *International Law and Freshwater. The Multiple Challenges*, edited by Laurence Boisson de Chazournes, Christina Leb, and Mara Tignino, 239–65. Cheltenham: Edward Elgar.

159 The ICJ has expressed itself in this sense in *Pulp Mills on the River Uruguay* (*Argentina v. Uruguay*): "the obligation to notify is intended to create the conditions for successful co-operation between the Parties, enabling them to assess the plan's impact on the river on the basis of the fullest possible information and, if necessary, to negotiate the adjustments needed to avoid the potential damage that it might cause." Pulp Mills on the River Uruguay (Argentina v. Uruguay), 2010 Judgment, I.C.J. Rep. 14 (April 20). Para. 113. For a deeper analysis on this aspect see McIntyre, "Procedural Rules and Protection of Transboundary Rivers," 252–256.

160 Pulp Mills on the River Uruguay (Argentina v. Uruguay), 2010 Judgment, I.C.J. Rep. 14 (April 20). Para. 174.

161 Ibid. Para. 177.

of an environmental nature, the obligation of prevention of transboundary harm, and especially the obligation of equitable and reasonable utilisation, are originally alien to the protection of the environment.[162] As seen above, environmental concerns have filtered into the obligations of equitable and reasonable utilisation and no-harm for instrumental reasons and, as such, might not be sufficient to protect the environment to the degree the principle of integration requires. Only an obligations of protection of international watercourses on an equal footing with the other substantive obligations of international watercourse law can ensure that use does not take precedence over protection.

This analysis captures one of the elements of the general two-fold configuration of the principle of integration in the specific domain of international watercourse law. Since the principle of integration depends on the balance between the classical substantive obligations of international watercourse law and the obligation of protection of international watercourses, the substantive obligations analysed earlier in this Chapter represent the interests at stake in an international watercourse which are involved in sustainable development. Therefore, the internal integration of these obligations is precisely the aim of legal integration as a dimension of the principle of integration. The following Chapter explores external integration as the adaptation into watercourse law of the other dimension of the principle of integration: institutional integration.

162 In fact, it can be argued that the shift in the relative weight between the principle of equitable and reasonable utilisation and the no harm principle could be related precisely with the increasing autonomy of the principle of protection of watercourses. In this regard, Movilla makes the reflection that "no sería tan descabellado considerar que la creciente consideración de los daños ambientales en las disputas relacionadas con los recursos hídricos pueda hacer inclinarse la balanza hacia una primacía de la prohibición de causar daños sensibles." Movilla "La Progresiva Ecologización Del Derecho Internacional de Los Cursos de Agua," 23.

CHAPTER 4

The Principle of Integration in the Framework of the Procedural Obligations Set by International Watercourse Law

The substantive obligations require a set of rules in order to be implemented in the international context. These norms are the procedural rules that provide the basic machinery for this cooperation to be effectively implemented and are analysed in the current Chapter. Their distinction from the substantive obligations analysed in the previous Chapter is somewhat artificial, since all of them might have the same level of bindingness, and non-compliance also gives rise to procedures for the termination of the breach.[1] Nevertheless, this distinction, in addition to being widely used in the legal literature on the subject,[2] is particularly appropriate for the purpose of this research, as it is directly related to one of the two dimensions of the principle of integration identified in Chapter 1. Consequently, the third Section focuses on the relationship between substantive and procedural norms in the context of international watercourse law.

The procedural rules of international watercourse law are an expression of the principle of cooperation and the mechanisms that enable the application of the other substantive obligations in this area of international law. Their relevance to the application of the principle of integration, however, lies in the fact that they are the tools to enable joint decision-making between the riparian States. As stated by Farrajota, "procedural obligations aim at ensuring participation of all interested States in the decision-making process concerning planned measures of new uses of the watercourse, thus enabling the States likely to be affected to express their concerns, to assess the effects of the proposed activities on the environment and on the territory of the other

1 See commentaries to Article 12 of the Draft articles on responsibility of States for internationally wrongful acts in Report of the Commission to the General Assembly on the work of its fifty-third session. In ILC, *Draft articles on responsibility of States for internationally wrongful acts*, A/CN.4/SER.A/2001/Add.1 (Part 2), at 76–77 (2001), https://legal.un.org/ilc/publications/yearbooks/english/ilc_2001_v2_p2.pdf. 54–57.

2 See, among others: Weiss, "Evolution of International Water Law"; Leb, Christina. 2013. *Cooperation in the Law of Transboundary Water Resources*. Cambridge: Cambridge University Press. 73–106; McCaffrey, *Law of International Watercourses*; Islam, *Law of Non-Navigational Uses of International Watercourses.*

 | DOI:10.1163/9789004736757_007

States, and to take adequate measures."[3] This Chapter presents an analysis of the procedural rules as they have been enshrined in the two global agreements on international watercourses. These are the obligation of prior notification of planned measures, the obligation to conduct an EIA, the obligation to consult with other riparian States on planned measures, and the obligation to exchange data and information.

1 The Procedural Obligations

Transboundary cooperation is based on the establishment of rules that determine when and how States must notify, consult and inform their coriparian States. This Section briefly introduces the procedural obligations of international watercourses law in order to be subsequently contrasted with the substantive obligations.

1.1 *The Obligation of Prior Notification of Planned Measures*

The obligation to notify measures or activities that might have significant adverse effects derives from the principles of good faith, good neighbourliness, and reciprocity and is "the only effective way for knowing about, and checking unilateral activities that may affect other riparian states."[4] Its rationale was clearly stated in the arbitral award on *Lac Lanoux* (*Espagne/France*), which noted that "[l]'Etat exposé à subir les répercussions des travaux entrepris par un Etat limitrophe est seul juge de ses intérêts, et si ce dernier n'en a pas pris l'initiative, on ne saurait méconnaître à l'autre le droit d'exiger notification des travaux ou concessions qui sont l'objet d'un projet."[5] In *Pulp Mills on the River Uruguay* (*Argentina v. Uruguay*), the ICJ also rejected mere formal compliance with this norm, stating that it was "intended to create the conditions for successful co-operation between the Parties, enabling them to assess the plan's impact on the river on the basis of the fullest possible information and, if

---

3 Farrajota, "Notification and Consultation in the Law Applicable to International Law, 290.

4 Salman, Salman M.A. 2015. "The Notification Process." In *International Water Law*, edited by Laurence Boisson de Chazournes and Mara Tignino, 105–60. Cheltenham: Edward Elgar. 105. See, generally: Leb, *Cooperation in the Law of Transboundary Water Resources*. 129–139; Caflisch, Lucius. 2019. "Prior Notice and Related Issues." In *Research Handbook on International Water Law*, edited by Stephen C. McAffrey and Riley T. Denoon, 109–25. Cheltenham: Edward Elgar; and Farrajota, "Notification and Consultation in the Law Applicable to International Law," 296–322.

5 Lac Lanoux (Espagne/France), 12 R.I.A.A (Perm. Ct. Arb. 1957). 314.

necessary, to negotiate the adjustments needed to avoid the potential damage that it might cause."[6]

This obligation is not exclusive to international watercourse law, as it widely adopted in environmental law.[7] In this area, soft law has played a role in establishing the obligation of prior notification. It was included in the Rio Declaration in the following terms: "States shall provide prior and timely notification and relevant information to potentially affected States on activities that may have a significant adverse transboundary environmental effect and shall consult with those States at an early stage and in good faith."[8] The statement is illustrative of the growing acceptance of this obligation, which is particularly relevant considering that it was not included in the Stockholm Declaration in 1972, largely due to the opposition of Brazil.

In conventional environmental law, the obligation of prior notification was adopted as early as the 1991 Convention on Environmental Impact Assessment in a Transboundary Context (hereinafter, Espoo Convention), which states that "the Party of origin shall, for the purposes of ensuring adequate and effective consultations under Article 5, notify any Party which it considers may be an affected Party as early as possible and no later than when informing its own public about that proposed activity.[9] The 1992 Convention on the Transboundary Effects of Industrial Accidents also contains a similar provision.[10]

However, this obligation did not appear in global environmental conventions until after the UNCED. In the CBD, for instance, it is foreseen that the Parties should regulate, through regional or multilateral agreements, mechanisms such as notification in relation to activities that might harm the biological diversity in areas beyond the limits of national jurisdiction.[11] An obligation of prior notification has also been included in the BBNJ Convention, stating that

---

6 Pulp Mills on the River Uruguay (Argentina v. Uruguay), 2010 Judgment, I.C.J. Rep. 14 (April 20). Para. 113.

7 On this topic see Sands et al. *Principles of International Environmental Law*, 633–635.

8 United Nations Conference on Environment and Development, *Rio Declaration on Environment and Development*, in Report of the United Nations Conference on Environment and Development, A/CONF.151/26 (Vol. I) (12 August 1992), undocs.org/en/A/CONF.151/26/Rev.1(vol. I). Principle 19.

9 Convention on Environmental Impact Assessment in a Transboundary Context, February 25, 1991, 1989 U.N.T.S. 309. Article 3.

10 Convention on the Transboundary Effects of Industrial Accidents, March 17, 1992, 2105 U.N.T.S. 457. Article 4.1.

11 "Promote, on the basis of reciprocity, notification, exchange of information and consultation on activities under their jurisdiction or control which are likely to significantly affect adversely the biological diversity of other States or areas beyond the limits of national jurisdiction, by encouraging the conclusion of bilateral, regional or multilateral

"Parties shall ensure timely public notification of a planned activity, including by publication through the Clearing-House Mechanism and through the secretariat, and planned and effective time-bound opportunities, as far as practicable, for participation by all States."[12]

In international watercourse law, the duty of prior notification is a consolidated customary norm.[13] As established in *Certain Activities Carried Out by Nicaragua in the Border Area* (*Costa Rica v. Nicaragua*) and *Construction of a Road in Costa Rica along the San Juan River* (*Nicaragua v. Costa Rica*),[14] the customary obligation to notify is only triggered if the planned activity poses a risk of significant harm to the other State.[15] It should be noted that the ICJ judgement on the *Dispute over the status and use of the waters of the Silala* downgraded the customary obligation of notification relative to the conditions set out in the UN Watercourses Convention. The Court considered that "Article 12 of the 1997 Convention does not reflect a rule of customary international law relating to international watercourses that is more rigorous than the general obligation to notify and consult contained in its own jurisprudence."[16]

Therefore, the inclusion of the notification obligation in the UN Watercourses Convention was made in more stringent terms than in customary law. In fact, this Convention is quite specific as to how this obligation must operate

---

arrangements, as appropriate". In Convention on Biological Diversity, June 5, 1992, 1760 U.N.T.S. 79. Article 14.1(d).

12 Agreement under the United Nations Convention on the Law of the Sea on the Conservation and Sustainable Use of Marine Biological Diversity of Areas beyond National Jurisdiction, June 19, 2023, N/A U.N.T.S. Article 32.

13 See in this regard: Sangbana, Komlan. 2018. "Notification and Consultation Concerning Planned Measures (Articles 11–19)." In *The UN Convention on the Law of the Non-Navigational Uses of International Watercourses: A Commentary*, edited by Laurence Boisson de Chazournes, Makane Moïse Mbengue, Mara Tignino, Komlan Sangbana, and Jason Rudall, 159–90. Oxford: OUP; or McCaffrey, *Law of International Watercourses*, 535.

14 Certain Activities Carried Out by Nicaragua in the Border Area (Costa Rica v. Nicaragua) and Construction of a Road in Costa Rica along the San Juan River (Nicaragua v. Costa Rica), Judgment, 2015 I.C.J. Rep. 665 (December 15). Para. 108.

15 Dispute over the status and use of the waters of the Silala (Chile v. Bolivia), Judgement, 2022 I.C.J. Rep. 614 (December 1). Paras. 114–115 and 118. See an analysis on this judgement in Sindico, Francesco, Laura Movilla, and Gabriel Eckstein. 2022. "Preliminary Reflections on the ICJ Decision in the Dispute between Chile and Bolivia Over the Status and Use of the Waters of the Silala." https://www.ejiltalk.org/preliminary-reflections-on-the-icj-decision-in-the-dispute-between-chile-and-bolivia-over-the-status-and-use-of-the-waters-of-the-silala/

16 Dispute over the status and use of the waters of the Silala (Chile v. Bolivia), Judgement, 2022 I.C.J. Rep. 614 (December 1). Para. 117.

between co-riparian countries. Article 12 establishes the general obligation in the following terms:

> Before a watercourse State implements or permits the implementation of planned measures which may have a significant adverse effect upon other watercourse States, it shall provide those States with timely notification thereof. Such notification shall be accompanied by available technical data and information, including the results of any environmental impact assessment, in order to enable the notified States to evaluate the possible effects of the planned measures.[17]

It must be noted that the threshold that triggers the obligation to notify under these articles of the UN Watercourses Convention is the potential "transboundary adverse effects", which the ILC has qualified as less than "significant harm". The purpose is to provide sufficient margin to avoid entering into the framework of Article 7,[18] as explained in the previous Section.

Other articles of the UN Watercourses Convention regulate several procedural aspects of the operationalisation of this obligation.[19] The level of detail in the regulation of this procedure is indicative of the importance given to it

---

17 Convention on the Law of the Non-Navigational Uses of International Watercourses, May 21, 1997, 2999 U.N.T.S. Article 12.

18 ILC, *Draft articles on the law of the non-navigational uses of international watercourses and commentaries thereto and resolution on transboundary confined groundwater*, A/CN.4/SER.A/1994/Add.l (Part 2) (1994) https://legal.un.org/ilc/texts/instruments/english/commentaries/8_3_1994.pdf, 111. Also relevant in terms of the principle of integration is the fact that the notification obligation applies not only to activities planned by the States, but also by private entities, as also clarified by the ILC.

19 Article 13 establishes a period of six months for the notified States to study and evaluate the potential effects of the planned measures, which can be extended for a further six months; Article 14 states that the notifying State must provide more information at the request of the notified State and refrain from implementing or permitting the planned measures while this information is being considered; Article 15 allows the notified States to send a document to the notifying State explaining the incompatibilities of the planned measures with the principles of equitable and reasonable utilisation and no harm, if any are found; Article 16 establishes that the notifying State may proceed with planned measures if it does not receive any reply during the period provided in Article 14, and that the expiry of this period allows the notifying State to compensate the costs of any action that would not have been undertaken if the notified State had replied within the period; finally, Article 18.1 establishes that if a State has enough evidence that a co-riparian State is planning measures that may have a significant adverse effect, it can request the application of Article 12. UN Watercourses Convention, *supra* note 17.

by the UN Watercourses Convention in the event of absence of an IRBO responsible for transmitting information on planned measures on the watercourse.

Since impacts on the watercourse are more commonly detected downstream, the duty to notify usually lies with upstream countries. However, the fact that downstream countries tend to develop their water resources earlier than upstream countries implies that upstream countries could be limiting the possibilities of downstream ones to develop their water resources in the future, and as already discussed, this could be considered a breach of the no-harm principle in certain circumstances. It follows, as argued by Salman, that downstream countries must also notify upstream countries of those measures potentially foreclosing the use of the international watercourse by an upstream country.[20] This makes the prior notification obligation much more reciprocal between the countries sharing the watercourse. In fact, most of the international basin agreements analysed in this research, especially the non-European ones, oblige the Parties to provide notification of planned measures whether they are upstream or downstream States.[21]

1.2 *The Obligation to Conduct an Environmental Impact Assessment*

The obligation to notify is closely related to the performance of EIAs. These instruments are analysed in depth in Chapter 12, so elements such as their specific content, the role of IRBOs and their regulation in international basin agreements are not examined here. However, their normative character must be briefly recalled for the purpose of this Section.

EIAs can be defined as a process conceived to give decision-makers the means to make informed decisions about the effects of a project or planned activity on the environment, sometimes also including social impacts. They generally include: criteria to determine the applicability of the process;

20 Salman, "Downstream Riparians Can Also Harm Upstream Riparians," 351–353.

21 See: The Niger Basin Water Charter, Article 20–21; Charter of Waters of the Senegal River, Article 24; Great Lakes Water Quality Agreement, Article 6; SADC Protocol on Shared Watercourses, Article 4; and Agreement on the establishment of the Zambezi Watercourse Commission, Article 16.1. Some international basin agreements have regulated this procedure with great detail. See in this regard the Water Charter of the Lake Chad Basin, Articles 52–60; and the Mekong Agreement, which counts on a separate procedure: MRC, *Procedures for Notification, Prior Consultation and Agreement* (30 November 2003), https://www.mrcmekong.org/wp-content/uploads/2024/08/Procedures-Notification-Prior-Consultation-Agreement.pdf. In relation to this procedure in the MRC regime see Rieu-Clarke, Alistair. 2014. "Notification and Consultation Procedures under the Mekong Agreement: Insights from the Xayaburi Controversy." *Asian Journal of International Law* 5 (1): 143–75.

assessment methods; a plan for the dissemination of results; a participatory process; and post-project follow-up provisions.

Although originally applied in the United States of America in the 1960s, they have been integrated into the national legislation of many countries and are the subject of significant regulation in regional and international sectoral treaties. As an obligation of international law, the obligation to conduct an EIA for activities potentially having a transboundary effect has been recognised by several international instruments.[22] In the soft law area, Principle 17 of the Rio Declaration[23] identifies it as an obligation of national authorities for activities likely to have a significant effect on the environment. Despite its non-binding nature and the lack of reference to transboundary damage, the inclusion of EIAs in the Rio Declaration is indicative of their importance for sustainable development.

Conventional international instruments do link the need to conduct an EIA to the possibility of transboundary impact.[24] Among them, Article 12 of the UN Convention on International Watercourses states that the notification of a planned measure "shall be accompanied by available technical data and information, including the results of any environmental impact assessment, in order to enable the notified States to evaluate the possible effects of the planned measures."[25] Given that States must determine if the planned measures are likely to have some sort of adverse transboundary effect in order to establish whether they are obliged to provide notification, the logical step would be to conduct a prior impact assessment.[26] Therefore, whether or not the State considers it necessary to notify the planned measures,

---

22 For a general introduction to Environmental Impact Assessments see, for instance: Craik, Neil. 2008. *The International Law of Environmental Impact Assessment.* Cambridge: Cambridge University Press; Hundloe, Tor. 2021. *Environmental Impact Assessment.* Cham: Springer; or Elias, Olufemi, and Meagan Wong. 2021. "Environmental Impact Assessment." In *Research Handbook on International Environmental Law*, edited by Malgosia Fitzmaurice, Marcel Brus, and Panos Merkouris, 188–208. Cheltenham: Edward Elgar.

23 Rio Declaration, *supra* note 8, Principle 17.

24 See CBD, *supra* note 11, Article 14; United Nations Framework Convention on Climate Change, May 9, 1992, 1771 U.N.T.S. 107. Article 4.1(f); and ILC, *Draft Articles on Prevention of Transboundary Harm from Hazardous Activities*, A/56/10 (2001), https://legal.un.org/ilc/texts/instruments/english/commentaries/9_7_2001.pdf. Article 7; ILC, *Draft Articles on the Law of Transboundary Aquifers with Commentaries*, A/63/10 (2008), https://legal.un.org/ilc/texts/instruments/english/commentaries/8_5_2008.pdf. Article 15.2.

25 UN Watercourses Convention, *supra* note 17, Article 12.

26 Certain Activities Carried Out by Nicaragua in the Border Area (Costa Rica v. Nicaragua) and Construction of a Road in Costa Rica along the San Juan River (Nicaragua v. Costa Rica), Judgment, 2015 I.C.J. Rep. 665 (December 15). Para. 104.

by the time such notification is issued the EIA will in most cases already have been prepared, as it will have been necessary to evaluate the need for notification.

The legal status of EIAs is even more clearly established in the UNECE Water Convention than in the UN Watercourses Convention,[27] as it obliges the Parties to the Convention that share a watercourse to undertake the necessary measures to conduct an EIA in certain circumstances.[28] In 1991, the Espoo Convention was adopted, the preamble to which clearly identifies the principle of integration as one of its underlying principles,[29] along with sustainable development.[30] This Convention is the most advanced international instrument to regulate EIAs, although it is not a universal instrument.[31]

EIAs have gained importance in international law in general and international watercourse law in particular as a necessary tool to prevent transboundary harm. By extension, they can be seen as a practical application of the principle of sustainable development and the precautionary principle as much as a necessary step to comply with the principle of 'good faith negotiations' in a transboundary context.[32] In this regard, the obligation to conduct EIAs has been recognised as an obligation of international law by the ICJ in *Pulp Mills on the River Uruguay (Argentina v. Uruguay)*.[33]

1.3 *The Obligation to Consult with Other Riparian States*

The obligation to enter into consultations with other States was included in the Rio Declaration alongside the obligation to notify in relation to activities that could have significant adverse transboundary environmental effects[34]

---

27 Convention on the Protection and Use of Transboundary Watercourses and International Lakes, March 17, 1992, 1936 U.N.T.S. 269. Article 3.1(h).

28 The complementarity between those two norms can be noticed in the explicit reference to the Espoo Convention in international watercourse agreements inspired in the UNECE Water Convention. See, for instance, Article 17 of the Dniester River Basin Treaty.

29 Espoo Convention, *supra* note 9, Preamble, first paragraph.

30 Ibid. Preamble, second paragraph.

31 On the relationship between the UNECE Water Convention and other UNECE environmental conventions see McIntyre, Owen. 2015. "The Water Convention Other UNECE Environmental Treaties." In *The UNECE Convention on the Protection and Use of Transboundary Watercourses and International Lakes*, edited by Attila Tanzi, Owen McIntyre, Alexandros Kolliopoulos, Alistair Rieu-Clarke, and Rémy Kinna, 73–87. Leiden: Brill Nijhoff.

32 McIntyre, *Environmental Protection of International Watercourses*, 369–370.

33 Pulp Mills on the River Uruguay (Argentina v. Uruguay), 2010 Judgment, I.C.J. Rep. 14 (April 20). Para. 204.

34 Rio Declaration, *supra* note 8, Principle 19.

and in several other international binding[35] and non-binding[36] environmental instruments.[37] This norm has had a significant development in the context of international watercourse law. After a riparian State provides notification of planned measures, normally including an EIA, the notified riparian State should be given the opportunity to answer and enter into a dialogue. If an obligation to enter into consultation did not follow, the obligation to notify would be deprived of a significant part of its sense. As argued by Leb, it is an underlying objective of notification that the response of the notified State be taken into account.[38] The arbitral tribunal in *Lac Lanoux (Espagne/France)* case understood consultations in the sense that:

> l'Etat d'amont a, d'après les règles de la bonne foi, l'obligation de prendre en considération les différents intérêts en présence, de chercher à leur donner toutes les satisfactions compatibles avec la poursuite de ses propres intérêts et de montrer qu'il a, à ce sujet, un souci réel de concilier les intérêts de l'autre riverain avec les siens propres.[39]

Leb has defined the content of this obligation in the following terms: "Consultation [...] is a process of information exchange that carries with it a legal consequence: the duty to take into account the information obtained throughout this process."[40] However, consultations are not only initiated in response to a notification: they can also be initiated by a direct petition from one of the States. As such, consultations can complete the obligation to notify but may also come into play without it.[41] In some regimes consultations are given a wider purpose in relation to the joint management of the shared watercourse,

35 See: Convention on Long-range Transboundary Air Pollution, November 13, 1979, 1302 U.N.T.S. 217, Article 5; and Convention on wetlands of international importance especially as waterfowl habitat, February 2, 1971, 996 U.N.T.S. 245, Article 5; CBD, *supra* note 11, Article 14.1(c); United Nations Convention on the Law of the Sea, December 10, 1982, 1833 U.N.T.S. 3. Article 66.2.

36 See: World Commission on Environment and Development, *Report of the World Commission on Environment and Development: "Our Common Future"*, A/42/427 (4 August 1987), undocs.org/en/A/42/427, Article 17; and ILC, *Draft principles on the allocation of loss in the case of transboundary harm arising out of hazardous activities*, A/61/10, at 66–67 (2006), undocs.org/en/A/61/10, Article 5(c).

37 On the topic of consultation in the context of environmental law, see Birnie, Boyle and Redgwell, *International Law and the Environment*, 177–180.

38 Leb, *Cooperation in the Law of Transboundary Water Resources*, 140.

39 Lac Lanoux (Espagne/France), 12 R.I.A.A (Perm. Ct. Arb. 1957). 315.

40 Leb, *Cooperation in the Law of Transboundary Water Resources*, 140.

41 Farrajota, "Notification and Consultation in the Law Applicable to International Law," 323.

for example in the implementation of pollution mitigation measures,[42] the use and allocation of water,[43] the establishment of alarm systems and emergency situations,[44] the implementation of IRBO decisions,[45] the maintenance and protection of installations,[46] or the settlement of disputes.[47]

The obligation to consult with other riparian States is also enshrined in the UN Watercourses Convention across several articles concerning a number of different situations.[48] In Article 6.2, this obligation is stated specifically in relation to the application of the principle of equitable and reasonable utilisation of Article 5 and for considering the relevant factors for its determination enumerated in Article 6.1.[49] Indeed, as McCaffrey suggests, regular consultations are necessary to comply effectively with the obligation of equitable and reasonable utilisation due to the nature of the latter.[50] Article 6(2) limits these consultations to "when the need arises", but it has been argued that "one can hardly imagine a situation falling within the purview of Articles 5 and 6 in which the rejection of a request for consultation could be upheld on the basis of any other provision of the Convention."[51] In any case, the obligation to enter into consultations is instrumental to the achievement of equitable and reasonable utilisation.

In a somewhat intuitive way, a similar claim can be made in relation to the avoidance of transboundary harm. The UN Watercourses Convention states the need to enter into consultations, not to avoid causing harm, but in order "to eliminate or mitigate such harm and, where appropriate, to discuss the question of compensation."[52] This preventive action, however, can be considered satisfied by the general regime of the obligation to notify. As seen above, the

42 Dniester River Basin Treaty, Article 8.2; SADC Protocol on Shared Watercourses, Article 4.2.b(iii).

43 MRC, *Procedures for Notification, Prior Consultation and Agreement* (30 November 2003), https://www.mrcmekong.org/wp-content/uploads/2024/08/Procedures-Notification-Prior-Consultation-Agreement.pdf. Article 5.1.

44 See: Water Charter of the Lake Chad Basin, Article 60; and Danube River Protection Convention, Article 6.1.

45 Convention on the Protection of the Rhine, Article 11.4.

46 Dniester River Basin Treaty, Article 11.

47 Agreement on the establishment of the Zambezi Watercourse Commission, Article 21.1.

48 See, in particular, articles 3(5), 6(2), 7(2), 11, 17(1), 18(2), 19(3), 21(3), 24(1) and 26(2) of the UN Watercourses Convention (*supra* note 17).

49 "In the application of article 5 or paragraph 1 of this article, watercourse States concerned shall, when the need arises, enter into consultations in a spirit of cooperation." UN Watercourses Convention, *supra* note 17, Article 6(2).

50 McCaffrey, *Law of International Watercourses*, 539–540.

51 Tanzi and Arcari, *United Nations Convention on the Law of International Watercourses*, 193.

52 UNECE Water Convention, *supra* note 27, Article 7(2).

arbitral tribunal in *Lac Lanoux* (*Espagne/France*) adopted a position in which the capacity to determine if a certain activity was harmful pertained solely to the affected State.[53] As noted by Tanzi and Arcari, however, this doctrine allows for abuse by the potentially affected State.[54] This problem is solved in the UN Watercourses Convention with the provision of Article 7(2) to eliminate or mitigate such harm in consultation with the affected State.

The inclusion in the UN Watercourses Convention of Article 17 on consultation with regard to planned measures caused no controversy,[55] which is indicative of the general acceptance of its customary nature.[56] This is supported by the ICJ itself, as in *Gabčikovo-Nagymaros Project* (*Hungary/Slovakia*) stated that consultation was an implicit obligation to define the implementation of the substantive obligations of environmental protection provided for in the 1977 Treaty. This obligation required "a mutual willingness to discuss in good faith actual and potential environmental risks."[57] In relation to the good faith requirement, in *Pulp Mills on the River Uruguay* (*Argentina v. Uruguay*), the Court also clarified that the notifying Party could not construct or authorise the construction of the planned facilities for the duration of the consultation period.[58] In the *Certain Activities Carried Out by Nicaragua in the Border Area* (*Costa Rica v. Nicaragua*) and *Construction of a Road in Costa Rica along the San Juan River* (*Nicaragua v. Costa Rica*) case, the issue was uncontentious, as both Parties concurred "on the existence in general international law of an obligation to notify, and consult with, the potentially affected State in respect of activities which carry a risk of significant transboundary harm."[59]

From the *Dispute over the status and use of the waters of the Silala*, on the other hand, it is interesting to note the close relationship between the obligations to

---

53 "A state wishing to do that which will affect an international watercourse cannot decide whether another state's interests will be affected; the other state is the sole judge of that." Lac Lanoux (Espagne/France), 12 R.I.A.A (Perm. Ct. Arb. 1957). 314.

54 Tanzi and Arcari, *United Nations Convention on the Law of International Watercourses*, 193.

55 UN Secretary-General, *Draft articles on the law of the non-navigational uses of international watercourses and resolution on confined transboundary groundwater, Report of the Secretary-General*, A/51/275 (6 August 1996), undocs.org/A/51/275.

56 On this question see Aura y Larios de Medrano, *La Regulación Internacional Del Agua Dulce*, 185–187.

57 Gabčikovo-Nagymaros Project (Hungary/Slovakia), Judgment, 1997 I.C.J. Rep. 7 (September 25). 112.

58 Pulp Mills on the River Uruguay (Argentina v. Uruguay), 2010 Judgment, I.C.J. Rep. 14 (April 20). Paras. 143–147.

59 Certain Activities Carried Out by Nicaragua in the Border Area (Costa Rica v. Nicaragua) and Construction of a Road in Costa Rica along the San Juan River (Nicaragua v. Costa Rica), Judgment, 2015 I.C.J. Rep. 665 (December 15). Para. 106.

notify and to enter into consultations. According to the reasoning of the Court, consultation is a consequence of a prior notification, which under customary law is only triggered when there is a risk of significant harm.[60]

In the UNECE Water Convention, there is less specific reference to consultations than in the UN Watercourses Convention. The obligation is only mentioned in Article 10, which is devoted to this particular form of cooperation and establishes it as a tool available at the request of any of the Parties.[61] It is important to note that the consultations are to be conducted through the joint body established under Article 9. This is not stipulated in the UN Watercourses Convention, where these organisations play a less central role than in the UNECE Water Convention. The higher degree of institutionalisation that the UNECE Water Convention provides for could also explain why the obligation to conduct consultations is not referred to explicitly as a cooperation mechanism in terms of compliance with other obligations, unlike in the UN Watercourses Convention.[62]

1.4 *The Obligation to Exchange Data and Information*

The obligation to exchange data and information might be considered a prerequisite for any intensified cooperation, inasmuch as it is "la base esencial para la toma de decisiones, formulación de políticas, y la consecución de una utilización equitativa y razonable y la no causación de daños sensibles en el ámbito de los cursos de agua internacionales."[63] This obligation, however, is not specific to international watercourse law and is usually included in instruments of international environmental law.[64]

60 See, in this regard, subsection b(i) in this Chapter.

61 "Consultations shall be held between the Riparian Parties on the basis of reciprocity, good faith and good-neighbourliness, at the request of any such Party. Such consultations shall aim at cooperation regarding the issues covered by the provisions of this Convention. Any such consultations shall be conducted through a joint body established under article 9 of this Convention, where one exists." (UNECE Water Convention, *supra* note 27, Article 10).

62 See Tanzi, Attila, and Cristina Contartese. 2015. "Establishment of an Implementation Mechanism under the Water Convention." In *The UNECE Convention on the Protection and Use of Transboundary Watercourses and International Lakes*, edited by Attila Tanzi, Owen McIntyre, Alexandros Kolliopoulos, Alistair Rieu-Clarke, and Rémy Kinna, 319–29. Leiden: Brill Nijhoff. 320–322.

63 Movilla, *La Dimensión Normativa de La Gobernanza Internacional Del Agua Dulce*. 161–163. See also Leb, *Cooperation in the Law of Transboundary Water Resources*. 115–124; McCaffrey, *Law of International Watercourses*, 540–541; and Leb, Christina. 2020. *Data Innovations for Transboundary Freshwater Resources Management. International Water Law*. Leiden: Brill.

64 Sands et al. *Principles of International Environmental Law*, 626–636.

Several environmental agreements mandate the exchange either directly between the concerned States or through international organisations.[65] The UNCLOS, for instance, provides that "States shall cooperate, directly or through competent international organizations, for the purpose of promoting studies, undertaking programmes of scientific research and encouraging the exchange of information and data acquired about pollution of the marine environment. They shall endeavour to participate actively in regional and global programmes to acquire knowledge for the assessment of the nature and extent of pollution, exposure to it, and its pathways, risks and remedies."[66] The Convention on the Conservation of Migratory Species of Wild Animals establishes that "[w]here appropriate and feasible, each AGREEMENT should provide for, but not be limited to: [...] the exchange of information on the migratory species concerned, special regard being paid to the exchange of the results of research and of relevant statistics."[67] In the soft law framework, it can be found in both the Stockholm Declaration[68] and the Rio Declaration,[69] among others.[70]

Article 9 of the UN Watercourses Convention also specifies that the exchange of data and information must be done on a regular basis and that it should include, at least, "the condition of the watercourse, in particular that of a hydrological, meteorological, hydrogeological and ecological nature and related to the water quality as well as related forecasts."[71] Since Article 9 is in Part II, it should be considered a general principle of the Convention. The principle is placed immediately after the general obligation of cooperation, which is not coincidental. It is reasonable to suggest that no cooperation can realistically take place without some significant exchange of data and information. In this regard, the ILC considers Article 9 a "specific application of the general obligation to cooperate laid down in article 8."[72] Moreover, this obligation may

65 See, for instance: CBD, *supra* note 11, Article 17.

66 United Nations Convention on the Law of the Sea, December 10, 1982, 1833 U.N.T.S. 3. Article 200.

67 Convention on the Conservation of Migratory Species of Wild Animals, June 23, 1979, 1651 U.N.T.S. Article V.5.d).

68 United Nations Conference on the Human Environment, *Declaration of the United Nations Conference on the Human Environment*, in Report of the United Nations Conference on the Human Environment, A/CONF.48/14/Rev.1. (5–16 June 1972), undocs.org/en/A/CONF.48/14/Rev.1. Principle 20.

69 Rio Declaration, *supra* note 8, Principle 9.

70 ILC, *Draft principles on the allocation of loss in the case of transboundary harm arising out of hazardous activities*, A/61/10, at 66–67 (2006), undocs.org/en/A/61/10. Article 12.

71 UN Watercourses Convention, *supra* note 17, Article 9.1.

72 ILC, *Report of the International Law Commission on the work of its forty-sixth session, 2 May–22 July 1994*, A/49/10 (1994), https://legal.un.org/ilc/documentation/english/reports/a_49_10.pdf. 107.

play a key role in achieving the equitable and reasonable utilisation of international watercourses. The ILC explicitly states that this information and data should enable States to comply with articles 5 to 7.[73]

For its part, the UNECE Water Convention also includes the obligation to exchange information, although in much more detail.[74] Article 13 of this Convention explicitly connects the exchange of information to the obligation to cooperate laid down in Article 9. This article also provides a far more comprehensive list than the UN Watercourses Convention of the data that the Parties must share.[75]

The regular exchange of data and information is regulated to a varying extent in several international basin agreements analysed in this research,[76] which, together with provisions in global conventions on the law applicable to international watercourses, makes it a widely accepted conventional rule.

However, whether it can be classed as customary law is less clear. This topic is not mentioned by the ILC in its commentaries on the draft articles regarding the law of non-navigational uses of international watercourses,[77] and international case law has not clarified the issue. In any case, much can be inferred from the ICJ's reasoning in relation to Article 11 of the UN Watercourses

73 Ibid. As noted by McCaffrey, "without data and information from co-riparian states concerning the conditions of the watercourse, it will be very difficult, if not impossible, for a state [...] to ensure that its utilization is equitable and reasonable vis-à-vis other states sharing the watercourse." (McCaffrey, *Law of International Watercourses*, 540.)

74 For a complete analysis of the obligation to exchange data and information under the UNECE Water Convention, see Lipponen, Annukka, and Lea Kauppi. 2015. "Monitoring and Assessment and the Duty of Cooperation under the Water Convention: Exchange of Information Among the Riparian Parties." In *The UNECE Convention on the Protection and Use of Transboundary Watercourses and International Lakes*, edited by Attila Tanzi, Owen McIntyre, Alexandros Kolliopoulos, Alistair Rieu-Clarke, and Rémy Kinna, 251–67. Leiden: Brill Nijhoff.

75 "(a) Environmental conditions of transboundary waters; (b) Experience gained in the application and operation of best available technology and results of research and development; (c) Emission and monitoring data; (d) Measures taken and planned to be taken to prevent, control and reduce transboundary impact; (e) Permits or regulations for waste-water discharges issued by the competent authority or appropriate body." (UNECE Water Convention, *supra* note 27, Article 13.1.)

76 Framework Agreement on the Sava River Basin, Article 4; Dniester River Basin Treaty, Article 18; Danube River Protection Convention, Article 12; Water Charter of the Lake Chad Basin, Appendix n° 5 on the exchange of data and information within the LCBC; SADC Protocol on Shared Watercourses, Article 3.6; and MRC, *Procedures for Data and Information Exchange and Sharing* (1 November 2001), https://www.mrcmekong.org/wp-content/uploads/2024/08/PDIES-3.pdf.

77 ILC Draft articles on the law of international watercourses, *supra* note 18, 107–109.

Convention on the exchange of information regarding the possible effects of planned measures on the condition of an international watercourse. Chile claimed that this article constituted customary law, but the Court rejected the assertion.[78]

2 External Integration of Substantive Obligations and Procedural Rules as the Basis for Institutional Integration

Closer to the core of this research is the integration of substantive obligations with procedural obligations.[79] In fact, part of the legal disagreement between Uruguay and Argentina in *Pulp Mills on the River Uruguay* (*Argentina v. Uruguay*) hinged on this aspect. Argentina argued that "a breach of the procedural obligations automatically entails a breach of the substantive obligations, since the two categories of obligations are indivisible."[80] Uruguay disagreed with that automatism, considering it 'artificial' and defending that it was for the Court to decide on the breach of each of the obligations separately.[81] The court did not accept Argentina's stance, arguing that "nowhere does the 1975 Statute indicate that a party may fullfil its substantive obligations by complying solely with its procedural obligations, nor that a breach of procedural obligations automatically entails the breach of substantive ones."[82]

From this reasoning, it could be interpreted that the ICJ was considering substantive and procedural rules as non-related norms. However, the Court did distinguish between the need to comply with each kind of norm irrespective of

78 Dispute over the status and use of the waters of the Silala (Chile v. Bolivia), Judgement, 2022 I.C.J. Rep. 614 (December 1). Paras. 111–112.

79 On this topic see, generally: Brunnée, "Procedure and Substance in International Environmental Law." On this topic in relation to international watercourses law: see McCaffrey, Stephen C. 2019. "Interwined General Principles." In *Research Handbook on International Water Law*, edited by Stephen C. McAffrey and Riley T. Denoon, 83–94. Cheltenham: Edward Elgar; McIntyre, "Procedural Rules and Protection of Transboundary Rivers"; and Tanzi, Attila. 2021. "Substantialising the Procedural Obligations of International Water Law between Compensatory and Distributive Justice." In *A Bridge Over Troubled Waters: Dispute Resolution in the Law of International Watercourses and the Law of the Sea*, edited by Hélène Ruiz Fabri, Erik Franckx, Marco Benatar, and Tamar Meshel, 351–76. Boston: Brill Nijhoff.

80 Pulp Mills on the River Uruguay (Argentina v. Uruguay), 2010 Judgment, I.C.J. Rep. 14 (April 20). Para. 72.

81 Ibid. Para. 74.

82 Ibid. Para. 78.

having fulfilled the other, with the actual existence of a "functional link."[83] This link would derive from the practical dependency of substantive obligations on procedural obligations: "The Court notes that the object and purpose of the 1975 Statute, set forth in Article 1, is for the Parties to achieve 'the optimum and rational utilization of the River Uruguay' by means of the 'joint machinery' for co-operation, which consists of both CARU and the procedural provisions contained in Articles 7 to 12 of the Statute."[84]

This argumentation would endorse McIntyre's claim that the ICJ had moved from seeing procedural and substantive rules as a collection of norms towards considering each body of rules as functionally connected to the other.[85] Moreover, the Court does not simply point out the existence of a link between the two categories of norms, but also adds a sense of intensity, stating that the fulfilment of the substantive norms requires a "continuous consultation between the Parties concerned."[86] In the *Dispute over the status and use of the waters of the Silala*, the ICJ reinstated the importance of procedural obligations in applying the substantive obligations under customary international law by referring to the judgment in *Pulp Mills on the River Uruguay (Argentina v. Uruguay)*, considering that they were of particular relevance when the shared resources could only be effectively protected through cooperation.[87]

External integration is intended to achieve the general objectives of international watercourse law. However, the Court also expressed in *Pulp Mills on the River Uruguay (Argentina v. Uruguay)* that procedural rules were a necessary element for the sustainable development of international watercourses.[88] It argued that, to comply with the substantive obligations that embody

83 Ibid. Para. 79.

84 Ibid. Para. 75.

85 McIntyre, "Procedural Rules and Protection of Transboundary Rivers," 242.

86 Pulp Mills on the River Uruguay (Argentina v. Uruguay), 2010 Judgment, I.C.J. Rep. 14 (April 20). Para. 77. Judge Vinuesa would have gone even further in his Dissenting Opinion by considering that non-compliance with procedural obligations would automatically imply the breach of substantive obligations (Pulp Mills on the River Uruguay (in Argentina v. Uruguay), 2010 Judgment, I.C.J. Rep. 14 (April 20) (Vinuesa, R., dissenting opinion), paras. 2–6 and 45–49). In a similar line of reasoining, judges Al-Khasawneh and Simma also criticised that the tribunal did not give enough weight to the recognition of the interdependence between procedural and substantive norms (in Pulp Mills on the River Uruguay (Argentina v. Uruguay), 2010 Judgment, I.C.J. Rep. 14 (April 20) (Al-Khasawneh, A.S. and Simma, B., joint dissenting opinion), paras. 26–28).

87 Dispute over the status and use of the waters of the Silala (Chile v. Bolivia), Judgement, 2022 I.C.J. Rep. 614 (December 1). Para. 100–101.

88 Pulp Mills on the River Uruguay (Argentina v. Uruguay), 2010 Judgment, I.C.J. Rep. 14 (April 20). Para. 177.

sustainable development, it would be necessary to take into account the interests of other riparian States through the fulfilment of the procedural norms. The Court thereby recognises the close relationship between substantive and procedural obligations although, as noted by McIntyre, "stopping short of finding the obligations contained therein to be indivisible."[89]

The stance adopted here is that external integration of the norms of international watercourse law – that is, the substantive and procedural obligations – is necessary for the achievement of sustainable development as it embodies the essence of the principle of integration in its procedural dimension. In other words, integrated decision-making in the governance of international watercourses is possible because external integration provides the necessary resources for its operation. This idea can be summarised in the concept of institutional integration put forward by the ILA in its work on the principle of integration.[90] From this point onwards and throughout this research, institutional integration is understood as the body of mechanisms established to allow an integrated decision-making process, which in the context of the governance of a shared resource includes external integration in the sense defined above. Therefore, Part III of the book delves further into the subject of institutional integration through the practice of IRBOs.

89 McIntyre, "Procedural Rules and Protection of Transboundary Rivers," 252.

90 ILA. Committee on International Law on Sustainable Development. 2006. "Report of the Toronto Conference." https://www.ila-hq.org/en_GB/documents/conference-report-toronto-2006-14. 7–12.

PART 2

Mechanisms for the Legal Integration of the Economic, Social and Environmental Dimensions in International Watercourse Regimes

Introduction

From a strictly legal perspective, the integration of economic, social and environmental aspects of sustainable development implies the accommodation of norms and values pertaining to those three domains, which respond to different interests and are usually designed with different objectives. This is a challenge that must be dealt with by the principle of integration. In international law, internormative issues are usually tackled from the perspective of the compatibility of norms. As such, conflicts between norms in general international law are usually resolved by applying rules of conflict of laws, which aim to provide a criterion to apply a certain norm instead of another one. The ILC Study Group on the fragmentation of international law identified as rules of conflict deriving from general international law the principle of *lex specialis derogare lege generali*, the principle of primacy of *lex posterior* over *lex prior*, and the *jus cogens*.[1]

However, the ILC also considered that according to the principle of harmonization, norms bearing on the same subject should, wherever possible, be interpreted so as to be translated into compatible obligations: "It is a generally accepted principle that when several norms bear on a single issue, they should, to the extent possible, be interpreted so as to give rise to a single set of compatible obligations."[2] The essence of this purpose is expressed in the principle of 'systemic integration', as enshrined in Article 31.3(c) of the Vienna Convention on the Law of the Treaties,[3] which, in contrast to the other rules of conflict, does not seek to apply one norm in place of another. Instead, it calls "to take into account the normative environment more widely"[4] when interpreting a norm. Under this principle, potentially conflicting norms can be considered as part of one same system and therefore potentially compatible if seen through a certain prism.

This aspect of systemic integration has obvious parallels with the principle of integration, but the two cannot be equated. In analysing the concept of 'legal

1 ILC, *Fragmentation of International Law: Difficulties Arising from the Diversification and Expansion of International Law, Report of the Study Group of the International Law Commission. Finalized by Martti Koskenniemi*, A/CN.4/L.682 (2006), undocs.org/A/CN.4/L.682.

2 ILC, *Fragmentation of International Law: Difficulties Arising from the Diversification and Expansion of International Law. Draft conclusions of the work of the Study Group. Finalized by Martti Koskenniemi*, A/CN.4/L.682/Add.1 (2 May 2006), undocs.org/A/CN.4/L.682/Add.1. Para. 4.

3 Vienna Convention on the Law of the Treaties, May 23, 1969, 1155 U.N.T.S. 331. Article 31.3(c).

4 Report finalized by Martti Koskenniemi, *supra* note 1, 209.

 | DOI:10.1163/9789004736757_008

integration', the principle of systemic integration should not be confused with the principle of integration – since the principle of integration has been defined as pertaining to the specific area of sustainable development – but neither should it be considered to embrace the full scope of legal integration, of which it is merely one of several instruments. *Legal integration as a dimension of the principle of integration* refers to the first dimension of the principle of integration, which is the focus of Part II of the book and whose elements will be analysed in the following pages. As seen earlier in this research, sustainable development comprises three inter-linked dimensions: economic, social and environmental, which are legally inter-connected in the framework of international watercourse law. When such dimensions are considered independently of one another, one dimension prevails over the others and the notion of sustainable development is subverted. Therefore, integration in this context must provide the legal techniques that allow for norms pertaining to the different dimensions to interact in such a manner that sustainable development is ensured.

For the sake of clarity, it may be useful to provide a previous disambiguation of legal integration in the sense explained above respect from two other similar concepts which nevertheless have different meanings. Firstly, the *principle of systemic integration in the context of the law of the treaties* is the principle referred to above, which is applied by interpreting norms taking into account other domains of the applicable law. That is, interpreting norms as forming part of a system. It is enshrined in Article 31.3(c) of the Vienna Convention of the Law of the Treaties and has been identified by the ILC as one of the means of resolving normative conflicts.[5]

Secondly, *normative integration in the context of international law* must be understood as one of the legal institutions that can help to preserve the unity of international law. Rodrigo has defined it as:

> [L]a incorporación en la redacción, en el contenido o en el proceso de interpretación y aplicación de una norma jurídica internacional de otras normas o de todo o parte del contenido de otras normas existentes en instrumentos de diversa naturaleza existentes en el mismo o en diferentes regímenes o en el Derecho internacional general con el objetivo de modificar los efectos jurídicos materiales, subjetivos o de otro tipo de las normas intervinientes. En síntesis, consiste en la incorporación en una norma jurídica internacional de normas externas a la misma que producen nuevos efectos jurídicos.[6]

5 Report finalized by Martti Koskenniemi, *supra* note 1, para. 492.
6 Rodrigo, "La Integración Normativa y La Unidad Del Derecho Internacional Público," 324.

Under this definition, normative integration is a general tool of international law. Obviously, it is a key element in the specific application of the principle of integration considered in this Part II of the book, since it can be applied in those cases where conflicts arise between norms pertaining to economic, social, or environmental domains, but it cannot be identified with legal integration as a dimension of the principle of integration as such. Instead, normative integration is one of the techniques through which legal integration operates.

Chapter 5 to 8 analyse the issue of legal integration in the context of international watercourses, both from the point of view of the legal frameworks established, its application and in the resolution of international disputes. Chapter 5 analyses international basin agreements in terms of their mandate for legal integration, either indirectly by establishing sustainable development as an objective of the treaty itself, or directly by establishing an especific obligation for legal integration, whether explicitly or implicitly.

The Chapter 6 analyses the use of normative integration techniques that can produce legal integration in the sense used in this book. On the one hand, these techniques can facilitate integration between specific rules that represent sustainable development interests. On the other hand, techniques of legal integration can operate through the establishment of links between international legal regimes that regulate different dimensions of sustainable development separately.

While Chapters 5 and 6 focus on legal measures that, having been introduced into a basin agreement, establish fixed links that produce legal integration, the Chapter 7 deals with legal mechanisms that operate in a variable way at the time of treaty implementation, since the extent to which these mechanisms operationalise legal integration and the manner in which they do so will depend to a significantly greater extent on the legal context in which they are applied. These are the following: the introduction of the different values of sustainable development into the international basin agreements; the introduction into international basin agreements of guiding principles that promote legal integration; and the legal integration operated by concepts developed in soft law instruments.

Legal integration can occur not only in the drafting or implementation of international basin agreements by governing bodies, but also in the resolution of international disputes. While this would be subsidiary to the prior mechanisms, international tribunals can employ a number of interpretation techniques, some of which can also produce legal integration. These techniques are analysed in Chapter 8: teleological interpretation; interpretation of evolving concepts; and interpretation of open-textured obligations.

CHAPTER 5

The Inclusion of a Mandate of Legal Integration in International Basin Agreements

One means of fostering legal integration for the achievement of sustainable development is to establish this aim as one of the objectives of a treaty. The analysis of international basin agreements shows that there are two ways in which this form of legal integration can be operated. On the one hand, legal integration can be mandated indirectly as a requirement to comply with an obligation formulated in broader or more specific terms to pursue sustainable development. On the other hand, legal integration can be mandated more directly, either explicitly through the incorporation of a clause on legal integration, or implicitly by including economic, social and environmental interests in the same treaty.

1 Indirect Inclusion of the Principle of Integration through Sustainable Development as a Goal of International Basin Agreements

A legislative technique that can propel legal integration is the explicit inclusion of sustainable development as an objective of the treaty. This might seem obvious at first glance, but sustainable development is a relatively recent concept and could not be included in older treaties. Among the first legal instruments to include sustainable development as a core objective were some important instruments in environmental law. See, for instance, the Convention to Combat Desertification[1] or the CBD,[2] which are basically centred on the protection of global environmental interests. It is increasingly common for treaties state the obligation to use a given natural resource in a sustainable manner, such

1 It refers to sustainable development as the overall objective of tackling desertification. In United Nations Convention to Combat Desertification in those Countries Experiencing Serious Drought and/or Desertification, Particularly in Africa, October 14, 1994, 1954 U.N.T.S. 3. Article 2.1.

2 It refers to sustainable use of the components of biological diversity. In Convention on Biological Diversity, June 5, 1992, 1760 U.N.T.S. 79. Article 1.

 | DOI:10.1163/9789004736757_009

as ecosystems,[3] wildlife,[4] or fisheries.[5] Included in this category are treaties referring to the conservation of natural resources – more common in environmental agreements on wildlife[6] – since such a formulation assumes the right to use those resources but with the condition that environmental concerns must be considered.[7]

The inclusion in a treaty of references to 'sustainable use' makes sense in view of the need to limit the principle of sovereignty over natural resources. Traditionally, conventional international law on this subject focused on securing the national sovereignty of the contracting Parties over the natural resources located exclusively in their territory and limited the scope of the agreement to shared resources.[8] As such, the limitation on sovereignty is by no means absolute but rather conditioned to the sustainability of the intended use of these natural resources.

Almost all of the international basin agreements adopted after 1992 refer in their preambles to sustainable development as an inspiring principle; while this has no legal effect, it expresses the general acceptance of sustainable development as a guiding concept. The Mekong Agreement and Procedures, for instance, reaffirms "the determination to continue to cooperate and promote in a constructive and mutually beneficial manner in the sustainable development, utilisation, conservation and management of the Mekong River Basin water and related resources [...]."[9]

In some international basin agreements, sustainable development is enshrined as the objective of the treaty. This is the case of many of the basin agreements analysed for the purpose of this research, such as those pertaining to the basins of the Niger, the Volta, the Chad Lake, the Dniester,

3 United Nations Convention on the Law of the Sea, December 10, 1982, 1833 U.N.T.S. 3. Article 194.5.

4 Convention on International Trade in Endangered Species of Wild Fauna and Flora, March 3, 1973, 993 U.N.T.S. 243.

5 Agreement for the Implementation of the Provisions of the United Nations Convention on the Law of the Sea of 10 December 1982 relating to the Conservation and Management of Straddling Fish Stocks and Highly Migratory Fish Stocks, December 4, 1995, 2167 U.N.T.S. 3.

6 For example, the Convention on the Conservation of Migratory Species of Wild Animals, June 23, 1979, 1651 U.N.T.S.

7 Redgwell, Catherine. 2018. "Sustainable Use of Natural Resources." In *Principles of Environmental Law*, edited by L. Krämer and E. Orlando, 115–24. Cheltenham: Edward Elgar. 119–120.

8 See, for instance, Fisheries Jurisdiction (United Kingdom v. Iceland), Judgment, 1974 I.C.J. Rep. 3 (25 July).

9 See, for instance: Mekong Agreement, Preamble.

the Sava, or the Rhine.[10] The basin agreement on the Dniester, for instance, states that:

> The objective of the present Treaty is to establish legal and institutional foundations for cooperation towards achieving rational and environmentally sound use and protection of water and other natural resources and ecosystems of the Dniester River basin in the interests of population and sustainable development of the states of the Contracting Parties.[11]

In some other treaties, sustainable development is not an objective of the treaty but constitutes an objective of the cooperation between the Parties,[12] although the two types of provision are not mutually exclusive. The Danube River Protection Convention establishes as the first of its "[o]bjectives and principles of cooperation" in which deployment "[t]he Contracting Parties shall strive at achieving the goals of a sustainable and equitable water management, including the conservation, improvement and the rational use of surface waters and ground water in the catchment area as far as possible."[13] Similarly, the Water Charter of the Lake Chad Basin states that "[t]he State Parties shall cooperate to achieve the sustainable management and development of Lake Chad in compliance with the rules and principles governing international lakes and watercourses."[14]

More rarely, sustainable development is an objective of the institutional mechanism established for the implementation of the basin agreement or of its bodies. For instance, the Agreement on the Establishment of the Zambezi Watercourse Commission establishes sustainable development as an objective of the Zambezi Watercourse Commission in general and as one of the tasks of the Council of Ministers in Article 5 and Article 8.1.a.[15]

---

10 In the same order: The Niger Basin Water Charter, Article 2; Water Charter of the Lake Chad Basin, Article 3; Draft Water Charter for the Volta River Basin, Article 1.1; Framework Agreement on the Sava River Basin, Article 2.1.b); Convention on the Protection of the Rhine, Article 3.1.

11 Dniester River Basin Treaty, Article 1.1.

12 See, for instance: Draft Water Charter for the Volta River Basin, Article 5,1; Mekong Agreement, Article 1.

13 Danube River Protection Convention, Article 2.

14 Water Charter of the Lake Chad Basin, Article 1.

15 Agreement on the establishment of the Zambezi Watercourse Commission, Articles 5 and 8.1.a.

Obviously, the mere insertion of sustainable development in a treaty in any of the above forms does not in itself produce integration, nor does it ensure sustainable development. Ultimately, this requires the implementation of more specific measures, which may or may not be foreseen in the text of the agreement. However, the importance of the inclusion of sustainable development – either explicitly or in any other form – should not be underestimated. If the principle of integration is instrumental for the achievement of sustainable development, the inclusion of this concept in a treaty can serve as a springboard for integration. In particular, it bolsters an integrative interpretation of the treaty that is coherent with the principle of integration. Even if the obligation to develop sustainably is considered an obligation of general international law, the explicit provision of sustainable development as an objective of the treaty would reinforce its application and underline the necessity to adopt measures for its effective achievement. In this sense, the specific inclusion of the concept in a treaty cannot be considered redundant since it would serve in all cases to reinforce the need for integration.

2 Direct Inclusion of the Principle of Integration in International Basin Agreements

Treaties can also explicitly include the principle of integration in a variety of ways. On the one hand, treaties can provide that national plans, programs, strategies, or policies in application of the norm must be formulated in a manner that entails the adoption of an integrated approach that encompasses different aspects of sustainable development. An example from international environmental law would be the United Nations Framework Convention on Climate Change, of which article 4.1.f) obliges the Parties to [t]ake climate change considerations into account, to the extent feasible, in their relevant social, economic and environmental policies and actions, and employ appropriate methods, for example impact assessment [...].[16]

This form of legal integration can also be found in several international basin agreements. The Niger Basin Water Charter, for instance, establishes that the Parties must develop and implement planning, protection, management,

16 United Nations Framework Convention on Climate Change, May 9, 1992, 1771 U.N.T.S. 107. Article 4.1.f). It is also the case of article 6.b) of the CBD (Convention on Biological Diversity, June 5, 1992, 1760 U.N.T.S. 79.) or Article 2.3 of the Kyoto Protocol (Kyoto Protocol to the United Nations Framework Convention on Climate Change, December 11, 1997, 2303 U.N.T.S. 162).

use, and development policies with the aim of achieving objectives which encompass both environmental, social and economic interests, such as the control of pollution, preservation of forestry and wetlands, or the planning of projects for the development of water resources.[17]

In a similar vein, the agreement between Moldova and Ukraine on the Dniester River Basin establishes that to implement the treaty, the Parties "shall adopt national and/or international Dniester River basin management plans, action plans, schemes and programs aimed at achieving sustainable water use, control of water pollution, prevention of adverse impacts of water,"[18] among other mesasures. This is also the case of the Danube River Protection Convention, which establishes that the measures planned at national or basin level should be aimed at "ensur[ing] the sustainable use of water resources for municipal, industrial and agricultural purposes as well as the conservation and restauration of ecosystems and to cover also other requirements occurring as to public health."[19] Possibly the basin agreement with the most detailed list is the Great Lakes Water Quality Agreement, which enumerates measures ranging from: the elaboration of pollution abatement, control, and prevention programs; aquatic invasive species programs and other measures; conservation programs; to enforcement actions and other measures to ensure the effectiveness of the programs.[20]

Other international basin agreements contain this mandate of integration as an obligation on the Parties to develop joint planning instruments. The Framework Agreement on the Sava River Basin requires the Parties to elaborate and implement joint plans and development programs in order to establish a navigation regime, which is primarily an economic interest, and for protection against floods, ice hazards, droughts, and incidents involving substances hazardous, which are mostly social and environmental concerns.[21]

Similarly, the Agreement on the Establishment of the Zambezi Watercourse Commission states that "Member States shall conduct their management and development plans, projects and programmes relating to the resources of the Zambezi Watercourse in accordance with the Strategic Plan."[22] The Strategic Plan, in turn, should set out the projects and programs for efficient management

17 The Niger Basin Water Charter, paragraphs 3° and 5° of Article 11.

18 Dniester River Basin Treaty, Article 6.1.

19 Danube River Protection Convention, Article 2.3.

20 Great Lakes Water Quality Agreement, Article 4.2.

21 Framework Agreement on the Sava River Basin, Paragraph 2 of Article 2 read jointly with paragraph 1.

22 Agreement on the establishment of the Zambezi Watercourse Commission, Article 14.9.

and sustainable development of the watercourse; that is, considering aspects from the three dimensions of sustainable development.[23]

The inclusion of such clauses in international basin agreements can be particularly helpful in ensuring an integrated implementation of the agreement in the sense that they give precise indications as to which instruments should be used. Their relevance can be better appreciated if contrasted with the method discussed in the previous Section. While the inclusion of sustainable development facilitates an interpretation of the treaty that can indirectly contribute to integration, the establishment of concrete obligations regarding the methods of implementation offers greater guarantees.

Several international basin agreements also contain provisions explicitly aimed at integrated management. The Volta Water Charter even establishes integrated management of water resources as one of the specific objectives of the treaty.[24] Nevertheless, integrated management is more commonly included as a method for the protection of the environment,[25] in particular as a means to achieve sustainable development of the basin.[26] In this regard, Article 11 of the Framework Agreement on the Sava River Basin, under the title 'Sustainable Water Management', states that:

> The Parties agree to cooperate on management of the waters of the Sava River Basin in a sustainable manner, which includes integrated management of surface and ground water resources, in a manner that shall provide for:
> a) Water in sufficient quantity and of appropriate quality for the preservation, protection and improvement of aquatic eco-systems (including flora and fauna and eco-systems of natural ponds and wetlands);
> b) Waters in sufficient quantity and of appropriate quality for navigation and other kinds of use/utilization;
> c) Protection against detrimental effects of water (flooding, excessive groundwater, erosion and ice hazards);
> d) Resolution of conflicts of interest caused by different uses and utilizations; and
> e) Effective control of the water regime.[27]

---

23 Ibid. Article 1.

24 Draft Water Charter for the Volta River Basin, Article 1.2.

25 Dniester River Basin Treaty, Article 4.2.

26 The Niger Basin Water Charter, Article 2; Draft Water Charter for the Volta River Basin, Article 5.2.a; Water Charter of the Lake Chad Basin, Article 3.

27 Framework Agreement on the Sava River Basin, Article 11.

What integrated management means is not always specified, but the Niger, the Volta, and the Chad Lake water charters adopt the literal definition provided by the Global Water Partnership[28] (hereinafter, GWP), according to which IWRM is "a process which encourages coordinated development and management of water, land and ancillary resources, in order to equitably maximise the resulting economic and social well-being without jeopardizing the sustainability of vital ecosystems."[29] Despite the open character of this definition, it is clear that the inclusion of a reference to IWRM might be decisive in determining the management model that is adopted in the application of an international basin agreement.

However, although it may be key to the application of the principle of integration, integrated management does not reflect the principle of integration understood in the sense of legal integration. Integrated management is analysed in Chapter 11 as one of the levels at which institutional integration operates, but it does not itself create links between norms or values pertaining to different regimes bearing on sustainable development. A thorough analysis of international basin agreements shows that clauses explicitly mandating legal integration are not commonly included in this type of treaty.

---

28 See: The Niger Basin Water Charter, Article 1.15; Draft Water Charter for the Volta River Basin, Article 3.25; Water Charter of the Lake Chad Basin, Article 2.

29 GWP. 2000. "Integrated Water Resources Management." *Technical Advisory Committee Background Papers*, no. 4. 4.

CHAPTER 6

Legal Integration through Normative Integration Techniques: Inter-Disciplinary Integration

International basin agreements are especially integrative legal instruments since they usually regulate both the uses of international watercourses for the satisfaction of economic and human needs and their environmental protection. Therefore, basin agreements cannot be regarded as instruments pertaining exclusively to the domain of environmental law,[1] nor to any domain of international law that could be classified under economic law. Since they focus on a specific natural environment, which is also a natural resource, international basin agreements aim to regulate the conflicting interests converging in the basin. They must provide the framework for balancing different legal goods, such as the protection of ecosystems, the provision of water for human consumption, or the utilisation of water for irrigation. In this regard, international basin agreements are potentially fertile ground for the use of normative techniques aimed at producing legal integration for sustainable development. This Chapter provides a classification of these techniques in the framework of the general theory on normative integration.

The relationship between different regimes is discussed extensively in legal doctrine. Some authors take a reactive approach, referring to 'regime interactions management',[2] which implies that this is an issue that must be tackled, or even prevented. Oberthür, for example, identifies a normative dimension of regime interactions management, the 'regulatory interplay management', which "may determine substantive standards of behaviour, for example by prescribing which rule to follow in the case of a rule conflict."[3]

1 International watercourses law is often classified as a branch of international environmental law by the doctrine. See, for instance, Sands et al. *Principles of International Environmental Law,* 303–340. However, the UN Watercourses Convention is not solely meant to protect the environment of watercourses, neither are the most of international basin agreements considered in this work.

2 See, for instance, Asselt, Harro van. 2014. *The Fragmentation of Global Climate Governance.* Cheltenham: Edward Elgar. 60–71.

3 Oberthür, Sebastian. 2009. "Interplay Management: Enhancing Environmental Policy Integration among International Institutions." *International Environmental Agreements: Politics, Law and Economics* 9 (4): 371–91.

 | DOI:10.1163/9789004736757_010

However, in the context of the principle of integration, the interactions between regimes are not so much something to be managed, but rather something to be enhanced and promoted. In other words, normative integration as a dimension of the principle of integration requires that legal techniques in the elaboration of treaties be used to enable those regime interactions rather than avoid them. Gradoni, for instance, identifies several "techniques de prise en compte des valeurs et intérêts environnementaux" of which some are consistent with this purposive approach to normative integration. These are exception,[4] harmonisation,[5] the *renvoi*, incorporation,[6] *contre-mesures "chevauchants",*[7] regulation of the jurisdictional scope,[8] and conflict norms expressly provided in an international instrument.[9]

Of those normative integration techniques, the *renvoi* is the only one that is sometimes used for the regulation of international watercourses. Also called rules of reference, *renvoi* consists of the insertion in one norm of a reference to another norm or a group of norms. This mechanism coincides to a large extent with the concept of inter-disciplinary integration described by the ILA.[10] An inter-normative disposition of this kind can refer either concretely or generically to norms with the same or different nature or incorporate the current

4 Gradoni, "Systèmes Juridiques Internationaux", 42–43. In relation to exceptions see also Bonet, Jordi. 2019. *La Internormatividad Entre Las Dimensiones Económica y Social Del Ordenamiento Jurídico Internacional. ¿Un Espacio Jurídico Para La Efectividad de Los Derechos Económicos, Sociales y Culturales?* Barcelona: Huygens Editorial. 148–149.

5 Gradoni, "Systèmes Juridiques Internationaux," 43–45.

6 It implies the integration of an external norm as if it was native to the adopting system. It might imply a rewriting of the external norm and an autonomation from it, so it becomes unaffected by ulterior changes in the external norm. In Ibid. 46–47.

7 If a legal system allows its norms to be breached as a countermeasure to a breach of an environmental obligation arising from an external norm, it predisposes itself to taking into account certain environmental interests and values codified outside the system. In Ibid. 49–50.

8 If the judicial bodies of a given legal system are given competency to interpret and apply external rules when this proves necessary to resolve a dispute relating primarily to the infringement of an internal rule, they implement a technique for taking into account external rules. In Ibid. 50.

9 If a conflict of norms is resolved on the basis of conflicting clauses expressly provided for in an international instrument, it may result in environmental interests and values being taken into account to a greater or lesser extent depending on whether the environmental norm is retained or set aside in favour of another norm underpinning different interests and values. In Ibid. 50.

10 ILA. Committee on International Law on Sustainable Development. 2006. "Report of the Toronto Conference." https://www.ila-hq.org/en_GB/documents/conference-report-toronto-2006-141. 16–17.

or potential content of certain identified norms.[11] This technique can operate in two ways: through inter-treaty references that link a treaty to dispositions or full texts of another treaty that is clearly identifiable; or through generic references to another regime. Opting for one or other of these mechanisms determines the openness of the normative integration operated. While an inter-treaty clause clearly identifies the norm referred to, a clause referring to another regime is much more vague and open to weighting. This Chapter analyses the application of the two normative integration techniques in the creation of international basin agreements.

Nevertheless, rules of reference are not the only means of linking treaties and regimes. As pointed out by Fajardo, sectoral principles such as those in the field of biodiversity also play an important role in mitigating the tension in fragmented regimes (e.g. between the CBD and the UNCLOS).[12] This function can be fulfilled not only intra-regime but also between different regimes and will be tackled in the next Chapter.

1 Treaty References to Specific Norms Regulating a Dimension of Sustainable Development: Inter-Treaty References

Inter-treaty references are references in one treaty to another treaty – or a norm forming part of another treaty – without reproducing its content.[13] On the one hand, this technique must be differentiated from intra-conventional references. For instance, Article 16.1 of the UN Watercourses Convention refers to articles 5 and 6 of the same convention as a condition to proceed with the planned measures if the notifying State has not received a response within the

---

11 Rodrigo, "La Integración Normativa y La Unidad Del Derecho Internacional Público," 327.

12 Fajardo del Castillo, Teresa. 2021. "Principles and Approaches in the Convention on Biological Diversity and Other Biodiversity-Related Conventions in the Post-2020 Scenario." In *Biological Diversity and International Law*, edited by Mar Campins Eritja and Teresa Fajardo del Castillo, 15–34. Cham: Springer. 18–21.

13 On this topic see, for instance: Lewald, Hans. 1929. "La Théorie Du Renvoi." *Collected Courses of the Hague Academy of International Law* 29: 515–620; Wolf, Francis. 1967. "L'interdépendence Des Conventions Internationales Du Travail." *Collected Courses of the Hague Academy of International Law* 121 (II): 2–217; Forteau, Mathias. 2003. "Les Renvois Inter-Conventionnels." *Annuaire Français de Droit International* 49 (1): 71–104; and Trevisanut, Seline. 2009. "La Convention Des Nations Unies Sur Le Droit de La Mer et Le Droit de l'Environnement : Développement Intrasystémique et Renvoi Intersystémique." In *La Circulation Des Concepts Juridiques : Le Droit International de l'environnement Entre Mondialisation et Fragmentation*, edited by Hélène Ruiz Fabri and Lorenzo Gradoni, 397–426. Paris: Société de législation comparée.

6 months.[14] This is an intra-treaty reference which does not constitute normative integration in the sense considered here.

On the other hand, inter-treaty reference must be differentiated from clauses that merely regulate the compatibility of treaties, which do not produce normative integration. An example would be Article 3.1 of the UN Watercourses Convention, which establishes that "[i]n the absence of an agreement to the contrary, nothing in the present Convention shall affect the rights or obligations of a watercourse State arising from agreements in force for it on the date on which it became a party to the present Convention."[15] This disposition is intended to prevent conflicts between this convention and prior agreements adopted by the Parties, but it does not create normative integration.

Therefore, for inter-treaty references to produce normative integration, they must establish a link between concrete and differentiated treaties.[16] In addition, if this normative integration is to be considered an expression of the principle of integration and not only an example of general normative integration in the framework of international law, the reference should link two dimensions of sustainable development.

Moreover, the doctrine distinguishes between two kinds of inter-treaty references depending on the identification of the integrated norm. If the norm is identified expressly, the content of the normative integration is realised in a closed manner. Another possibility is that the reference is made with an open formulation, in which case the content is variable.[17]

Analysis of international basin agreements shows that legal integration through inter-treaty references is rarely applied in this area of international law. Only the Great Lakes Water Quality Agreement and the Water Charter for the Volta River Basin use this technique. In the first case, two treaties related to the pollution of water are referred to determine the substances which are to be considered a "hazardous polluting substance" in the terms of the agreement:[18] the International Convention for the Prevention of Pollution from Ships[19] and the International Convention on Liability and Compensation for

14 Convention on the Law of the Non-Navigational Uses of International Watercourses, May 21, 1997, 2999 U.N.T.S. Article 16.1.

15 Ibid. Article 3.1.

16 Rodrigo, "La Integración Normativa y La Unidad Del Derecho Internacional Público," 328–330.

17 Ibid. 330–333.

18 Great Lakes Water Quality Agreement, Annex 5, D.8.

19 Absorbed by the Protocol of 1978 relating to the International Convention for the prevention of pollution from ships, February 17, 1978, 1340, 1341 U.N.T.S. 61, 3.

Damage in Connection with the Carriage of Hazardous and Noxious Substances by Sea.[20]

In the case of the Water Charter for the Volta River Basin,[21] international treaties pertaining to three specific areas of law are referred to explicitly, of which two are clearly environmental. In relation to the control of pollution from agriculture, mining, and due to foreign hazardous waste, it is established that the Parties are to strengthen the enforcement of the Convention on the control of transboundary movements of hazardous wastes and their disposal;[22] the Bamako Convention on the prohibition of hazardous waste imports and the control of their transboundary movement in Africa;[23] the Rotterdam Convention on the Prior Informed Consent Procedure for Certain Hazardous Chemicals and Pesticides in International Trade;[24] the Stockholm Convention on persistent organic pollutants; and the Minamata Convention on mercury.[25]

Seemingly, the Water Charter for the Volta River Basin refers to four international treaties from the biodiversity protection domain. The CBD[26] is taken as the reference to comply with the commitment to "identify, take inventory and regularly keep watch over/monitor the biological diversity of the Basin's aquatic and terrestrial ecosystems and to take all appropriate conservation measures, with special attention to endangered species and species offering the greatest potential for sustainable utilisation"[27] and for the sharing of the benefits from the use of genetic resources.[28] Also in relation to this last purpose, the Charter refers to the Nagoya Protocol on Access to Genetic Resources and the Fair and Equitable Sharing of Benefits Arising from their Utilization to the Convention on Biological Diversity.[29] With regard to the management

20 Superseded by the Protocol of 2010 to the International Convention on Liability and Compensation for Damage in Connection with the Carriage of Hazardous and Noxious Substances by Sea, 30 April 1996, https://www.hnsconvention.org/wp-content/uploads/2018/08/2010-HNS-Protocol_e.pdf [not yet in force].

21 Draft Water Charter for the Volta River Basin, Article 37.1.

22 Basel Convention on the Control of Transboundary Movements of Hazardous Wastes and their Disposal, March 22, 1989, 1673 U.N.T.S. 57.

23 Bamako Convention on the Ban of the Import into Africa and the Control of Transboundary Movement and Management of Hazardous Wastes within Africa, January 30, 1991, 2101 U.N.T.S. 177.

24 Rotterdam Convention on the Prior Informed Consent Procedure for Certain Hazardous Chemicals and Pesticides in International Trade, September 10, 1998, 2244 U.N.T.S. 337.

25 Stockholm Convention on Persistent Organic Pollutants, May 22, 2001, 2256 U.N.T.S. 119.

26 Convention on Biological Diversity, June 5, 1992, 1760 U.N.T.S. 79.

27 Draft Water Charter for the Volta River Basin, Article 38.1.

28 Ibid. Article 133.1.

29 Nagoya Protocol on Access to Genetic Resources and the Fair and Equitable Sharing of Benefits Arising from their Utilization to the Convention on Biological Diversity, October 29, 2010, 3008 U.N.T.S.

of the internationally listed ecosystems, it is simply stated that the Parties must abide by the ratified conventions on the subject,[30] which are the Ramsar Convention[31] and the Convention for the protection of the world cultural and natural heritage.[32]

Albeit rare, inter-treaty references are the most reliable way of ensuring legal integration since they do not leave much room for doubt as to the extent to which the referred norm must be applied. However, it is precisely this legal uncertainty that might be considered their main weakness, since it does not allow for an evolutionary interpretation. Only if the referred norm is modified will the referring norm be adapted to the new standards and needs. In this regard, inter-regime references might provide a more balanced option to ensure inter-disciplinary integration in international basin agreements.

2 General Treaty References to Regimes Regulating a Dimension of Sustainable Development: Inter-Regime References

This technique consists of a generic reference to the content of a norm regulating a certain issue. According to Rodrigo, this option has three main characteristics. First, the integrating norm must be conventional, but the referred norms can be either conventional law or customary law or may even refer to soft law acts. Second, since the reference is generic, it obliges to identify the affected norms or acts. Third, the content of the referred norms can vary, which gives the integrating norm a dynamic nature.[33] This type of inter-regime reference might be considered an application of the principle of integration as long as the linked regimes can be framed in different dimensions of sustainable development. An example of this technique from international environmental law

30 Draft Water Charter for the Volta River Basin, Article 42.2.

31 Convention on wetlands of international importance especially as waterfowl habitat, February 2, 1971, 996 U.N.T.S. 245.

32 Convention for the protection of the world cultural and natural heritage, November 16, 1972, 1037 U.N.T.S. 151.

33 Rodrigo, "La Integración Normativa y La Unidad Del Derecho Internacional Público," 327. On the topic of interactions between regimes see, for instance, Casanovas, "Aproximación a Una Teoría de Los Regímenes En Derecho Internacional Público"; Young E., Margaret. 2011. *Trading Fish, Saving Fish: The Interaction between Regimes in International Law*. Cambridge University Press; Asselt, *The Fragmentation of Global Climate Governance*, 44–59; Trevisanut, Seline, Nikolaos Giannopoulos, and Rozemarijn Roland Holst. 2020. "Introduction: Regime Interaction in Ocean Governance." In *Regime Interaction in Ocean Governance*, edited by Seline Trevisanut, Nikolaos Giannopoulos, and Rozemarijn Roland Holst, 1–21. Leiden: Brill Nijhoff.

would be Article 16.2 of the CBD[34] as it refers to the legislation on the protection of intellectual property in order to regulate access to and transfer of biotechnology between the Parties to the treaty. This article states that:

> Access to and transfer of technology referred to in paragraph 1 above to developing countries shall be provided and/or facilitated under fair and most favourable terms, including on concessional and preferential terms where mutually agreed, and, where necessary, in accordance with the financial mechanism established by Articles 20 and 21. In the case of technology subject to patents and other intellectual property rights, such access and transfer shall be provided on terms which recognize and are consistent with the adequate and effective protection of intellectual property rights.[35]

In the law regulating international watercourses, very few instances of this technique could be found. From the two universal conventions, only two provisions are relevant in relation to this Section. On the one hand, Article 29 of the UN Watercourses Convention refers to the principles and international norms applicable in the event of armed conflict to affirm that they also protect international watercourses and related installations, facilities, and other works.[36] With that provision, the clauses regarding the environment in instruments such as the 1949 Protocol additional to the Geneva Conventions of 12 August 1949 and relating to the Protection of Victims of International Armed Conflicts (Protocol I)[37] become directly applicable to international watercourses.

On the other hand, Article 8 of the UNECE Water Convention establishes that the obligation to share information under this convention must respect the "applicable supranational regulations to protect information related to industrial and commercial secrecy, including intellectual property."[38] This clause might refer at least to the 26 treaties administered by the World Intellectual Property Organisation (WIPO).[39]

34 Convention on Biological Diversity, June 5, 1992, 1760 U.N.T.S. 79. Article 16.2.

35 Ibid.

36 Convention on the Law of the Non-Navigational Uses of International Watercourses, May 21, 1997, 2999 U.N.T.S. Article 29.

37 Protocol additional to the Geneva Conventions of 12 August 1949, and relating to the Protection of Victims of International Armed Conflicts (Protocol I), June 8, 1977, 1125 U.N.T.S. 3.

38 Convention on the Protection and Use of Transboundary Watercourses and International Lakes, March 17, 1992, 1936 U.N.T.S. 269. Article 8.

39 For a full list of all those treaties see the WIPO website. WIPO. n.d. "WIPO-Administered Treaties." Accessed June 22, 2023. https://www.wipo.int/treaties/en/.

Regarding the law applicable to basin agreements, possibly the clearest uses of references to other regimes as an integration technique are those made in two international basin agreements to the international regulations on the protection of the marine environment. On the one hand, the treaty between Moldova and Ukraine on the protection of the Dniester River Basin establishes that the measures for the protection of the Black Sea should be adopted "taking into account applicable international norms and standards."[40] Such a provision constitutes a reference to the regime of protection of the Black Sea, which might include both general treaties on protection of biodiversity (e.g. the CBD or the Ramsar Convention) or regional treaties on the protection of specific areas, such as the Mediterranean Sea (e.g. the Convention for the Protection of the Mediterranean Sea Against Pollution)[41] or the Black Sea itself (e.g. the Convention on the Protection of the Black Sea Against Pollution).[42]

On the other hand, the Great Lakes Water Quality Agreement between Canada and the United States of America provides that the programs and measures adopted to prevent and control vessel discharges that are harmful to the quality of water must "take into account relevant standards and guidance issued under the auspices of the International Maritime Organization (IMO)", in relation to discharges of oil and hazardous polluting substances, of garbage, and of aquatic invasive species and pathogens as a result of biofouling and from antifouling systems. This provision refers to a regime that might include up to nine different multilateral treaties.[43]

40 Dniester River Basin Treaty, Article 14. In that case, the applicable norms might range from the CBD to the Ramsar Convention.

41 Convention for the protection of the Mediterranean Sea against pollution (with annex and Protocols for the prevention of pollution of the Mediterranean Sea by dumping from ships and aircraft and Protocol concerning co-operation in combating pollution of the Mediterranean Sea by oil and other harmful substances in cases of emergency), February 16, 1976, 1102 U.N.T.S. 27.

42 Convention on the Protection of the Black Sea Against Pollution, April 21, 1992, 1764 U.N.T.S.

43 Great Lakes Water Quality Agreement, Annex 5, Article B.3 and, section Discharges, 1(c)(i), 2(b), 4 and 5. The treaties included in the regime referred by this provision are: the 1972 Convention on the Prevention of Marine Pollution by Dumping of Wastes and Other Matter; the 1973 International Convention for the Prevention of Pollution from Ships; the 1974 International Convention for the Safety of Life at Sea; the 1983 United Nations Convention on the Law of the Sea; the 1990 International Convention on Oil Pollution Preparedness, Response and Co-operation and its Protocol adopted in 2000; the 2001 International Convention on the Control of Harmful Anti-fouling Systems on Ships; the 2004 International Convention for the Control and Management of Ships' Ballast Water and Sediments; and the 2009 Hong Kong International Convention for the Safe and Environmentally Sound Recycling of Ships.

Examples of integration through references to other regimes also include the provisions of two international basin agreements referring to the applicable environmental law. In the case of the Water Charter of the Lake Chad Basin, the reference to "all applicable environmental norms" is made to establish the need to conduct regular environmental audits.[44] In the case of the Water Charter for the Volta River Basin, a reference is made in general terms to the responsibility of all the Parties in the "application of legislation and regulations on water resources and the environment."[45] In both cases, international environmental law is not mentioned explicitly, but it might be deemed to be included insofar as it is applicable in the basin.

Finally, the Danube River Protection Convention refers to the supranational and international regulation of EIAs.[46] Given that all the Danube Basin States are members of the UNECE and Parties to the Espoo Convention, this instrument should be considered the minimum referred norm of this regime, which is in turn applicable to any planned developmental activity in the basin with transboundary impact. This is also the case of the Water Charter for the Volta River Basin, which states that in order to prevent pollution at the source, the Parties, the Authority, and other stakeholders must conduct environmental assessments according to the regulations applicable in each country. Since the Espoo Convention is not applicable to the basin States of the Volta and international law does not regulate the content of EIAs, this provision of the Water Charter for the Volta River Basin is not affected by international law beyond the obligation to conduct EIAs in due diligence.

In this regard, it must be recalled that in *Pulp Mills on the River Uruguay (Argentina v. Uruguay)* the ICJ considered that, although each State is responsible for determining its own rules concerning impact assessments, it deemed as implicit in the due diligence that, "where necessary", the environmental impact of a project should be monitored throughout its life.[47] In the same case, Argentina alleged that Uruguay had failed to comply with Article 41(a) of the 1975 Statute of the Uruguay River,[48] which in turn required the application of

44 Water Charter of the Lake Chad Basin, Article 46.

45 Draft Water Charter for the Volta River Basin, Article 159.2.

46 Danube River Protection Convention, Article 7(5)(f).

47 Pulp Mills on the River Uruguay (Argentina v. Uruguay), 2010 Judgment, I.C.J. Rep. 14 (April 20). Para. 205.

48 This article reads: "Sin perjuicio de las funciones asignadas a la Comisión en la materia, las Partes se obligan a: a) Proteger y preservar el medio acuático y, en particular, prevenir su contaminación, dictando las normas y adoptando las medidas apropiadas, de conformidad con los convenios internacionales aplicables y con adecuación, en lo pertinente, a las pautas y recomendaciones de los organismos técnicos internacionales." In Statutes of the River Uruguay, February 26, 1975, 1295 U.N.T.S. 331, Article 41(a).

the CITES Convention, the Biodiversity Convention, and the Ramsar Convention. Since this Article does not refer to the three conventions explicitly and just contains an obligation to protect and preserve the aquatic environment in conformity with the applicable international conventions, it can be considered an inter-regime reference. Although the Court did not find that Uruguay had breached this obligation, it did affirm that those conventions were applicable according to Article 41(a) of the 1975 Statute.[49]

Another form of linking regimes for integration is the inclusion in a treaty of references to principles that are specific to another regime. The principle thus becomes applicable in a different legal context. If the treaty containing the reference pertains to a different regime to the referred principle, and both regimes can be identified as bearing on two different dimensions of sustainable development, then it produces legal integration in the sense of the principle of integration. This can be considered a regime-linking technique since the interpretation of the referred principle will be subject to its development in its context of origin. However, the integration is not with the whole of the other regime, but with an undetermined part of it: the part that regulates the principle. It could therefore be argued that this is an intermediate measure between an inter-treaty reference and an inter-regime reference.

In the specific area of international basin agreements, the references to principles from another regime that could be identified are taken exclusively from international environmental law. The most frequent reference is to the polluter-pays principle, which is present in the vast majority of the agreements analysed here[50] and is a well-established principle of international environmental law. It was included among the principles of the Rio Declaration of 1992,[51] has been extensively applied by the EU in several policy domains,[52] and

49 Pulp Mills on the River Uruguay (Argentina v. Uruguay), 2010 Judgment, I.C.J. Rep. 14 (April 20). Para. 262–264.

50 The Niger Basin Water Charter, Article 8; Charter of Waters of the Senegal River, Article 18; Water Charter of the Lake Chad Basin, Article 7.d°); Danube River Protection Convention, Article 2(4); Dniester River Basin Treaty, Article 4.2.d); Great Lakes Water Quality Agreement, Article 2.4(h); Convention on the Protection of the Rhine, Article 4(d); Draft Water Charter for the Volta River Basin, Article 4.n.

51 United Nations Conference on Environment and Development, *Rio Declaration on Environment and Development*, in Report of the United Nations Conference on Environment and Development, A/CONF.151/26 (Vol. 1) (12 August 1992), undocs.org/en/A/CONF.151/26/Rev.1(vol. I). Principle 16.

52 See, for instance: EU Water Framework Directive (Directive 2000/60/EC of the European Parliament and of the Council of 23 October 2000 establishing a framework for Community action in the field of water policy, 2000 O.J. (L 327) 1, 73.); Directive 2004/35/CE of the European Parliament and of the Council of 21 April 2004 on environmental liability with regard to the prevention and remedying of environmental damage, 2004 O.J. (L 143) 56,

has also been applied by Organisation for Economic Co-operation and Development (hereinafter, OECD) countries, largely guided by soft law instruments developed by this organisation.[53] The polluter-pays principle is firmly established in international environmental law,[54] and its inclusion in an international basin agreement allows for its application in this specific framework of cooperation according to international standards, notwithstanding any specific regulations the Parties may have established in the agreement itself, or through another instrument.

Beyond the polluter-pays principle, it only remains to mention the principles of prevention and precaution, which are also enshrined in several of the international basin agreements analysed. They are not discussed further here as they are the subject of Chapter 7 on 'integrative treaty principles'. However, it can be derived from this that nothing prevents a principle enshrined in a treaty being both integrative in nature and serving the principle of integration as an inter-regime reference in the sense given in this Chapter. This is certainly the case of the principles of prevention and precaution, which are integrative due to their inherent characteristics but are also well-established principles of international environmental law.[55] As such, the inclusion of integrative principles in international basin agreements also works as a link with a specific

75; Directive 2010/75/EU of the European Parliament and of the Council of 24 November 2010 on industrial emissions, 2010 O.J. (L 334) 17, 119; Directive 2008/98/EC of the European Parliament and of the Council of 19 November 2008 on waste and repealing certain Directives, 2008 O.J. (L 312) 3, 30; Directive 2012/18/EU of the European Parliament and of the Council of 4 July 2012 on the control of major-accident hazards involving dangerous substances, amending and subsequently repealing Council Directive 96/82/EC Text with EEA relevance, 2012 O.J. (L 197) 1, 37; Directive 2009/147/EC of the European Parliament and of the Council of 30 November 2009 on the conservation of wild birds, 2010 O.J. (L 20) 7, 25; Council Directive 92/43/EEC of 21 May 1992 on the conservation of natural habitats and of wild fauna and flora, 1992 O.J. (L 206) 7, 50.

53 See, for instance: OECD, 2022, *Recommendation of the Council on the Implementation of the Polluter-Pays Principle*, OECD/LEGAL/0132 (14 November 1974), https://legalinstruments.oecd.org/en/instruments/11; and OECD, *The Polluter-Pays principle: Analyses and Reccommendations*, OCDE/GD(92)81 (1992), https://one.oecd.org/document/OCDE/GD(92)81/En/pdf.

54 On the legal status of the polluter-pay principle see Schwartz, Priscilla. 2018. "The Polluter-Pays Principle." In *Principles of Environmental Law*, edited by Ludwig Krämer and Emanuela Orlando, 260–72. Cheltenham: Edward Elgar. 264.

55 For a complete explanation on the legal status of the principle of prevention see Duvic-Paoli, Leslie-Anne. 2018. "Principle of Prevention." In *Principles of Environmental Law*, edited by Ludwig Krämer and Emanuela Orlando, 161–73. Cheltenham: Edward Elgar. For a complete explanation on the legal status of the precautionary principle see Sands et al. *Principles of International Environmental Law*, 217–228.

regime that can be included in the environmental dimension of sustainable development.

3 Other Integrative Inter-Disciplinary Techniques

It might also be found in some international basin agreements references to other two types of instruments different from treaties or regimes which might be considered inter-disciplinary integration techniques as long as they create links between economic, social and environmental dimensions. The first type are the references in one international basin agreement to soft law instruments, although it should be acknowledged that these are rather rare cases. This can be found, on the one hand, in the Great Lakes Water Quality Agreement, which refers to the Rio Declaration to determine the sense of the polluter-pays and precaution principles.[56] On the other hand, the Water Charter of the Volta River Basin makes reference to two regulatory acts of the Economic Community of West African States (ECWAS) on the issue of transhumance: the Decision A/DEC-5/10/98 of 31 October 1998 on the regulation of transhumance between the member States of the Economic Community of West African States; and Rule C/REG.3/01/03 of 28 January 2003 on the enforcement of transhumance regulations among the member States of the Economic Community of West African States.[57] While it is difficult to classify the ECWAS acts in one of the sustainable development dimensions, these references together with the one to the CBD might have legal effects as they become compulsory sources of interpretation for the Charter.

The second type is the inclusion in an international basin agreement of a mandate to cooperate with an international organisation. This is the case of the Framework Agreement on the Sava River Basin, Article 12 of which states that in the application of the agreement, the Parties must cooperate with the International Commission for Protection of Danube River, the Danube Commission, the UNECE, and the EU.[58] The integrative character of this mandate with inter-treaty references is given first and foremost by the fact that, as international bodies, each of the four organisations is constituted by a treaty, but also by the fact that the latter two cover a wide range of issue-areas pertaining to the different domains of sustainable development. As such, a mandate to cooperate can be considered an indirect reference to a treaty, which in turn

56 Great Lakes Water Quality Agreement, Article 2.4(h) and 2.4(i).

57 Draft Water Charter for the Volta River Basin, Article 76.2.

58 Framework Agreement on the Sava River Basin, Article 5.

might produce normative integration as long as the grounds for cooperation concern a part of the referred treaty pertaining to a dimension of sustainable development. It should be recalled in this regard that several IRBOs have signed memorandums of understanding with international organisations to regulate the conditions of their cooperation.[59]

59 See, for instance, the Memorandum of Understanding between the International Commission for the Protection of the Black Sea (ICPBS) and the International Commission for the Protection of the Danube River (ICPDR) on common strategic goals, Document No.: IC/027 Version: FINAL; or the MRC. (2010). Memorandum of Understanding (MoU) Between the Mekong River Commission Secretariat and the ASEAN Secretariat. Vientiane: MRC Secretariat. https://doi.org/10.52107/mrc.ajhypd

CHAPTER 7

Legal Integration through Norms that Promote the Consideration of Economic, Social and Environmental Values in the Application of International Basin Agreements

Intentional Integration

Conceptually, intentional integration refers to norms whose purpose is to promote the integration of sustainable development dimensions in a given area, process or level of governance. The ILA report mentions this form of legal integration *en passant* and does not elaborate on it beyond stating that it consists of "the elaboration of rules – and concepts – that are purposely devised to promote the interrelationship between subject areas in the furtherance of a particular issue."[1] Rodrigo defines intentional integration as "una modalidad de integración en la que la norma exige a los Estados que, cuando adopten las medidas que sean pertinentes en cada caso, consideren, incorporen y evalúen sus repercusiones, incluidos beneficios, desventajas y costes, respecto a los aspectos económicos, sociales y ambientales."[2]

Intentional integration could therefore be understood as the use of legal techniques that oblige those entitled to apply the rule to apply it in an integrative manner, even if there is no explicit or implicit mandate to do so. In other words, the existence of such legal techniques would impede the application of norms that do not consider the three dimensions of sustainable development, even where no specific mandate exists, as in the cases explained in sections 1 and 2 of this Chapter.

Three legal integration techniques can be identified for the operationalisation of intentional integration. The first, and possibly the strongest guarantee of an effective application of the principle of integration, is the inclusion in a treaty of the different interests and values of sustainable development. This measure is independent of the inclusion of the objective of sustainable development or an explicit reference to the principle of integration.

---

1 ILA. Committee on International Law on Sustainable Development. 2006. "Report of the Toronto Conference." https://www.ila-hq.org/en_GB/documents/conference-report-toronto-2006-14. 17.

2 Rodrigo, *El Desafío Del Desarrollo Sostenible*, 157.

 | DOI:10.1163/9789004736757_011

The second technique is the derivation of integrative effects from the specific features of certain principles meant to govern a treaty. In other words, some principles might necessarily imply integration to a certain extent although it is not their main aim. Examples include the principles of prevention and precaution.

Finally, integration can be operationalised through the use in a given instrument of concepts originally developed in soft law instruments, whose use and acknowledgment by the States requires an integrated approach. Relevant examples are ecosystem services and the concept of security applied to water resources.

1 The Inclusion of the Different Values of Sustainable Development in International Basin Agreements: Intra-Treaty Integration

Treaties can include the principle of integration indirectly by enshrining economic development and environmental protection as legally protected global goods, either in the same clause or in separate dispositions throughout the treaty. This is partially coincident with the concept of intra-treaty integration used by the ILA.[3] However, from its definition it is unclear whether the mere inclusion of sustainable development in a treaty would also amount to intra-treaty integration. In any case, these are sufficiently distinct mechanisms as to be classified in different categories. In this research, intra-treaty integration is only understood in the sense described in the current Section.

The UN Watercourses Convention, for instance, considers on an apparently equal footing social and economic interests together with "[g]eographic, hydrographic, hydrological, climatic, ecological and other factors of a natural character."[4] The principle of integration might be found indirectly embedded in international basin agreements, since all of them protect to a certain extent interests of two or all three dimensions of sustainable development. In order to analyse the relevant instruments in an orderly manner, the environmental aspects will be analysed first and the social aspects second. The economic dimension is not addressed specifically as it is assumed that economic interests have traditionally been the main drivers of international watercourse use.

Most of the international basin agreements considered here contain a generic reference to environmental protection. Environmental protection is

3 ILA Report of the Toronto Conference, *supra* note 1, 14–16.

4 Convention on the Law of the Non-Navigational Uses of International Watercourses, May 21, 1997, 2999 U.N.T.S. Article 6.1, Paras. (a) and (b).

usually formulated as a general objective of the treaty itself. The Parties to the Mekong Agreement, for instance, agree "[t]o protect the environment, natural resources, aquatic life and conditions, and ecological balance of the Mekong River Basin from pollution or other harmful effects resulting from any development plans and uses of water and related resources in the Basin."[5] However, environmental protection can also be included in international basin agreements as an aspect to be taken into account in specific areas of cooperation, such as the regulation of pollution[6] or the marine environment.[7]

All basin agreements also contain provisions for the protection of specific environmental aspects, albeit to a varying degree. First, it is common for ecosystems to be protected either in general terms,[8] through provisions against water pollution[9] and invasive species,[10] or as a parameter to determine the ecological flow.[11] The Treaty between the Government of the Republic of Moldova and the Cabinet of Ministers of Ukraine on Cooperation in the Field of Protection and Sustainable Development of the Dniester River Basin, for instance, refers to ecosystems in each of these senses.[12]

Moreover, some international basin agreements also regard the state of ecosystems as a parameter to determine the equitable and reasonable use of the international watercourse[13] or the prohibition of causing environmental damage.[14] Article 7 of the Mekong Agreement, for instance, obliges the Parties "[t]o make every effort to avoid, minimise and mitigate harmful effects that might occur to the environment, especially the water quantity and quality, the aquatic (eco-system) conditions, and ecological balance of the river system,

5 Mekong Agreement, Article 3. See also in this regard: Dniester River Basin Treaty, Article 1.1; The Niger Basin Water Charter, Article 2; Charter of Waters of the Senegal River, Article 4; Water Charter of the Lake Chad Basin, Article 8; Treaty for Amazonian Cooperation, July 3, 1978, ECOLEX TRE-000515, Articulo 1.

6 Draft Water Charter for the Volta River Basin, Article 24.2.a).

7 Dniester River Basin Treaty, Article 14.

8 Charter of Waters of the Senegal River, Article 2, para. 3; The Niger Basin Water Charter, Article 2, para. 7; Water Charter of the Lake Chad Basin, Article 4.d); Danube River Protection Convention, Article 2(3) and 5; Draft Water Charter for the Volta River Basin, Articles 1.2.c).

9 Draft Water Charter for the Volta River Basin, Article 24.2.

10 Water Charter of the Lake Chad Basin, Article 30; Charter of Waters of the Senegal River, Article 16, para. 4.

11 Framework Agreement on the Sava River Basin, Article 11.a).

12 See articles 8, 9.2, 12.2 and 12.3 of the Dniester River Basin Treaty.

13 Water Charter of the Lake Chad Basin, Articles 10 and 13.c°); Draft Water Charter for the Volta River Basin, Articles 13.1.d).

14 Danube River Protection Convention, Article 5(1) in relation to 1(c); Water Charter of the Lake Chad Basin, Article 29.

from the development and use of the Mekong River Basin water resources or discharge of wastes and return flows."[15]

Second, and closely related to the examples above, protection of biodiversity is often the object of protection by such agreements, either as an objective of the treaty[16] or as a specific reason for pollution control.[17] Sometimes the concept is not explicitly included but may be derived from the treaty's own definition of environmental protection. The Senegal Water Charter, for example, sets the objective to "déterminer les règles relatives à la préservation et à la protection de l'environnement, particulièrement en ce qui concerne la faune, la flore, les écosystèmes des plaines inondables et des zones humides."[18]

Third, wetlands are also an object of protection, most often in relation to the protection of their particular ecosystems,[19] the need to maintain the necessary flow of water,[20] as a parameter to balance the equitable and reasonable utilisation of the international watercourse,[21] or to set the water quality standards for their maintenance.[22] Annex III of The Danube River Protection Convention, for instance, mentions wetlands specifically as an example of the objectives of establishing quality standards for water. In this regard, Parties shall "[t]ake into account specific requirements regarding sensitive and specially protected waters and their environment, e.g. lakes, zones for the protection of bank-filtered water and wetlands."[23]

Finally, other specific environmental interests may also appear in international watercourse agreements, such as the protection against desertification,[24] the protection of soils[25] or the fight against climate change.[26] One of the most

15 Mekong Agreement, Article 7.

16 The Niger Basin Water Charter, Article 12, para. 10; Water Charter of the Lake Chad Basin, Article 4.d); Draft Water Charter for the Volta River Basin, Article 1.2.c); Dniester River Basin Treaty, Article 1.2.c).

17 Water Charter of the Lake Chad Basin, Article 24; Draft Water Charter for the Volta River Basin, Article 29.2.

18 Charter of Waters of the Senegal River, Article 2, para. 3.

19 Charter of Waters of the Senegal River, Article 2, para. 3; Water Charter of the Lake Chad Basin, Article 4.b); Dniester River Basin Treaty, Article 12.3; Great Lakes Water Quality Agreement, Article 3.1(a)(v).

20 The Niger Basin Water Charter, Article 4, para. 14; Framework Agreement on the Sava River Basin, Article 11.a).

21 Water Charter of the Lake Chad Basin, Article 13.c°); Draft Water Charter for the Volta River Basin, Article 13.d).

22 Framework Agreement on the Sava River Basin, Article 11.a).

23 Danube River Protection Convention, Annex III(d).

24 Water Charter of the Lake Chad Basin, Article 29.

25 Water Charter of the Lake Chad Basin, Article 31; Draft Water Charter for the Volta River Basin, Articles 1.2.c) and 43–46.

26 The Niger Basin Water Charter, Article 12, paragraph 4; Great Lakes Water Quality Agreement, annexes 3, 2, 4, 6, 7, 8, 9; Draft Water Charter for the Volta River Basin, Articles 13.1.q) and 53–56.

comprehensive agreements in this regard is the Water Charter of the Lake Chad Basin, Article 29 of which states: "The State Parties and the Commission undertake all necessary measures to prevent damage-causing situations affecting the ecosystems in the Lake Chad Basin, such as silting, erosion, bank degradation, flooding, drought, desertification or deforestation."[27]

In relation to soil protection, Article 31 states: "The State Parties undertake all necessary measures to prevent and control soil degradation by adopting long-term, integrated soil conservation and sustainable management strategies, and to control erosion, improper use of soils and the degradation of their physical, chemical, biological and economic properties."[28] Also relevant is Article 13, which establishes that the State Parties shall, in the pursuit of the obligation of equitable and sustainable utilisation, take into account factors including "[t]he effects of climate variability and climate change."[29]

From another perspective, the protection of interests that can be framed in the social dimension of sustainable development is also present in international basin agreements. Of these interests, the most directly related to water and the most widely enshrined in this kind of instrument is access to water by the populations dependent on the watercourse. In fact, several of the international basin agreements that provide a list of factors to be taken into account to determine the equitable and reasonable utilisation of the watercourse include the population dependent on the basin as one of these factors.[30]

For example, the Agreement on the Establishment of the Zambezi Watercourse Commission establishes that "[i]n the application of [Equitable and Reasonable Utilisation] the Technical Committee shall take into account all the relevant factors, and circumstances including the following: [...] (c) the population dependent on the Zambezi Watercourse in each Member State."[31] Such consideration might be considered inspired by Article 6 of the UN Watercourses Convention also fixing as a parameter of equitable and reasonable utilisation "[t]he population dependent on the watercourse in each watercourse State."[32]

Particularly in African international basin agreements, access to water is a key parameter to be considered in the equitable and reasonable utilisation of the watercourse. This is usually stated in terms of the right to water of the

27 Water Charter of the Lake Chad Basin, Article 29.

28 Ibid. Article 31.

29 Ibid. Article 13.r°).

30 Water Charter of the Lake Chad Basin, Article 13.d°); The Niger Basin Water Charter, Article 4, para. 6; Draft Water Charter for the Volta River Basin, Article 13.1.c).

31 Agreement on the establishment of the Zambezi Watercourse Commission, Article 13.3.c).

32 UN Watercourses Convention, *supra* note 4. Article 6.1(c).

population living in the basin.[33] In line with the recognition of this right to water, it is also common to find a clause intended to secure access to water for human needs in cases where there is competition between uses.[34] The Charter of Waters of the Senegal River, for instance, states that:

> L'Organisation, en fonction des demandes des utilisateurs, fixe les priorités entre les besoins, ainsi que la consommation d'eau nécessaire. Aucun usage ne bénéficie d'une priorité par rapport aux autres conformément aux principes du droit international.
>
> Toutefois, en cas de pénurie de la ressource, une attention particulière sera accordée à l'approvisionnement en eau potable et aux usages domestiques de l'eau.[35]

This is coherent with the UN Watercourses Convention, of which Article 10, titled "Relationship between different kinds of uses", establishes that "[i]n the absence of agreement or custom to the contrary, no use of an international watercourse enjoys inherent priority over other uses."[36]

Similarly, in the framework of the UNECE Water Convention, Article 6 of the UNECE Protocol on Water and Health[37] is relevant as it lays down priority to access to drinking water and provision of sanitation "within a framework of integrated water-management systems aimed at sustainable use of water resources, ambient water quality which does not endanger human health, and protection of water ecosystems."[38] However, unlike the Water Convention, this Protocol has not been opened to signature by non-members of the UNECE, hence it cannot become applicable elsewhere.

Closely related to the questions of access to drinking water and poverty is the regulation of the uses of water to satisfy food necessities. Soft law instruments such as the Johannesburg Declaration put special emphasis on combating poverty: "We recognize that poverty eradication, changing consumption

33 Water Charter of the Lake Chad Basin, Article 13.0°); The Niger Basin Water Charter, Article 4, para. 12; Draft Water Charter for the Volta River Basin, Article 13.1.0) and 127.

34 Dniester River Basin Treaty, Article 4.3; Water Charter of the Lake Chad Basin, Article 14; The Niger Basin Water Charter, Article 15; Draft Water Charter for the Volta River Basin, Article 15.

35 Charter of Waters of the Senegal River, Article 9.

36 UN Watercourses Convention, *supra* note 4, Article 10.1.

37 Protocol on Water and Health to the 1992 Convention on the Protection and Use of Transboundary Watercourses and international Lakes, June 17, 1999, 2331 U.N.T.S. 202. Article 5(b).

38 Ibid. Article 6.1.

and production patterns, and protecting and managing the natural resource base for economic and social development are overarching objectives of, and essential requirements for sustainable development."[39] In this regard, it is relevant that some international basin agreements also contain the eradication, reduction or prevention of poverty as a goal.[40]

Moreover, in some basin agreements food production is not considered an industrial activity and, depending on the socio-economic structure of the basin, the use of water to grow vegetables or to feed the livestock might be foreseen for "domestic use". African international basin agreements in particular provide quite comprehensive definitions of domestic use. The Water Charter of the Lake Chad Basin defines it as "abstractions to meet the needs of human beings, limited to the quantities necessary for human consumption, hygiene, and livestock or vegetable production for family use only,"[41] while the Charter of Waters of the Senegal River understands *usages domestiques* as "les prélèvements ou les rejets ayant pour objet la satisfaction des besoins des personnes physiques, et limités aux quantités nécessaires à l'alimentation, à l'hygiène et aux productions animales ou végétales destinées à l'usage familial."[42]

Also relevant as a social interest protected by international basin agreements is human health. In some cases, the protection of public health is enshrined as one of the main objectives of the treaty[43] and of the elements comprised in the concepts of damage or transboundary impact,[44] but it is more commonly associated with the prevention and control of pollution.[45] For instance, Annex III of the Treaty between the Government of the Republic of Moldova and the Cabinet of Ministers of Ukraine on Cooperation in the Field of Protection and Sustainable Development of the Dniester River Basin establishes a long list of activities which "shall be primarily considered when defining priorities in

39 World Summit on Sustainable Development, *Johannesburg Declaration on Sustainable Development*, in Report of the World Summit on Sustainable Development, A/CONF.199/20 (26 August-4 September 2002), undocs.org/en/A/CONF.199/20. Para. 11.

40 Charter of Waters of the Senegal River, Article 5.1°, para. 3; Water Charter of the Lake Chad Basin, Article 4.k)(v); Draft Water Charter for the Volta River Basin, Article 5.2.g).

41 Water Charter of the Lake Chad Basin, Article 2.

42 Charter of Waters of the Senegal River, Article 1.18°. See also in this regard: The Niger Basin Water Charter, Article 1.35; Draft Water Charter for the Volta River Basin, Article 3.52.

43 Danube River Protection Convention, Article 2(3); Agreement on the establishment of the Zambezi Watercourse Commission, Article 14.2.

44 Charter of Waters of the Senegal River, Article 16; Water Charter of the Lake Chad Basin, Article 2; Draft Water Charter for the Volta River Basin, Article 3.29.

45 The Niger Basin Water Charter, Article 10.1° and 2°; Water Charter of the Lake Chad Basin, Article 21.a); Great Lakes Water Quality Agreement, Articles 3.1.(a)(iv), 3.1.(b)(ii) and Annex 3; Draft Water Charter for the Volta River Basin, Article 29.2.

developing plans, programs and measures for reduction, control and elimination of pollution" in relation to their effects on human health, among other elements.[46]

In other, more anecdotal, cases, agreements foresee the protection of human health from diseases,[47] the protection from impacts derived from environmental damage,[48] or even the coordination of health systems.[49] In some agreements, the protection of human health is also established as one of the reasons to implement emergency measures through an abbreviated notification procedure.[50]

These norms related to health are in line with some provisions contemplated in the two universal conventions on international watercourses. On the one hand, the UN Watercourses Convention provides that "[w]atercourse States shall, individually and, where appropriate, jointly, prevent, reduce and control the pollution of an international watercourse that may cause significant harm to other watercourse States or to their environment, including harm to human health or safety […]."[51] The UN Watercourses Convention also foresees that protection of human health can justify an immediate implementation of planned measures without complying with the notification procedure.[52]

---

46 "1. water industry and land reclamation; 2. crop production; 3. livestock farming; 4. aquaculture; 5. cement production; 6. sewage sludge disposal; 7. dredging and dock operations; 8. electronics industry; 9. hydroelectric and thermoelectric power generation; 10. fertilizer industry; 11. food industry; 12. forestry; 13. metallurgical industry; 14. mining operations; 15. other organic and inorganic chemical industries; 16. paper and pulp industry; 17. oil refining; 18. oil products pipelines; 19. pharmaceutical industry; 20. development and production of biocides; 21. waste treatment; 22. shipbuilding and ship repair; 23. leather goods industry; 24. textile industry; 25. tourism; 26. transportation; 27. management of domestic solid waste collection and disposal; 28. incineration of wastes and disposal of combustion products; 29. sewage treatment and disposal; 30. activities leading to alteration of riverside natural conditions or to the destruction of habitats" (Dniester River Basin Treaty, Annex I).

47 The Niger Basin Water Charter, Articles 2, paragraph 8 and 10.°; Dniester River Basin Treaty, Article 8.1.c); Water Charter of the Lake Chad Basin, Article 49; Draft Water Charter for the Volta River Basin, Articles 63–64.

48 Dniester River Basin Treaty, Annex II, Article B.1.b).

49 Treaty for Amazonian Cooperation, July 3, 1978, ECOLEX TRE-000515, Article VIII.

50 The Niger Basin Water Charter, Article 24; SADC Protocol on Shared Watercourses, Article 4.1(i), by reference in Agreement on the establishment of the Zambezi Watercourse Commission; Water Charter of the Lake Chad Basin, Article 60; Draft Water Charter for the Volta River Basin, Article 95.

51 UN Watercourses Convention, Article 21.

52 Ibid. Article 19.

On the other hand, the UNECE Water Convention includes the effects on human health in its definition of "transboundary impact,"[53] which seems to have inspired some of the transboundary river basin agreements mentioned above. More important for the development of the UNECE Water Convention in relation to human health is the adoption in 1999 of the UNECE Protocol on Water and Health,[54] the main objective of which is:

> [T]o promote at all appropriate levels, nationally as well as in transboundary and international contexts, the protection of human health and well-being, both individual and collective, within a framework of sustainable development, through improving water management, including the protection of water ecosystems, and through preventing, controlling and reducing water-related disease.[55]

The mere elaboration of such an instrument is already telling of the importance the Parties of the UNECE give to international watercourses for the protection of human health.

Also relevant as social concerns embedded in international basin agreements are the references to education. They are rare and are mostly foreseen as means of promoting the sustainable use of water resources specifically[56] or the natural resources of the basin more generally. The Water Charter of the Lake Chad Basin, for instance, provides that "[t]he State Parties, in cooperation with the Commission, shall take the measures needed to encourage and facilitate awareness-raising in local communities to increase accountability and awareness with a view to better participation in the integrated, sustainable management of water and other natural resources in the Basin,"[57]

Finally, it is relevant to note the inclusion of references to cultural aspects in international basin agreements. Such references are less common, but they can be found in relation to the protection of historical monuments and cultural heritage from transboundary impacts.[58] The Treaty between the

---

53 Convention on the Protection and Use of Transboundary Watercourses and International Lakes, March 17, 1992, 1936 U.N.T.S. 269. Article 1.2.

54 UNECE Protocol on Water and Health, *supra* note 37.

55 Ibid. Article 1.

56 Charter of Waters of the Senegal River, Article 13; Great Lakes Water Quality Agreement, Annex 6, B.2(d); Dniester River Basin Treaty, Annex IV, B2.a); Draft Water Charter for the Volta River Basin, Article 1.3.1) and 148.

57 Water Charter of the Lake Chad Basin, Article 81.

58 Water Charter of the Lake Chad Basin, Article 2; Agreement on the establishment of the Zambezi Watercourse Commission, Article 119; Draft Water Charter for the Volta River Basin, Article 2.29.

Government of the Republic of Moldova and the Cabinet of Ministers of Ukraine on Cooperation in the Field of Protection and Sustainable Development of the Dniester River Basin, for instance, defines transboundary impact as significant adverse effect on the environment, which includes effects on:

> human health and safety, flora, fauna, soil, air, water, climate, landscape, ecosystems and historical monuments or other physical structures or the interaction among these factors; they also include effects on the cultural heritage or social and economic conditions resulting from alterations of those factors.[59]

In a similar vein, some international basin agreements make reference to the importance of safeguarding traditional knowledge related to water[60] or the protection of sacred waters.[61]

Nevertheless, there is a striking lack of consideration of other social interests that are affected by international watercourses. One of the most notorious omissions, especially in the most recent agreements, is perhaps gender equality, which is only included in the Water Charter of the Lake Chad Basin[62] and the Water Charter for the Volta River Basin.[63]

2 Integrative Principles Guiding the Implementation of International Basin Agreements

Most international basin agreements contain lists of principles – in some cases particularly comprehensive ones – that are intended to guide the implementation of the treaty. Given their capacity to inform in a general sense any action that takes place within the framework of cooperation established by the treaty, these principles can potentially have a decisive integrating effect.[64]

---

59 Dniester River Basin Treaty, Article 3.

60 Water Charter of the Lake Chad Basin, Article 75 and 80; Great Lakes Water Quality Agreement, Article 2.4(l) and Annex 10; Draft Water Charter for the Volta River Basin, Article 133.

61 Draft Water Charter for the Volta River Basin, Article 132.3.

62 Water Charter of the Lake Chad Basin, Article 74.

63 Draft Water Charter for the Volta River Basin, Articles 4.g and 131.

64 In relation to this function of principles see Lostal, Marina. 2013. "The Role of Specific Discipline Principles in International Law: A Parallel Analysis between Environmental and Cultural Heritage Law." *Nordic Journal of International Law* 82 (3): 391–415; and Fajardo del Castillo, Teresa. 2018. "Environmental Law Principles and General Principles of

A first obvious example is sustainable development when it is enshrined as a guiding principle, as is the case of the rivers Zambezi, Volta and Rhine, Lake Chad, and the Great Lakes Water Quality Agreement between Canada and the United States of America.[65] The Charter of Waters of the Senegal River is a particular case because although sustainable development is referred to in Article 4, which lays down the guiding principles on water distribution, it is established not as a principle *per se* but as the 'perspective' from which the principles must be interpreted:

> Les principes directeurs de toute répartition des eaux du Fleuve visent à assurer aux populations des Etats riverains, la pleine jouissance de la ressource, dans le respect de la sécurité des personnes et des ouvrages, ainsi que du droit fondamental de l'Homme à une eau salubre, dans la perspective d'un développement durable.[66]

Another principle that might be included in international basin agreements is equitable and reasonable utilisation. It has already been identified as a key element of the law of international watercourses that is related to sustainable development. In this case, however, equitable and reasonable utilisation is only referred as a guiding principle for the implementation of the agreement, rather than as an obligation for the States. Nevertheless, the fact that the principle is enshrined in such a sense does not preclude its use as an obligation in the same treaty.[67] The Water Charter for the Volta River Basin, for instance, establishes the following guiding principle:

> To implement the present Water Charter, the State Parties shall be guided by the following fundamental principles: [...] The principle of equitable and reasonable utilisation of shared water resources: each country has the right to an equitable and reasonable share of water allowing it to

International Law." In *Principles of Environmental Law*, edited by Ludwig Krämer and Emanuela Orlando, 38–51. Cheltenham: Edward Elgar. 54–47.

65 Draft Water Charter for the Volta River Basin, Article 2.4.d); Agreement on the establishment of the Zambezi Watercourse Commission, Article 12(a); Convention on the Protection of the Rhine, Article 4(g); Water Charter of the Lake Chad Basin, Article 7.a°; Great Lakes Water Quality Agreement, Article 2.4(m).

66 Charter of Waters of the Senegal River, Article 4.

67 See, for instance, the Agreement on the establishment of the Zambezi Watercourse Commission, *supra* note 25, Articles 12.1.h) and 13.

> draw the maximum benefit while causing the least possible disadvantage to other countries.[68]

However, Part 2 of Section 2 of this same treaty extensively regulates the equitable and reasonable utilisation of the watercourse and establishes the specific obligation of:

> Considering their common interests in the sustainable management of the Basin, the State Parties shall equitably and reasonably utilise the Basin's surface and ground water in their respective national jurisdictions to obtain optimal, sustainable benefits that are compatible with the legitimate interests of all the countries in the Basin and with the protection of watercourses, aquifers and aquatic and terrestrial ecosystems.[69]

Another principle present in various international agreements, such as those pertaining to the Volta, the Zambezi, Chad Lake, the Niger and the Rhine,[70] is the principle of prevention.[71] Prevention is a principle of environmental law that can be considered to be related to integration, given that its application requires the early detection of the effects of a specific act on the environment in a given context. It is one of the principles behind the obligation to perform an EIA prior to actions that may have an environmental impact. The principle of prevention, therefore, constitutes a link between actions that respond to economic or social interests and the protection of the environment. In this sense, it is also closely related to the obligation not to cause harm, which is fundamental in the law of international watercourses.

The conditionality of prevention on the effective performance of an EIA has been recognised by the ICJ, which in its judgement on *Pulp Mills on the*

---

68 Draft Water Charter for the Volta River Basin, Article 4.d).

69 Ibid. Article 12.

70 Ibid. Articles 2.4.d). See also: Agreement on the establishment of the Zambezi Watercourse Commission, Article 12.1.(c); Water Charter of the Lake Chad Basin, Article 7.bº; Great Lakes Water Quality Agreement, Article 2.4(j); The Niger Basin Water Charter, Article 7; Convention on the Protection of the Rhine, Article 4(b).

71 For a complete definition of the principle of prevention, see Duvic-Paoli, Leslie-Anne. 2018. "Principle of Prevention." In *Principles of Environmental Law*, edited by Ludwig Krämer and Emanuela Orlando, 161–73. Cheltenham: Edward Elgar. On the principle of prevention see also: Sadeleer, Nicolas De. 2021. "The Principles of Prevention and Precaution in International Law: Two Sides of the Same Coin?" In *Research Handbook on International Environmental Law*, 151–87. Cheltenham: Edward Elgar; and Jardim Oliveira, Thiago B. 2013. "La Diligence Due Dans La Prévention Des Dommages à l'environnement." *Brazilian Yearbook of International Law* 2 (13): 205–42.

River Uruguay (*Argentina v. Uruguay*) stated that "due diligence, and the duty of vigilance and prevention which it implies, would not be considered to have been exercised, if a party planning works liable to affect the regime of the river or the quality of its waters did not undertake an environmental impact assessment on the potential effects of such works."[72] Therefore, the inclusion of prevention as a guiding principle for the implementation of an agreement contributes to normative integration in that it requires a prior assessment of the uses of international watercourses, taking into account factors that are different from those that originally motivated the uses in question.

Closely related to the principle of prevention, the precautionary principle is also present in some basin agreements, either in a section on 'principles' or under another similar title.[73] When the treaty provides a definition of the principle of precaution, as in the case of agreements on the Volta, the Dniester, the Niger, Chad Lake and in the Great Lakes Water Quality Agreement between Canada and the United States of America,[74] it largely restates the definition given by Principle 15 of the Rio Declaration: "Where there are threats of serious or irreversible damage, lack of full scientific certainty shall not be used as a reason for postponing cost-effective measures to prevent environmental degradation."[75]

Although the precautionary principle is different from the prevention principle, its capacity to foster integration in the application of an international basin agreement relies on the same aspect. Precaution is to be applied where there is scientific uncertainty as to the effects of a certain activity on the environment.[76] Therefore, it also requires the application of some sort of

72 Pulp Mills on the River Uruguay (Argentina v. Uruguay), 2010 Judgment, I.C.J. Rep. 14 (April 20). Para. 204.

73 See, for instance: Agreement on the establishment of the Zambezi Watercourse Commission, Article 12.1(d); Convention on the Protection of the Rhine, Article 4(a).

74 See: Draft Water Charter for the Volta River Basin, Article 2.4.q); Dniester River Basin Treaty, Article 4.2.c); The Niger Basin Water Charter, Article 6; Water Charter of the Lake Chad Basin, Article 7.hº); Great Lakes Water Quality Agreement, Article 2.4(i).

75 United Nations Conference on Environment and Development, *Rio Declaration on Environment and Development*, in Report of the United Nations Conference on Environment and Development, A/CONF.151/26 (Vol. I) (12 August 1992), undocs.org/en/A/CONF.151/26 /Rev. 1(vol. I). Principle 15.

76 For a complete explanation on the precautionary principle see, generally: Freestone, David, and Ellen Hey, eds. 1996. *The Precautionary Principle and International Law: The Challenge of Implementation*. The Hague: Kluwer Law International; Sands et al. *Principles of International Environmental Law*, 217–228; Sadeleer, "Principles of Prevention and Precaution in International Law"; Wiener, Jonathan B. 2018. "Precautionary Principle." In *Principles of Environmental Law*, edited by Ludwig Krämer and Emanuela Orlando, 174–85. Cheltenham: Edward Elgar.

mechanism to evaluate the cause-effect relationship between a 'developmental' activity and the environment, even if it is to conclude that these effects cannot be determined.

A few international basin agreements also include the principle of participation.[77] The Water Charter for the Volta River Basin understands it as "the permanent, responsible involvement of all the stakeholders in the design, development and implementation, and in the monitoring and evaluation of all sustainable management activities for water resources and the environment in the Basin."[78] This principle also has significant integrative potential. In practice, the integration of the economic, social and environmental dimensions implies coordination with different State and non-State actors representing different interests, such as public institutions, NGOs, water users associations and companies, among others. Even conducting an EIA requires consultation with these actors. This aspect will be further discussed in Part III of the book, but it can be stated here that the more participative the application of an agreement, the greater the guarantee of an integrated outcome, as more stakeholders representing different interests will be taken into account.

The inclusion of principles related to social aspects in international basin agreements is minimal compared to that of environmental principles. Only the Chad Lake and the Volta basin agreements incorporate the principle of gender equality,[79] while no other principles pertaining to social interests or human rights can be found. As noted by Mbengue:

> Les instruments de régulation des cours d'eau transfrontières ne sont pas a priori des instruments de protection des droits de l'homme. C'est là une étape majeure dans la mise en relation du droit international africain de l'eau avec d'autres régimes juridiques internationaux tels le droit international des droits de l'homme.[80]

This mechanism to propel integration, therefore, is clearly underused and represents an opportunity for the development of future basin agreements or for the review of current agreements.

---

77 Water Charter of the Lake Chad Basin, Article 7.g°.

78 Draft Water Charter for the Volta River Basin, Articles 4.j).

79 Water Charter of the Lake Chad Basin, Article 7.n°; Draft Water Charter for the Volta River Basin, Articles 2.4.g).

80 Mbengue, Makane Moïse. 2013. "Les Chartes de l'eau: Vers Une Nouvelle Conception de La Gestion Des Ressources En Eau Partagees En Afrique ?" In *Liber Amicorum Raymond Ranjeva : L'Afrique et Le Droit International : Variations Sur l'organisation Internationale*, edited by M Kamga and M. M. Mbengue, 201–13. Paris: Pedone. 230.

3 The Use in International Basin Agreements of Integrative Approaches Developed by Soft Law Instruments

Treaties in general and international basin agreements in particular might include approaches developed in other fora that introduce dynamic content in a legal text. The advantage of this technique is the capacity it provides to adapt to new scientific and policy advances despite the inherently static nature of a treaty.[81] While integrative approaches do not offer legal certainty, they might facilitate adaptability in the application of the overarching norm. Integrative approaches in the sense used in this research have three characteristics.

First, these approaches must have been developed through soft law instruments – possibly with contributions by the doctrine – and that their content is therefore developed outside binding normative instruments. Second, their content should promote integration, whether between economic, social and environmental aspects at the same time, or between at least two of them. The degree of this integration will depend on whether the approach was developed in soft law instruments, such that it is potentially possible to find more or less integrative visions of the same approach. It therefore falls to the applier and interpreter of the norm to decide which version of the approach is more in line with the sense in which it was included in the legal instrument. Finally, the approach should not be integrative for the sake of it but should be intended to facilitate integration with the purpose of enhancing sustainability. It can therefore be expected that international basin agreements will contain approaches that meet the two prior conditions but do not contribute to sustainable governance of international watercourses. In this case, however, they would not serve the purpose of the principle of integration.

One integrative approach used in international basin agreements is ecosystems services. As mentioned earlier, most of these instruments refer to ecosystems as an object of protection and give them a central role in the integrity of the international watercourse and its capacity to provide the various benefits for the dependent population. Precisely in line with this utilitarian perspective on ecosystems, three international basin agreements include the 'ecosystem services' approach, which is also integrative according to the criteria used here.

Ecosystem services can be found in Annex 7 of the Great Lakes Water Quality Agreement, where their maintenance is directly related to the achievement of the general and specific objectives of the treaty, which encompass

81 See in this regard the adaptive function of soft law in Atapattu, Sumudu. 2012. "International Environmental Law and Soft Law: A New Direction or a Contradiction?" *Non-State Actors, Soft Law and Protective Regimes* 12 (1991): 200–226.

environmental (e.g. protection of aquatic ecosystem health), social (e.g. provision of drinking water; protection of human health) and economic (e.g. protect the food chain from pollution) aspects.[82] Furthermore, this agreement provides a specific definition of ecosystem services according to which they can be considered a strongly integrative approach, given that it establishes numerous relationships of dependence between various aspects pertaining to the different dimensions of sustainable development.[83] However, this approach has also been extensively developed in soft law instruments by various types of entities, such as UN bodies such as the UNECE,[84] an international organisation such as the EU,[85] independent scientific initiatives such as IPBES[86] and, in particular, through the work of the CBD,[87] as well as discussed in doctrine.[88] In this sense, what is understood by ecosystem services may vary depending on the moment at which the above-mentioned basin agreements are applied or the

82 Great Lakes Water Quality Agreement, Article 3.1.

83 "[T]he benefits people obtain from ecosystems such as: energy, food and water, biomedicines, flood prevention, biodiversity, climate regulation, erosion control, pest and pathogen control, soil formation, nutrient cycling, recreation, heritage, spiritual or personal fulfillment and other non-material benefits." (Ibid. Annex 7, Article E).

84 UNECE. 2007. *Recommendations on Payments for Ecosystem Services in Integrated Water Resources Management*. New York and Geneva: United Nations.

85 European Commission, *The Role of the CFP in Implementing an Ecosystem Approach to Marine Management*, COM(2008) 187 final (11 April 2008). 3.

86 UNEP, *Conceptual Framework for the Intergovernmental Science-Policy Platform on Biodiversity and Ecosystem Services Annex Conceptual Framework for the Intergovernmental Science-Policy Platform on Biodiversity and Ecosystem Services*, Decision IPBES/2/4 (2014), https://www.ipbes.net/sites/default/files/downloads/Decision%20IPBES_2_4.pdf

87 See, for instance: Conference of the Parties of the CBD, *Tenth Meeting, Nagoya, Japan, 18–29 October 2010, Decision X/29, 'Marine and Coastal Biodiversity'*, UNEP/CBD/COP/10/27 (29 October 2010), https://www.cbd.int/doc/decisions/cop-10/cop-10-dec-29-en.pdf

88 From a point of view of policy analysis, see, for instance: Muradian, R., M. Arsel, L. Pellegrini, F. Adaman, B. Aguilar, B. Agarwal, E. Corbera, et al. 2013. "Payments for Ecosystem Services and the Fatal Attraction of Win-Win Solutions." *Conservation Letters* 6 (4): 274–79; and Berbés-Blázquez, Marta, José A. González, and Unai Pascual. 2016. "Towards an Ecosystem Services Approach That Addresses Social Power Relations." *Current Opinion in Environmental Sustainability* 19: 134–43. From an economic point of view see, for instance: Pascual, Unai, Jacob Phelps, Eneko Garmendia, Katrina Brown, Esteve Corbera, Adrian Martin, Erik Gomez-Baggethun, and Roldan Muradian. 2014. "Social Equity Matters in Payments for Ecosystem Services." *BioScience* 64 (11): 1027–36. From a legal perspective see, for instance: McIntyre, Owen. 2014. "The Protection of Freshwater Ecosystems Revisited: Towards a Common Understanding of the 'ecosystems Approach' to the Protection of Transboundary Water Resources." *Review of European, Comparative and International Environmental Law* 23 (1): 88–95; Lucia, Vito De. 2018. "A Critical Interrogation of the Relation between the Ecosystem Approach and Ecosystem Services." *Review of European, Comparative and International Environmental Law* 27 (2): 104–14.

specific conditions of the basin, especially in agreements that do not provide their own definition of the concept. Indeed, there is variability among the definitions that could potentially be taken as a reference for an eventual interpretation: while the IPBES considers ecosystem services to be "all the benefits that humanity obtains from nature,"[89] the UNECE is more detailed in its definition:

> 'Ecosystem services' means the benefits people obtain from ecosystems. These include provisioning services such as food, water, timber and fibre; regulating services that affect climate, floods, disease, wastes and water quality; cultural services that provide recreational, aesthetic and spiritual benefits; and supporting services such as soil formation, photosynthesis and nutrient cycling.[90]

The Water Charter of the Lake Chad Basin refers to the services provided by ecosystems as a criterion for assessing the minimum flow to be maintained: "The State Parties undertake to maintain environmental flows at key points in the Basin to protect and preserve the aquatic ecosystems and services rendered by such ecosystems."[91] Similarly, the Water Charter for the Volta River Basin links ecosystem services to the maintenance of minimum streamflows[92] and measures to control pollution of the watercourse.[93] In addition, this instrument links the maintenance of ecosystem services to the principle of equitable and reasonable use by stating ecosystem protection requirements as a factor to be considered in the maintenance of a minimum flow.[94]

---

89 UNEP, *Conceptual Framework for the Intergovernmental Science-Policy Platform on Biodiversity and Ecosystem Services Annex Conceptual Framework for the Intergovernmental Science-Policy Platform on Biodiversity and Ecosystem Services*, Decision IPBES/2/4 (2014), https://www.ipbes.net/sites/default/files/downloads/Decision%20IPBES_2_4.pdf. Annex, Section B, paragraph 8.

90 UNECE. 2007. *Recommendations on Payments for Ecosystem Services in Integrated Water Resources Management*. New York and Geneva: United Nations. 2.

91 Water Charter of the Lake Chad Basin, Article 12 and 13.c°). Precisley in this same excerpt of the Water Charter of the Lake Chad Basin another integrative approach is mentioned: the minimum flow for the protection of ecosystems. While Appendix 2 "establishes the maximum quantities of water abstracted from the Lake's tributaries, their alluvial aquifers, aquifers linked to the Lake and the Lake itself" (Ibid. Appendix 2, 2.1), Appendix 3 allows minimum flows to be established for each measuring station along the river (See Appendix n° 3 of the Water Charter of the Lake Chad Basin, Article 3.2).

92 Draft Water Charter for the Volta River Basin, Articles 3.15, 14.1 and 106.3.a).

93 Ibid. Articles 26.2.

94 Ibid. Articles 13.d).

The condition of aiming to achieve sustainable development in order to be an integrative approach is quite clear in the case of "ecosystem services". Since its overall purpose is to underline the importance of ecosystems for human life, it can be considered to implicitly encompass sustainability in the use of ecosystems. In this regard, it is relevant to note the manner in which this approach is introduced in the Basin Development Strategy for the Mekong River Basin 2021–2030.[95] This document is clearly concerned with protecting wetlands and the watershed because of the services they provide to society and therefore establishes a set of indicators to evaluate how they are impacted by human activities (the extension of the wetland area; the condition of riverine, estuarine and coastal habitats; the condition and status of ecologically significant areas, and the condition and status of fisheries and other aquatic resources).[96] The objective of these vigilance measures is to safeguard the ecosystem services provided by wetlands and watersheds to ensure that a series of economic and social necessities are met. Therefore, as stated in the Strategy, it is expected that:

> By 2030, regional and national development plans are informed by valuation of environmental assets and ecosystem services and agreed limits of acceptable change to ecological conditions, helping to ensure the continuation of the ecosystem services. Forested areas of watersheds are increasing. The key environmental assets of the basin provide a range of ecosystem services including provisioning (e.g. food, fuel, timber), regulating (e.g. flood control, water quality), supporting (e.g. habitat, carbon sequestration), and cultural (e.g. traditional and aesthetic values) services. These services contribute social and economic benefits to basin communities, particularly for poor, resource dependent people in vulnerable situations.[97]

Another type of integrative approach that can be found in the analysed international basin agreements are those deriving from theories on the security of natural resources or the security of aspects and sectors relevant to human life. This is the case of references to food security and energy security, which only appear in the Water Charter of the Lake Chad Basin and the Water Charter for

95 MRC. 2021. *Basin Development Strategy for the Lower Mekong Basin 2021–2030 and the MRC Strategic Plan 2021–2025*. Vientiane: MRC Secretariat. https://www.mrcmekong.org/wp-content/uploads/2024/08/BDS-2021-2030-and-MRC-SP-2021-2025-3.pdf.

96 Ibid. 89.

97 Ibid.

the Volta River Basin. The first agreement mentions food security among the objectives of the treaty and as a way of "[i]mproving the socio-economic conditions of the populations."[98] The second mentions both food and energy security as two criteria to balance the admissible amounts of water abstractions.[99]

These are two of the most recent international basin agreements, which might suggest a tendency towards the inclusion of this approach in agreements regulating cooperation on international basins.

The term 'security' can be understood in the classical sense of national security or in the sense of 'human security'. In accordance with the first sense, several international basin agreements express concerns regarding national and/or public security as a means of limiting the scope of the obligation to share information.[100] Under the Great Lakes Water Quality Agreement, for instance, a limit is set on the US-Ca IJC's powers to request information from the States.[101]

In fact, this exception to the general obligation to exchange information is already included in the two universal conventions on international watercourses. The UN Watercourses Convention provides that "[n]othing in the present Convention obliges a watercourse State to provide data or information vital to its national defence or security,"[102] while the UNECE Water Convention states that "[t]he provisions of this Convention shall not affect the rights or the obligations of Parties in accordance with their national legal systems and applicable supranational regulations to protect information related to industrial and commercial secrecy, including intellectual property, or national security."[103]

However, the sense of the term that can be considered an integrative approach of the kind discussed here is that of human security. While it is true that both food and energy security may *a priori* be of concern from a human security perspective, this does not preclude consideration of their social and economic implications, which would be closely linked to sustainable development. Despite the adoption of human security paradigm by the UN Security

98 Water Charter of the Lake Chad Basin, Article 4.k).

99 Draft Water Charter for the Volta River Basin, Article 15.

100 See: Water Charter of the Lake Chad Basin, Article 5.3.; the Agreement on the establishment of the Zambezi Watercourse Commission, Article 15.4.; the Mekong Agreement, Article 3.; the Danube River Protection Convention, Article 12(5).

101 Great Lakes Water Quality Agreement, Article 7.2.

102 UN Watercourses Convention, *supra* note 4, Article 31.

103 Convention on the Protection and Use of Transboundary Watercourses and International Lakes, March 17, 1992, 1936 U.N.T.S. 269. Article 8.

Council at the late 1990s,[104] its conceptual development has been largely mediated by the annual reports of the UNDP, the first of which, published in 1994, provided a synthetic definition:

> Human security can be said to have two main aspects. It means, first, safety from such chronic threats as hunger, disease and repression. And second, it means protection from sudden and hurtful disruptions in the patterns of daily life – whether in homes, in jobs or in communities. Such threats can exist at all levels of national income and development.[105]

The concerns of food and energy clearly fit within this definition and are considered extensively in other parts of the report, although food constitutes a much greater concern in terms of human security. This same pattern can be seen in the last of 2022.[106]

It must next be asked why food and energy security from a human security perspective should be considered integrative approaches, especially considering that both the energy and the food sectors contribute significantly to the predation of the environment. The answer might be found in the development of the two concepts through soft law instruments. For example, a widely accepted definition of food security is the one forwarded by the Food and Agriculture Organization (hereinafter, FAO) and included in the Declaration of the World Summit on Food Security:[107]

> Food security exists when all people, at all times, have physical, social and economic access to sufficient, safe and nutritious food to meet their dietary needs and food preferences for an active and healthy life. The four pillars of food security are availability, access, utilization and stability. The nutritional dimension is integral to the concept of food security.[108]

---

104 On the role of the UN Security Council in relation to human security see, for example, Dedring, Jürgen. 2004. "Human Security and the UN Security Council." In *Conflict and Human Security: A Search for New Approaches of Peace-Building*, edited by Hideaki Shinoda and Ho-Won Jeong, 45–95. Hiroshima: Institute for Peace Science, Hiroshima University.

105 UNDP. 1994. *Human Development Report 1994*. Oxford: OUP. In relation to human security see also Newman, Edward. 2011. "A Human Security Peace-Building Agenda." *Third World Quarterly* 32 (10): 1737–56.

106 UNDP. 2022. *2022 Special Report on Human Security – New Threats to Human Security in the Anthropocene: Demanding Greater Solidarity*. UNDP.

107 World Summit on Food Security, *Declaration of the World Summit on Food Security*, WSFS 2009/2 (16–18 November 2009), https://www.fao.org/3/k6050e/k6050e.pdf.

108 See footnote 1. In Ibid.

According to this definition, food security requires not only production of sufficient amount and quality but also the stability of production over time.[109]

This same Declaration establishes five principles as a basis for the States to commend their efforts to seek food security, the third of which is especially relevant here, as it expresses the commitment to:

> [S]trive for a comprehensive twin-track approach to food security that consists of: 1) direct action to immediately tackle hunger for the most vulnerable and 2) medium- and long-term sustainable agricultural, food security, nutrition and rural development programmes to eliminate the root causes of hunger and poverty, including through the progressive realization of the right to adequate food.[110]

Among the objectives for the achievement of the second track of this approach are "protection of the environment, conservation of the natural resource base and enhanced use of ecosystem services."[111] In line with these objectives, there is growing acknowledgement of the dependency between food production and the environment, since most of the processes that bring food to the table rely on it.[112] From this point of view, the integrative character of food security seems beyond doubt, together with its aim to contribute to the sustainable governance of spaces such as international basins. In fact, in the governance of international watercourses, the concept of food security spans beyond the framework of sustainable development. The LCBC describes ensuring food security as a potential means of tackling the challenges deriving from a context of armed conflict. In this regard, the 2015 Lake Chad Development and Climate Resilience Action Plan acknowledges the disrupting effects of the armed

---

109 In relation to food security, see Pons Ràfols, Xavier. 2013. "La Seguridad Alimentaria Mundial: La Acción Política e Institucional de La FAO." In *Alimentación y Derecho Internacional. Normas, Instituciones y Procesos*, edited by Xavier Pons Ràfols, 28–81. Madrid: Marcial Pons.; and Pérez de Armiño, Karlos. 2013. "La Gobernanza Global de La Seguridad Alimentaria: Debilidades, Disparidades e Iniciativas de Reforma." In *Alimentación y Derecho Internacional. Normas, Instituciones y Procesos*, edited by Xavier Pons Ràfols, 83–117. Madrid: Marcial Pons.

110 World Summit on Food Security, *Declaration of the World Summit on Food Security*, WSFS 2009/2 (16–18 November 2009), https://www.fao.org/3/k6050e/k6050e.pdf. 3.

111 Ibid. 5.

112 See, for instance, FAO, IFAD, UNICEF, WFP, and WHO. 2022. *The State of Food Security and Nutrition in the World 2022. Repurposing Food and Agricultural Policies to Make Healthy Diets More Affordable*. Rome: FAO.

conflict with Boko Haram on the continuation of activities related to livestock, fishing and farming.[113]

Energy security is more debatable as an integrative approach in the sense considered in this Section. Although the development of the concept has been mostly mediated by a national security approach due to the critical role of energy in the power balances in international relations,[114] the connections between human energy needs and environmental consequences – and their implications for the economy – are undeniable. However, the declining availability of fossil fuels and the increasing affordability of renewable energy technologies make renewable energy more and more attractive in terms of national security. Somewhat paradoxically, then, energy security developed from the perspective of national security could potentially (though unintentionally) contribute to sustainable development.[115]

Nevertheless, the use of this approach by the Water Charter for the Volta River Basin – the only international basin agreement that contains it – suggests that the meaning is coherent with a human security approach, since it establishes that the Parties are to respect an upper limit on the extraction of water to ensure "energy security for their people."[116] The concept of energy security has therefore developed during the last four decades, as exemplified by the International Energy Agency (IEA). If the concept with which it was founded in 1974 by OECD members was focused mainly on the supply of oil,[117] the current IEA's definition of energy security encompasses the idea of sustainability, albeit in a non-explicit manner.[118]

---

113 LCBC, *The Lake Chad Development and Climate Resilience Action Plan*, 102851 v2 (13 November 2015), https://doi.org/10.1596/23793. 2. See also: LCBC. 2018. "Regional Strategy for the Stabilization, Recovery & Resilience of the Boko Haram-Affected Areas of the Lake Chad Basin Region." https://cblt.org/download/rss-strategy/. 36.

114 See, for instance, military approach undertaken by the NATO on energy security. In NATO. 2008. "Bucharest Summit Declaration. Issued by the Heads of State and Government Participating in the Meeting of the North Atlantic Council in Bucharest on 3 April 2008." 2008. https://www.nato.int/cps/en/natohq/official_texts_8443.htm.

115 Fleming, Ruven C. 2021. "The Energy Trilemma." In *Energy Law, Climate Change and the Environment*, edited by Martha M. Roggenkamp, Kars J. de Graaf, and Ruven C. Fleming, 31–40. Cheltenham: Edward Elgar. 34–35.

116 Draft Water Charter for the Volta River Basin, Article 15.

117 OECD, *Decision of the Council Establishing an International Energy Agency of the Organisation. Adopted by the Council at its 373rd Meeting on 15th November* (15 November 1974), https://iea.blob.core.windows.net/assets/ba8c3ef8-f5b3-45db-86d2-719502e8d4ef/decesionofthecouncil.pdf.

118 "[T]he uninterrupted availability of energy sources at an affordable price. Energy security has many aspects: long-term energy security mainly deals with timely investments to supply energy in line with economic developments and environmental needs. On the

Seemingly, in the latest ministerial declaration of the Parties of the IEA, the preoccupation for the sustainability of energy supply in terms of greenhouse gas emissions and the promotion of renewable energy sources is more clear,[119] at least at a rhetorical level, and is added to the initial idea of the mere supply of energy. In this declaration, for instance, the Parties stated that they "call on the IEA to continue to play a leading role in the energy sector transformation in light of climate change, concentrating on helping countries achieve net zero emissions by 2050, and expansion of related job opportunities";[120] and that they "highlight the growing role of zero-emitting gases or hydrogen, with particular attention to renewable forms, in helping to enhance energy security, while reducing emissions."[121]

Since this declaration, the concept used by the IEA appears to be much closer to the one expressed by the Water Charter for the Volta River Basin, but it also seems more coherent with SDG 7, which aims to "[e]nsure access to affordable, reliable, sustainable and modern energy for all."[122] From this point of view, it can be argued that energy security, together with food security, is an integrative approach in the terms described in this Section.

Related to both national security and human security, the concept of environmental security has also gained relevance since its appearance in the early 1980s. However, it does not seem to have been adopted in cooperation in international watercourses since it does not appear in any international basin agreements. This approach has not only been developed by the doctrine, it has also been adopted by the EU in its climate policy, development aid policy, and the Common Foreign and Security Policy.[123]

---

other hand, short-term energy security focuses on the ability of the energy system to react promptly to sudden changes in the supply-demand balance." The definition can be found in the IEA website, although it does not seem to derive from an official declaration adopted by the parties. However, it is in line with the latest ministerial declarations. See, for instance, IEA. n.d. "Energy Security." Accessed October 27, 2022. https://www.iea.org/areas-of-work/ensuring-energy-security.

119 IEA, *IEA Ministerial Communiqué*, (24 March 2022), https://iea.blob.core.windows.net/assets/1899b4ca-933d-4dee-8327-7c12f65b6190/IEA2022Ministerial_Finalcommunique_24March2022.pdf.

120 Ibid. Para. 11.

121 Ibid. Para. 21.

122 United Nations summit for the adoption of the post-2015 development agenda, *Transforming our world: the 2030 Agenda for Sustainable Development*, A/RES/70/1 (21 October 2015), undocs.org/en/A/RES/70/1. Goal 7.

123 For a complete study on this topic see: Schellekens-Gaiffe, Marie-Ange. 2017. "La Sécurité Environnementale Dans Les Relations Extérieures de l'Union Européenne." Université La Rochelle. See also Brunnee, Jutta, and Stephen J. Toope. 1997. "Environmental Security

Finally, and again in relation to the use of the term 'security' in the framework of human security, it is striking that none of the international basin agreements analysed here refers to the 'water security'.[124] A widely accepted definition would be:

> [T]he capacity of a population to safeguard sustainable access to adequate quantities of acceptable quality water for sustaining livelihoods, human well-being, and socio-economic development, for ensuring protection against water-borne pollution and water-related disasters, and for preserving ecosystems in a climate of peace and political stability.[125]

UNESCO had also defined this approach in very similar terms, identifying it with "[t]he capacity of a population to safeguard access to adequate quantities of water of acceptable quality for sustaining human and ecosystem health on a watershed basis, and to ensure efficient protection of life and property against water related hazards – floods, landslides, land subsidence) and droughts."[126]

It is surprising that international water law has not even discussed this approach. This could be due to its relative newness, and international basin agreements adopted in the coming years will possibly be more likely to include it. In any case, the approach is undeniably integrative in terms of linking elements from the three dimensions of sustainable development. It is extensively used, for example, in instruments adopted by IRBOs, such as the Basin Development Strategy for the Mekong River Basin 2021–2030.[127]

---

and Freshwater Resources: Ecosystem Regime Building." *American Journal of International Law* 91 (1): 26–59.

124 For a general analysis of the relationship between water and international security see: Tignino, Mara. 2010. "Water, International Peace, and Security." *International Review of the Red Cross* 92 (879): 647–74; or Huici Sancho, Laura. 2018. "Water and International Security: The Conceptual Framework." In *Agua, Recurso Natural Limitado. Entre El Desarrollo Sostenible y La Seguridad Internacional*, edited by Ana M. Badia Martí and Laura Huici Sancho, 173–84. Madrid: Marcial Pons.

125 UN Water. 2013. *Water Security & the Global Water Agenda: A UN-Water Analytical Brief.* Hamilton, Canada: United Nations University. 1.

126 UNESCO, *International Hydrological Programme (IHP) Eighth Phase: Water Security: Responses to Local, Regional and Global Challenges, Strategic Plan, IHP-VIII (2014–2021)*, IHP/2012/IHP-VIII/1Rev (2012), https://unesdoc.unesco.org/ark:/48223/pf0000218061.locale=en. 5.

127 Basin Development Strategy for the Lower Mekong Basin 2021–2030 and the MRC Strategic Plan 2021–2025, *supra* note 95.

CHAPTER 8

Legal Integration through Mechanisms for the Resolution of International Watercourse Disputes

The resolution of disputes between States concerning the uses of shared water resources may involve the application of rules pertaining to the different areas of sustainable development. One the one hand, then, problems may arise regarding the compatibility between these norms. On the other hand, problems may emerge concerning the way in which each norm should be interpreted in the light of norms also applicable to other dimensions of sustainable development. The first type of problem is usually resolved in accordance with the rules of conflict applicable in international law, which make it possible to determine which of two conflicting rules is applicable in a specific case and which, in turn, would not be applied. The result of applying rules of conflict would therefore be the opposite of normative integration, since if the conflict were to arise between rules belonging to different dimensions of sustainable development, one would prevail over the other.

However, not all regulatory conflicts are resolved through the non-application of one of the conflicting norms since interpretation can provide alternative mechanisms for resolution. As emphasised by the ILC, "when several norms bear on a single issue they should, to the extent possible, be interpreted so as giving rise to a single set of compatible obligations."[1] In this Chapter, therefore, the aim is to analyse which legal interpretation techniques serve the purpose of the principle of integration.

Before analysing these questions, however, it is necessary to delimit the cases under study. Given that the aim is to analyse the interpretation of rules, the disputes analysed must be resolved in accordance with the law. Most disagreements over the use and management of international watercourses are resolved through political or diplomatic mechanisms, provided that they allow the parties to maintain political control of the resolution of the dispute. IRBOs play an important role in those cases by providing a negotiation forum,

1 ILC, *Fragmentation of International Law: Difficulties Arising from the Diversification and Expansion of International Law. Draft conclusions of the work of the Study Group. Finalized by Martti Koskenniemi*, A/CN.4/L.682/Add.1 (2 May 2006), undocs.org/A/CN.4/L.682/Add.1. Para. 4.

 | DOI:10.1163/9789004736757_012

establishing pre-defined mechanisms and technical guidance.[2] However, since in these cases the parties in the dispute seek an agreement of convenience which does not necessarily have to be based on international law, such resolutions cannot be considered to reflect the state of international law. Instead, the resolution of disputes through jurisdictional or arbitral mechanisms will be relevant as an expression of international law: judgments of the ICJ; awards of arbitration courts; or rulings issued by the bodies of the international treaty organisations that have dispute settlement powers.

Regarding the jurisdiction of the ICJ in disputes between States over an international watercourse, there are several international basin agreements that provide for recourse to this court if other mechanisms do not work, such as the Charter of Waters of the Senegal River, the Niger Basin Water Charter, the Framework Agreement on the Sava River Basin, and the Danube River Protection Convention.[3] However, as the ICJ itself has determined, the fact that a treaty does not provide for this recourse does not preclude the Court from declaring itself competent if the parties to the dispute so agree.[4]

International arbitration is also a mechanism to which the parties can resort in a dispute in order to have it resolved by an arbitral tribunal in accordance with the law. It is provided for in some basin agreements, such as the Framework Agreement on the Sava River Basin, the Water Charter of the Lake Chad Basin, the Convention on the Protection of the Rhine, the Boundary Waters Treaty, and the Danube River Protection Convention;[5] although in practice the States have resorted even less to arbitration than to the ICJ in resolving disputes relating to shared watercourses.

Finally, although there is a growing trend towards the internalisation of dispute resolution by IRBOs, few such organisations currently have a body of a jurisdictional nature or with similar attributions. One example is the US-Ca

2 On this matter see: Schmeier, Susanne, and Ivan Zavadsky. 2020. "Managing Disagreements in European Basins What Role for River Basin Organizations in Water Diplomacy?" In *River Basin Organizations in Water Diplomacy*, edited by Anoulak Kittikhoun and Susanne Schmeier, 275–92. Abingdon: Routledge.

3 See: Charter of Waters of the Senegal River, Article 30; Water Charter of the Lake Chad Basin, Article 89; Framework Agreement on the Sava River Basin, Article 22.2; Draft Water Charter for the Volta River Basin, Article 155; The Niger Basin Water Charter, Article 31; Danube River Protection Convention, Article 24.2.a), para. 1.

4 Land and Maritime Boundary between Cameroon and Nigeria (Cameroon v. Nigeria), Preliminary Objections, Judgement, 1998 I.C.J. Rep. 275 (June 11). Para 68.

5 Framework Agreement on the Sava River Basin, Article 22.2; Water Charter of the Lake Chad Basin, *sup*Article 89; Convention on the Protection of the Rhine, Article 16.2; Boundary Waters Treaty, Article X; Danube River Protection Convention, Article 24.2.a), para. 2.

IJC, which on some occasions has been granted quasi-jurisdictional capacities.[6] However, this mechanism is increasingly uncommon both in the framework of the US-Ca IJC and in other IRBOs considered in this work.

1 Integration through Teleological Interpretation of Treaties

Ascertaining the purpose of the parties is a traditional interpretation technique,[7] which is foreseen in Article 30.1 of the Vienna Convention on the Law of the Treaties in stating that "[a] treaty shall be interpreted in good faith in accordance with the ordinary meaning to be given to the terms of the treaty in their context and in the light of its object and purpose."[8] Interpretation according to the purpose might not seem *a priori* a technique leading to an integrated interpretation, but the analysis reveals that this can be the case if the treaty being interpreted is aimed at creating a framework for cooperation.

In *Gabčikovo-Nagymaros Project (Hungary/Slovakia)*, the ICJ finds that the Treaty between Hungary and Slovakia establishes a regime for the coordinated operation of the jointly owned system of locks, whose benefits must be equally shared. Therefore, the Court considers that the alternative system that Czechoslovakia had started to build to counterbalance the inaction of Hungary, the so-called 'Variant C', should be integrated into the joint regime established by the Treaty. Moreover, the Court states that this is possible because considering Variant C as part of the regime allows complying with Article 9 of the Treaty, which provides that the Parties must participate in the cost and benefits of the system of locks, while accommodating both economic and environmental concerns.[9] In this case, the ICJ is making a teleological interpretation with integrative effects since the reason to include Variant C in the regime is to allow the system to provide the benefits that it seeks in the form of electricity, while also respecting environmental standards.

The teleological interpretation of such a treaty is not surprising. The Treaty of 16 September 1977 concerning the construction and operation of the Gabčikovo-Nagymaros Project System of Locks, which is the object of interpretation in this case, encompasses both economic concerns, such as energy

6 See Sangbana, *La Protection Des Eaux Douces Transfrontières Contre La Pollution*, 269–274.

7 Jennings, R. Y. 1967. "General Course on Principles of International Law." *Collected Courses of the Hague Academy of International Law* 121 (II): 323–619. 544–547. On this topic see Linderfalk, Ulf. 2007. *On the Interpreation of Treaties*. Dordrecht: Springer. 203–234.

8 Vienna Convention on the Law of the Treaties, May 23, 1969, 1155 U.N.T.S. 331. Article 31.1.

9 Gabčikovo-Nagymaros Project (Hungary/Slovakia), Judgment, 1997 I.C.J. Rep. 7 (September 25). Paras. 142–146.

production, and environmental protection. The ICJ considered that all of the objectives had to be given proper consideration:

> As the Court has already had occasion to point out, the 1977 Treaty was not only a joint investment project for the production of energy, but it was designed to serve other objectives as well: the improvement of the navigability of the Danube, flood control and regulation of ice-discharge, and the protection of the natural environment. None of these objectives has been given absolute priority over the other, in spite of the emphasis which is given in the Treaty to the construction of a System of Locks for the production of energy. None of them has lost its importance. In order to achieve these objectives the parties accepted obligations of conduct, obligations of performance, and obligations of result. […]
>
> The Court is of the opinion that the Parties are under a legal obligation, during the negotiations to be held by virtue of Article 5 of the Special Agreement, to consider, within the context of the 1977 Treaty, in what way the multiple objectives of the Treaty can best be served, keeping in mind that all of them should be fulfilled.[10]

In this sense, the Treaty provides a legal context that is conducive to an integrative interpretation. According to his interpretation, Zarbiev distinguishes between three types of treaties.[11] The first are purely environmental treaties, which pose no difficulty for teleological interpretation, but which would not allow integration through teleological interpretation. The second type are treaties that do not contain any reference to environmental interests. In these cases, the teleological interpretation in the sense of integrating environmental and economic or social values would be limited to a *téléo-systémique* interpretation in relation to a broader legal framework. This would be the case, for example, of the interpretations of the Court of Justice of the European Union in relation to EU law as a whole.[12] This type of teleological interpretation, however, is highly unlikely in international basin agreements, as they are not, as a rule, part of a broader legal framework, such as the legal system constituted by EU law. Possibly the only exception among the international basin agreements analysed in this research is the Agreement on the Establishment of the

10 Ibid. Para. 135 and 139.

11 Zarbiev, "L'interprétation Téléologique Des Traités," 220–223.

12 See, for instance, the reasoning of the Court of Justice of the European Union to recognise the direct effect of Directives under certain circumstances: Case 41/74, Yvonne van Duyn v. Home Office, 1974 E.C.R. 133.

Zambezi Watercourse Commission, which could be interpreted according the Revised Protocol on Shared Watercourses in the Southern African Development Community.

The interpretation of the ICJ in *Gabčikovo-Nagymaros Project* (*Hungary/Slovakia*) can be considered to have been made in the context of a third type of treaty – situated in the middle ground between the two previous types – in which both environmental and economic or social values are included. Given that international basin agreements tend to incorporate both environmental and developmental concerns, this is a legal area conducive to teleological interpretations in the sense of the principle of integration.[13]

A limit to teleological interpretation is set in *Pulp Mills on the River Uruguay* (*Argentina v. Uruguay*), where Argentina argued that the 1975 Statute on the river Uruguay covered aspects beyond the quality of the waters of the river. Its claim was based on Article 36, which states: "Las Partes coordinarán, por intermedio de la Comisión, las medidas adecuadas a fin de evitar la alteración del equilibrio ecológico y controlar plagas y otros factores nocivos en el Río y sus áreas de influencia."[14] Argentina claimed that, according to this provision, the ICJ had jurisdiction to rule on the alleged air pollution and visual pollution caused by one of the mills constructed by Uruguay since the treaty was aimed at protecting the *régime* of the river generally. The argument was that these two types of pollution would negatively affect the recreational uses of the river, especially at the Gualeguaychú resort. Argentina was therefore defending a teleological interpretation of the instrument by including non-aquatic pollution in the scope of the treaty.

The Court, however, refused to interpret Article 36 as encompassing air pollution and visual pollution and declared itself not competent to rule on the matter on the basis of the 1975 treaty.[15] Moreover, in the case of the alleged air pollution, the Court argued that only if it was demonstrated that the aquatic

13 In the context of the WTO there is extensive evidence of this type of teleological interpretation, especially in the reference to sustainable development in the preamble of the Agreement establishing the World Trade Organization (Agreement establishing the World Trade Organization, April 15, 1995, 1867 U.N.T.S.). On this topic see Fernández Pons, Xavier. 2006. *La OMC y El Derecho Internacional.* Madrid: Marcial Pons, 218–227; and Tomkiewicz, Vincent. 2009. "L'interprétation Téléologique Au Sein de l'OMC." In *La Circulation Des Concepts Juridiques : Le Droit International de l'environnement Entre Mondialisation et Fragmentation*, edited by Hélène Ruiz Fabri and Lorenzo Gradoni, 243–66. Société de législation comparée.

14 Statutes of the River Uruguay, February 26, 1975, 1295 U.N.T.S. 331. Article 36.

15 Pulp Mills on the River Uruguay (Argentina v. Uruguay), 2010 Judgment, I.C.J. Rep. 14 (April 20). Paras. 49–52.

environment had been polluted indirectly through the air could the matter be considered under the provisions of the treaty.[16]

2 Integration through Interpretation of Evolutionary Terms

Another form of integration through interpretation occurs through concepts embedded in a treaty that, due to their open and dynamic nature, require an evolutionary interpretation.[17] As a particular form of application of the principle of systemic integration enshrined in Article 31.3.c) of the Vienna Convention on the Law of the Treaties,[18] the ILC acknowledged the need for this type of interpretation "where (a) the concept is one which implies taking into account subsequent technical, economic or legal developments; (b) the concept sets up an obligation for further progressive development for the parties; or (c) the concept has a very general nature or is expressed in such general terms that it must take into account changing circumstances."[19] The relevance of this mechanism as a means of applying the principle of integration is clear, since the introduction of new concepts in the sustainable development discourse is a common practice.

Environmental law and policy is an especially prolific area for the emergence and development of new concepts.[20] Some of them have been already addressed in this Chapter in relation to their inclusion in international basin agreements, such as the ecosystem services approach and the security approach applied to several aspects related to human needs. However, there are other concepts whose interpretation by jurisdictional or arbitral bodies produces integration between values related to sustainable development if considered in the light of the most recent knowledge. One example of such a mechanism is the interpretation of 'exhaustible natural resources' by the Appellate Body of

---

16 Ibid. Para. 263.

17 On this topic see Gardiner, Richard. 2008. *Treaty Interpretation*. New York: OUP. 252–256; and Alland, "L'interprétation Du Droit International Public," 207–215.

18 In relation to this principle see Andrés, "El Principio de Integración Sistémica y La Unidad Del Derecho Internacional"; or Cazala, Julien. 2009. "Le Rôle de l'interprétation Des Traités à La Lumière de Toute Autre « règle Pertinente de Droit International Applicable Entre Les Parties » En Tant Que « passerelle » Jetée Entre Systèmes Juridiques Différents." In *La Circulation Des Concepts Juridiques : Le Droit International de l'environnement Entre Mondialisation et Fragmentation*, edited by Hélène Ruiz Fabri and Lorenzo Gradoni, 95–136. Paris: Société de législation comparée.

19 Report finalized by Martti Koskenniemi, *supra* note 1. Para. 23.

20 Rodrigo, "La Integración Normativa y La Unidad Del Derecho Internacional Público," 337–339.

the World Trade Organisation (hereinafter, WTO) in *United States – Import Prohibition of Certain Shrimp and Shrimp Products,*[21] which considered the term to include both living and non-living resources as opposed to the moment of the creation of the norm: "The words of Article XX(g), "exhaustible natural resources", were actually crafted more than 50 years ago. They must be read by a treaty interpreter in the light of contemporary concerns of the community of nations about the protection and conservation of the environment."[22] On the basis of this argument, the Appellate Body referred to other treaties created outside the WTO system, such as UNCLOS and the CBD, and soft law instruments such as the Rio Declaration and Agenda 21.[23]

Another case is the interpretation of the concept of 'maximum sustainable yield' in the context of international sea-fisheries law.[24] It is included in the UNCLOS[25] and in the 1995 Agreement on Conservation and Management of Straddling Fish Stocks and Highly Migratory Fish Stocks.[26] Although this concept has been criticised for being based not on a scientific knowledge of fisheries but on a policy favouring the interests of fishermen,[27] it has been interpreted in an integrative sense by the International Tribunal on the Law of the Sea. This tribunal refers to maximum sustainable yield in relation to the specific cooperation obligations of the Parties of the Sub-Regional Fisheries Commission in regard to the general obligation enshrined in Article 61.3 of the UNCLOS to ensure the sustainable management of shared fish stocks in their exclusive economic zones. In that sense, the International Tribunal on the Law of the Sea points out that:

21 Appellate Body Report, *United States – Import Prohibition of Certain Shrimp and Shrimp Products*, WTO Doc. WT/DS58/AB/R (adopted October 12, 1998). For a commentary on this judgment, see Fernández Pons, Xavier. 2006. *La OMC y El Derecho Internacional.* Madrid: Marcial Pons. 232–237.

22 Ibid. Para. 129.

23 Ibid. Para. 130.

24 For a discussion on the concept of maximum sustainable yield see Hey, Ellen. 2012. "The Persistence of a Concept: Maximum Sustainable Yield." *International Journal of Marine and Coastal Law* 27 (4): 763–71.

25 Articles 61.3 and 119.1.a.

26 Agreement for the Implementation of the Provisions of the United Nations Convention on the Law of the Sea of 10 December 1982 relating to the Conservation and Management of Straddling Fish Stocks and Highly Migratory Fish Stocks, December 4, 1995, 2167 U.N.T.S. 3. Article 5(b).

27 For a review of those critics see Arif, Abdullah Al. 2017. "Legal Status of Maximum Sustainable Yield Concept in International Fisheries Law and Its Adoption in the Marine Fisheries Regime of Bangladesh: A Critical Analysis." *International Journal of Marine and Coastal Law* 32 (3): 544–69.

> To comply with these obligations, the [Sub-Regional Fisheries Commission] Member States, pursuant to the Convention, specifically articles 61 and 62, must ensure that: [...] conservation and management measures are designed to maintain or restore stocks at levels which can produce the maximum sustainable yield, as qualified by relevant environmental and economic factors, including the economic needs of coastal fishing communities and the special needs of the [Sub-Regional Fisheries Commission] Member States, taking into account fishing patterns, the interdependence of stocks and any generally recommended international minimum standards, whether subregional, regional or global.[28]

Understood in this way, maximum sustainable yield requires an evolutionary interpretation since it might vary depending on environmental and economic factors; it may even vary depending on social factors, since the needs of coastal fishing communities are to be taken into account.

To date, no judgement of the ICJ or any arbitration tribunal has been based on this particular form of evolutionary interpretation in disputes regarding international watercourses. However, due to the increasing number of open and dynamic concepts being introduced in basin agreements, it is reasonable to assume that the resolution of a dispute will eventually rely to some extent on the interpretation of one or more of these concepts. In fact, the arbitral tribunal in *The South China Sea Arbitration* (*The Republic of Philippines v. The People's Republic of China*)[29] had to interpret the concept of ecosystem as used in the UNCLOS.[30] It then resorted to relevant international law applicable between the Parties: "An 'ecosystem' is not defined in the [UNCLOS], but internationally accepted definitions include that in Article 2 of the CBD, which defines ecosystem to mean 'a dynamic complex of plant, animal and micro-organism communities and their non-living environment interacting as a functional unit'"[31] Seemingly, the Tribunal referred to the CITES to interpret

28 Request for Advisory Opinion (Sub-Regional Fisheries Commission), Case No. 21, Advisory Opinion of April 2, 2015, 19 ITLOS Rep. 4. Para. 219.6.

29 The South China Sea Arbitration (The Republic of Philippines v. The People's Republic of China). Final award, 33 R.I.A.A (Perm. Ct. Arb. 2016).

30 In relation to this interpretation, see Paine, Joshua. 2020. "The Judicial Dimension of Regime Interaction beyond Systemic Integration." In *Regime Interaction in Ocean Governance*, edited by Seline Trevisanut, Nikolaos Giannopoulos, and Rozemarijn Roland Holst, 184–221. Leiden: Brill Nijhoff. 192–194.

31 The South China Sea Arbitration (The Republic of Philippines v. The People's Republic of China). Final award, 33 R.I.A.A (Perm. Ct. Arb. 2016). Para. 945.

the concept of "depleted, threatened or endangered species"[32] as used in the UNCLOS. Nothing would prevent these same arguments being followed in relation to the ecosystems of an international watercourse.

The closest an international court has come to making an evolutionary interpretation of a concept in order to resolve a case concerning an international watercourse was perhaps the ICJ in the *Dispute over the status and use of the waters of the Silala*. Bolivia initially claimed that the Silala springs – a diverted channel crossing the border with Chile – should not be recognised as part of the watercourse. It was argued that the channel was merely an "artificially enhanced watercourse" to which customary law on the use of international watercourses was not applicable, thus ensuring Bolivia's full sovereignty over the diverted waters.[33]

The outcome of the *Dispute over the status and use of the waters of the Silala*, then, depended greatly on how the concept of international watercourse was defined. It has been seen that the concept of 'international watercourse' is a contested one, with divergences between the two global conventions on the matter, especially in relation to whether it should include the drainage basin and groundwater. In the *Dispute over the status and use of the waters of the Silala*, the Court had an opportunity to advance international law in terms of the concept of international watercourse. However, it merely found that in the course of the proceedings, Bolivia had moved its position closer to that of Chile, which understood that the channel was part of the international watercourse, so it did not rule on this question on the grounds that the claim had lost its object.[34]

3 Integration through the Interpretation of Open-Textured Obligations

As the ILC has pointed out, another situation in which the interpretation of a treaty may take into account the norms of other treaties is when the obligation is described in very general terms. In such cases, the obligation would operate as a *renvoi* to the state of the law at the time of its application.[35] The same

---

32 United Nations Convention on the Law of the Sea, December 10, 1982, 1833 U.N.T.S. 3. Article 192.5.

33 Dispute over the status and use of the waters of the Silala (Chile v. Bolivia), Judgement, 2022 I.C.J. Rep. 614 (December 1). Paras. 50–58.

34 Ibid. Para. 59.

35 Report finalized by Martti Koskenniemi, *supra* note 1. Para. 478. In relation to that topic see also Virally, Michel. 1985. "La Distinction Entre Textes Internationaux de Portée Juridique

could be said in relation to other values not included in the treaty. This was the situation in which, in *Gabčikovo-Nagymaros Project (Hungary/Slovakia)*, the ICJ had to address the question of whether Czechoslovakia had breached articles 15 and 19 of the Treaty of 16 September 1977 concerning the construction and operation of the Gabčikovo-Nagymaros Project System of Locks. According to Article 15, the Parties "shall ensure, by the means specified in the joint contractual plan, that the quality of the water in the Danube is not impaired as a result of the construction and operation of the System of Locks", while Article 19 states that "[t]he Contracting Parties shall, through the means specified in the joint contractual plan, ensure compliance with the obligations for the protection of nature arising in connection with the construction and operation of the System of Locks."[36]

The integrative effect at interpreting open-textured obligations is also operationalised by the ICJ itself, in the first place by establishing an explicit link to sustainable development as the key concept behind the obligation to reconcile development and environmental protection.[37] The Court also states that the solution to be reached after applying the new environmental norms must be agreed upon by the Parties and must be (emphasis added) integrated: "It is for the Parties themselves to find an agreed solution that takes account of the objectives of the Treaty, which must be pursued in a joint and integrated way, as well as the norms of international environmental law and the principles of the law of international watercourses."[38]

Therefore, articles 15 and 19 of the Treaty of 16 September 1977 introduce the obligations to protect the quality of the waters and of the environment. The Court assumed that their formulation was "designed to accommodate change"[39] and it ultimately stated that, while they do not constitute a specific obligation of performance, the articles obliged the Parties to "take new environmental norms into consideration when agreeing upon the means to be specified in the Joint Contractual Plan."[40] Moreover, the Court considered that an evolutionary interpretation of the provisions contained in the articles is compulsory, as:

---

et Textes Internationaux Dépourvus de Portée Juridique." *Yearbook of the Institute of International Law* 60 (1): 328–57. 332; and Fernández de Casadevante Romani, Carlos. 2007. *Sovereignty and Interpretation of International Norms*. Berlin Heidelberg: Springer. 37–43.

36 Cited in Gabčikovo-Nagymaros Project (Hungary/Slovakia), Judgment, 1997 I.C.J. Rep. 7 (September 25). Para. 18.

37 Ibid.

38 Ibid. Para. 141.

39 Ibid. Para. 104.

40 Ibid. 112.

> In order to evaluate the environmental risks, current standards must be taken into consideration. This is not only allowed by the wording of Articles 15 and 19, but even prescribed, to the extent that these articles impose a continuing – and thus necessarily evolving – obligation on the parties to maintain the quality of the water of the Danube and to protect nature.[41]

This issue was also commented on by Weeramantry and Bedjoui in separate opinions regarding ICJ's resolution on *Gabčikovo-Nagymaros Project* (*Hungary/Slovakia*).[42] While the former is quite optimistic about the solution provided by the Court, the latter is more cautious about the possibilities of an evolutionary interpretation and considers that although the interpretation is a necessary one, the Court should have clarified its extent further and recalled that the general rule remains that of Article 31 of the Vienna Convention on the Law of the Treaties. The two judges appear to differ in their assumption of the legal basis for the evolutionary interpretation in question.

For Weeramantry, the interpretation is naturally based on Article 31.3(c) of the Vienna Convention on the Law of the Treaties,[43] while Bedjoui understands that the Court did not invoke that article, though he believes that it should have done.[44] Certainly, the judgement does not make direct reference to the article at any point. In any case, the incorporation of environmental norms for the interpretation of older treaties considered by the ICJ in *Gabčikovo-Nagymaros Project* (*Hungary/Slovakia*) seems to have been established in international law to some extent, since it was later assumed by the arbitral tribunals in *Arbitration Regarding the Iron Rhine* (*IJzeren Rijn"*) *Railway* (*Belgium/Netherlands*)[45] and the *Indus Waters Kishenganga Arbitration* (*Pakistan vs. India*).[46]

---

41 Ibid. Para. 140.

42 See Gabčikovo-Nagymaros Project (Hungary/Slovakia), Judgment, 1997 I.C.J. Rep. 7 (September 25) (Weeramantry, C.G., separate opinion); and Gabčikovo-Nagymaros Project (Hungary/Slovakia), Judgment, 1997 I.C.J. Rep. 7 (September 25) (Bedjaoui, M., separate opinion).

43 Gabčikovo-Nagymaros Project (Hungary/Slovakia), Judgment, 1997 I.C.J. Rep. 7 (September 25) (Weeramantry, C.G., separate opinion). 110–112.

44 Gabčikovo-Nagymaros Project (Hungary/Slovakia), Judgment, 1997 I.C.J. Rep. 7 (September 25) (Bedjaoui, M., separate opinion). Paras. 12–19.

45 Arbitration Regarding the Iron Rhine ("Ijzeren Rijn") Railway (Belgium/Netherlands), 27 R.I.A.A (Perm. Ct. Arb. 2005). Paras. 58–59 and 79.

46 Indus Waters Kishenganga Arbitration (Pakistan vs. India). Final award, 31 R.I.A.A (Perm. Ct. Arb. 2013). Para. 85.

The only other recourse to Article 31.3(c) of the Vienna Convention[47] on the Law of the Treaties for the application of a treaty in a case relating to the interpretation of a norm of international watercourses law was that of Argentina in *Pulp Mills on the River Uruguay (Argentina v. Uruguay)*. Argentina argued that 1975 Statute on the River Uruguay had to be interpreted "in the light of principles governing the law of international watercourses and principles of international law ensuring protection of the environment."[48] However, the Court refused to consider this matter, deeming it to be outside the scope of the jurisdiction conferred to it under Article 60 of the Statute.

Nevertheless, evolutionary interpretations do not necessarily need to be based on Article 31.3(c) of the Vienna Convention, as can be seen in *Pulp Mills on the River Uruguay (Argentina v. Uruguay)*. This is apparent in the ICJ's reasoning in relation to the obligation enshrined in the Statute establishing the Administrative Commission of the River Uruguay "[t]o protect and preserve the aquatic environment and, in particular, to prevent its pollution, by prescribing appropriate rules and measures in accordance with applicable international agreements and in keeping, where relevant, with the guidelines and recommendations of international technical bodies."[49] The Court considered that this obligation had "to be interpreted in accordance with a practice, which in recent years has gained so much acceptance among States that it may now be considered a requirement under general international law to undertake an environmental impact assessment."[50] In other words, the general formulation of such a conventional obligation had to be interpreted taking into account the evolution of international law, which, unlike the time at which the Statute was adopted, now required an EIA to be conducted.

---

47 Vienna Convention on the Law of the Treaties, May 23, 1969, 1155 U.N.T.S. 331. Article 31.3.c).

48 Pulp Mills on the River Uruguay (Argentina v. Uruguay), 2010 Judgment, I.C.J. Rep. 14 (April 20). Para. 55.

49 Statutes of the River Uruguay, February 26, 1975, 1295 U.N.T.S. 331. Article 41(a).

50 Pulp Mills on the River Uruguay (Argentina v. Uruguay), 2010 Judgment, I.C.J. Rep. 14 (April 20). Para. 204.

PART 3

Mechanisms of Institutional Integration of the Economic, Social and Environmental Dimensions in International Watercourses Regimes

Introduction

Beside legal integration, sustainable development depends largely on institutional mechanisms which ensure that decisions are made in such a way that they integrate economic, social and environmental interests. This dimension of the principle of integration is referred to here as 'institutional integration'. The ILA has argued that institutional integration is the closest concept to what the drafters of the Rio Declaration on Environment and Development[1] had in mind when they wrote the fourth principle, which states that "[i]n order to achieve sustainable development, environmental protection shall constitute an integral part of the development process and cannot be considered in isolation from it."[2]

Seemingly, institutional integration aligns most closely with Article 17 of the IUCN Draft International Covenant on Environment and Development, which states that "Parties shall, at all stages and at all levels, integrate environmental conservation into the planning and implementation of their policies and activities giving full and equal consideration to environmental, economic, social and cultural factors,"[3] which in turn requires the Parties to "establish or strengthen institutional structures and procedures to integrate environmental and developmental issues in all spheres of decision-making."[4] This conceptualisation of institutional integration would therefore imply the establishment of both procedural and substantive obligations for an integrated governance framework of (for instance) international watercourses, as well as requiring a suitable organisational set-up of the institutions affecting sustainable development.

Part III of the book is organised along the two variables that determine the extent of institutional integration. The high complexity of institutional

---

1 ILA. Committee on International Law on Sustainable Development. 2006. "Report of the Toronto Conference." https://www.ila-hq.org/en_GB/documents/conference-report-toronto-2006-14. 7.

2 United Nations Conference on Environment and Development, *Rio Declaration on Environment and Development*, in Report of the United Nations Conference on Environment and Development, A/CONF.151/26 (Vol. I) (12 August 1992), undocs.org/en/A/CONF.151/26/Rev.1 (vol. I).

3 IUCN Commission on Environmental Law. 2015. *Draft International Covenant on Environment and Development: Implementing Sustainability*. Gland: IUCN. Article 17.2. The concept of 'policy integration' in the Draft International Covenant on Environment and Development should not be confused with policy integration as used in the next Chapter, which is more specific.

4 Ibid. Article 17.2.c).

 | DOI:10.1163/9789004736757_013

integration calls for mechanisms to ensure an informed and participatory decision-making process, so these will be cross-cutting dimensions throughout the four following chapters. Chapter 9 focuses on determining the general conditions of institutional integration and defines its main features. First, it analyses the mandate and capacity requirements placed on institutions responsible for integration, focusing particularly on IRBOs. Second, it examines the institutional set-up of IRBOs and how this facilitates informed decision-making, as well as the institutional mechanisms for public participation in the decision-making process.

In the following chapters, the analysis is structured according to the levels at which institutional integration may (and should) occur: policy-, management- and project-specific integration. Ideally, integration would be applied at each of these levels sequentially so that management decisions would result from a specific policy and integration at the project level would fit into a broader management framework (as is commonly the case of governance cycles at national levels). Thus, while Chapter 10 looks at institutional integration at the level of international river basin policy making, Chapter 11 shifts focus to the integrated management of international watercourses. Finally, Chapter 12 addresses institutional instruments aimed at achieving integration at the project level for initiatives affecting international watercourses.

CHAPTER 9

Institutional Conditions for an Integrated Decision-Making Process

The organisational dimension is key for the effective application of the principle of integration, since an informed and participatory decision-making process requires the existence of a suitable institutional structure. In this sense, Boisson de Chazournes states that "les principes du développement durable et de la gestion intégrée des ressources en eau dont ces instruments sont porteurs, appellent à une coopération institutionnelle plus étoffée et plus outillée dans ses modes d'intervention, requérant des organismes et commissions de bassin l'exercice d'un noyau commun de fonctions."[1] In the case of the governance of international watercourses, this reinforced institutional cooperation increasingly translates into the establishment of IRBOs with more extensive competences and resources. This Chapter focuses on determining which aspects of the mandate, structure and functions of IRBOs are conducive to an informed and participatory decision-making process that allows to integrate the economic, social and environmental dimensions.[2]

1 Conditions for International River Basin Organisations to Promote Integration: Mandate and Capacity

The feasibility of integrated governance derives largely from the existence of an organisation that provides the means for informed decision-making and the participation of relevant stakeholders. For IRBOs to provide those means,

1 Boisson de Chazournes, "Organismes et Commissions de Bassin," 439.

2 Take into account that this is not a study on the effectiveness of the institutional mechanisms described, but rather an analysis of the institutional integrative practices currently applied by IRBOs. For an analysis in terms of effectiveness of IRBOs see, for instance: Schmeier, *Governing International Watercourses*; Meijerink, Sander, and Dave Huitema. 2017. "The Institutional Design, Politics, and Effects of a Bioregional Approach: Observations and Lessons from 11 Case Studies of River Basin Organizations." *Ecology and Society* 22 (2); and Schulze, Sabine, and Susanne Schmeier. 2012. "Governing Environmental Change in International River Basins: The Role of River Basin Organizations." *International Journal of River Basin Management* 10 (3): 229–44.

 | DOI:10.1163/9789004736757_014

however, they must have a suitable mandate and possess sufficient resources and human capacity. This Section analyses these two questions.

Considering the cross-sectoral nature of sustainable development, any organisation responsible for the governance of a natural resource such as an international watercourse must have the power to intervene in all – or at least a substantive part – of its aspects. As such, IRBOs should have a mandate that encompasses enough issue-areas to be able to integrate the many dimensions that determine the sustainable development of a watercourse, which can range from water quantity and water quality to environmental protection and socioeconomic development. This will depend on the mandate given to them in the watercourse agreement or subsequent revisions established by the relevant States.

According to Schmeier, only 27 IRBOs around the world focus on one specific issue, while a majority of 57 address more than one issue. Only 26 IRBOs focus on multiple issue-areas, which usually are located in the developing world: for instance, the OMVS or the VBA. It must be noted, however, that this is a changing process and the scope of issue-areas governed by an IRBO can be expanded (for instance, the International Commission for the Protection of the Rhine), which is more often the case. The increasing scarcity of fresh water may possibly be the reason for the tendency of IRBOs to cover more issue-ares. However, although it happens rarely, the scope of IRBOs might also be restricted to some extent (for instance, the MRC initiated a process to rationalise the scope of its functions).[3]

Depending on the extent of the cooperation agreed between the Parties for the governance of the international watercourse, the IRBO will have a different institutional design. The literature classifies IRBOs in three categories: Committees, Commissions and Authorities.[4] They will be analysed from the point of view of their capacity to foster integration of the economic, social and environmental dimensions.

Committees (also called councils) are the most basic type, consisting of an official group of representatives of the Parties who meet to discuss the state of the watercourse and advise their government, but which do not have any permanent staff. In terms of the principle of integration, Committees are clearly unfit for purpose: integrated decision-making requires mechanisms for

3 Schmeier, *Governing International Watercourses*. 83–84.

4 It is used the classification proposed by Lautze et al. after a comparative analysis of IRBOs. In Lautze, Jonathan, Kai Wegerich, Jusipbek Kazbekov, and Murat Yakubov. 2013. “International River Basin Organizations: Variation, Options and Insights.” *Water International* 38 (1): 30–42. 31–33.

the gathering of information on the watercourse and mechanisms to enable stakeholder participation, which in turn is contingent on a certain level of institutionalisation, which Committees clearly do not provide. In addition, Committees tend to have the narrowest mandates of any IRBO, which, as seen above, is also a constraint on integration.

The second type of IRBO, Commissions, have permanent staff and focus on monitoring (e.g. data collection), regulation (e.g. coordination, harmonisation) and planning, while the third type, Authorities, also have permanent staff as well as a technical office, and their functions typically include the development and operation of projects.[5] Commissions are the most common type of institutional structure, accounting for 78 of 113 IRBOs, while there are only 13 IRBOs consistent with the definition of Authority,[6] most of which are found in West Africa (e.g. the NBA or the VBA). Since Authorities usually assume the functions assigned to Commissions in addition to their additional functions, it can be concluded that integration is feasible within both types of structure. On the one hand, the development and operation of projects, which is the defining trait of Authorities, is not a necessary function for integration. It might be argued that the greater an IRBO's responsibility for the implementation of planned measures, the greater the chance of an integrated outcome.

However, implementation is usually a matter of national authority, not only in international watercourse governance but in any shared interest in which States choose to cooperate in the framework of international law. As such, the effective application of the principle of integration cannot reasonably be achieved by the direct implementation of projects by IRBOs. This said, at first glance, the functions of Committees seem to encompass some of the basic requirements for integration, such as monitoring, which is as central to integrated management as planning.

Another aspect determining the broadness of scope of IRBOs, which affects their integrative capacity, is the geographical scope of their mandate. This is obviously largely parallel with the issue-area aspect. Those IRBOs focusing only on navigation, for instance, deal only with the river itself, whereas IRBOs covering additional issue-areas such as socio-economic development are more likely to extend their coverage to the whole basin. The comparative analysis conducted by Schemeier reveals that only 34 of 110 IRBOs cover the transboundary basin (including the river or not), of which 22 belong to the 'multi-issue' group.[7]

5 Lautze et al., "International River Basin Organizations," 31–33.

6 Schmeier, *Governing International Watercourses*. 88.

7 Ibid. 84–85.

It is also possible that IRBOs act on a more restricted scale which does not directly correspond to the basin or river. Some IRBOs are created for the management of a specific project, while others oversee only a specific part of a basin. The latter case can arise when not all of the States whose territory is occupied by the basin form part of the IRBO (e.g. the MRC, of which China is not a member), or when the organisation is created to manage only a tributary river of the main channel (e.g. the International Sava River Basin Commission, where the Sava is a tributary of the Danube). The partial geographic scope of many IRBOs is not only inconsistent with the law of international watercourses, which clearly identifies the basin as the desired area for transboundary cooperation,[8] it also limits the feasibility of applying the principle of integration in many international watercourses, as sustainable development is unlikely to be determined only by factors pertaining to the watercourse.

Once they are given the adequate mandate, IRBOs need to be empowered with the capacity to carry out their functions, given that integration is resource-consuming in material and human terms. From a general organisational point of view, it is revealing to consider the internal reforms undertaken by the World Bank in order to promote integration of the economic, social and environmental dimensions in its decision-making process regarding its lending functions. The solution devised in the late 1980s, following the financing of certain development projects with serious environmental consequences, was to create a central department with a mandate to monitor and sanction the actions that the World Bank intended to undertake, which in practice meant converting the Environment, Science and Technology Unit into the Environment Department and creating Regional Environmental Divisions in each of the World Bank's regional vice-presidencies.[9] This reform gave the Environment Department a more central role and a stronger mandate, but also increased its staff requirements.[10] This led to a dramatic increase in the number of environmental economists, biologists and environmental engineers employed during the 1990s. With those changes, "the board could be more certain that Bank staff

8 See Chapter 2 of this book.

9 World Bank Group Archives Catalog. n.d. "Records of the Environment Sector – World Bank Group Archives Catalog." Accessed December 11, 2024. https://archivesholdings.worldbank.org/records-of-environment-sector.

10 Mucklow, Fiona. 2000. "The Integration of Environmental Principles into the World Bank." *Review of European Community and International Environmental Law* 9 (2): 100–111. 104.

now had the ability to analyse the environmental impact of projects, but also the interest in seeing that its new goals were realized."[11]

Among the challenges for successful integration in the context of international watercourse governance, Bréthaut also points to "the size of the financial resources that have to be invested in order to establish and monitor the activities of a river basin organisation, the time and human resources needed to understand complex systems and to plan multipurpose solutions, and finally the volume of data and information that has to be collected in order to identify effective arrangements."[12] In other words, any serious attempt an IRBO makes to implement institutional integration must be supported by sufficient resources.

In terms of human resources, however, capacity should be measured not only in terms of the number of staff employed by the IRBO but also, more specifically, by its training.[13] In addition, the amount of staff required depends on the functions foreseen in the IRBO's mandate. In this sense, a pattern can be observed in that the European IRBO secretariats tend to be considerably smaller than those of African organisations, as the former tend to perform a coordinating role while the latter have a broader mandate.[14]

However, the higher resource demands of many African IRBOs are not always matched by sufficient funding. In fact, many organisations, such as the Okavango River Basin Water Commission, have been largely dependent on international funding to carry out their functions.[15] It is therefore reasonable to assume that several IRBOs lack the resources to effectively pursue an integrated governance approach of the basin.

Institutional capacity-building for cooperation on international watercourses has been the object of a considerable number of projects in the Global South, supported by international lending institutions, international organisations and by national development aid agencies from the Global North. These projects may focus on the most basic elements of cooperation (especially in cases with a weaker cooperation framework), such as the drafting of a

---

11 Nielson, Daniel L., and Michael J. Tieraey. 2003. "Delegation to International Organizations: Agency Theory and World Bank Environmental Reform." *International Organization* 57 (2): 241–76. 264.

12 Bréthaut, Christian, and Géraldine Pflieger. 2020. *Governance of a Transboundary River: The Rhône*. Cham: Palgrave Macmillan. 42.

13 Schmeier, *Governing International Watercourses*. 200.

14 Ibid. 95.

15 Schmeier, Susanne. 2015. "The Institutional Design of River Basin Organizations – Empirical Findings from around the World." *International Journal of River Basin Management* 13 (1): 51–72. 58–59.

watercourse agreement or the initial setting-up of the IRBO. An example of the first is the project "VSIP project del Volta" initiated in 2013 and financed by The World Bank among other funders, had as one of its outputs the elaboration of a Draft Water Charter for the Volta Basin.[16] An example of the second is the project "Strategic Action Programme for the Dniester River Basin 2021–2035", financed by the GEF, which allowed the setting up of the Commission on Sustainable Use and Protection of the Dniester River,[17] or the project "Chu-Talas I 2003–2006", supported by the OECD, the UNECE and the United Nations Economic and Social Commission for Asia and the Pacific, which led to the inauguration of the Chu and Talas Commission.[18]

Other projects provide support for capacity-building in a wide array of areas. The "Projet Appui ABN – GIZ", for example, was launched with the general objective of supporting the NBA,[19] while the project "Sustainable Water Resources Management in the Lake Chad Basin (GIZ) – Module: "Organizational advisory services for the Lake Chad Basin Commission" implemented in cooperation with the German Federal Institute for Geosciences and Natural Resources had the aim of supporting the LCBC in its organizational development and to strengthen its planning, cooperation, and communication capacities.[20]

A further group focus on the establishment and enhancement of monitoring capacities, sometimes with the creation of an observatory. It is an example of the first type the project "Une composante du Système Mondial d'Observation du Cycle Hydrologique (WHYCOS)" implemented between the OMVS and the World Meteorological Organisation (hereinafter, WMO) for the establishment of a system of observation of the hydrological cycle of the River Senegal.[21] As examples of the second type are the UNEP/GEF Volta River Basin

16 VBA. n.d. "VSIP Project." Accessed December 11, 2024. http://abv.int/en/vsip-project/.

17 Report annex to: Dniester Commission, *Joint Statement on the Strategic Action Programme for the Dniester River 2021–2035* (31 March 2021), https://dniester-commission.org/wp-content/uploads/2021/04/joint-statement-signed-4-languages-SAP_Eng.pdf.

18 OSCE. 2021. "Support for the Creation of a Transboundary Water Commission on the Chu and Talas Rivers between Kazakhstan and Kyrgyzstan: Final Project Report." 2021. https://unece.org/DAM/env/water/Chu-Talas/OSCE_Chu_Talas_Final_Report.pdf.

19 NBA. 2022. "Transboundary Water Resource Management in the Niger Basin." 2022. http://www.abn.ne/images/documents/FME2022/gestion_re_transfrontalieres_en.pdf.

20 LCBC. n.d. "Sustainable Water Resources Management in the Lake Chad Basin (GIZ) – Module: 'Organizational Advisory Services for the Lake Chad Basin Commission.'" Accessed August 3, 2022. https://cblt.org/sustainable-water-resources-management-in-the-lake-chad-basin-giz-module-organizational-advisory-services-for-the-lake-chad-basin-commission/.

21 OMVS. n.d. "HYCOS – OMVS." Accessed December 11, 2024. https://www.omvs.org/projet/hycos/.

Project for "Addressing Transboundary Concerns in the Volta River Basin and its Downstream Coastal Area", which had the aim of "promoting a more sectorialy-coordinated management approach, based on Integrated Water Resource Management (IWRM) principles";[22] and the project "UCC-Water: Speedup of the IWRM-2005 Objectives Implementation in Central Asia", which had the objective of conducting a diagnostic and drawing a roadmap for IWRM in the Ferghana Valley countries.[23]

Finally, there is another stream of projects concerned with the planning and development of a framework for integrated water resources management in the basin. For instance, the project "Observatoire des ressources en eau et des milieux associés", which aimed at creating an observatory for the Volta basin to contribute to the mandate of the VBA.[24] In all those cases, the focus illustrates the importance given to capacity-building in IRBOs as a condition for efficient governance of international watercourses.

2 Mechanisms for an Informed Decision-Making Process that Enable Institutional Integration

In relation to informed decision-making, it is important to consider that pursuing the integration of the economic, social and environmental dimensions significantly increases the difficulty of predicting the effects of any 'developmental' action affecting the environment or society. This leads to a greater need for a "reliable and continuing flow of information about the environmental, social, and economic effects of human activities,"[25] but also ensures that these effects are better understood. Therefore, institutional integration depends, firstly, on a broader array of environmental, social and economic indicators and, secondly, on the procedural mechanisms for obtaining and sharing information.

Well-established instruments such as EIAs respond to the need for mechanisms for integrated decision-making,[26] while instruments for integrated

22 GEF-Volta. n.d. "Welcome to the UNEP/GEF Volta River Basin Project." Accessed December 11, 2024. http://gefvolta.iwlearn.org/.

23 CAWATER. n.d. "UCC-Water: Sub-Regional Programme for Central Asia." Accessed December 11, 2024. http://cawater-info.net/ucc-water/index_e.htm.

24 VBA. n.d. "Observatory | VBA." Accessed December 11, 2024. http://abv.int/en/observatoire-2/.

25 Dernbach, "Achieving Sustainable Development," 273.

26 Bürgi Bonanomi, Elisabeth. 2015. *Sustainable Development in International Law Making and Trade*. Cheltenham: Edward Elgar. 87.

analysis and modelling of a growing body of data are increasingly used for the governance of international watercourses.[27] International environmental law generally prescribes several of these techniques, such as information exchange, reporting, consultation (between States), notification of emergency situations, and monitoring.[28] The obtention of accurate information as a premise for good governance has been a key aspect of international environmental law and policy for some years,[29] and most environment-related agreements lay down obligations regarding the exchange of information.[30]

In fact, the claim that the principle of integration is the most practical part of sustainable development rests to a large extent on the mechanisms enabling

---

27 Leb, *Data Innovations for Transboundary Freshwater Resources Management.*

28 Sands et al. *Principles of International Environmental Law,* 623–664.

29 Principle 20 of the Stockholm Declaration already pledged that "the free flow of up-to-date scientific information and transfer of experience must be supported and assisted, to facilitate the solution of environmental problems," (United Nations Conference on the Human Environment, *Declaration of the United Nations Conference on the Human Environment,* in Report of the United Nations Conference on the Human Environment, A/CONF.48/14/Rev.1. (5–16 June 1972), undocs.org/en/A/CONF.48/14/Rev.1. Principle 20) while Principle 9 of the 1992 Rio Declaration calls for "exchanges of scientific and technological information" (United Nations Conference on Environment and Development, *Rio Declaration on Environment and Development,* in Report of the United Nations Conference on Environment and Development, A/CONF.151/26 (Vol. I) (12 August 1992), undocs.org/en/A/CONF.151/26/Rev.1(vol. I)). Agenda 21 devotes Chapter 40 to "Information for deci sion-making" and Chapter 35 to the role of science for the management of the environment and development (United Nations Conference on Environment and Development, *Agenda 21,* in *Report of the United Nations Conference on Environment and Development,* A/CONF.151/26 (Vol. I) (12 August 1992), undocs.org/en/A/CONF.151/26/Rev.1(vol. I).). On this topic see, for instance: the series Handbooks on biodiversity information management, edited by the World Conservation Monitoring Centre, especially the Volume 1, 2, 6 and 7; Timmerman, Jos G., and Sindre Langaas. 2005. "Water Information: What Is It Good for? The Use of Information in Transboundary Water Management." *Regional Environmental Change* 5 (4): 177–87; Funtowicz, Silvio.O., and J.R. Ravetz. 1999. "Information Tools for Environmental Policy under Conditions of Complexity." *Environmental Issues Series – European Environment Agency,* no. 9: 1–34; and Gerlak, Andrea K., Jonathan Lautze, and Mark Giordano. 2011. "Water Resources Data and Information Exchange in Transboundary Water Treaties." *International Environmental Agreements: Politics, Law and Economics* 11 (2): 179–99.

30 See, for instance: Article 244 of the UNCLOS (United Nations Convention on the Law of the Sea, December 10, 1982, 1833 U.N.T.S. 3.); Article 13 of the 1989 Basel Convention (Basel Convention on the Control of Transboundary Movements of Hazardous Wastes and their Disposal, March 22, 1989, 1673 U.N.T.S.); Article 17 of the CBD (Convention on Biological Diversity, June 5, 1992, 1760 U.N.T.S. 79.); or Article 14 of the 1998 Chemicals Convention (Rotterdam Convention on the Prior Informed Consent Procedure for Certain Hazardous Chemicals and Pesticides in International Trade, September 10, 1998, 2244 U.N.T.S. 337).

an informed decision-making process. In this regard, Sands affirms that "[i]n many ways [the principle of integration] is the most legalistic: its formal application requires the collection of appropriate environmental information and its dissemination and the conduct of appropriate environmental information and its dissemination and the conduct of appropriate environmental impact assessments."[31]

In compliance with the general obligation to exchange information and data, IRBOs are generally tasked with collecting and processing data on the international watercourse in order to provide the necessary information. Put differently, IRBOs are also meant to assist in bringing scientific rigour to the decision-making process. The creation of a joint mechanism – the IRBO – to carry out this function is not compulsory, nor is it intrinsically indispensable, but comparative analysis of international watercourses demonstrates that information and data are more effectively exchanged where a joint body is established for the purpose.[32]

The specific activities that IRBOs can carry out to facilitate a science-based decision-making process are as follows: measuring and monitoring the current state of the basin; forecasting potential future states of the basin; developing new understandings of the basin; and reviewing the state of knowledge.[33] Information and data are generally collected by the States and then communicated to the IRBO, which is responsible for treating and sharing it with all the Parties in a meaningful and orderly manner.[34]

To do this, the IRBO must have been provided with the relevant knowledge and the necessary technical and human resources. Technical capacitation is the aim of several projects carried out in collaboration with international organisations.[35] A key example is the WHYCOS System of the WMO, which aims to strengthen the technical, human and institutional capacities of bodies

---

31 Sands, "International Law in the Field of Sustainable Development: Emerging Legal Principles," 61.

32 UNECE. 2011. *Second Assessment of Transboundary Rivers, Lakes and Groundwaters*. New York and Geneva: United Nations.

33 Milman, Anita, and Andrea K. Gerlak. 2020. "International River Basin Organizations, Science, and Hydrodiplomacy." *Environmental Science and Policy* 107 (November 2019): 137–49. 141.

34 See, for instance, Article 99 of the Draft Water Charter for the Volta River Basin.

35 See, for instance, the Project WISDOM (Water related Information System for the Sustainable Development of the Mekong Delta) on the creation of an environmental information system, funded by Germany and Vietnam: German Aerospace Center. n.d. "ProjectCoastalx." Accessed July 10, 2022. https://www.wisdom.eoc.dlr.de/coastalx/#/bookmarks.

including national hydrological services[36] and has been implemented for several large international watercourses around the world as, for example, the projet Sénégal-HYCOS for the establishment of an information system on the hydrologic cycle of River Senegal, with the participation of the WMO.[37]

Ensuring informed decision-making in the management of a complex system such as a watercourse usually requires the intervention of experts, who in the IRBO structure are usually organised in expert groups. The LCBC has a Water Resources Advisory Committee which serves as the committee of experts with an advisory function for several procedures regarding the notification of planned measures.[38] The VBA provides for the creation of a Panel of Independent Experts which has a general mandate to act as the "advisory body in charge of providing the Authority with scientifically justified opinions on all aspects of sustainable management of water and the environment in the Basin,"[39] although according to the Charter it also has the specific function of examining the planned measures announced by the Parties.[40]

In some cases, the participation of experts is organised across thematic expert groups. The Statute of the ISRBC foresees the creation of both permanent and *ad hoc* expert groups.[41] There are currently six permanent groups, specialised in river basin management, flood prevention, accident prevention and control, navigation, geographic information systems, and hydrology and meteorology. There are also three *ad hoc* expert groups on legal issues, financial issues, and information system.[42] In the latter case, the experts are chosen by the ISRBC following proposals by the representatives of the Parties.[43] At the time of writing, the first Sava River Basin Management Plan is being updated.

36 WMO. Hydrohub. n.d. "World Hydrological Cycle Observing System (WHYCOS) | Hydro-Hub." Accessed July 10, 2022. https://hydrohub.wmo.int/en/world-hydrological-cycle-observing-system-whycos.

37 OMVS. n.d. "HYCOS – OMVS." Accessed August 3, 2022. https://www.omvs.org/projet/hycos/

38 Water Charter of the Lake Chad Basin, Articles 2, 52, 56 and 57.

39 Draft Water Charter for the Volta River Basin, Article 137.

40 Ibid. Article 91.

41 Framework Agreement on the Sava River Basin, Annex I, containing the Statute of the International Sava River Basin Commission, Article 1.2.

42 ISRBC. n.d. "Expert Groups – International Sava River Basin Commission." Accessed July 13, 2022. https://www.savacommission.org/about-us/structure-and-functioning/expert-groups/241.

43 ISRBC, *Rules of Procedure of the International Sava River Basin Commission*, Doc. No: WD-20-12/2-3 (29 December 2020), https://www.savacommission.org/UserDocsImages/05_documents_publications/basic_documents/ISRBC%20Rules%20of%20Procedure.pdf.

At the expert level, this task is being carried out mainly by the permanent group for River Basin Management and the permanent expert group for GIS.[44]

As mentioned, it is increasingly common for IRBOs to establish environmental observatories as separate bodies for the monitoring and measurement of biodiversity and other environmental aspects of the watercourse. Indeed, the creation of observatories is foreseen in some of the most recent international watercourse agreements in West Africa, such as the Water Charter of the Lake Chad Basin, the Niger Basin Water Charter, and the Draft Water Charter for the Volta River Basin,[45] and also in international watercourses of other regions, such as the Observatorio Regional Amazónico[46] of the Organización del Tratado de Cooperación Amazónica, and the *Observatoire de l'Environnement* of the OMVS.[47] The Draft Water Charter for the Volta River Basin also provides for the creation of research institutes to conduct research in areas of interest of the basin.[48]

It is common practice for IRBOs to develop and maintain an online tool (although not always in open access) with the available data, which is usually equipped with a GIS-based information system.[49] A good example is the MRC Data and Information Service Portal,[50] created under the legal provisions of the 2001 Procedures for Data and Information Exchange and Sharing[51] and in accordance with the 2002 Guidelines on Custodianship and Management

44 ISRBC. "River Basin Management Plan – International Sava River Basin Commission." Accessed July 13, 2022. https://www.savacommission.org/sava-river-basin-management-planning/river-basin-management-plan-1965/1965.

45 See: Article 66 of the Water Charter of the Lake Chad Basin; Article 18 of the The Niger Basin Water Charter; and Article 100 of the Draft Water Charter for the Volta River Basin.

46 Organización del Tratado de Cooperación Amazónica. "Observatorio Regional Amazónico." Accessed February 13, 2023. https://oraotca.org/en/home/.

47 OMVS. n.d. "Environnement – OMVS." Accessed December 11, 2024. https://www.omvs.org/environement/.

48 Draft Water Charter for the Volta River Basin, Article 119.

49 See, for instance: ISRBC. n.d. "Sava GIS Geoportal." Accessed December 11, 2024. http://savagis.org/; and LCBC. n.d. "Lake Chad Information System." Accessed February 13, 2023. https://lis.cblt.org/lis/km. See, also, the Water Information Systems facilitating transboundary management in the Rhine River basin and the project "Water Accountability in Transboundary Chu-Talas River Basins", in INBO, and IOWater. 2018. *The Handbook on Water Information Systems. Administration, Processing and Exploitation of Water-Related Data.* Paris: INBO and UNESCO. 106 and 96–67.

50 MRC. n.d. "MRC – Data Portal." Accessed February 13, 2023. https://portal.mrcmekong.org/home.

51 MRC, *Procedures for Data and Information Exchange and Sharing* (1 November 2001), https://www.mrcmekong.org/wp-content/uploads/2024/08/PDIES-3.pdf.

of the Mekong River Commission Information System.[52] The MRC information system provides the necessary information for planning, development, decision-making, and monitoring in the basin, using an integrated database, models and other data processing tools and institutional and technical mechanisms for data and information sharing and exchange. The Portal is the channel through which this information is made available to the Parties and other stakeholders, who hold varying levels of access rights.

This key role of IRBOs in providing the information required for informed decision-making in the governance of international watercourses can be bolstered by advances in satellite sensing and earth observation, technology that is becoming cheaper and more accurate.[53] Satellite data on international watercourses have the potential to lessen the impact of the lack of exchange of information between riparian countries due to lack of trust. These data are usually openly accessible and therefore become available regardless of the willingness of States to share them. As suggested by Leb, this growing volume of easily available data will make it more necessary and more beneficial to establish IRBOs with the skilled staff to operationalize satellite datasets and time series and to process the data through complex modelling tools.[54]

3 Mechanisms for a Participatory Decision-Making Process that Enable Institutional Integration

Integration also depends on the participation of the different stakeholders that affect or are affected by sustainable development. Since public participation in general terms, and its application in the field of international watercourses in particular, goes beyond the question of its role in relation to the principle of integration, this Section focuses first on defining in what sense

---

52 MRC. 2002. "Guidelines on Custodianship and Management of the Mekong River Commission Information System". https://www.mrcmekong.org/wp-content/uploads/2024/08/PDIES-3.pdf.

53 On this topic see, for example: Eugenio, Francisco, Javier Marcello, and Javier Martín. 2020. "Multiplatform Earth Observation Systems for Monitoring Water Quality in Vulnerable Inland Ecosystems: Maspalomas Water Lagoon." *Remote Sensing* 12 (2): 284.; and Kitambo, Benjamin, Fabrice Papa, Adrien Paris, Raphael M Tshimanga, Stephane Calmant, Ayan Santos Fleischmann, Frederic Frappart, et al. 2022. "A Combined Use of in Situ and Satellite-Derived Observations to Characterize Surface Hydrology and Its Variability in the Congo River Basin." *Hydrology and Earth System Sciences* 26 (7): 1857–82.

54 Leb, *Data Innovations for Transboundary Freshwater Resources Management.*

public participation is central to the principle of integration. Secondly, the role of IRBOs to provide the means for public participation is explored.

3.1 *Framing Public Participation for Institutional Integration*

The recognition of public participation in a legally binding international instrument varies by region. In the context of the UNECE, it is enshrined in the Convention on Access to Information, Public Participation in Decision-Making and Access to Justice in Environmental Matters[55] (hereinafter, Aarhus Convention); while in the Latin America and Caribbean region it has been regulated in the Regional Agreement on Access to Information, Public Participation and Justice in Environmental Matters in Latin America and the Caribbean[56] (hereinafter, Escazú Agreement).

In broad terms, public participation can be defined as "the practice of consulting and involving members of the public in the agenda-setting, decision-making, and policy-forming activities of organizations or institutions responsible for policy development."[57] This topic can be considered from two perspectives.

On the one hand, the involvement of the affected actors in decision-making on environmental activities might be framed in the field of human rights. The three procedural rights in relation to the environment are: the right to environmental information, public participation in environmental decision-making, and the right to a remedy for environmental harm.[58] An authoritative instrument in this regard is the Rio Declaration, which Principle 10 states that:

---

55 Convention on Access to Information, Public Participation in Decision-Making and Access to Justice in Environmental Matters, June 25, 1998, 2161 U.N.T.S. 447. In relation to this convention, see Pigrau Soler, Antoni, and Susana Borràs Pentinat. 2008. "Diez Años Del Convenio de Aarhus Sobre El Acceso a La Información, La Participación y El Acceso a La Justicia En Materia de Medio Ambiente." In *Acceso a La Información, Participación Pública y Acceso a La Justicia En Materia de Medio Ambiente: Diez Años Del Convenio de Aarhus*, edited by Antoni Pigrau Soler, 21–84. Barcelona: Atelier; or Peñalver i Cabré, Alexandre. 2014. "El Derecho Humano Al Medio Ambiente y Su Protección Efectiva." *Revista Vasca de Administración Pública / Herri-Arduralaritzarako Euskal Aldizkaria*, no. 99–100 (December): 2333–57.

56 Regional Agreement on Access to Information, Public Participation and Justice in Environmental Matters in Latin America and the Caribbean, March 4, 2018, 3397 U.N.T.S. In relation to this agreement see Médici Colombo, Gastón. "El Acuerdo Escazú: La Implementación Del Principio 10 de Río En América Latina y El Caribe." *Revista Catalana de Dret Ambiental* 9, no. 1 (2018): 1–66.

57 Rowe, Gene, and Lynn J. Frewer. 2004. "Evaluating Public-Participation Exercises: A Research Agenda." *Science, Technology, & Human Values* 29 (4): 512–57. 512.

58 Kiss, Alexander, and Dinah Shelton. 2004. *International Environmental Law*. Third Edit. Ardsley, NY: Transnational Publishers. 668–678.

> At the national level, each individual shall have appropriate access to information concerning the environment that is held by public authorities, including information on hazardous materials and activities in their communities, and the opportunity to participate in decision-making processes. States shall facilitate and encourage public awareness and participation by making information widely available. Effective access to judicial and administrative proceedings, including redress and remedy, shall be provided.[59]

The status of public participation in environmental decision-making is contested though, with a division of opinion among the doctrine. Some authors stand unambiguously for the status of public participation as a human right, while others are more cautious in this regard.[60]

The UNECE Water Convention does recognise public right of access to information regarding "the conditions of transboundary waters, measures taken or planned to be taken to prevent, control and reduce transboundary impact, and the effectiveness of those measures."[61] However, this provision is only applicable to the Parties and does not extend to participation in the decision-making process.[62] Therefore, it cannot be said that there is a universally applicable human right to public participation in this particular area of international law; even less so the specific right to involvement in the decision-making process.[63]

---

59 United Nations Conference on Environment and Development, *Rio Declaration on Environment and Development*, in Report of the United Nations Conference on Environment and Development, A/CONF.151/26 (Vol. I) (12 August 1992), undocs.org/en/A/CONF.151/26/Rev.1(vol. I). Principle 10.

60 In relation the former ones see, for instance: Boyle, Alan. 2012. "Human Rights and the Environment: Where Next?" *European Journal of International Law* 23 (3): 613–42. In relation the the latter ones see, for instance: Spijkers, Otto. 2021. "Participation of Non-State Actors and Global Civil Society in International Environmental Law-Making and Governance." In *Research Handbook on International Environmental Law*, edited by Malgosia Fitzmaurice, Marcel Brus, and Panos Merkouris, 45–61. Cheltenham: Edward Elgar. For a general comment on this topic see Tsioumani, Elsa. 2018. "Public Participation in Environmental Decision-Making." In *Principles of Environmental Law*, edited by L. Krämer and E. Orlando, 366–78. Cheltenham: Edward Elgar.

61 Convention on the Protection and Use of Transboundary Watercourses and International Lakes, March 17, 1992, 1936 U.N.T.S. 269. Article 16.

62 See a complete analysis on this topic in: Vykhryst, Serhiy. 2015. "Public Information and Participation under the Water." In *The UNECE Convention on the Protection and Use of Transboundary Watercourses and International Lakes*, edited by Attila Tanzi, Owen McIntyre, Alexandros Kolliopoulos, Alistair Rieu-Clarke, and Rémy Kinna, 268–284. Leiden: Brill Nijhoff.

63 Tsioumani, "Public Participation in Environmental Decision-Making," 373.

The situation is less clear regarding public participation in the development of policies and the management of international watercourses, where there is no homogeneous or consistently applied practice,[64] despite the claims from different forums.[65] The UN Watercourses Convention makes no reference to this type of rights, except for the prohibition of discriminating by nationality "in granting to such persons, in accordance with its legal system, access to judicial or other procedures, or a right to claim compensation or other relief in respect of significant harm caused by such activities carried on in its territory."[66]

On the other hand, and more importantly for the purpose of this study, public participation is also a key aspect for integration because the information and contributions received from the public are indispensable when the decisions under discussion will have a bearing on complex eco-social systems. It is unlikely that any authority in the pursuit of sustainable development can take into consideration all the interests concerned and obtain all the necessary information on its own. As argued by Troell et al, Local communities and non-governmental organizations often have detailed knowledge of their environment that is not available to governments or institutions [...], including traditional knowledge that conventional approaches overlook.[67] Therefore, it is not only a matter of public participation in terms of individual or community rights – which is usually the primary focus of public participation in the context of environmental law – but also a requirement for "ensuring that social and environmental considerations and goals are integrated into governmental decision-making."[68]

This practical approach to public participation is already present in a general sense in the Rio Declaration, which states that "[e]nvironmental issues are

64 Movilla, *La Dimensión Normativa de La Gobernanza Internacional Del Agua Dulce*, 211.

65 See, in this regard, articles 4 and 18 of the ILA's Berlin Rules (ILA. Committee on Water Resources Law 2004. "Report of the Berlin Conference." https://www.ila-hq.org/en_GB/documents/conference-report-berlin-2004-5).

66 Convention on the Law of the Non-Navigational Uses of International Watercourses, May 21, 1997, 2999 U.N.T.S. Article 32.

67 Troell, Jessica, Carl Bruch, Angela Cassar, and Scott Schang. 2005. "Transboundary Environmental Impact Assessment as a Tool for Promoting Public Participation in International Watercourse Management." In *Enhancing Public Participation and Governance in Water Resources Management*, edited by Libor Jansky and Juha I. Uitto, 53–82. Tokyo: United Nations University Press. 55–56; In the same vain, see Mbengue, Makane M, and Mara Tignino. 2005. *Transparency, Public Participation, and Amicus Curiae in Water Disputes*. Edited by Edith Brown Weiss, Laurence Boisson de Chazournes, and Nathalie Bernasconi-Osterwalder. *Fresh Water and International Economic Law*. Oxford: OUP. 373–374.

68 Dernbach, "Achieving Sustainable Development," 256.

best handled with the participation of all concerned citizens, at the relevant level";[69] it is more specifically provided for in Agenda 21,[70] Section III of which concerns 'strengthening the role of major groups', specifically women, children and youth, indigenous people, NGOs, local authorities, workers and their trade unions, business and industry, the scientific and technological community, and farmers.[71]

Despite its focus on recognising a human right to public participation in environmental matters, the practical approach is also recognised in the Preamble of the Aarhus Convention, which states that "in the field of the environment, improved access to information and public participation in decision-making enhance the quality and the implementation of decisions."[72] This can be regarded as a particular manifestation of a "problem-solving approach" to public participation as defined by Steele: the deliberation process is not considered as a means for tackling pluralism, but an opportunity to better achieve goals such as sustainability.[73] In addition, this instrumental application of public participation is increasingly appreciated by decision-makers, both because of the intrinsic value of local knowledge and due to the lack of resources and staff that affects some organisations responsible for managing natural resources.[74]

It is necessary to distinguish between those mechanisms merely providing a one-way communication channel and mechanisms that enable stakeholders to really get involved in the decision-making process and exert a certain degree of influence.[75] If we take as a reference Arnstein's classical "ladder of participation", the levels at which stakeholders could potentially contribute to the decision-making process would be all those above the 'informing' rung. This would exclude the levels at which stakeholders are mere spectators or passive recipients of information and include levels ranging from consultation,

69 Rio Declaration, *supra* note 59. Principle 10.

70 United Nations Conference on Environment and Development, *Agenda 21,* in *Report of the United Nations Conference on Environment and Development,* A/CONF.151/26 (Vol. I) (12 August 1992), undocs.org/en/A/CONF.151/26/Rev.1(vol. I).

71 Ibid. Para. 23.1–32.14.

72 Aarhus Convention, *supra* note 55. Preamble, paragraph 9.

73 Steele, J. 2001. "Participation and Deliberation in Environmental Law: Exploring a Problem-Solving Approach." *Oxford Journal of Legal Studies* 21 (3): 415–42. 417–418.

74 Geoghegan, Tighe. 2002. "Participatory Forest Management in the Insular Caribean: Current Status and Progress to Date." *CANARI Technical Report,* no. 310. 7.

75 Schulze, Sabine. 2012. "Public Participation in the Governance of Transboundary Water Resources? Mechanisms Provided by River Basin Organizations." *L'Europe En Formation* 3 (365): 49–68. 65–66.

at which they are merely asked for an opinion, to those at which stakeholders have control of the decision-making process.[76]

3.2 *International River Basin Organisations as Frameworks for Public Participation*

With regard to the specific operalisation of public participation, relevant to the analysis undertaken here are both the more or less formalised public participation methods[77] but also the institutionalised mechanisms foreseen in international watercourse agreements. In fact, in the case of cooperation on international watercourses, IRBOs are the mechanisms that must provide the institutional means through which stakeholders can take part in the decision-making process.[78]

The first public participation function of IRBOs is the provision of information. Although this cannot perhaps be considered a public participation mechanism *per se*, as access to information creates a unidirectional relationship in which the stakeholders are mere recipients, it is nevertheless a precondition for further stakeholder involvement. Indeed, all of the IRBOs analysed in current and following chapters have a website through which information regarding the state of the basin and governance actions is made available. Although IRBOs vary considerably in the amount of information they provide and the ease with which it can be accessed, all of them provide relevant information on the basin according to their functional scope.[79]

The OMVS, for instance, created the *Centre de documentation et des archives*, the content of which is openly accessible online through its website.[80] Although

---

76 Arnstein, Sherry R. 1969. "A Ladder Of Citizen Participation." *Journal of the American Planning Association* 35 (4): 216–24.

77 The theory on public participation identifies some of those methods available, which are a good guidance for the current analysis: referenda, public hearings/inquires, public opinion surveys, negotiated rule making, consensus conference, citizens jury/panel, citizens/public hearing committee or focus groups. In Rowe, Gene, and Lynn J Frewer. 2000. "Public Participation Methods: A Framework for Evaluation." *Science, Technology, & Human Values* 25 (1): 3–29. 8–9.

78 In this regard, Lautze distinguishes between four types of public participation mechanisms provided by IRBO: "[m]echanisms which ensure that citizens and other stakeholders have 'access to information', participation in form of stakeholder 'consultation processes', active involvement in 'program and/or project planning' as well as public participation in 'decision-making processes'." Schulze, "Public Participation in the Governance of Transboundary Water Resources?" 63–64.

79 Exception made of the Chu-Talas Water Commission, of which no website could be found.

80 OMVS. n.d. "Cda – Centre de Documentation et Des Archives." Accessed February 13, 2023. https://cda-omvs.org/.

the search mechanism of this portal could be improved, it provides access to many documents, studies, articles and data on the basin and the work of the OMVS. Other IRBOs provide more limited access. Information, however, can also be obtained through other channels, such as awareness-raising and information campaigns. See, for instance, the awareness raising and information campaign in the Chu-Talas basin conducted by the local NGO BIOM.[81]

Stakeholder participation can take place through mechanisms entailing direct involvement in the decision-making process, either through merely consultative procedures or through organic participation.

Consultation processes have the double objective of informing the stakeholders of an IRBO's activities and strategies and of providing the opportunity for those stakeholders to give their opinion in return. What characterises this form of participation is that the inputs provided by the stakeholders do not necessarily influence the decision-making process of IRBOs, which in turn limits the stakeholders' interest in taking part. It will be further analysed how consultations can be conducted at each level of watercourse governance: project, policy and management. In any case, as a form of public involvement, consultations continue to be rather *ad hoc* and are rarely endowed with a permanent structure, remaining part of the EIA process or carried out as specific opinion-gathering activities in the wider framework of the planning process.

In order for stakeholders to have a real impact on the decision-making process of IRBOs they need to have a specific and permanent role in the governing bodies. In this respect, their capacity to influence decisions will be determined by the structure of the IRBO and the stakeholders' role in each of these decision-making bodies (if they are given one). According to their functions, as seen above, IRBOs can be categorised as committees, commissions or authorities. If we consider only the second and the third types, they may be formed by the following kind of bodies, although with considerable variation across international watercourses: 'Heads of State', which is more common in authority type of IRBOs; a 'political council', comprising ministers or other State representatives; a 'technical committee', which examines issues and advises the political council; and a 'secretariat', which assumes administrative functions and is able to advance an organisational agenda beyond the meetings of representatives.[82]

81 UNECE. n.d. "Transboundary Cooperation in Chu and Talas River Basin | UNECE." Accessed July 21, 2022. https://unece.org/environment-policy/water/areas-work-convention/transboundary-cooperation-chu-and-talas-river-basin.

82 Lautze et al., "International River Basin Organizations," 35.

Stakeholder participation in basin summits at which Heads of State are present is rare in the comparative analysis of IRBOs. However, a good example is the public participation scheme of the MRC. It provides for stakeholders to participate in both the MRC Summit, which is held every four years and brings together the Heads of State of all Parties, and in the MRC International Conference, which precedes each MRC Summit.[83] It should be noted, though, that 'non-State' stakeholders wishing to attend the MRC Summit must be invited previously, which may create a bias in terms of which stakeholders are given the opportunity to ultimately influence the decision-making process via this channel. Moreover, the participation of stakeholders is meant to facilitate "exchange" on transboundary water management, hence it is essentially a consultative mechanism.

The participation of stakeholders in political councils is a little more common. The MRC foresees their participation in the annual Council Meeting although, again, attendance is by invitation only. The regime governing management of the Dniester also allows stakeholders to participate in the parallel bodies established under the two agreements regulating the basin, the meeting of the Plenipotentiaries and the Commission.[84] According to the regulations on public participation applicable to both agreements, a register of stakeholders must be created, which is open to public authorities of all levels, NGOs and public associations; the only requirement is that stakeholders must have a legitimate interest in issues of transboundary water management within the mandate and activities of the Plenipotentiaries (or the Commission).[85]

These stakeholders have the right to be informed prior to each meeting of the Plenipotentiaries and the Commission, receiving the agenda and any draft document to be discussed. According to Article 6.1, they can participate in three ways: "[s]takeholder participation shall include initiation of issues for consideration by the Plenipotentiaries, submission of written and/or verbal comments on document drafts, and also submission of written and/or verbal proposals concerning changes or amendments to such drafts."[86] More

---

83 MRC. 2021. *Handbook for Stakeholder Engagement At the Mekong River Commision*. 1st ed. Vientiane: MRC Secretariat. https://doi.org/10.52107/mrc.qx5yns.

84 See: Agreement between the Government of Ukraine and the Government of Moldova on joint boundary waters management and protection, November 23, 1994, LEX-FAOC065455, 1994, Article 16; and Dniester River Basin Treaty, Article 6.4.

85 Dniester Commission, *Regulation on Stakeholder Participation in the Activities of the Institution of Plenipotentiaries* (19 December 2007), https://dniester-commission.org/wp-content/uploads/2018/12/11regulation-on-stakeholder-participation-in-the-activities.doc. Articles 2 and 4.

86 Ibid. Article 6.1.

importantly, the regulations also establish that the Plenipotentiaries (and the Commission) must give reasoned replies to stakeholders' proposals within 30 calendar days[87] and that comments submitted by stakeholders in relation to draft documents must be duly considered in making final decisions.[88] In this case, therefore, the regime established for stakeholder participation contains guarantees to ensure that their contributions have an impact on the decision-making process.

In addition to the mechanisms for direct stakeholder participation in the governing bodies of IRBOs, there are also mechanisms for indirect participation – either through organs directly foreseen in the international watercourse agreement, through subsidiary bodies, or through decentralised bodies.

The first form of indirect participation, that is through organs directly foreseen in the international watercourse agreement, may operate through two kinds of consultative bodies attached to the political council, which can either allow the participation of stakeholders in addition to other actors or are constituted with the specific aim of forming a consultative body of stakeholders to inform the political council. The OMVS has both kinds. The *Commission permanente des eaux*[89] is an example of the first type, in which 'observer' status may be given to users' representatives, representatives of territorial collectives, representatives of NGOs or representatives of decentralised management committees.[90] This status is granted on the condition that the entities have a direct concern with the issues addressed by the *Commission*, ensuring that their participation is efficient.[91] The *Comité de bassin* of the OMVS is an example of the second type of consultative body. It is formed by water and electricity companies, farming societies, transport operators, NGOs, users' associations and representatives of the scientific community with the expertise to advise the political council on the general aspects of the management policy for the basin, which in the OMVS is called the Council of Ministers.[92]

87 Ibid. Article 6.3.
88 Ibid. Article 7.3.
89 Charter of Waters of the Senegal River, Articles 19 and 21.
90 Ibid. Article 23.
91 Sangbana, Komlan. 2017. "The Role of Non-State Actors in the Development and Implementation of International Water Law." In *Routledge Handbook of Water Law and Policy*, edited by Alistair Rieu-Clarke, Andrew Allan, and Sarah Hendry, 287–96. Abingdon: Routledge. 288.
92 Sangbana, Komlan. 2015. "La Participation Du Public Dans Le Cadre de l'Organisation Pour La Mise En Valeur Du Fleuve Sénégal." In *Public Participation and Water Resources Management: Where Do We Stand in International Law?*, edited by Mara Tignino and Komlan Sangbana, 77–83. Paris: UNESCO. 81.

The second form of indirect participation is the inclusion of stakeholders in specialised or technical bodies, which are established thematically to tackle particular issues or areas of interest of the IRBO. These may be referred to as working groups or task forces, which will be analysed in detail in Chapter 11 and to which we refer regarding their functions and examples. In any case, it must be underlined that they are a very common way of involving stakeholders in the governance of international watercourses, also in cases in which they are not permitted to participate in the political bodies of the IRBO. They usually are subsidiary bodies that the Parties can create or dissolve depending on the changing needs of the basin. Would be examples of this type of organs the Health Professionals Advisory Board or the Great Lakes Science Advisory Board of the US-Ca IJC.[93]

A third form of participation is used in those cases where the extension of the basin and/or the large number of Parties are more conducive to decentralised stakeholder involvement. It consists of the establishment of national or local committees which enable more grassroots public involvement. In the framework of the OMVS, this approach has been applied through the establishment of a National Coordination Committee in each State for monitoring and coordinating the activities of the OMVS bodies and participating in the implementation of programmes, but also to facilitate the participation of civil society through NGOs and local community representatives.

During the 2000s, several Local Coordination Committees were created in each State specifically to enable stakeholders and local populations of the regions bordering the river to participate in OMVS activities.[94] As stated by Sangbana, "En raison de sa zone de compétence géographique, les [Local Coordination Committees] sont considérés comme la plateforme de participation par excellence des populations locales. En pratique ces comités servent de cadre de consultation entre l'OMVS et les populations locales."[95] Representatives of Local Coordination Committees also participate in National Coordination Committees, of which they are native members.

The institutional structure of the NBA also establishes a decentralised framework for the participation of local civil society in basin policy: the *vision partagée*. Between 2005 and 2014, this policy led to the creation in each State

---

93 IJC. n.d. "Boards, Studies, and Committee." Accessed December 11, 2024. https://ijc.org/en/who/boards.

94 INBO. 2018. *The Handbook for the Participation of Stakeholders and the Civil Society in the Basins of Rivers, Lakes and Aquifers*. Paris: INBO. 37–38.

95 Sangbana, "La Participation Du Public Dans Le Cadre de l'Organisation Pour La Mise En Valeur Du Fleuve Sénégal," 82.

of a *Coordination Nationale des Usagers* together with a *Coordination Régionale des Usagers*. Together, these bodies "servent d'interface entre les acteurs et usagers et les autres parties prenantes au développement et à la préservation des ressources du bassin."[96] They were set up following an initial process to identify non-State stakeholders by topic (e.g. agriculture, fisheries, sanitation, etc.) in order to select legitimate representatives of a wide spectrum of water users.[97]

---

96 Dessouassi, Robert. 2015. "État Du Processus de Gestion Intégrée Des Ressources En Eau Dans Le Bassin Du Niger : Expériences de l'implication Des Acteurs Non Étatiques et de La Prévention Des Conflits Entre Usagers de Ressources." In *Public Participation and Water Resources Management: Where Do We Stand in International Law?*, edited by Mara Tignino and Komlan Sangbana, 69–76. Paris: UNESCO. 73.

97 INBO. 2018. *The Handbook for the Participation of Stakeholders and the Civil Society in the Basins of Rivers, Lakes and Aquifers*. Paris: INBO. 14–15.

CHAPTER 10

Institutional Integration in the Elaboration of an International Basin Policy: Policy-Specific Integration

As projects are often driven by interests that do not necessarily respond to sustainability criteria, integration at the project level has important limitations. This is why the ILA, citing Cordonier and Khalfan,[1] suggested the need to apply the principle of integration at the level of the determining factors of sustainable development, when a holistic approach is still possible.[2] In other words, there is a need to apply the principle of integration in policy-making. This is a problematic issue, since policy-making is, obviously, an eminently political activity in which the claim that it should be conditioned by a legal principle confers a constitutional dimension.

This Chapter addresses the question of what is entailed in applying the principle of integration in policy-making, analysing the instruments that make it possible in the field of international watercourses, such as SEAs, information exchange and public participation. Finally, the integrated approaches applicable to the governance of international watercourses will be tackled. Prior to that, however, it must be stressed that the issue of policy integration in the context of international watercourse governance raises some initial problems.

Firstly, a prior clarification should be made to determine what is understood by 'policy', which is the element that is supposed to be integrated in the context of international watercourse cooperation. Despite the polysemic nature of the term, it can be distinguished from management precisely in that it involves some sort of political decision, while management would instead be the combination of implementing acts following a political act. The complexity of the matter allows for several angles of analysis: policy as a process, policy as an output, policy as a general objective, or policy as the decision of a government.[3] Here the focus is on the concept of policy as a process. As the

1 Cordonier and Khalfan, *Sustainable Development Law*. 180–181.

2 ILA. Committee on International Law on Sustainable Development. 2006. "Report of the Toronto Conference." https://www.ila-hq.org/en_GB/documents/conference-report-toronto-2006-14. 11.

3 Persson, Å. 2004. "Environmental Policy Integration: An Introduction." *Policy Integration for Sustainability*, no. June: 54.

 | DOI:10.1163/9789004736757_015

analysis undertaken here has an institutional focus, the aim is to capture how the decision-making process regarding the creation and implementation of a policy serves to apply the principle of integration in the framework of international watercourses.

Secondly, we must consider what it means for policies to be 'integrated'. Policy integration is a broad term that identifies a whole stream of academic literature on public environmental policy but also a wider academic field of policy analysis. The article on marine policy by Underdal[4] is usually referred to as a seminal text on this topic. For this author, policy integration requires that all stages of the policy-making process meet three qualities: "comprehensiveness to the input stage; aggregation to the processing of inputs; and consistency to outputs".

Comprehensiveness is defined as the inclusion of a broad perspective over time (consequences of the policy from a long-term perspective), space (large geographical area for which policy consequences are considered), issues (interdependent issues) and actors (reference group) in the evaluation of policy alternatives. This comprehensive approach derives from the idea that all policy consequences should be taken into account in order to be integrated. In Underdal's words, "the scope of policy premises should equal the scope of policy consequences."[5] The author warns that this open policy scope will usually be constrained by the extent of the knowledge held about the cause-effect relationships.[6]

The second quality, aggregation, is understood as the consideration of a certain policy from a general perspective, taking into account all the elements identified in the previous stage. This is not simply a technical decision, and a certain degree of negotiation and interest-balancing will be required eventually.

Lastly, consistency refers to both the vertical and horizontal dimensions of the provisions through which a policy is implemented. The vertical dimension of the consistency of a policy is understood in relation to other policy levels, while the horizontal dimension is considered in relation to other policy domains. In this sense, for a specific policy to be consistent, it must be subsumed into general guidelines of some sort.

4 Underdal, Arild. 1980. "Integrated Marine Policy. What? Why? How?" *Marine Policy* 4 (3): 159–69.
5 Ibid. 160.
6 Ibid. 161.

Since the 1980s, several other concepts similar to policy integration have appeared. Meijers[7] identifies some of these broadly synonymous concepts: integrated policy-making, coherent policy-making, cross-cutting policy-making, concerted decision-making, holistic government, joined-up policy and joined-up government. These concepts are not always used consistently in the literature, but Meijers establishes a hierarchical order in which policy integration is the most demanding option for stakeholders involved in the design and implementation of a policy.

At the base of this hierarchy are those approaches based on co-operation among the actors, who work together with the aim of achieving their own goals, which are not necessarily shared. Coordination, however, is defined as a more formal means of cooperation in which there is more interdependence and the joint outcome decisions can possibly diverge from those preferred by the actors at the beginning of the process. Finally, integration would encompass cooperation and coordination but, going a step forward, requires "more interaction, accessibility and compatibility, leads to more interdependence (and also follows from more interdependence regarding the issue at stake), needs more formal institutional arrangements, involves more resources, requires stakeholders to give up more autonomy and is more comprehensive in terms of time, space and actors". This type of process will lead to the development of a new joint policy by the sectors involved instead of a set of policies that align to a greater or lesser degree.

Therefore, 'integrated policy' is understood, on the one hand, in terms of its characteristics; that is, whether it combines the qualities of comprehensiveness, aggregation and consistency described by Underdal. The term is also understood according to its incremental character, implying a deepened relationship between sectors in the sense explained by Meijers. Moreover, as the concern of this research is the application of the principle of integration, the "integratedness" of the policy must satisfy the overall objective of sustainable development.

Policy-integration in the context of international watercourse cooperation is hampered by a specific difficulty: since a watercourse is shared by several States, the decision-making process will take place in the international sphere. To establish a policy in this context requires negotiation in which all of the States reach a common agreement, which will not necessarily be binding. In

7 Meijers, Evert, and Dominic Stead. 2004. "Policy Integration: What Does It Mean and How Can It Be Achieved? A Multi-Disciplinary Review." In *Berlin Conference on the Human Dimensions of Global Environment Change: Greening of Policies – Interlinkages and Policy Integration, Berlin*, 1–15. Berlin.

addition, the implementation phase of the resulting policy will also be far removed from that of a national policy. If no common institution is foreseen for this purpose, such as an IRBO, policy implementation will be completely decentralised and carried out by the States. If such an instrument does exist, the IRBO will participate in the implementation of the policy to some extent depending on its mandate.

The recent experiences of West-African international watercourses are good examples of the development of integrated policies for shared water resources. The respective processes started with a declaration at ministerial level or from the Head of State and led primarily to the creation of "water charters,"[8] which are formal international treaties under the terms of the 1969 Vienna Convention on the Law of Treaties. The west-African water charters represent a major change from the previous treaties regulating those international watercourses. As explained by Mbengue, what distinguishes the "charters" is their object and objective, as they are mostly instruments for the protection of the shared water resources, while the older treaties intended to establish the framework for a common exploitation in a rational and reasonable manner.[9]

They are also, however, central instruments of the policy pertaining to the international watercourses concerned. As argued by Sangbana, "[l]es chartes sont utilisées par les institutions africaines comme outil de politique régionale dans l'administration de la gestion des ressources en eau partagées."[10] The case of the Niger basin is illustrative. In February 2002, the Member States of the NBA decided to develop a policy of integrated water resource management for the sustainable development of the basin.[11] With this decision, a process of negotiation began under the name of *Vision partagée*,[12] which would involve the governments, financial institutions and civil society. One of its outputs would be The Niger Basin Water Charter,[13] together with other non-binding instruments and institutional mechanisms.[14]

---

8 See, for instance the 2002 Ministerial Declaration of the members of the NBA, in NBA Executive Secretariat. 2008. *La Vison Partagée Du Basin Du Niger*. Niamey: NBA. 13.

9 Mbengue, Makane Moïse. 2013. "Les Chartes de l'eau : Vers Une Nouvelle Conception de La Gestion Des Ressources En Eau Partagees En Afrique ?" In *Liber Amicorum Raymond Ranjeva : L'Afrique et Le Droit International : Variations Sur l'organisation Internationale = Africa and International Law : Reflections on the International Organization*. Paris: Editions A. Pedone. 226–227.

10 Sangbana, *La Protection Des Eaux Douces Transfrontières Contre La Pollution*. 195.

11 NBA Executive Secretariat. 2008. *La Vison Partagée Du Basin Du Niger*. Niamey: NBA. 13.

12 Ibid.

13 The Niger Basin Water Charter.

14 For a complete explanation of the process, see also Dessouassi, "État Du Processus de Gestion Intégrée Des Ressources En Eau Dans Le Bassin Du Niger", 72–73.

However, the final outcome of the international policy-making process is not prescribed, and there are several examples of policy-making processes that did not lead to the adoption of a binding instrument. The 2003 *Declaration de Nouakchott*,[15] for instance, opened a process for the establishment of a deeper involvement of basin stakeholders in the management of the watercourse, but it did not lead to the adoption of any further binding agreement. In fact, this policy built on the Charter of Waters of the Senegal River adopted the year before.

1 Methods for Informed Decision-Making Processes Regarding Public Policies

In the context of environmental law and policy, tools have been created for securing an informed decision-making process in the elaboration of public policies. The most well known and widely employed are SEAs, while Sustainability Impact Assessments can also be included in this category. Despite their general character, those instruments can also be applied in the context of cooperation on international watercourses. Therefore, in this Section they will be analysed from the theoretical point of view and from practice in international watercourses, if any.

1.1 *Strategic Environmental Assessments*

Strategic Environmental Assessment have a special role to play in the application of the principle of integration at the policy level, since they are intended to tackle the impact on the environment in earlier stages of planning, in order to facilitate a more holistic approach. This instrument was originally developed by the EU through the Directive 2001/42/EC of the European Parliament and of the Council of 27 June 2001 on the assessment of the effects of certain plans and programmes on the environment.[16] Under this Directive, the Parties to the EU must conduct a SEA when developing plans or programmes on a variety of sectors (e.g. agriculture, transport, fisheries, water management, etc.)

15 OMVS, *Declaration de Nouakchott relative au cadre d'orientation strategique pour l'OMVS*, adopted by the Conference of Heads of State and Government, Resolution N° 00010/CCEG (21 May 2003), http://archives-omvs.org/collectionsdigitales/flipsupports/conventions/declaratnouakchott/2/.

16 Directive 2001/42/EC of the European Parliament and of the Council of 27 June 2001 on the assessment of the effects of certain plans and programmes on the environment, 2001 O.J. (L 197) 30, 37.

or when implementing certain norms.[17] In this regard, the SEAs usually are to set the framework for development consent of projects under an EIA, which will be analysed in relation to projects. However, in this Chapter SEAs are not referred as in their particular regulation in the EU context. Since this method has been adopted in other regions of the world not regulated by EU law, here it is considered its application to the cooperation on any non-EU international watercourse.

The ILA highlights the emergence of SEAs as a response to accusations of the excessively narrow scope of EIAs and as an instrument for policy-specific integration.[18] Like EIAs, SEAs are a structured approach for obtaining and evaluating environmental information to be used in decision-making relating to development activities. With this information it should be possible to predict changes in the environment as a result of the planned action, as well as to propose alternative actions and their potential consequences. The difference is the scope of the analysis. While EIAs are conducted as part of the planning process of a particular project (e.g. the construction of a dam), SEAs are conducted in the framework of actions at a higher level, such as laws, policies, programmes and plans.[19]

In this sense, SEAs can play a complementary role as they "respond to the criticism that project-based EIA tends to occur after broader social and economic policy decisions have been made."[20] In fact, Article 7(2) of the Espoo Convention[21] refers briefly to the former type when determining the applicability of the latter:

> Environmental impact assessments as required by this Convention shall, as a minimum requirement, be undertaken at the project level of the proposed activity. To the extent appropriate, the Parties shall endeavour to apply the principles of environmental impact assessment to policies, plans and programmes.[22]

17 For instance, Council Directive 92/43/EEC of 21 May 1992 on the conservation of natural habitats and of wild fauna and flora, 1992 O.J. (L 206) 7, 50. Articles 6 and 7.

18 ILA Report of the Toronto Conference, *supra* note 2. 11.

19 Abaza, Hussein, Ron Bisset, and Barry Sadler. 2004. *Environmental and Strategic Environmental Assessment: Towards an Integrated Approach*. Geneva: UNEP. 87.

20 Craik, *International Law of Environmental Impact Assessment*, 156.

21 Convention on Environmental Impact Assessment in a Transboundary Context, February 25, 1991, 1989 U.N.T.S. 309. In relation to this convention see generally Marsden, Simon. 2008. *Strategic Environmental Assessment. International & European Law*. Sterling: Earthscan.

22 Espoo Convention, *supra* note 21. Article 2(7).

From the wording of this article, it can be understood that the principles of EIA established in this convention are to be considered universal to some extent. This enabled the Meeting of the Parties of the Espoo Convention to draw up the Protocol on Strategic Environmental Assessment to the Convention on Environmental Impact Assessment in a Transboundary Context[23] (hereinafter, Kyiv Protocol), which was adopted in Kyiv in 2003.[24]

Like the Espoo Convention, the Kyiv Protocol is only accessible to members of the UNECE. However, it is highly relevant as it is the main international legal instrument that requires the assessment of strategic proposals,[25] and although it is mainly concerned with national SEAs, it is also an important reference for transboundary SEAs as it contains provisions regarding the consultations to be undertaken if the party of origin considers that the plans or programmes may have transboundary environmental effects (including effects on health).[26] The Kyiv Protocol is very explicit on the purpose of SEAs as tools for enabling sustainable development through the integration of environmental and health concerns.[27] It establishes the formal requirement for the Parties to conduct SEAs for programmes and plans,[28] while its provisions on policies are more recommendatory in nature.[29]

In practice, SEAs differ substantially depending on whether they are applied to programmes and plans or to policies. In the first case they usually take the form of fixed procedures based on EIA legislation. By contrast, SEAs of a proposed policy tend to be less regulated and more flexible, as policy-making processes have less defined limits. At the same time, as noted by Abaza *et al.*, this

23 Protocol on Strategic Environmental Assessment to the Convention on Environmental Impact Assessment in a Transboundary Context, May 21, 2003, 2685 U.N.T.S. 140.

24 The elaboration of the Kyiv Protocol was greatly influenced by the EU SEA Directive (Directive 2001/42/EC of the European Parliament and of the Council of 27 June 2001 on the assessment of the effects of certain plans and programmes on the environment, 2001 O.J. (L 197) 30, 37), adopted two years before, and also by the Aarhus Convention (Convention on Access to Information, Public Participation in Decision-Making and Access to Justice in Environmental Matters, June 25, 1998, 2161 U.N.T.S. 447.). Due to the importance of public participation for conducting a SEA, the relationship of this Protocol with the Aarhus Convention will be reviewed latter.

25 Marsden, Simon. 2008. *Strategic Environmental Assessment. International & European Law.* Sterling: Earthscan. 93.

26 Kyiv Protocol, *supra* note 23. Article 10.

27 The Protocol clearly states as one of its objectives: "Integrating by these means environmental, including health, concerns into measures and instruments designed to further sustainable development." In Ibid. Article 1(e).

28 Ibid. Article 4.

29 Ibid. Article 13(1). Note that policies were not included as object of SEA in the EU SEA Directive.

greater flexibility usually entails a certain lack of rigour, less transparency and less consistent application.[30] In any case, from the point of view of the principle of integration, and similarly to EIAs, the most relevant part of a SEA is the scoping phase. This is where the comprehensiveness of the analysis will be determined, by defining the impacts and issues that will influence the decision-making process.[31] Needless to say that, as in the case of EIAs, consultation with a wide range of stakeholders is crucial to obtaining a full picture of the effects of the proposed policy. The issue of public participation in policy-making will be addressed in more depth later in the Chapter.

SEAs are not foreseen in either of the two global conventions on international watercourses, nor are they mentioned in the majority of international watercourse agreements. In fact, only two treaties of those analysed in this study mention SEAs in relation to policies (in addition to programmes and plans). Unsurprisingly, these are two of the most recent examples: the Water Charter of the Lake Chad Basin[32] and the Draft Water Charter for the Volta River Basin.[33] The treaty regarding the Volta River is particularly comprehensive, providing that SEAs should be specifically regulated at the level of the basin.[34]

Nevertheless, SEAs are also conducted in basins in which no specific regulatory framework exists. For example, between 2009 and 2010, the MRC carried out a SEA of the proposed construction of 12 hydropower stations along the lower Mekong. This assessment identified the long-term impacts of the planned facilities on several aspects, including non-environmental ones, such as social systems and navigation. It also yielded an array of recommendations for both the Parties of the MRC and the Commission itself.[35]

---

30 Abaza, Bisset and Sadler, *Environmental and Strategic Environmental Assessment*, 88.

31 For a detailed explanation of the phases of SEAs see: Ibid. 106–108.

32 It states that "Policies, programmes and plans for the development of water resources and the environment in the Basin shall be subject to strategic environmental assessment prior to implementation". In Water Charter of the Lake Chad Basin, Article 47.

33 See Draft Water Charter for the Volta River Basin, Articles 77–78.

34 It states that "Through their cooperation with the Authority, the State Parties shall effectively implement agreed environmental management frameworks for strategic environmental assessment." In Draft Water Charter for the Volta River Basin, Article 78.

35 The Final Report can only be found in the four languages of the MRC. In: MRC. n.d. "Results of Strategic Environmental Assessment of Hydropower on the Mekong Mainstream Released." Accessed February 13, 2023. https://www.mrcmekong.org/news-and-events/news/results-of-strategic-environmental-assessment-of-hydropower-on-the-mekong-mainstream-released/. A summary of the Final Report can be found in: MRC. 2010. "MRC Strategic Environmental Assessment (SEA) of Hydropower on the Mekong Mainstream:

1.2 *Sustainability Impact Assessments*

Another available methodology for the assessment of policies is Sustainability Impact Assessment. Although it is not common in the area of water resources and no examples of its application to international watercourses could be found, this type of assessment is conceptually interesting because it effectively embodies the idea of informed decision-making for sustainable development. The methodology originated in the context of the WTO[36] and it has been applied mainly in EU in the specific area of trade policy.[37] However, Sustainability Impact Assessments have also been promoted by the OECD, which published a guideline document for their implementation in any policy area, not only in trade-related contexts.[38]

Like the other assessments tools referred to above, Sustainability Impact Assessments are also structured in several phases. Those are: Step 1. Screening the proposal; Step 2. Scoping the assessment; Step 3. Selecting tools or methodologies to match the scoping; Step 4. Ensuring stakeholder participation; Step 5. Analysing the economic, environmental and social impacts; Step 6. Identifying synergies, conflicts and trade-offs across these impacts; Step 7. Proposing mitigating measures to optimise positive outcomes; Step 8. Presenting the results and options to policy makers.[39] They are also governed by a set of principles (sustainability, focus beyond numbers, stakeholder involvement, transparency and accountability, proportionate analysis and responsibility).[40]

Their characteristic feature is a wider focus, aimed at assessing the combined economic, social and environmental effects of the proposed policy. As

---

Summary of the Final Report." https://icem.com.au/documents/envassessment/mrc_sea_hp/SEA_Final_Report_Oct_2010.pdf

36 See George, Clive, and Colin Kirkpatrick. 2009. "Have Sustainability Impact Assessments of Trade Agreements Delivered on Development Issues: A Reflexive Analysis of the Emergence and Main Contributions of Trade SIAs." In *Trade, Globalization and Sustainability Impact Assessment: A Critical Look at Methods and Outcomes*, edited by Paul Ekins and Tancrède Voituriez, 63–84. London: Earthscan.

37 See the European Commission, Directorate-General for Trade. 2016. *Handbook for Trade Sustainability Impact Assessment.* European Commission. On this topic see, for instance: Kirkpatrick, Colin, and Clive George. 2006. "Methodological Issues in the Impact Assessment of Trade Policy: Experience from the European Commission's Sustainability Impact Assessment (SIA) Programme." *Impact Assessment and Project Appraisal* 24 (4): 325–34; and Hoekman, Bernard, and Hugo Rojas-Romagosa. 2022. "EU Trade Sustainability Impact Assessments: Revisiting the Consultation Process." *Journal of International Economic Law* 25 (1): 45–60.

38 OECD. 2010. *Guidance on Sustainability Impact Assessment.* Paris: OECD.

39 Ibid.

40 Ibid. 4–6.

such, Segger and Khalfan consider the Sustainability Impact Assessment to be the most integrated tool of its kind and the natural evolution of the growing application of EIAs (and SEAs), which have progressively incorporated social concerns along with economic and environmental ones. In fact, they consider Sustainability Impact Assessments the "fourth degree of integration", as the clearest example of a highly integrated mechanism.[41] Since Sustainability Impact Assessments are arguably the most comprehensive approach to assessing the impacts of policies, programmes and plans,[42] they could be of great help in the assessment of proposed policies pertaining to international watercourses. Not surprisingly, the process relies heavily on stakeholder participation.

2 Involvement of Stakeholders in Policy Development

Agenda 21 notes the importance of participation by NGOs in the development and implementation of policies, both at UN and national level, and calls on the UN system to adopt measures to enhance the contribution of NGOs to policy design and decision-making.[43] More specifically, this same instrument states that policy-making on the management of water resources should be based on an approach of full public participation, including women, youth, indigenous people and local communities.[44] Seemingly, the Committee on Economic, Social and Cultural Rights of the UN Economic and Social Council linked the right of individuals and groups to participate in the decision-making of any policy which could affect their right to water.[45] In this Section, the forms in which the public can participate in the development of policies in the context of cooperation on international watercourses will be analysed.

41 Cordonier and Khalfan, *Sustainable Development Law*. 175–176 and 184–187.

42 Bürgi, *Sustainable Development in International Law Making and Trade*. 94.

43 United Nations Conference on Environment and Development, *Agenda 21*, in *Report of the United Nations Conference on Environment and Development*, A/CONF.151/26 (Vol. I) (12 August 1992), undocs.org/en/A/CONF.151/26/Rev.1(vol. I). Paras. 27.6, 27.9.a) and b).

44 Ibid. Paras. 18.9.c).

45 UN Committee on Economic, Social and Cultural Rights, *Substantive issues arising in the implementation of the International Covenant on Economic, Social and Cultural Rights. General Comment No. 15 (2002). The right to water (arts. 11 and 12 of the International Covenant on Economic, Social and Cultural Rights)*, E/C.12/2002/11 (20 January 2003), undocs .org/en/E/C.12/2002/11.

2.1 *Public Participation in Processes Leading to International Watercourse Agreements*

Public participation in the negotiation of treaties on international watercourses remains a very rare practice. Only two cases could be found, in which public participation was channeled through environmental NGOs. One case, as mentioned above, is the *Vision partagée*[46] process of the Niger basin, which led to the adoption of The Niger Basin Water Charter in 2008. Civil society requested significant involvement in this process in 2005 with the *Déclaration de Bamako des Acteurs de la Société Civile*, and this was subsequently acknowledged by the Council of Ministries of the NBA in 2006 in its 25th ordinary session.[47] From this moment, all users' associations were representated at all technical meetings and the meetings of all decision-making organs of the NBA.[48] This required the elaboration of a previous study to identify and characterise the users of the Niger basin from the different sectors concerned, which included agriculture and stockbreeding, fishing, navigation, drinking water and sanitation, protection of ecosystems, dams, tourism, mining, and industry and crafts.[49]

The second case is the process leading to the negotiation of the Dniester Treaty.[50] After the collapse of the Soviet Union, Ukraine and Moldova signed a bilateral agreement on the management and protection of the Dniester.[51] The shortcomings of this instrument in relation to environmental protection raised early claims for amendment from NGOs, which led to the consideration of a new 'Dniester Convention' in 1999 at the International Conference on environmental problems of the Dniester river basin. Although the draft convention was ultimately not signed, the event drew significant participation from NGOs and gave rise to the so-called 'Dniester process',[52] which would end in the ratification by both countries of the Dniester Treaty in 2012.[53] This

46 NBA Executive Secretariat. 2008. *La Vison Partagée Du Basin Du Niger*. Niamey: NBA.

47 Dessouassi, "État Du Processus de Gestion Intégrée Des Ressources En Eau Dans Le Bassin Du Niger", 74.

48 Ibid.

49 Ibid. 28.

50 The Niger Basin Water Charter.

51 Agreement between the Government of Ukraine and the Government of Moldova on joint boundary waters management and protection, November 23, 1994, LEX-FAOC065455.

52 Vykhryst emphisies the importance of NGOs in the initiation of the development of the Dniester River Basin Treaty and its development. In Vykhryst, Serhiy. 2013. "Public Participation in the Dniester River Basin Management." In *Public Participation and Water Resources Management: Where Do We Stand in International Law?*, edited by Mara Tignino and Komlan Sangbana. Paris: UNESCO, 68.

53 Dniester River Basin Treaty.

process was led primarily by the Organization for Security and Co-operation in Europe (hereinafter, OSCE), the UNEP and the UNECE, and was structured in three phases with significant public participation,[54] both through consultations[55] and through the participation of NGOs in meetings.[56]

2.2 *Public Participation in Strategic Environmental Assessments*

Another important mechanism through which civil society can influence the design of a policy regarding an international watercourse is in the process of a SEA. As mentioned above, there is no general standard for conducting SEAs, while they are more extensively regulated in the context of the UNECE. The Aarhus Convention is an important instrument in the region to determine the extent of public participation in SEAs, but it is also an important reference for non-UNECE members.[57] Article 7 of the Aarhus Convention places a strong focus on public participation in the development of plans and programmes, detailing the conditions in which this participation is to take place,[58] but makes less specific provision for public participation in the preparation of policies, stating only that: "[t]o the extent appropriate, each Party shall endeavour to provide opportunities for public participation in the preparation of policies relating to the environment."[59] Hence, this convention does not indicate how

54 Note that in 1999 46 NGOs of both Ukraine and Moldova created the International Environmental Association of River Custodians "Eco-TIRAS" registered in Moldova. In UNECE, and OSCE. 2005. "Transboundary Diagnostic Study for the Dniester River Basin, November 2005." https://www.osce.org/files/f/documents/d/6/38320.pdf.

55 UNECE, and OSCE. 2007. "Action Programme to Improve Transboundary Cooperation and Sustainable Management of the Dniester River Basin: Project Results." Accessed February 14, 2023. http://dniester-basin.org/wp-content/uploads/2009/06/4dniester-ii-publication_engl_with-cover.pdf.

56 See the lists of participants in the meeting reports of the project Plenipotentiaries of the Republic of Moldova and Ukraine. n.d. "Dniester III | Dniester Basin." Accessed February 13, 2023. http://dniester-basin.org/materials/dnestr3/.

57 Morgera, Elisa. 2005. "An Update on the Aarhus Convention and Its Continued Global Relevance." *Review of European Community and International Environmental Law* 14 (2): 138–47.

58 "Each Party shall make appropriate practical and/or other provisions for the public to participate during the preparation of plans and programmes relating to the environment, within a transparent and fair framework, having provided the necessary information to the public. Within this framework, article 6, paragraphs 3, 4 and 8, shall be applied. The public which may participate shall be identified by the relevant public authority, taking into account the objectives of this Convention." In Convention on Access to Information, Public Participation in Decision-Making and Access to Justice in Environmental Matters, June 25, 1998, 2161 U.N.T.S. 447. Article 7.

59 Ibid.

public participation should be included in the case of the preparation of policies, leaving it to the Parties to establish the necessary mechanisms.[60] As SEAs can be part of that policy-making process, it would also be encumbent on the Parties to determine how public input should be incorporated.

Apparently, no SEAs were conducted in the cooperative framework of the international watercourses mentioned above which foresee the use of such assessments.[61] Instead, a SEA was conducted by the four members of the MRC in 2010, despite not being regulated in any international watercourse agreement or protocol.[62] Note that the aim of that SEA was to evaluate the potential regional distribution of costs and benefits with respect to economic development, social equity and environmental protection of a set of twelve hydropower dams to be constructed in the territory of three different countries. In this regard, the object of assessment was a wide policy of hydropower development of the river and not just the impacts of a particular project. The process was carried out with consistent participation of civil society, mostly through the organisation of workshops: four national workshops were held with line agencies and sector institutes, five national and local workshops for NGOs and civil society organisations, and three regional multi-stakeholder workshops,[63] which in sum involved a total of 40 NGOs.[64]

The SEA final report also points out the lack of time and resources to reach all necessary stakeholders and recommends further dissemination of the SEA report and another multi-stakeholder forum to discuss it.[65] Nevertheless, the overall process was useful to harvest the opinions of regional stakeholders and to raise awareness of the potential impacts of the planned hydropower development activities. Although it is too early to ascertain the impact of the contribution of SEAs in the context of international watercourses, they are

60 However, the convention's implementation guide states that the establishment of public participation procedures in the context of SEA would be a valuable tool for the implementation of Article 7. In UNECE. 2014. *The Aarhus Convention: An Implementation Guide.* Second. Geneva: United Nations. 174.

61 See the first section of this Chapter.

62 MRC. n.d. "Results of Strategic Environmental Assessment of Hydropower on the Mekong Mainstream Released." Accessed February 13, 2023. https://www.mrcmekong.org/news-and-events/news/results-of-strategic-environmental-assessment-of-hydropower-on-the-mekong-mainstream-released/. A summary of the Final Report can be found in: MRC. 2010. "MRC Strategic Environmental Assessment (SEA) of Hydropower on the Mekong Mainstream: Summary of the Final Report." https://icem.com.au/documents/envassessment/mrc_sea_hp/SEA_Final_Report_Oct_2010.pdf.

63 Ibid. 37.

64 Ibid. 9.

65 Ibid. 150.

undoubtedly a useful tool to channel public participation in the policy design process.

3 Integrated Policy Approaches

Integrated policy-making has been tackled from several perspectives, with varying degrees of centrality given to water. The same approaches may also be applied in the context of an international watercourse. The most recently developed examples have been largely promoted by UN institutions (e.g. the WEF Nexus approach); while others are explicitly mentioned in international watercourse agreements (e.g. the ecosystem approach). Some approaches, however, are not especifically applied in the context of cooperation frameworks on international watercourses but are recognised as a general principle or mechanism in a regional legal system (e.g. environmental policy integration; policy coherence for sustainable development). This Section presents a review of the most relevant examples to determine the extent to which they facilitate application of the principle of integration.

3.1 *The Water-Energy-Food Nexus Approach*

In the last decade, the Water-Energy-Food Nexus paradigm (hereinafter WEF Nexus) has become mainstream in the sustainable development literature. The use of the word 'nexus' to refer to the interlinkages between natural resources can be traced back, at least, to 1983 with the launch of the Food-Energy Nexus Programme of the United Nations University, which focused mainly on the challenges arising from the dependency between the food and energy sectors in developing countries.[66] It was not until the 2011 conference leading to the 2012 Rio+20 conference with the document *Understanding the Nexus. Background paper for the Bonn2011 Nexus Conference* that the WEF Nexus debate gained momentum.[67] Since then, it has been adopted by several organisations, both at national and international level, to conduct analyses of sectoral sustainability.

66 Mcgrane, Scott J., Michele Acuto, Francesca Artioli, Po Yu Chen, Robert Comber, Julian Cottee, Geremy Farr-Wharton, et al. 2018. "Scaling the Nexus: Towards Integrated Frameworks for Analysing Water, Energy and Food." *Geographical Journal*, no. March 2018: 419–31.

67 Hoff, Holger. 2011. *Understanding the Nexus. Background Paper for the Bonn2011 Nexus Conference*. Stockholm: Stockholm Environment Institute.

The main objective of the WEF Nexus approach is to ensure water security, energy security and food security and to foster the transition to a green economy.[68] Similarly to other approaches, it aims to overcome the "silo thinking" that characterises the dominant economic model. As such, the analysis is made in terms of security, and the focus is placed on the negative inter-sectoral impacts that put at risk the human well-being, while environmental sustainability is treated in a more instrumental way as a necessary element for granting ecosystem services.

The WEF Nexus is seen as an element of concern that requires an integrated approach due to the increasing interconnectedness of the three sectors.[69] In a situation of water and land abundance, the relationship between sectors would be unimportant, but in a context of scarcity or uneven distribution of resources, the use of one resource by one sector can easily harm another sector.[70] For example, the use of water resources by certain countries to produce hydropower may compete with the use of water for irrigation by other countries sharing a watercourse.

Among the factors putting pressure on natural resources and thus on the three sectors of the WEF Nexus, advocates of this approach mention: inequality between countries during the rapid development of the last half-century; the growth of urbanisation and globalisation; climate change; degradation of the natural resource base; and scarcity of water, land and other resources. Where these factors put a particular stress on the WEF Nexus, their governance will be of the utmost importance. Conversely, the WEF Nexus approach may not be necessary or suitable relative to other approaches in cases where there is a relative abundance of water resources or in which there are no energy and agricultural sectors dependent on these resources.

Perhaps the main contribution of the WEF Nexus approach is its focus on interdisciplinarity. Comparing it with a prior approach in the water sector, Allouche *et al.* state that "[w]hile IWRM was asking of (water) sector managers to be more broad-based and accommodating in their approach, the nexus is asking managers to think like managers of other resources, imbibe their

---

68 The UNEP defines the Green Economy as "one that results in improved human well-being and social equity, while significantly reducing environmental risks and ecological scarcities". In UNEP. 2011. *Towards a Green Economy: Pathways to Sustainable Development and Poverty Eradication – A Synthesis for Policy Makers*. St-Martin-Bellevue, France: UNEP.

69 Hoff, Holger. 2011. *Understanding the Nexus. Background Paper for the Bonn2011 Nexus Conference*. Stockholm: Stockholm Environment Institute.

70 Bazilian, Morgan, Holger Rogner, Mark Howells, Sebastian Hermann, Douglas Arent, Dolf Gielen, Pasquale Steduto, et al. 2011. "Considering the Energy, Water and Food Nexus: Towards an Integrated Modelling Approach." *Energy Policy* 39 (12): 7896–7906.

concerns and then only decide measures in their own sectors". The plasticity of the 'nexus' concept has prompted many variations with differing levels of comprehensiveness. Some authors only consider the nexus between two of the sectors, water and energy,[71] but include their contribution in the WEF Nexus debate; while others refer to soil or land instead of food.[72] It is also a common practice to include other sectors in the analysis, such as climate[73] or ecosystems.[74]

By definition, the WEF Nexus is only a partial approach, but it has certain practical qualities. For some, it is analytically attractive as its more limited scope and its trade-offs versus synergies logic make it easier to quantify and more suitable for modelling than other frameworks.[75] For others, the WEF Nexus approach is a feasible tool for implementing the SDGs, and several authors and institutions find the sectoral perspective especially adaptable to the structure of goals.[76]

However, the WEF Nexus approach has not been free from criticism. It has been accused of securitising the sustainable development debate towards a managerial approach aimed at keeping unsustainable economic interests

71 Sixt, Gregory N., Claudia Strambo, Jingjing Zhang, Nicholas Chow, Jie Liu, and Guoyi Han. 2020. "Assessing the Level of Inter-Sectoral Policy Integration for Governance in the Water-Energy Nexus: A Comparative Study of Los Angeles and Beijing." *Sustainability (Switzerland)* 12 (17): 1–19.

72 Karabulut, Armağan Aloe, Eleonora Crenna, Serenella Sala, and Angel Udias. 2018. "A Proposal for Integration of the Ecosystem-Water-Food-Land-Energy (EWFLE) Nexus Concept into Life Cycle Assessment: A Synthesis Matrix System for Food Security." *Journal of Cleaner Production* 172: 3874–89.

73 Sušnik, Janez, Chengzi Chew, Xavier Domingo, Simone Mereu, Antonio Trabucco, Barry Evans, Lydia Vamvakeridou-Lyroudia, Dragan A. Savić, Chrysi Laspidou, and Floor Brouwer. 2018. "Multi-Stakeholder Development of a Serious Game to Explore the Water-Energy-Food-Land-Climate Nexus: The SIM4NEXUS Approach." *Water (Switzerland)* 10 (2): 139.

74 Strasser, Lucia De, Annukka Lipponen, Mark Howells, Stephen Stec, and Christian Bréthaut. 2016. "A Methodology to Assess the Water Energy Food Ecosystems Nexus in Transboundary River Basins." *Water (Switzerland)* 8 (2): 1–28.

75 See in this regard, the numerous tool proposals for nexus modelling. In Dargin, Jennifer, Bassel Daher, and Rabi H. Mohtar. 2019. "Complexity versus Simplicity in Water Energy Food Nexus (WEF) Assessment Tools." *Science of the Total Environment* 650 (2019): 1566–75.

76 See for instance: FAO. 2018. *Accelerating SDG 7 Achievement. Policy Brief 09. Water-Energy-Food Nexus for the Review of SDG 7.* New York: United Nations; and Weitz, Nina, Måns Nilsson, and Marion Davis. 2014. "A Nexus Approach to the Post-2015 Agenda: Formulating Integrated Water, Energy, and Food SDGs." *SAIS Review of International Affairs* 34 (2): 37–50.

intact.[77] Others question its novelty, arguing that its basic principles were already present in approaches such as IWRM or EPI.[78] It has also been criticised for lacking its self-proclaimed holistic perspective, showing instead a bias towards the Global North.[79]

The biggest gaps in the WEF Nexus approach are probably its governance and its legal dimensions.[80] The "Nexus debate" is strongly influenced by systems thinking and system theories since it departs from the idea of the interrelated nature of the different sectors involved (e.g. water, energy and food). Translating the dynamicity of complex systems into the policy-making processes and into law is a major challenge for three reasons: first, because of the intrinsic complexity of the interrelationship between the WEF Nexus sectors; second, in regard to governance, because of the sectoral focus that governments tend to adopt; and third, because legal systems tend to favour legal security over flexibility.

Governance remains an underdeveloped aspect of the WEF Nexus literature, where three elements need to be further explored: first, no definition is offered of the conditions that would incentivise and facilitate the collaboration and coordination of sectors, institutions and actors; second, if the horizontal dimension of the WEF Nexus governance referred to above is not sufficiently well defined, the vertical dimension is even less clear; third, the call for optimisation of resources of the WEF Nexus approach is understood differently in each sector, reflecting their different interests, but the WEF Nexus literature does not address the problem of balancing opposing interests,[81] largely relying on all-accommodating technical solutions.

One of the few attempts to deal with these questions suggests three governance schemes for the WEF Nexus: the first is a governance model for horizontal integration of the three WEF Nexus sectors, consisting of the participation in joint actions of all relevant actors from each sector. The classification of

---

77 Leese, Matthias, and Simon Meisch. 2015. "Securitising Sustainability? Questioning the 'Water, Energy and Food-Security Nexus.'" *Water Alternatives* 8 (1): 695–709.

78 Benson, David, Animesh K. Gain, and Josselin J. Rouillard. 2015. "Water Governance in a Comparative Perspective: From IWRM to a 'nexus' Approach?" *Water Alternatives* 8 (1): 756–73.

79 Wiegleb, Viviana, and Antje Bruns. 2018. "What Is Driving the Water-Energy-Food Nexus? Discourses, Knowledge, and Politics of an Emerging Resource Governance Concept." *Frontiers in Environmental Science* 6 (128): 1–15.

80 Yihdego, Zeray, and Julie Gibson. 2020. *Implementing International Watercourses Law through the WEF Nexus and SDGs*. Leiden: Brill.

81 Weitz, Nina, Claudia Strambo, Eric Kemp-Benedict, and Måns Nilsson. 2017. "Closing the Governance Gaps in the Water-Energy-Food Nexus: Insights from Integrative Governance." *Global Environmental Change* 45 (2017): 165–73.

Al-Saidi and Elagib calls this the "incorporation framework."[82] It would require the creation of a central (supra-sectoral or supra-ministerial) authority with a strong mandate in order to be able to effectively implement a WEF Nexus policy.[83] The proposal can be clearly defined as a policy integration scheme but does not add much to older integrated governance frameworks aside from its particular sectoral focus, since it is rather similar – albeit in a simplified way – to Underdal's policy integration model mentioned above.

The second option for policy integration focuses more specifically on the links between sectors. Its aim is to allow the prioritisation of issues and the identification of cooperation needs, but without aspiring to as comprehensive an approach as the incorporation model.[84]

The third option is based on vertical integration or, to quote again from Al-Saidi and Elagib, "assimilation". This model would consist in each sector carrying out an independent WEF Nexus analysis that would identify trade-offs and synergies with the other sectors. The sectoral policy would then be defined according to this analysis in a "nexus smart" way. They consider this to be a cooperation model, but this is questionable. It is true that it tackles the "silo thinking" that the WEF Nexus approach tries to overcome, but the sectors do not cooperate at the governance level. The sectoral stakeholders are invited to contribute their opinion, but separate sectoral analysis "involving relevant actors from each of the three sectors into the decision-making process within one sector,"[85] even if they are "nexus aware", can still lead to different outcomes. This third approach is precisely the one adopted by the NBA, which will be analysed in more depth later in Chapter 12. In this case, it is the sectoral actor representing the interests of the water sector (the IRBO) that conducts the WEF Nexus assessment autonomously.

If the governance of the WEF Nexus is under-explored, the legal dimension is even less developed, with only few studies on the law of international watercourses focusing on this topic. In this area of study, the WEF Nexus approach is considered to facilitate the application of the substantive principles of

82 Al-Saidi, Mohammad, and Nadir Ahmed Elagib. 2016. "Towards Understanding the Integrative Approach of the Water, Energy and Food Nexus." *Science of the Total Environment* 574 (2017): 1131–39. 1135.

83 Märker, Carolin, Sandra Venghaus, and Jürgen Friedrich Hake. 2018. "Integrated Governance for the Food – Energy – Water Nexus – The Scope of Action for Institutional Change." *Renewable and Sustainable Energy Reviews* 97 (July): 290–300.

84 Al-Saidi and Elagib, "Towards Understanding the Integrative Approach."

85 Märker, Carolin, Sandra Venghaus, and Jürgen Friedrich Hake. 2018. "Integrated Governance for the Food – Energy – Water Nexus – The Scope of Action for Institutional Change." *Renewable and Sustainable Energy Reviews* 97 (July): 290–300.

international watercourses law and to foster cooperation in this matter. In relation to the equitable and reasonable utilisation principle, it is argued that the WEF Nexus approach can help in the following ways: by determining water needs and weighing different uses;[86] by granting the right to access to water and sanitation;[87] by identifying unsustainable uses of the watercourse;[88] and by providing ground for the application of the principle of systemic integration in case of a conflict of norms pertaining to the domains of the WEF Nexus.[89]

In respect to the "no harm principle", the WEF Nexus approach can also make an important contribution. On the one hand, it can provide trans-sectoral criteria for determining the 'significance threshold' of what is to be considered harm in a particular case under the UN Watercourses Convention,[90] as much as determining 'significant adverse effect' under the UNECE Water Convention.[91] On the other hand, it can alleviate the traditional disagreement between upstream and downstream countries, with the former usually prioritising the equitable utilisation principle and the latter prioritising the no harm rule.[92] Finally, the WEF Nexus approach facilitates application of the principle of cooperation as it can raise awareness of the advantages of cooperation to "maximise mutual benefits or avert potential risks through the identification of, and acting upon, trade-offs."[93]

Until now, the application of the WEF Nexus approach in relation to international watercourses has been rather limited. The institutional mechanism of the UNECE Water Convention has been a main supporter of this approach in the context of international watercourses, with WEF Nexus studies conducted

86 Belinskij, Antti. 2015. "Water-Energy-Food Nexus within the Framework of International Water Law." *Water (Switzerland)* 7 (10): 5396–5415. 5405.

87 Olawuyi, Damilola. 2019. "Sustainable Development and the Water-Energy-Food Nexus: Legal Challenges and Emerging Solutions." *Environmental Science and Policy* 103 (2020): 1–9. 4.

88 Pallàs Secall, Pol. 2023. "Contribuciones Del Enfoque Del Nexo Agua-Energía- Alimentación Al Derecho de Los Cursos de Agua Internacionales." In *Derecho y Agua En El Horizonte 2030*, edited by Marta Fernández Prieto, 459–80. Pamplona: Aranzadi. 467.

89 Ibid.

90 Yihdego, Zeray, and Julie Gibson. 2020. *Implementing International Watercourses Law through the WEF Nexus and SDGs: An Integrated Approach Illustrated in the Zambezi River Basin*. Leiden: Brill. 43.

91 Pallàs, "Contribuciones Del Enfoque Del Nexo Agua-Energía-Alimentación," 468.

92 Ibid.

93 Yihdego, Zeray, and Julie Gibson. 2020. *Implementing International Watercourses Law through the WEF Nexus and SDGs: An Integrated Approach Illustrated in the Zambezi River Basin*. Leiden: Brill. 44.

in six international watercourses[94] and the development of its own WEF Nexus methodology,[95] but there are few examples to date of its adoption by IRBOs. The most clear case is the guidelines on WEF Nexus assessment adopted by the NBA.[96] Apart from these cases, the concept appears only sporadically in the context of cooperation on international watercourses.

The first instance is the 2021–2030 Basin Development Strategy of the MRC, which envisages the WEF Nexus approach as a way "to go beyond identifying and sharing information to avoid duplication in areas of 'common interest' and focus on strategic win-win outcomes in areas of 'complementary interest'."[97] However, no further activities on this topic can be recalled. The second, which is also largely declaratory, is the joint statement in May 2022 by the heads of water agencies of the Republic of Kazakhstan, the Republic of Tajikistan, Turkmenistan and the Republic of Uzbekistan concerning the management of the water-food-energy-environment nexus through the implementation of IWRM.[98] The third, which is considerably more developed, is the Nexus Roadmap for the Drina River basin,[99] which was agreed by representatives of all the

94 See UNECE. 2015. *Reconciling Resource Uses in Transboundary Basins: Assessment of the Water-Food-Energy-Ecosystems Nexus*. New York and Geneva: United Nations; and UNECE. 2020. *Reconciling Resource Uses: Assessment of the Water-Food-Energy-Ecosystems Nexus in the North Western Sahara Aquifer System. Part A-"Nexus Challenges and Solutions"*. New York and Geneva: United Nations.

95 UNECE. 2018. *Methodology for Assessing the Water-Food-Energy-Ecosystems Nexus in Transboundary Basins and Experiences from Its Application: Synthesis*. New York and Geneva: United Nations.

96 Those guidelines will be analysed specifically in Subsection 4.4.a) as they are devised as nexus assessments for projects and can be considered, therefore, a method of informed decision-making for project-specific integration.

97 MRC. 2021. *Basin Development Strategy for the Lower Mekong Basin 2021–2030 and the MRC Strategic Plan 2021–2025*. Vientiane: MRC Secretariat. https://www.mrcmekong.org/wp-content/uploads/2024/08/BDS-2021-2030-and-MRC-SP-2021-2025-3.pdf.

98 ICWC. Interstate Commission for Water Coordination of Central Asia. n.d. "Joint Statement of the Heads of Water Agencies of the Republic of Kazakhstan, the Republic of Tajikistan, Turkmenistan and the Republic of Uzbekistan." Accessed August 5, 2022. http://www.icwc-aral.uz/statute15.htm. In relation to the cooperation regime on shared watercourses between these countries, see Campins Eritja, Mar, and Aurèlia Mañé Estrada, eds. 2014. *Building a Regional Framework in Central Asia. Between Cooperation and Conflict*. Barcelona: Institut Català Internacional per la Pau; and Campins Eritja, Mar, Jaume Saura Estapá, and Xavier Pons Ráfols. 2015. "Towards Improved Regional Co-Operation over Water Uses in Central Asia: The Case of Hydroelectric Energy and Inland Fisheries." *Asian Journal of International Law* 6 (1): 119–58.

99 Slides presented at the 3rd Meeting of the Drina Nexus SC: GWP. 2022. "The Draft Nexus Roadmap for the Drina River Basin (and Suggested Draft Joint Statement)."

Parties in May 2022 and which largely builds on the previous WEF Nexus assessment of the Drina basin conducted by the UNECE.[100]

Finally, the WEF Nexus approach can be considered to be present in the Water Charter of the Volta Basin, Article 15.1 of which states that the Parties "undertake to maintain the total amounts abstracted from the water resources in the Basin within a set maximum in order to balance the uses of water while ensuring drinking water supplies, food security and energy security for their people as well as securing the minimum requirements for ecosystems". The fact that this is a relatively new instrument – and the key concepts it uses – suggests that the WEF Nexus approach must have been considered in the drafting of the Charter.

3.2 *The Ecosystems Approach*

Ecosystems have attracted increasing focus as an object of protection by international environmental law,[101] a fact contributed to by the growing tendency to adopt integrated approaches to environmental protection.[102] This is likely due to the interconnected nature of the elements that form an ecosystem: it is natural to extend the protection of certain elements (e.g. a particular animal species) to the rest of the elements that constitute their habitat. Rather than viewing ecosystems as an object of protection, this study focuses on their relevance as a particular way of perceiving nature that informs the development of policies and law: that is, as the basis of an approach. In De Lucia's words "is a style of research characterized by the qualifier 'an ecosystem approach to …', and it may be equally applied to environmental management, to public education, to human well-being, to fisheries, or to urban development."[103]

The adoption of the ecosystem approach is widespread, for example, among international organisations and agencies pertaining to different

https://www.gwp.org/globalassets/global/gwp-med-files/news-and-activities/see/3rd-sc-drina-river-basin-meeting/nexus-roadmap-for-the-drina-river-basin_gwp-med.pdf.

100 UNECE. 2015. *Reconciling Resource Uses in Transboundary Basins: Assessment of the Water-Food-Energy-Ecosystems Nexus*. New York and Geneva: United Nations.

101 McIntyre, Owen. 2019. "Environmental Protection and the Ecosystem Approach." In *Research Handbook on International Water Law*, edited by Stephen C. McAffrey and Riley T. Denoon, 126–46. Cheltenham: Edward Elgar. 129–132.

102 Boer, Ben. 1995. "Implementation of International Sustainability Imperatives at a National Level." In *Sustainable Development and Good Governance*, edited by Konrad Ginther and Erik Denters, 111–36. Dordrecht: Martinus Nijhoff. 637.

103 De Lucia, Vito. 2015. "Competing Narratives and Complex Genealogies: The Ecosystem Approach in International Environmental Law." *Journal of Environmental Law* 27 (1): 91–117. 98.

environmental regimes. Examples include EU policy on fisheries,[104] FAO policy on agriculture,[105] Arctic Council marine policy,[106] and the approach of the Water Convention secretariat to the protection of international watercourses.[107] However, the main development of the concept has taken place in the area of international protection of biodiversity. In 2000, the 5th Conference of the Parties of the CBD described the ecosystem approach as a "strategy for the integrated management of land, water and living resources that promotes conservation and sustainable use in an equitable way."[108] It seems that a certain consensus is now being reached regarding some core aspects,[109] although there is no universally accepted definition of 'ecosystem approach' as yet.

In any case, the integrative nature of the ecosystem approach was clearly recognised by the Parties of the CBD. Twelve principles were devised, of which the Principle 10 states that "[t]he ecosystem approach should seek the appropriate balance between, and integration of, conservation and use of biological diversity."[110] This integrative dimensions of the ecosystems approach was further developed in the Conference of the Parties 11 of the CBD held in 2012, where the Parties added several guidelines for the implementation of Principle 10.[111] These guidelines link the application of the ecosystem approach to an

---

104 Regulation (EU) No 1380/2013 of the European Parliament and of the Council of 11 December 2013 on the Common Fisheries Policy, amending Council Regulations (EC) No 1954/2003 and (EC) No 1224/2009 and repealing Council Regulations (EC) No 2371/2002 and (EC) No 639/2004 and Council Decision 2004/585/EC, 2013 O.J. (L 354) 22, 61.

105 FAO, *Report of the Conference of the FAO. Fortieth Session, 3–8 July 2017*, C 2017/REP (10 July 2017), https://www.fao.org/3/mu208e/mu208e.pdf.

106 Arctic Council. 2015. *Arctic Marine Strategic Plan.* Akureyri: PAME International Secretariat. In relation to the adoption of the ecosystem approach by the Arctic Council, see Campins Eritja, Mar. 2021. "The Arctic Ocean: Ecosystem Approach in a Context of Extreme Vulnerability." In *Biological Diversity and International Law*, edited by Mar Campins Eritja and Teresa Fajardo del Castillo. Cham, Switzerland: Springer.

107 UNECE, *Meeting of the Parties to the Convention on the Protection and Use of Transboundary Watercourses and International Lakes, Report of the Meeting of the Parties on its sixth session*, ECE/MP.WAT/37 (23 July 2013), undocs.org/ECE/MP.WAT/37.

108 Conference of the Parties of the CBD, *Fifth meeting, Nairobi, 15–26 May 2000, Annex III, Decision V/6 'Ecosystem Approach'*, UNEP/CBD/COP/5/23 (15 – 26 May 2000), https://www.cbd.int/doc/decisions/cop-05/full/cop-05-dec-en.pdf. Annex, Article 1.

109 De Lucia, "Competing Narratives and Complex Genealogies," 97.

110 Conference of the Parties of the CBD, *Fifth meeting, Nairobi, 15–26 May 2000, Annex III, Decision V/6 'Ecosystem Approach'*, UNEP/CBD/COP/5/23 (15–26 May 2000), https://www.cbd.int/doc/decisions/cop-05/full/cop-05-dec-en.pdf. Annex, Article 6, Principle 10.

111 "10.1 Develop integrated natural resource management systems and practices to ensure the appropriate balance between, and integration of, the conservation and use of biological diversity, taking into account long- and short-term, direct and indirect, benefits of protection and sustainable use as well as management scale.

integrative practice with the final objective of reconciling the uses of natural resources with the preservation of ecosystems, which can be identified with sustainable development. In this regard, integration is a key aspect of the ecosystem approach, which "promotes the integration, within a transversal ecosystem perspective, of fragmented jurisdictional and political boundaries, and of the social and ecological aspects of environmental governance."[112]

From the legal point of view, the ecosystem approach could lead to integration between substantive norms of different regimes that regulate elements pertaining to the same ecosystem (e.g. biodiversity and international watercourses) or between these norms and others that protect the same elements (e.g. biodiversity and air pollution). In this regard, it has been suggested that the ecosystem approach could be understood as an interstitial norm in the sense proposed by Lowe.[113] Therefore, despite the lack of normative autonomy as an interstitial principle, it could provide coherence, legitimacy, and an interpretative base for environmental rules.[114] The legal status of the ecosystem approach is still being defined and does not seem to have been crystallised in a legal principle,[115] but it should be considered at least a specific management principle in the framework of biodiversity-related conventions.[116]

10.2 Develop policy, legal, institutional and economic measures that enable the appropriate balance and integration of conservation and use of ecosystems components to be determined. 10.3 Promote participatory integrated planning, ensuring that the full range of possible values and use options are considered and evaluated.
10.4 Seek innovative mechanisms and develop suitable instruments for achieving balance appropriate to the particular problem and local circumstances. 10.5 Manage areas and landscapes in a way that optimises delivery of ecosystem goods and services to meet human requirements, conservation management and environmental quality. 10.6 Determine and define sustainable use objectives that can be used to guide policy, management, and planning, with broad stakeholder participation. Identify solutions which relieve sectoral pressure on existing resources." (Conference of the Parties of the CBD, *Eleventh meeting, Hyderabad, India, 8–19 October 2012, Decision XI/11 'Ecosystem Approach'*, UNEP/CBD/COP/DEC/VII/11 (8–19 October 2012), https://www.cbd.int/doc/decisions/cop-11/full/cop-11-dec-en.pdf. Annex I, Principle 10).

112 De Lucia, "Critical Interrogation," 105.

113 Lowe, Vaughan. 2000. "The Politics of Law-Making: Are the Method and Character of Norm Creation Changing?" In *The Role of Law in International Politics*, edited by Michel Byers, 207–26. New York: OUP.

114 Futhazar, Guillaume. 2021. "The Normative Nature of the Ecosystem Approach: A Mediterranean Case Study." *Transnational Environmental Law* 10 (1): 109–33.

115 Koester, Veit. 2018. "Environmental Principles and Concepts in Biodiversity Treaties." In *Principles of Environmental Law*, edited by Ludwig Krämer and Emanuela Orlando, 538–56. Cheltenham: Edward Elgar. 551.

116 Fajardo del Castillo, Teresa. 2021. "Principles and Approaches in the Convention on Biological Diversity and Other Biodiversity-Related Conventions in the Post-2020 Scenario."

From a procedural perspective, McIntyre notes that it is indispensable to establish a river basin commission if the ecosystem approach is to be effectively applied in the context of an international watercourse. This is due to the increased interstate cooperation that the approach involves, which encompasses four main elements: the establishment of environmental flows; a common understanding by all riparian countries of the ecosystem services provided by the watercourse; adaptive management to respond to the changing conditions of the watercourse and the uncertainty regarding complex socio-ecological systems; and the need to establish benefit-sharing arrangements.[117]

The ecosystem approach is increasingly acknowledged in the cooperation on international watercourses to the extent that it is enshrined in some modern international watercourse agreements. While the Dniester Treaty mentions the ecosystem approach among the principles of cooperation,[118] the water charters of the Chad Lake and the Volta, instead, refer to the ecosystem services – which is a concept closely related to the ecosystem approach – as factors of equitable and reasonable utilisation of the watercourse.[119]

However, the ecosystem approach is central to international watercourse initiatives in which it is not explicitly foreseen in the corresponding watercourse agreement. This is the case of the International Watersheds Initiative (IWI) of the US-Ca IJC, which was endorsed in 1998 by the governments of Canada and the United States of America to overcome the narrow view on transboundary watercourse issues. By adopting the ecosystem approach, the watershed commissions would tackle all issues affecting the watershed in an integrated manner, including both biophysical and human aspects.[120] The formula adopted to implement the ecosystem approach was the establishment of "watershed boards" with the mission of coordinating governmental institutions at different levels; acquiring expertise, knowledge and information on the ecosystems of the watershed; consulting and involving stakeholders; and providing the capacity to identify and address unforeseen developments.

In *Biological Diversity and International Law*, edited by Mar Campins Eritja and Teresa Fajardo del Castillo. Springer. 28–30.

117 McIntyre, "The Legal Role and Context of River Basin Organizations."

118 In fact, this treaty states that the Parties must "protect, utilize and manage water and other natural resources and ecosystems based on the integrated approach". In Dniester River Basin Treaty, Article 4.2.e.

119 Water Charter of the Lake Chad Basin, Article 13.c°; Draft Water Charter for the Volta River Basin, Article 13.1.d.

120 IJC. 1997. "The IJC in the 21st Century." https://ijc.org/sites/default/files/ID1011.pdf.

3.3 *Other Integrated Policy Approaches*

Although the Nexus approach and the ecosystems approach are the most widely applied in the elaboration of integrated policies on international watercourses, there are some other integrated policy approaches that might also be relevant in this area. Perhaps the one that has gained more adherence in environmental policy-making is environmental policy integration (usually referred as EPI), which is usually defined in contrast to 'policy coordination.[121] Kivimaa and Mickwitz,[122] but also Briassoulis,[123] for instance, understand policy integration as the inclusion of one sectoral policy in another sectoral policy. This is the most common idea behind EPI, an issue that has generated a large body of literature, especially in the context of EU environmental policy. In the Single European Act, it was provided that "environmental protection requirements shall be a component of the Community's other policies,"[124] a stance that gained importance in the successive treaty reforms and is currently enshrined in Article 11 of the TFEU.[125] Since then, an intense debate has developed over how it should be applied in the context of EU policies, from a legal and a public policy perspective and in both academia and policy-making circles.

The origin of EPI as a concept can be found in the 1980s, broadly concurrent at the UN level with the UNCED process and in the EU, as already mentioned. The basic concept is simple: the integration of environmental policy objectives into another or several other policies as it can be derived from article 11 TFEU. Lafferty and Hovden[126] focus on the policy-making process of EPI in a government-centred scheme, leaving aside the outcomes of the policies implemented for those governmental actors and their effects on society. They differentiate two dimensions of EPI: vertical and horizontal.

---

121 Bauer, A., and E. Rametsteiner. 2007. "Policy Integration and Co-Ordination: Theoretical, Methodical and Conceptual Aspects." In *Proceeding of the 1st COST Action E51 Joint MC and WG Meeting*, edited by Ewald Rametsteiner, 31–48. Vienna: University of Natural Resources and Applied Life Sciences. 36–37.

122 Kivimaa, Paula, and Per Mickwitz. 2006. "The Challenge of Greening Technologies-Environmental Policy Integration in Finnish Technology Policies." *Research Policy* 35 (5): 729–44.

123 Briassoulis, Helen. 2004. "Policy Integration for Complex Policy Problems: What, Why and How." In *Berlin Conference on the Human Dimensions of Global Environmental Change: Greening Greening of Policies – Interlinkages and Policy Integration*, 1–30. Berlin.

124 Single European Act, February 17, 1986, O.J. (L 169) 1, 28. Article 130.r.2).

125 Consolidated Version of the Treaty on the Functioning of the European Union, May 9, 2008, 2008 O.J. (C 115) 47.

126 Lafferty, William M., and Eivind Hovden. 2003. "Environmental Policy Integration: Towards an Analytical Framework." *Environmental Politics* 12 (3): 1–22.

Vertical EPI refers to the extent to which environmental concerns are included in a sectoral department of a government together with its other sectoral objectives, usually known as the "greening" of a department's decision-making process. This vertical integration is not understood in its administrative sense (government, region, local) but as the expression of two opposites, with the government actor on one side and the sectoral actors, such as individuals or companies, on the other.

Horizontal EPI, on the other hand, refers to the "extent to which a central authority has developed a comprehensive cross-sectoral strategy for EPI."[127] Assuming that each sectoral department will have its own objectives and interests along the three axes of sustainable development (economic, social and environmental), these authors consider that a cross-sectoral strategy for EPI should involve a "principled-priority" in favour of the environment.

The latter dimension of EPI, which prioritises the environment over other concerns, is what Jordan and Lenschow define as a "strong reading" of EPI.[128] As seen above in the words of Bauer and Rametsteiner,[129] there are also "weaker" conceptualisations of EPI that are more broadly aligned with the notions of policy cooperation and coordination, according to which the prioritisation of a set of sectoral objectives (e.g. environmental goals) is not feasible and the focus is put on integration to reach win-win solutions, generate synergies or ensure reciprocity between policies without any sense of preference between their objectives.

Another important approach that must be recalled here is policy coherence for sustainable development (hereinafter, PCSD). PCSD is an approach to policy-making developed by the OECD following the adoption of Agenda 2030 in 2015.[130] Previously, the focus of this approach had been on the North-South effects of policies, expressing the idea that trade, agriculture or any other sectoral policies of the donor should not counter the objectives of aid to developing countries.[131] From 2015 on, the OECD shifted the concept to target sustainable development generally and to be applicable both in the relationships between countries and also internally:

127 Ibid.14.

128 Jordan, Andrew, and Andrea Lenschow. 2008. *Innovation in Environmental Policy? Integrating the Environment for Sustainability*. Cheltenham: Edward Elgar.

129 Bauer and Rametsteiner, "Policy Integration and Co-Ordination," 36–37.

130 OECD. 2015. *Better Policies for Development 2015*. Paris: OECD Publishing.

131 See, for instance: OECD, *Ministerial Declaration On Policy Coherence For Development*, C/MIN(2008)2/FINAL (4 June 2008), https://one.oecd.org/document/C/MIN(2008)2/FINAL/en/pdf.

> "PCSD is defined as an approach and policy tool – relevant to all countries – to integrate the economic, social, environmental and governance dimensions of sustainable development at all stages of domestic and international policy making. It aims to increase governments' capacities to identify synergies, consider policy trade-offs between multiple objectives, for example between economic growth, environmental protection, and reduction of carbon emissions; and address the potential spillovers of domestic policies."[132]

This broad definition has been largely developed by the OECD as a way to achieve the SDGs and includes a detailed framework for its application.[133] The concept is rather ambitious, consisting of a sort of 'pan-sectoral' approach that cannot be applied solely from the water sector or in the context of cooperation in an international watercourse, instead requiring the capacity to intervene horizontally in all sectoral policies that may affect each other.

Examples of its adoption range from the establishment of PCSD in development programmes at national level (e.g. Mexico, Switzerland or Poland), the appointment of coordinators for sustainable development across all Ministries (e.g. Germany), the establishment of a centralised organ to ensure a whole-of-government approach to SDG implementation (e.g. the "SDGs Promotion Headquarters" led by the Prime Minister of Japan) or the creation of a coordination unit inside the Government (e.g. Canada or Chile).[134]

Nevertheless, the concept of PCSD is so wide that could even be confused with that of 'policy integration', which questions its ability to provide new insights into how to implement integration. In fact, policy integration is regarded by the OECD as a particular institutional approach for PCSD,[135] but the former is poorly defined by this institution and is difficult to differentiate from the latter. In any case, no particular experiences of the application of the PCSD were found that would include cooperation in the management of an international watercourse, a domain in which it remains a merely theoretical approach.

---

132 OECD. 2015. *Better Policies for Development 2015*. Paris: OECD Publishing. 40–41.

133 See: OECD. 2017. *Policy Coherence for Sustainable Development 2017*. Paris: OECD Publishing; and OECD. 2018. *Policy Coherence for Sustainable Development 2018*. Paris: OECD Publishing.

134 OECD. 2019. *Policy Coherence for Sustainable Development 2019*. Paris: OECD Publishing. 73–75.

135 Ibid. 76–80.

CHAPTER 11

Institutional Integration in the Management of International River Basins: Management-Specific Integration

The management of watercourses is another level at which integration must be pursued if the objectives of integrated policy-making are to be effectively achieved. The water sector has developed well-known approaches to the management of water resources such as the IWRM, which will be examined later. There are many different definitions of management in the literature and practices vary considerably between administrations or management cultures; the specific domain of watercourse management is no exception.

However, attempts have been made to codify general management practices. Article 24 of the UN Watercourses Convention states that "Watercourse States shall, at the request of any of them, enter into consultations concerning the management of an international watercourse, which may include the establishment of a joint management mechanism."[1] This disposition leaves it largely to the States to establish the specific terms and model of management, with few predetermined elements.

In the following paragraph, management is defined very simply as including "(a) Planning the sustainable development of an international watercourse and providing for the implementation of any plans adopted and (b) Otherwise promoting the rational and optimal utilization, protection and control of the watercourse."[2] It can be concluded from this article that management under the UN Watercourses Convention entails three activities: planning (of sustainable development of the international watercourse), implementation (of that previous planning) and promotion (of rational and optimal utilisation, protection and control).

However, this enumeration presents a clear weakness, since central aspects of management, such as protection and control of the watercourse, are not stated in a "command-and-control" manner but rather presented as aspects that must be promoted by the States or by the joint management mechanism that may have been established. This does not prevent the States from giving

1 Convention on the Law of the Non-Navigational Uses of International Watercourses, May 21, 1997, 2999 U.N.T.S. Article 24.1.

2 Ibid. Article 24.2.

 | DOI:10.1163/9789004736757_016

the joint management mechanism more stringent capacities, but it does leave greater scope for non-compliance with planned actions. Nevertheless, since the planning of the development must be sustainable, as stipulated by Article 24.2.(a) of the UN Watercourses Convention, there is room for the adoption of an integrated approach.

Mention should be made at this point of the link between management and river basin commissions, which Article 24.1. of the UN Watercourses Convention foresees as an optional mechanism for the joint management. However, previous versions of this article provided that such mechanisms must be compulsory[3] and specify their functions as management institutions. The draft articles presented by the Special Rapporteur Jens Evensen provided a first enumeration of the functions of these commissions.[4] With some variations, the Special Rapporteur Stephen McCaffrey proposed in the second paragraph of Article 26 of the draft articles of the Sixth Report the following management functions to be carried out by joint organisations:

a. implementation of the obligations of the watercourse States under the present articles, in particular the obligations under parts II and III of the articles;
b. facilitation of regular communication, and exchange of data and information;
c. monitoring international watercourse(s) [systems] on a continuous basis;
d. planning of sustainable, multi-purpose and integrated development of international watercourse[s] [systems];

3 See, for instance, the first version of article 15 on the establishment of 'permanent institutional machinery'. In ILC, *Third report on the law of the non-navigational uses of international watercourses*, by Mr. Stephen M. Schwebel, Special Rapporteur, A/CN.4/348 and Corr.1 (1982), https://legal.un.org/ilc/documentation/english/a_cn4_348.pdf. Para. 471.

4 "(a) to collect, verify and disseminate information and data concerning utilization, protection and conservation of the international watercourse or watercourses; (b) to propose and institute investigations and research concerning utilization, protection and control; (c) to monitor the international watercourse on a continuous basis; (d) to recommend to watercourse States measures and procedures necessary for the optimum utilization and the effective protection and control of the watercourse; (e) to serve as a forum for consultations, negotiations and other procedures for peaceful settlement entrusted to such commissions by watercourse States; (f) to propose and operate control and warning systems with regard to pollution, other environmental effects of water uses, natural hazards or other hazards which may cause damage or harm to the rights or interests of watercourse States." (ILC, *Second report on the law of the non-navigational uses of international watercourses, by Mr. Jens Evensen, Special Rapporteur*, A/CN.4/381 and Corr.1 and Corr.2. (1984), https://legal.un.org/ilc/documentation/english/a_cn4_381.pdf. Para. 7).

e. proposing and implementing decisions of the watercourse States concerning the utilization and protection of international watercourse[s] [systems]; and

f. proposing and operating warning and control systems relating to pollution, other environmental effects of the utilization of international watercourse[s] [systems], emergency situations, or water-related hazards and dangers.[5]

The definitive version of the paragraph, however, presented fundamental changes. On the one hand, the Drafting Committee decided to dissociate management from joint commissions, as they considered that management could be carried out in a less formal way. On the other, it found the enumeration of paragraph 2 too elaborate and decided to reformulate it "in a synthetic rather than an analytical way", leaving its further definition for the commentaries.[6] From the commented version, it can be seen that the Drafting Committee included in its definition of management functions: the "planning of sustainable, multipurpose and integrated development of international watercourses; facilitation of regular communication and exchange of data and information between watercourse States; and monitoring of international watercourses on a continuous basis."[7] Although the commentaries are not binding, they clearly express a common understanding of what constitutes the elements of management.

However, the lack of a universal definition has left room for the adoption of specific management approaches such as the IWRM, which is viewed as a general standard for water management that has been adopted by many countries to improve water management practices[8] and has also been incorporated into target 5 of the SDG 6 of Agenda 2030.[9] As Ziganshina argues, Article 24 of the

---

5 ILC, *Sixth report on the law of the non-navigational uses of international watercourses, by Mr. Stephen C. McCaffrey, Special Rapporteur*, A/CN.4/427 & Corr.1 and Add.1 (1990), https://legal.un.org/ilc/documentation/english/a_cn4_427.pdf. Para. 19.

6 ILC, *Summary record of the 2229th meeting*, A/CN.4/SR.2229 (1991), https://legal.un.org/ilc/documentation/english/summary_records/a_cn4_sr2229.pdf. Para. 30. The version of Article 26 of the Drafting Committee would be left unchanged subsequently and the version of the current Article 24 of the UN Watercourses Convention (*supra* note 1) is identical.

7 ILC, *Draft articles on the law of the non-navigational uses of international watercourses and commentaries thereto and resolution on transboundary confined groundwater*, A/CN.4/SER.A/1994/Add.l (Part 2) (1994) https://legal.un.org/ilc/texts/instruments/english/commentaries/8_3_1994.pdf. 125.

8 Ziganshina, "Protection, Preservation, and Management", 222.

9 It reads "implement integrated water resources management at all levels, including through transboundary cooperation as appropriate". In United Nations summit for the adoption of the post-2015 development agenda, *Transforming our world: the 2030 Agenda for Sustainable Development*, A/RES/70/1 (21 October 2015), undocs.org/en/A/RES/70/1.

UN Watercourses Convention should evolve based on the experiences of planning, implementation and monitoring practices in international watercourses around the globe.[10]

The UNECE Water Convention does not contain an article on management, nor does it indicate what elements the concept of management should encompass. It does, however, establish that transboundary waters should be managed in an ecologically sound and rational way to prevent, control and reduce any transboundary impact.[11] The text also states as a guiding principle to achieve the objectives of the convention that water resources must be managed "so that the needs of the present generation are met without compromising the ability of future generations to meet their own needs";[12] in other words, with the objective of ensuring the sustainable development of the watercourse.

Taking as a starting point the aspects of management enumerated in the UN Watercourses Convention definition and as stated by the Drafting Committee, and in light of the extended practice of including the public in decision-making concerning the management of international watercourses, this Chapter is divided into Sections on the following elements: planning; exchange of information and monitoring; and public participation. Finally, these elements are considered alongside the approaches that respond to the need for integrated management.

1 Methods for Informed Management of International Watercourses

Integrated planning has been called for in the international agenda for sustainable development from the beginning. The Stockholm Declaration makes extensive reference to integrated planning, enshrining it as one of its principles.[13] It also recommends that the UN, other international organisations, and the States jointly develop methods for the integrated planning and management of natural resources.[14] Agenda 21 refers to integrated planning throughout the text, while Chapter 18 offers the following definition of integrated

10 Ziganshina, "Protection, Preservation, and Management", 224.

11 Convention on the Protection and Use of Transboundary Watercourses and International Lakes, March 17, 1992, 1936 U.N.T.S. 269. Article 2.2(b).

12 Ibid. Article 2.5(c).

13 United Nations Conference on the Human Environment, *Declaration of the United Nations Conference on the Human Environment*, in Report of the United Nations Conference on the Human Environment, A/CONF.48/14/Rev.1. (5–16 June 1972), undocs.org/en/A/CONF.48/14/Rev.1. Principle 13.

14 Ibid. Recommendation 68.

planning in the specific context of integrated water resources development and management:

> Water resources development and management should be planned in an integrated manner, taking into account long-term planning needs as well as those with narrower horizons, that is to say, they should incorporate environmental, economic and social considerations based on the principle of sustainability; include the requirements of all users as well as those relating to the prevention and mitigation of water-related hazards; and constitute an integral part of the socio-economic development planning process. A prerequisite for the sustainable management of water as a scarce vulnerable resource is the obligation to acknowledge in all planning and development its full costs. Planning considerations should reflect benefits investment, environmental protection and operation costs, as well as the opportunity costs reflecting the most valuable alternative use of water. Actual charging need not necessarily burden all beneficiaries with the consequences of those considerations. Charging mechanisms should, however, reflect as far as possible both the true cost of water when used as an economic good and the ability of the communities to pay.[15]

According to this definition, integrated planning can be considered to encompass four aspects: sustainability; consideration of the interests of all users; cross-sectoral integration of water in all socio-economic planning; and cost distribution of water resources use.

As seen above, the UN Watercourses Convention identifies planning as the first element in the management of an international watercourse, although it does not provide a further definition. Planning can be understood as a coordination mechanism which, according to Grigg, "provides a neutral forum for problem-solving in the search for win-win solutions in conflict scenarios among stakeholders."[16] Since the focus is on the conflict between stakeholders, their participation in the process will be of the utmost importance. As such, planning must be organised as a bottom-up process which allows all stakeholders to agree on a shared goal; in a top-down process, stakeholders may not perceive the need for planning and the plan may eventually fail. The first step

15 United Nations Conference on Environment and Development, *Agenda 21*, in *Report of the United Nations Conference on Environment and Development*, A/CONF.151/26 (Vol. 1) (12 August 1992), undocs.org/en/A/CONF.151/26/Rev.1(vol. I). Para. 18.16.

16 Grigg, Neil S. 2016. *Integrated Water Resource Management: An Interdisciplinary Approach*. Cham: Palgrave Macmillan. 67.

is for all stakeholders to agree on a "focal point goal" that will clearly define the purpose of the management plan. The stakeholders should share some common interest or problem, such as watershed improvement, river basin, estuary restoration, lake recovery, aquifer overdraft, instream flow or a river corridor improvement. Planning can also be supported by the intervention of scientific and engineering activities.[17]

The planning process for an international watercourse can be divided in two stages. First, a transboundary analysis is carried out to obtain a detailed picture of the state of the basin and the challenges that the management plan must tackle. Second, the management plan is drawn up to define the actions that each State must implement. These stages will be analysed in more detail next.

1.1 *Informed Planning Process*

The planning process should be performed by a joint body and lead to the adoption of a common 'management plan.' In this regard, the UNECE recommends that the process be initiated by conducting a Transboundary Diagnostic Analysis of the basin to identify the "current state of water resources and uses, challenges, and opportunities."[18] This requirement is not explicitly foreseen in international watercourse agreements, but all water management plans that have received the support of the GEF have been preceded by a Transboundary Diagnostic Analysis,[19] as have others not receiving GEF funding.[20] These preliminary analyses vary significantly in the comprehensiveness of the issues considered, but they generally cover the following aspects: a biophysical description of the basin which includes its geologic, hydrographic, climatic and biodiversity characteristics; a socio-economic analysis including its demography, key economic sectors and cultural and health aspects; its legal and institutional framework; and problematic issues, such as ecosystem degradation,

---

17 Grigg, Neil S. 2011. *Governance and Management for Sustainable Water Systems*. London: IWA Publishing. 164–166.

18 UNECE. 2021. *Practical Guide for the Development of Agreements or Other Arrangements for Transboundary Water Cooperation*. Geneva: United Nations. 48.

19 See, for instance: Barnes, J., R. Saraiva, G. Mmopelwa, J. Mbaiwa, D. Wamunyima, and L. Magole. 2009. "Okavango River Basin Transboundary Diagnostic Analysis: Socio-Economic Assessment. Final Report." Accessed February 15, 2023. https://iwlearn.net/resolveuid/4f82de663916daa53318dc2c964e6546. See, also, GEF, and The World Bank. 1998. "Aral Sea Basin Program (Kazakhstan, Kyrgyz Republic, Tajikistan, Turkmenistan and Uzbekistan). Water and Environmental Management Project." http://www.cawater-info.net/library/eng/reports/wemp.pdf.

20 See, for instance: NBA. 2007. "Elaboration of an Action Plan for the Sustainble Development of the Niger Basin – Phase 1 Assessment and Analysis. Final Report." 2007. http://www.abn.ne/images/documents/textes/padd/phase_1_en.pdf.

extreme hydrological events, water quality concerns, invasive species or overuse of water resources, among others.[21] All Transboundary Diagnostic Analysis involve a wide range of stakeholders.[22]

Management plans are intended to define the actions to be implemented by the riparian States that have some sort of transboundary nature, and which commonly include aspects such as: hydropower generation, irrigation, navigation, low water replenishment, ecosystem preservation, floods and drought control, and pollution.[23] They can take many different forms across international watercourses and are often structured hierarchically through instruments that establish a cascade of objectives from general to more specific. Three levels of instruments can be differentiated, although in most cases only one or two of them are used. In the practice of IRBOs, the terms used to refer to these instruments vary considerably, so the content and purpose of each instrument must be considered in order to classify them. These levels are the 'strategy' as the most general level of planning, the 'master plan' as the second level, and the 'action plan' as the third level.

In the most detailed planning processes, strategies are adopted for periods of between ten and 20 years,[24] usually with the explicit purpose of providing a foundation for the elaboration of the management plan. This is the case of the ISRBC, which in 2011 adopted the Strategy on Implementation of the Framework Agreement on the Sava River Basin. This instrument had the general mission of defining the measures for the implementation of the framework agreement and establishing the means of public participation and stakeholder involvement.[25] Specifically, one of the implementation measures was the elaboration of the master plan, which would be approved in 2014.[26]

---

21 See, for instance: GEF. 2019. "Transboundary Diagnostic Analysis of the Dniester River Basin." https://drive.google.com/file/d/1_EohwFL-prbz_LV_MB__tZ7VGlkxYfF2/view. See also NBA. 2007. "Elaboration of an Action Plan for the Sustainble Development of the Niger Basin – Phase 1 Assessment and Analysis. Final Report." 2007. http://www.abn.ne/images/documents/textes/padd/phase_1_en.pdf.

22 See, for instance: UNEP-GEF Volta Project. 2013. "Volta Basin Transboundary Diagnostic Analysis. Final Report." *UNEP/GEF/Volta/RR 4/2013*. http://gefvolta.iwlearn.org/project-resources/studies-reports/tda-final/regional-tda/volta-basin-tda-english.

23 GWP, and INBO. 2012. *The Handbook for Integrated Water Resources Management in Transboundary Basins of Rivers, Lakes and Aquifers*. Paris: GWP & INBO. 83.

24 GWP, and INBO. 2009. *A Handbook for Integrated Water Resources Management in Basins*. Paris: GWP & INBO. 65.

25 ISRBC, *Strategy on Implementation of the Framework Agreement on the Sava River Basin*, Doc. No. 1S-26-O-11-4/2-2 (April 2011), https://www.savacommission.org/UserDocsImages/05_documents_publications/basic_documents/strategy_on_implementation_of_the_fasrb_2011.pdf.

26 ISRBC, *Sava River Basin Management Plan* (2 December 2014), https://www.savacommission.org/UserDocsImages/05_documents_publications/water_management/eng/SavaRBMPlan/sava_river_basin_management_plan_approved_eng.pdf.

Master plans are the central instrument of planning, and national plans affecting parts of the international watercourse must be coherent with them. This is explicitly stated, for instance, in the Draft Water Charter for the Volta River Basin: "[t]he Authority and the State Parties shall ensure that national legislation, regulations and strategies on the management of water resources and the environment are harmonized."[27] They are documents establishing the actions to be implemented by the States, the costs of which must be divided proportionally between them. Master plans are iterative documents, intended to be revised periodically in a time frame that can be set in the plan itself.[28] Their adoption is only foreseen in the most recent international watercourse agreements,[29] but it is already a generalised practice.[30]

When master plans are developed with the help of the GEF, they take the name of 'Strategic Action Plan',[31] which have the advantage of being highly standardised. This quality, according to the International Network of Basin Organisations (hereinafter, INBO), "enables a clear distinction between actions with purely national benefits and those addressing transboundary concerns

---

27 Draft Water Charter for the Volta River Basin, Article 6.1.

28 UNECE. 2021. *Practical Guide for the Development of Agreements or Other Arrangements for Transboundary Water Cooperation.* Geneva: United Nations. 49.

29 For instance: Article 141 of the Draft Volta Water Charter establishes that the VBA must develop and implement a "master plan for the development and management of water at basin scale"; Article 1 and 11 of the The Niger Basin Water Charter in relation to the adoption of Sustainable Development Action Plans; Article 12 of the Framework Agreement on the Sava River Basin; and Article 6.1 of the 2012 Dnister Treaty.

30 See, for instance, the adoption in 2021 of the Basin Development Strategy for the Lower Mekong Basin 2021–2030 and the MRC Strategic Plan 2021–2025 (MRC. 2021. *Basin Development Strategy for the Lower Mekong Basin 2021–2030 and the MRC Strategic Plan 2021–2025.* Vientiane: MRC Secretariat. https://www.mrcmekong.org/wp-content/uploads/2024/08/BDS-2021-2030-and-MRC-SP-2021-2025-3.pdf). See, also: ICPDR. 2021. "Danube River Basin Management Plan (DRBMP) Update 2021 | ICPDR – International Commission for the Protection of the Danube River." https://www.icpdr.org/main/publications/danube-river-basin-management-plan-drbmp-update-2021. See, also: Comité Intergubernamental Coordinador de los Países de la Cuenca del Plata. 2016. "Programa Marco de La Cuenca Del Plata. Proceso de Ejecución y Principales Resultados." 2016. https://cicplata.org/wp-content/uploads/2017/09/programa_marco_de_la_cuenca_del_plata.pdf.

31 See, for instance: GEF, The World Bank, UNDP, LCBC, and UNOPS. 2008. "Strategic Action Programme for the Lake Chad Basin: Agreed by the LCBC Member States of Cameroon, Central African Republic, Chad, Niger, and Nigeria." https://iwlearn.net/resolveuid/2cc8f6b24b896184e77164ab75cbf7b1. See also the Strategic Action Programme for Chu and Talas River Basins, which was elaborated in 2018 by the Chu-Talas Water Commission with the funding of GEF and is pending approval by the States (Chu-Talas Water Commission. n.d. "Enabling Transboundary Cooperation and Integrated Water Resources Management in the Chu and Talas River Basins." Accessed July 8, 2022. https://erc.undp.org/evaluation/managementresponses/detail/9846).

with global benefits. Another key element involves the development of institutional mechanisms at the regional and national levels for implementing the Strategic Action Plan and monitoring and evaluation procedures to measure effectiveness of the outcomes of the process."[32] Moreoever, as already mentioned, they are always based on a previous Transboundary Diagnostic Analysis.

Finally, it is also a common practice for IRBOs to draw up action plans for the implementation of the master plan, especially when the master plan is not sufficiently detailed.[33] Strategic Action Plans, for instance, do not require any further implementing instrument. It is also possible to adopt sectoral plans of actions for concrete topics, such as for floods[34] in the Danube. A legal basis for the use of Strategic Action Plans is only provided in the Draft Water Charter for the Volta River Basin.[35]

SEAs have already been analysed in the Chapter 10 on policy-specific integration. However, they are also applicable to the elaboration of plans and programmes, purposes for which they are foreseen in both the Lake Chad and the Volta water charters.[36] In the case of Danube and the Sava river basins, planning is subject to Directive 2001/42/EC of the European Parliament and of the Council of 27 June 2001 on the assessment of the effects of certain plans and programmes on the environment.[37] Until now, SEAs have been used mainly by

---

32 GWP, and INBO. 2012. *The Handbook for Integrated Water Resources Management in Transboundary Basins of Rivers, Lakes and Aquifers*. Paris: GWP & INBO. 84.

33 See, for instance: NBA. 2016. "Plan Operationnel 2016 - 2024. Document Principal." http://www.abn.ne/images/documents/PO/plan_operationnel_%20abn_vf11032016.pdf.
See also: Comité Intergubernamental Coordinador de los Países de la Cuenca del Plata. 2016. "Programa de Acciones Estratégicas de La Cuenca Del Plata." Accessed February 15, 2023. https://cicplata.org/wp-content/uploads/2017/09/programa_de_acciones_estrategicas_de_la_cuenca_del_plata.pdf.
See, also, the MRC Strategic Plan 2021–2025, In: Basin Development Strategy for the Lower Mekong Basin 2021–2030 and the MRC Strategic Plan 2021–2025, *supra* note 30. See, also: ISRBC, *Joint Plan of Actions for the Sava River Basin* (15 June 2017), https://www.savacommission.org/UserDocsImages/05_documents_publications/basic_documents/ISRBC_Joint Plan of Actions for the Sava RB.pdf.

34 ICPDR. 2004. "Flood Action Programme. Action Programme for Sustainable Flood Protection in the Danube River Basin." https://www.icpdr.org/sites/default/files/ICPDR_Flood%20_Action_Programme.pdf.

35 Draft Water Charter for the Volta River Basin, Article 145.

36 Water Charter of the Lake Chad Basin, Article 47; Draft Water Charter for the Volta River Basin, Article 77.

37 Directive 2001/42/EC of the European Parliament and of the Council of 27 June 2001 on the assessment of the effects of certain plans and programmes on the environment, 2001 O.J. (L 197) 30, 37.

the World Bank to assess the environmental and social effects of its investment programmes[38] and only to a much lesser extent in the context of international watercourse planning. In this regard, SEAs are an underexploited opportunity for a more integrated management of international watercourses.

1.2 *Definition of the Information System*

Both the UN Watercourses Convention and the UNECE Water Convention contain the obligation for the watercourse States to exchange information and data,[39] the legal framework for which has been analysed in Chapter 6. This aspect is very important for the integrated management of international watercourses since its effective implementation requires that sufficient and adequate information and data regarding the basin are shared by the riparian States. A constant flow of information is necessary in the planning phase in order to obtain an accurate picture of the state of the basin and the challenges that must be tackled, but also in the implementation phase and subsequent revisions of the plan. Stakeholders will also need reliable information for all other management activities, such as monitoring, assessment, or prevention activities.[40] The production and exchange of information requires the establishment of an information system at basin level, which has an institutional and a technical dimension.

The information system should be established on the basis of the information and data requirements for integrated management.[41] It is first necessary to agree on the amount and kind of information that should be provided by each riparian State in accordance with the specific information needs. International watercourse agreements always contain provisions regarding the exchange of information since it is one of the classical procedural obligations,[42] but they do not define what information this should be in any significant detail. This is usually left to the Parties to establish in further agreements.

Therefore, for most basins, the first step in establishing an information system is to determine what information is required in terms of: the qualitative

38 Abaza, Bisset and Sadler, *Environmental and Strategic Environmental Assessment*, 97–98.

39 Article 9 of the UN Watercourse Convention; Convention on the Protection and Use of Transboundary Watercourses and International Lakes, March 17, 1992, 1936 U.N.T.S. 269. Article 6.

40 GWP, and INBO. 2012. *The Handbook for Integrated Water Resources Management in Transboundary Basins of Rivers, Lakes and Aquifers*. Paris: GWP & INBO. 51.

41 UNECE Task Force on Monitoring & Assessment. 2000. *Guidelines for Water Quality Monitoring and Assessment of Transboundary Rivers*. Lelystad: Institute for Inland Water Management and Waste Water Treatment. 21.

42 See, in this regard, Chapter 4 above.

and quantitative status of the watercourse; the uses of the watercourse and their impacts on the quality of water and its ecosystems; the issues that are relevant for management, such as floods, sediments, pollution, etc.; and the measures in place to address the issues detected. In the case of the Volta basin this is directly regulated in the watercourse agreement to a great extent, since it establishes a very comprehensive list of information required that includes the following types: water resources flows, abstractions, meteorology, lessons learnt about floods, quality, discharge, irrigation schemes, land occupancy and soil conditions, environmental issues, water providing facilities, navigation, policies and legislation and socio-economic conditions.[43] In fact, the determination of the necessary information and finding the sources of information will be largely conditioned by the planning of the basin, since they encompass both a prior analysis and definition of the measures that need to be applied.

Determining the necessary information is also an iterative process that must be revised as information needs change, but some general considerations can be made for all international watercourses. On the one hand, according to Garcia *et al.*, the integrated management of water resources requires, regardless of the context, the monitoring of 17 variables: precipitation, temperature, evapotranspiration (ET), normalized difference vegetation index (NDVI), streamflow, soil moisture, wind speed, groundwater recharge, groundwater level, surface water level, snow or ice cover, snow or ice water equivalent, land cover change, pumping and groundwater change, land subsidence, elevation, and water quality.[44]

On the other hand, integrated management also requires sharing information beyond the physical aspects of the watercourse. A minimum standard list of these other aspects is provided by the UN Watercourses Convention, Article 6.1 of which contains a non-exhaustive set of factors to determine the equitable and reasonable utilisation of the international watercourse. According to this list, Leb categorises the data and information requirements in four groups, of which three do not concern the natural characteristics of a water system: the socio-economic needs; the protection, conservation of water and water systems and related costs: as general information and related to the effects of

43 VBA, *Appendix 1 to the Water Charter for the Volta River Charter related to the procedure for producing, collecting, exchanging and utilising data and information* (August 2019), http://abv.int/wp-content/uploads/2022/02/Annex1_Exchanging_data_information_Eng.pdf. Article 5.

44 García, Luis; Rodríguez, Juan Diego; Wijnen, Marcus; Pakulski, Inge. 2016. Earth Observation for Water Resources Management: Current Use and Future Opportunities for the Water Sector. Washington, DC: World Bank.

the use or uses considered; and the alternatives available within the various countries and with respect to the considered use or uses.[45]

Next, the data collected on each side of the border must be harmonised to make it comparable. This is regulated in the UNECE Water Convention[46] but is not generally mentioned in international watercourse agreements. The only exceptions are the Draft Water Charter for the Volta River Basin[47] and the Water Charter of the Lake Chad Basin,[48] which oblige the States to harmonise their methods to produce and collect the data to be shared. This is a significant fact, since these are among the most recent and comprehensive examples of international agreements, perhaps suggesting an emerging trend in the management of international watercourses. The two charters, together with the Mekong Agreement, include annexes establishing in significant detail the characteristics of the information that the Parties must collect, the methods to be used for its collection, and procedural provisions such as the desired frequency of information exchange.[49]

Even when such regulations are not explicitly laid down in a watercourse agreement, data harmonisation measures can be taken according to the characteristics of the basin and the management model adopted. The US-Ca IJC, for instance, created a Transboundary Hydrographic Data Harmonization Task Force with the aim of harmonising the datasets relating to a "swath" of binational drainage areas along the international boundary.[50] The harmonised information framework created by this task force facilitates integrated management by the boards and the other stakeholders operating in the shared basins. It also allows data to be processed for modelling, using applications including the SPARROW system,[51] and other applications.

45 Leb, *Data Innovations for Transboundary Freshwater Resources Management*, 19.

46 Convention on the Protection and Use of Transboundary Watercourses and International Lakes, March 17, 1992, 1936 U.N.T.S. 269. Article 11.4.

47 Draft Water Charter for the Volta River Basin, Article 98.

48 Lake Chad Basin Commission, 2011, Article 63.

49 See: VBA, *Appendix 1 to the Water Charter for the Volta River Charter related to the procedure for producing, collecting, exchanging and utilising data and information* (August 2019), http://abv.int/wp-content/uploads/2022/02/Annex1_Exchanging_data_information_Eng.pdf; and Water Charter of the Lake Chad Basin, Appendix n° 5 on the exchange of data and information within the Lake Chad Basin Commission; and MRC, *Procedures for Data and Information Exchange and Sharing* (1 November 2001), https://www.mrcmekong.org/wp-content/uploads/2024/08/PDIES-3.pdf.

50 IJC. n.d. "The Approach | International Joint Commission." Accessed December 11, 2024. https://ijc.org/en/iwi/data/approach.

51 IJC. n.d. "SPARROW | International Joint Commission." Accessed December 11, 2024. https://ijc.org/en/what/iwi/sparrow.

1.3 *Monitoring and Assessment*

Once the kind of information required has been determined and the institutional infrastructure has been established, the methods for gathering and processing the data should be set accordingly to ensure the effective retrieval of the information. The sources of information can be both primary, such as monitoring programmes or model predictions with expert judgement, and secondary, for example resources containing statistical or administrative information.[52] In practice, monitoring is the main source of information.

As explained by the GWP, there are two main channels of monitoring and assessment: "The first produces data to assess the status of water resources, and the current and potential driving forces and pressures on the resource in terms of water intake and pollution. The second monitors and assesses basin management to assess progress to meet strategy aims and to learn lessons for improving the effectiveness of the IRBO."[53] In the first case, which focuses on the status of the water resources, information can be gathered through permanent research programmes, *ad hoc* studies at the request of any of the Parties, measurement stations, or networks of experts. These are well-established mechanisms that allow for the monitoring of accurate information on the ecological and chemical state of the water resources.[54]

The UN Watercourses Convention does not go into detail regarding monitoring, merely stating the need to exchange and process information[55] without referring to any specific monitoring task or subsequent use of the data. By contrast, Article 11 of the UNECE Water Convention is devoted to monitoring and assessment of the conditions of transboundary waters and transboundary impact.[56] In fact, the institutional structure of the Convention includes a Working Group on Monitoring and Assessment to assist States "in establishing and implementing joint programmes for monitoring and assessing the pressures on and the conditions of those transboundary waters,"[57] which is indicative of

52 UNECE Task Force on Monitoring & Assessment. 2000. *Guidelines for Water Quality Monitoring and Assessment of Transboundary Rivers*. Lelystad: Institute for Inland Water Management and Waste Water Treatment. 12.

53 GWP, and INBO. 2009. *A Handbook for Integrated Water Resources Management in Basins*. Paris: GWP & INBO. 93.

54 For a complete description of those mechanisms see Sangbana, *La Protection Des Eaux Douces Transfrontières Contre La Pollution*. 167–170.

55 UN Watercourses Convention, *supra* note 1, Article 9.3.

56 UNECE Water Convention, *supra* note 46, Article 11.

57 Description and information on its activity available online: UNECE. n.d. "Working Group on Monitoring and Assessment | UNECE." Accessed July 10, 2022. https://unece.org/environment-policy/water/about-the-convention/convention-bodies/working-group-monitoring-and-assessment.

the importance of this aspect for the implementation of the UNECE Water Convention. The UNECE recommends that Parties conduct joint research and studies, exchange knowledge and use of models, set up monitoring regulations, and establish harmonised monitoring and assessment programmes.[58]

In practice, international watercourse agreements – particularly the most recent – usually contain provisions on monitoring the quality of the water resources and other aspects.[59] The most comprehensive of these agreements is again the Draft Water Charter for the Volta River Basin, which obliges the Parties to monitor several aspects of the basin, such as the abstraction of water from the watercourses, the quality of the surface and groundwater resources, effluent discharges, biological diversity, ecology, sedimentation, transboundary aquifers, fishing resources, transboundary audits and the safety of hydraulic infrastructure.[60]

Subsequently, these provisions must be translated in a monitoring system. The TransNational Monitoring Network established under the Danube River Protection Convention and launched by the ICPDR in 1996 is a good example of an arrangement for the monitoring of information relating to water quality and pollution. The network has 101 monitoring stations and three sampling points, and results are published annually.[61]

For the integrated management of international watercourses, it is not only the physical state of the water that is relevant; social, economic, political and technical factors, which vary considerably across watercourses, must also be assessed to determine their possible effect on watercourses ecosystems and vice versa.[62] This integrated approach requires information on human activities and uses of the watercourse, which in turn can only be obtained through

58 UNECE. 2021. *Practical Guide for the Development of Agreements or Other Arrangements for Transboundary Water Cooperation*. Geneva: United Nations. 79.

59 See, for instance: Article 9 of the Danube River Protection Convention; Article 16 of the 2012 Dniester River Basin Treaty; the separate Procedures for Water Use Monitoring (PWUM) of the 1995 Mekong Agreement; Article 4.9 of the Statute of the Commission of the Republic of Kazakhstan and the Kyrgyz Republic on the Use of Water Management Facilities of Intergovernmental Status on the Rivers Chu and Talas, 2006; or Article 27 of the Water Charter of the Lake Chad Basin.

60 See, in this order, articles 21, 22–23, 25, 33, 38, 41, 46, 51, 73, 83 and 105 of the Draft Water Charter for the Volta River Basin.

61 ICDPR. n.d. "TNMN – TransNational Monitoring Network." Accessed February 13, 2023. https://www.icpdr.org/main/activities-projects/tnmn-transnational-monitoring-network.

62 UNECE Task Force on Monitoring & Assessment. 2000. *Guidelines for Water Quality Monitoring and Assessment of Transboundary Rivers*. Lelystad: Institute for Inland Water Management and Waste Water Treatment. 27.

stakeholder involvement in the process, including the public administrations of the riparian States and non-governmental actors.[63] Integration increases the complexity and the cost of the assessment, what is probably why few examples of its application are found.[64] However, there are some documented cases of international watercourse assessments that include social and economic factors in the modelling approach.[65]

Monitoring systems, however, are not limited to the collection of data; it should also be defined how the information will be analysed, communicated and used by all stakeholders involved in the management of the basin.[66] Consequently, the monitoring phase should be followed by an analysis of the data, which will usually lead to the establishment of indicators. In turn, these indicators will inform the planning process or the development of policies regarding transboundary management.[67] The information obtained through monitoring also provides the input for predicting the effects of water quality change on human activities and vice versa.[68]

2 Involvement of Stakeholders for Integrated Management of International Watercourses

Public participation is a key aspect of integrated management. It has been already explained that the monitoring process requires the involvement of

---

63 GWP, and INBO. 2012. *The Handbook for Integrated Water Resources Management in Transboundary Basins of Rivers, Lakes and Aquifers*. Paris: GWP & INBO. 53.

64 Bonzi, Christopher, Janina Onigkeit, Holger Hoff, Brian Joyce and Katja Tielbörger. 2016. "Analysing Stakeholder Driven Scenarios with a Transboundary Water Planning Tool for IWRM in the Jordan River Basin". In *Integrated Water Resources Management: Concept, Research and Implementation*, edited by Borchardt, Dietrich, Janos J. Bogardi, and Ralf B. Ibisch, 413–434. Cham: Springer.

65 See, for instance, the project "RIVERTWIN-A Regional Model for Integrated Water Management in Twinned River Basins" (ICWC. Scientific-Information Center ICWC. n.d. "RIVERTWIN." Accessed July 11, 2022. http://cawater-info.net/rivertwin/index.htm).

66 GWP, and INBO. 2009. *A Handbook for Integrated Water Resources Management in Basins*. Paris: GWP & INBO. 92.

67 UNECE Working Group on Monitoring and Assessment. 2003. *Guidelines on Monitoring and Assessment of Transboundary and International Lakes. Part B: Technical Guidelines*. Helsinki: Finnish Environment Institute. 92–94.

68 See, for instance the SPARROW (SPAtially Referenced Regression On Watershed attributes) watershed model used by the IJC, which allows to track contaminants and nutrients along the watershed in order to inform the decision-making regarding the reduction of loads and protection measures. In IJC. n.d. "SPARROW | International Joint Commission." Accessed July 11, 2022. https://ijc.org/en/what/iwi/sparrow.

stakeholders, especially when the uses of the watercourse and the social and economic effects need to be included in the subsequent assessment. The planning process is the centre of this dynamic, since management plans are usually drawn up with the involvement of the general public and other stakeholders to some extent, but particular forms of participation can also be envisaged for the subsequent implementation phase.

Public participation in the management of international watercourses is much more advanced in the practice of States and in basin agreements than an initial analysis of global agreements in this domain would suggest. The UN Watercourses Convention simply refers to the right of individuals having been affected by transboundary harm to not be discriminated against on the grounds of nationality in terms of access to justice or the right to claim compensation.[69] The UNECE Water Convention contains a complete provision regarding the right of the public to be granted access to the following type of information: water-quality objectives; permits issued together with the conditions necessary for their obtention; and the results of monitoring.[70] Moreover, it provides that this information must be made available free of charge and at any reasonable time.[71]

However, access to information is the most basic element of public participation. It is a precondition for more intensive public participation mechanisms, but it is unlikely to affect the decision-making process regarding the management of international watercourses by itself. Beyond the matter of access to information, international watercourse agreements usually contain provisions regarding public participation, which foresee varied methods and refer to different domains of decision.[72] Also, the practice of IRBOs reveals that public participation can take place in other forms that are not always foreseen in the watercourse agreement. The different forms of public participation are explored in the following two Sections.

2.1 *Public Participation Mechanisms for Integrated Management*

There are several ways in which stakeholders can participate and influence (to a varying degree) the decision-making process pertaining to management of

69 UN Watercourses Convention, *supra* note 1. Article 32.

70 UNECE Water Convention, *supra* note 46. Article 16.1.

71 Ibid. Article 16.1.

72 See, for instance: Chapter VII of the The Niger Basin Water Charter. Seemingly, Article 5.3 of the Procedures for Water Quality of the Mekong Agreement state that the Parties must promote public participation in maintaining acceptable/good water quality. In MRC, *Procedures for Water Quality*. (26 January 2011), https://www.mrcmekong.org/wp-content/uploads/2024/08/PWQ.pdf.

the basin. The status of observer is a common way of formalising stakeholder participation in the decision-making process and is foreseen in several international watercourse agreements.[73] This figure is addressed in some detail in the ICPDR, which currently encompasses 24 accredited organisations, including NGOs, international environment protection organisations and other regional stakeholders.[74] They have the right to participate in all plenary meetings and the meetings of all expert groups and task groups "with the possibility to express their position and views, and to have them reflected in the relevant documents."[75] As noted by Sangbana, this right confers enough powers to the observers, since they can influence the final recommendations.[76] They are also entitled to submit documents and make proposals to the ICPDR and can be invited to participate in any programme or project.[77] The ICPDR's statute of observer is a good model for facilitating stakeholder participation in a context where the cooperation framework is focuses predominantly on the protection of the watercourse.

The Charter of Waters of the Senegal River also foresees the participation as observers in the *Commission Permanente des Eaux*[78] of entities pertaining to the riparian States as representatives of users, territorial collectives, NGOs or decentralised management committees.[79] Nevertheless, participants are not granted stable status but are rather subject to selection. They must be accepted by the Council of Ministers after being proposed by the High-Commissioner and they need to have a particular interest to participate, hence their participation is sporadic.[80] In addition, their right to participate "de manière effective aux travaux de la Commission Permanente des Eaux"[81] seems to be limited

73 Article 93 of The Water Charter of the Lake Chad Basin, for instance, accepts NGOs with consultative status; the Framework Agreement on the Sava River Basin in Article 3.5 provides that observers may be invited to its sessions.

74 ICDPR. n.d. "Observers | ICPDR – International Commission for the Protection of the Danube River." Accessed July 13, 2022. https://www.icpdr.org/main/icpdr/observers.

75 ICPDR, *Guidelines for Observers to the ICPDR*, IC/185 (6 November 2014), https://www.icpdr.org/sites/default/files/nodes/documents/ic_185_-_guidelines-for-observers.pdf.

76 Sangbana, "The Role of Non-State Actors," 289.

77 ICPDR, *Guidelines for Observers to the ICPDR*, IC/185 (6 November 2014) https://www.icpdr.org/sites/default/files/nodes/documents/ic_185_-_guidelines-for-observers.pdf.

78 The Commission Permanente des Eaux is in charge of "*définir, conformément aux dispositions de la présente Charte et de ses annexes, les principes et les modalités de la répartition des eaux entre les différents secteurs d'utilisation*". Charter of Waters of the Senegal River, Article 19.

79 Ibid. Article 23.

80 Sangbana, "La Participation Du Public Dans Le Cadre de l'Organisation Pour La Mise En Valeur Du Fleuve Sénégal," 81.

81 Charter of Waters of the Senegal River, Article 23.

to a right to speak and provide clarifications on topics with which they are concerned.[82]

The OMVS also accepts the participation of observers in the Basin Committees, which were created in 2009 and bring together public and private actors. Their role is to give their opinion on the general axes of the management policy to the Basin Committee,[83] which in turn issues advisory opinions to the Council of Ministers on the management, development, impacts and planning of water resources and the environment.[84]

In contrast to the ICPDR, the OMVS model of observer status is more open to users and stakeholders beyond those groups with a specific interest in the protection of the watercourse. This is due to the greater dependency of the population on those water resources and the wider scope of the cooperation framework, which is characteristic of Western Africa. However, the different nature of the goals of the watercourse agreement should not necessarily translate into a lesser weight of observers in the decision-making process.

Working groups, also called thematic committees or task groups, are usually established by IRBOs to advise on specific issues and challenges faced by the basin, such as flood control or climate change adaptation. These bodies can be formed by both stakeholders acting as experts[85] and by representatives of civil society and the economic sector. The ICPDR has four task groups, which focus on more specialised topics than the expert groups, such as groundwater, nutrients, economy and hydro-morphology.[86] They are created by the expert groups or by the International Commission and are formed by experts and representatives of the observer organisations.[87]

82 Sangbana, "La Participation Du Public Dans Le Cadre de l'Organisation Pour La Mise En Valeur Du Fleuve Sénégal," 81.

83 Ibid.

84 INBO. 2018. *The Handbook for the Participation of Stakeholders and the Civil Society in the Basins of Rivers, Lakes and Aquifers*. Paris: INBO. 25.

85 See, for instance, the working groups of the Dniester Commission, which are merely constituted by experts from governmental institutions. In that case, they could be considered as expert groups, although the name may be misleading. In Dniester Commission. n.d. "Working Groups." Accessed December 11, 2024. https://dniester-commission.org/en/joint-management/dniester-commission/working-groups/.

86 ICPDR. n.d. "Task Groups | ICPDR – International Commission for the Protection of the Danube River." Accessed December 11, 2024. https://www.icpdr.org/main/icpdr/task-groups.

87 ICPDR, *Rules of Procedure of the ICPDR*, Rev3 – FINAL IC/002 (13 April 2006), https://www.icpdr.org/sites/default/files/Final%20IC%20002-Rev3%20-%20RoP.pdf.

The US-Ca IJC may create advisory boards,[88] which function as working groups and involve a wide spectrum of stakeholders. The mandate and membership of those Advisory Boards may differ significantly. Some of those bodies could be rather considered experts groups (e.g. Health Professionals Advisory Board; Great Lakes Science Advisory Board), while others have a monitoring mandate (e.g. International Kootenay Lake Board of Control).[89] See, for instance, the Great Lakes Water Quality Board created in 2012 under the Great Lakes Water Quality Agreement with the mandate of assessing the implementation of this agreement and advising on emerging issues affecting the basin. The regulation on membership guarantees highly diverse representation from both countries of governmental agencies, civil society, local authorities and populations (including, specifically, Tribal Governments, First Nations, Métis) and agricultural and economic sectors.[90]

The ISRBC has also undertaken two innovative initiatives to integrate the opinion of stakeholders in its decision-making process. On the one hand, in 2015 it created the Sava Water Council, which provides for the participation of a wide spectrum of sectoral stakeholders. It has not met regularly since its creation, but the focus of its discussions has been highly integrative.[91] The ISRBC also created the Sava Youth Parliament, which enables young people to be involved in its work. The considerations forwarded by this organisation are communicated to the Meeting of the Parties, the ISRBC and to thematic workshops.[92]

Finally, mention should be made of the many kinds of measures and initiatives implemented to promote public participation in the management of international watercourses. The UN Watercourses Convention, for example, states that as part of the management of international watercourses the Parties should promote the "the rational and optimal utilization, protection and

88 IJC, *Rules of Procedure of the International Joint Commission* (2011), https://www.ijc.org/sites/default/files/2018-08/RULES%20OF%20PROCEDURE%20OF%20THE%20INTERNATIONAL%20JOINT%20COMMISSION.pdf.

89 IJC. n.d. "Boards, Studies, and Committee | International Joint Commission." Accessed December 11, 2024. https://ijc.org/en/who/boards.

90 IJC. n.d. "IJC Directive to the Great Lakes Water Quality Board | International Joint Commission." Accessed December 11, 2024. https://ijc.org/en/wqb/who/mandate.

91 See the meetings in 2016 in: ISRBC. n.d. "Sava Water Council – International Sava River Basin Commission." Accessed December 11, 2024. https://www.savacommission.org/activities/stakeholders-involvement/sava-water-council/1956.

92 ISRBC. n.d. "Sava Youth Parliament – International Sava River Basin Commission." Accessed December 11, 2024. https://www.savacommission.org/activities/stakeholders-involvement/sava-youth-parliament/1955.

control of the watercourse."[93] Some international watercourse agreements make explicit provision for this promotional function.[94] The different actions include the creation of outreach materials,[95] publication of guides,[96] educational activities,[97] workshops for the development of knowledge and capacities of stakeholders,[98] and river-dedicated days,[99] among others.

2.2 *Public Consultation Mechanisms for Integrated Management*

Consultation mechanisms are intended to engage a wider scope of actors with a legitimate interest in the management of the basin. Unlike public participation mechanisms, which are necessarily constrained by the more formal procedures in which they are conveyed, public consultation forums aim to facilitate public involvement to the greatest possible extent.[100] They offer a more passive role as a trade-off for capturing a much broader array of opinions and gaining legitimacy. There are two major consultation mechanisms, stakeholder forums and public consultations, which will be analysed below. The boundary

---

93 UN Watercourses Convention, *supra* note 1. Article 24.2(b).

94 See, for instance: Article 13 of the Charter of Waters of the Senegal River; and MRC, *Procedures for Water Quality*. (26 January 2011), https://www.mrcmekong.org/wp-content/uploads/2024/08/PWQ.pdf. Article 5.3.

95 The publication of a magazine by river commissions is a manner to rise-awareness on their activities and current challenges of the basin. See, for instance, the OMVS – Le Journal, which was published annually until 2017 (OMVS. n.d. "Collection – OMVS Le Journal (2006–2017)." Accessed December 11, 2024. http://archives-omvs.org/collectionsdigitales/omvslejournal.htm), or the *Danube Watch*, which is published every four months (ICDPR. n.d. "Danube Watch Magazine." Accessed December 11, 2024. https://www.icpdr.org/library/publications/danube-watch-magazine).

96 See, for instance, the MRC. 2012. "Manual for Training Trainers in Integrated Water Resources Management in the Mekong Basin". https://www.mrcmekong.org/wp-content/uploads/2024/08/Manual-for-Training-Trainers-in-Integrated-Water-Resources-Management-in-the-Mekong-Basin.pdf.

97 See, for instance, the development by the ICPDR of the "Danube Adventure online game" as a tool to promote the knowledge about the Danube among children in a playful way. In ICPDR. n.d. "Danube Adventure Online Game | ICPDR – International Commission for the Protection of the Danube River." Accessed December 11, 2024. https://www.icpdr.org/main/activities-projects/danube-adventure-online-game.

98 Article 79 of the Water Charter of the Lake Chad Basin is dedicate to the capacity building of the stakeholders involved in the management of the shared waters, specifying that special attention should be given to "women, youths, civil society organisations and grassroots community organisations".

99 See, for instance the "Danube Day", which the ICPDR celebrates each 29th of June since 2004. In ICDPR. n.d. "Danube Day | ICPDR – International Commission for the Protection of the Danube River." Accessed February 13, 2023. https://www.icpdr.org/main/activities-projects/danube-day.

100 Sangbana, *La Protection Des Eaux Douces Transfrontières Contre La Pollution*. 184.

between these two mechanisms can become blurred on some occasions, as stakeholder forums can serve as the basis for public consultations, but they can be sufficiently differentiated to be examined separately.

As a general rule, stakeholder forums are not foreseen in transboundary agreements on international watercourse management. The only exception is the Draft Water Charter for the Volta River Basin, which makes a passing reference to this mechanism in its "definitions and use of terms."[101] The Statutes of the Volta Basin Authority further determine that the Forum of Stakeholders is an advisory body with the functions of providing the Council with the opinions and proposals of the stakeholders involved in the development of the basin and contributing to the work of the VBA through education and raising-awareness activities. The list of stakeholders called to be part of this body is very comprehensive:

a. The representatives of various categories of water users; Civil Society involved in water resources management; and decentralized local authorities in each portion of the basin of the State Parties,
b. The representatives of the National Focal Bodies,
c. The representatives of the neighbouring trans-boundary basin organizations,
d. The representatives of research centres operating in the water and environment sector.[102]

In the context of the NBA, the 1er Forum Régional des Acteurs Usagers des Ressources du bassin (FOREAU) was held in 2006. The following year, it was decided by the Council of Ministers that this body would meet every four years. The second edition of the FOREAU, held in 2012, was attended by 200 participants, among them users, local authorities, state representatives and technical and financial partners.[103] In 2017, the Regional Stakeholder Forum on Water Governance in the Niger Basin was held. The event had a wider focus than the FOREAU and allowed more types of stakeholders to participate. Its main purpose was to provide a space for stakeholders to exchange experiences with representatives of the NBA on good governance of the basin and to formulate recommendations on a series of matters.[104]

101 Draft Water Charter for the Volta River Basin, Article 2.23.

102 Statuts de l'Autorité du Bassin de la Volta [Statutes of the Volta Basin Authority], November 16, 2007, FAOLEX LEX-FAOC180706. Article 7.

103 Dessouassi, "État Du Processus de Gestion Intégrée Des Ressources En Eau Dans Le Bassin Du Niger", 74–75.

104 INBO. 2018. *The Handbook for the Participation of Stakeholders and the Civil Society in the Basins of Rivers, Lakes and Aquifers*. Paris: INBO. 56–57.

Under the Agreement between Canada and the United States of America on Great Lakes Water Quality, the Great Lakes Public Forum is held every three years for "(a) the Parties to discuss and receive Public comments on the state of the lakes and binational priorities for science and action to inform future priorities and actions; and (b) the [US-Ca IJC] to discuss and receive Public input on the Progress Report of the Parties."[105] Article 1(f) of this Agreement includes in its definition of the public "the individuals and organizations such as public interest groups, researchers and research institutions, and businesses and other non-governmental entities."[106]

These stakeholder forums are an assembly-like mechanism providing a very flexible and open space for the IRBOs to consult the stakeholders, but they are also a channel for a wide representation of stakeholders to deliver their opinions, suggestions and demands to the Parties. This mechanism can be of great value to integrated management in that it provides for the greatest possible gathering of actors involved in each activity affecting the watercourse. The presence of the majority of stakeholders ensure that the forums are a unique occasion for discussing conflicting uses of the international watercourse, ensuring that Parties are not as likely to be relegated to less central organs.

The second mechanism, public consultations, is characterised by being *ad hoc*. They are organised when IRBOs need to gather stakeholders' opinions on a particular matter, such as a specific project or the elaboration of a plan. Only two international watercourse agreements use the term 'public consultation'. The Draft Water Charter for the Volta River Basin and the Water Charter of the Lake Chad Basin define them in exactly the same words as: "activities consisting of asking the opinion of the local populations and/or social groups affected by a project, among others, to help determine the impacts a project is likely to cause, as well as the acceptability of the solutions that can be offered to compensate for them, or the most appropriate mitigation measures."[107] From this definition, it can be inferred that these mechanisms are closely related to the consultation process of both EIAs and SEAs. In fact, the Draft Water Charter for the Volta River Basin makes this link explicitly, referring to the participation of NGOs in environmental assessments through public consultations.[108]

Public consultations might also be framed in the planning process. Hare et al., for instance, list the following available methodologies: for large groups they

105 Great Lakes Water Quality Agreement, Article 5.1.

106 Ibid. Article 1(f).

107 Article 2.11. of the Draft Water Charter for the Volta River Basin; Article 2 of the Water Charter of the Lake Chad Basin.

108 Draft Water Charter for the Volta River Basin, Article 122.2.a).

can be used large group response exercise, questionnaires/surveys, web site provision; in small- and medium-sized groups or individuals they can be used card sorting, focus groups, cognitive mapping, interviews, joint use of models and role playing methods.[109] In the practice of IRBOs, it is also very common to conduct public consultations as part of the planning process, which can take place at different stages and are channelled through different methodologies.

The system used by the ICPDR to formulate its Danube River Basin Management Plan,[110] for instance, gives stakeholders the opportunity to participate in three stages: first, in determining the schedule of the planning process itself; second, in identifying the significant water management issues, to serve as the basis for the drafting of the Danube River Basin Management Plan; and third, in preparing the draft itself.[111] In all three stages, but particularly the first and the second, the stakeholders' opinions are received by the ICPDR through online questionnaires and comments submitted in writing. In the third stage, however, a workshop with more than 80 stakeholders is held at which participants can express their opinion on the draft Danube River Basin Management Plan. The event is structured in groups directed by a facilitator and a rapporteur in order to grant each participant the time to intervene and for each topic to be discussed.[112]

---

109 In Hare, Matt P., Olivier Barreteau, Beck M. Bruce, Rebecca A. Letcher, Erik Mostert, J. David Tàbara, Dagmar Ridder, Valerie Cogan, and Claudia Pahl-Wostl. 2006. "Methods for Stakeholder Participation in Water Management." In *Sustainable Management of Water Resources: An Integrated Approach*, edited by Carlo Giupponi, Anthony J. Jakeman, Derek Karssenberg, and Matt P. Hare, 177–231. Cheltenham: Edward Elgar. 183–187.

110 Note that Article 14 of the EU Water Framework Directive must be applied in the context of the Danube. However, the process is relevant also from an international law perspective since the process envisaged by the ICPDR surpasses the minimum requirements set by this Directive.

111 ICPDR. 2018. "WFD & FD Public Participation Plan regarding Public Consultation and Communication in the Course of Developing the 3rd Danube River Basin Management Plan and the 2nd Flood Risk Management Plan for the Danube River Basin, Both for the Implementation Cycle 2." IC 209 Revised. https://www.icpdr.org/sites/default/files/2024-07/WFD-FD_Public_Participation_Plan%20%28Draft%29.pdf.

112 See the ICPDR. 2015. "Voice of the Danube ICPDR Stakeholder Consultation Workshop 2015. Workshop Report. 2–3 July 2015, Zagreb, Croatia." https://www.icpdr.org/sites/default/files/nodes/documents/icpdr-voice-of-the-danube-final-report.pdf. See also the "Stakeholder Consultation Workshop: Our Opinion – Our Danube" celebrated in 2021 for the elaboration of the Danube River Basin Management Plan 2022–2027, which took place online. In ICPDR. n.d. "Stakeholder Consultation Workshop: Our Opinion – Our Danube | ICPDR – International Commission for the Protection of the Danube River." Accessed December 11, 2024. https://www.icpdr.org/main/activities-projects/stakeholder-consultation-workshop-our-opinion-our-danube.

A similar process was conducted by the OMVS during the period 2009–2011 for the preparation of its *Schéma Directeur d'Aménagement et gestion des eaux*. To engage the public, a campaign was launched which included radio programmes and the publication of an image-based guide. The feedback was obtained through the organisation of national and regional workshops in which representatives of users and the wider population could participate.[113]

The US-Ca IJC organises public consultations on several topics regarding the management of shared watercourses, the focus of which is usually the planning of specific aspects. See, for instance, the "Public Consultation on Plan of Study"[114] for the review of the water supply and flood operating plan of the International Souris River Board in 2013; the public consultation for the "Review of Environmental Emergency Planning, Preparedness and Response in the Rainy-Lake of the Woods Drainage Basin" in 2019;[115] or the public consultation in relation to the "Watershed Management Plans to Reduce Nutrient Pollution in Lake Erie" in 2018.[116] The interested stakeholders can usually provide their comments through the website, by email or by standard mail.

3 Integrated Management Approaches

There is a vast body of literature on the integrated management of specific natural resources or specific natural environments. For instance, integrated management is commonly proposed for coastal areas, ecosystems, mountains, forests, solid waste, river basins, landscapes, or small islands, which are usually governed at lower administrative levels or under the jurisdiction of a particular agency in charge of management, but which are also considered in transboundary contexts. The concepts of Integrated Environmental Management (hereinafter, IEM)[117] or "integrated environmental management

113 INBO. 2018. *The Handbook for the Participation of Stakeholders and the Civil Society in the Basins of Rivers, Lakes and Aquifers*. Paris: INBO. 29.

114 IJC. n.d. "2013 Public Consultation on Plan of Study | International Joint Commission." Accessed December 11, 2024. https://ijc.org/en/srb/news/past-consultations.

115 IJC. n.d. "The IRLWWB Invites Comment on Its Review of Environmental Emergency Planning, Preparedness and Response in the Rainy-Lake of the Woods Drainage Basin." Accessed December 11, 2024. https://ijc.org/en/rlwwb/public-comment/env-emerg.

116 IJC. n.d. "Watershed Management Plans to Reduce Nutrient Pollution in Lake Erie." Accessed December 11, 2024. https://ijc.org/en/watershed-management-plans-reduce-nutrient-pollution-lake-erie.

117 Margerum, Richard D., and Stephen M. Born. 1995. "Integrated Environmental Management: Moving from Theory to Practice." *Journal of Environmental Planning and Management* 38 (3): 371–92.

and planning"[118] have been proposed to classify this kind of management approach, from which some common patterns can be identified.

Born and Sonzogni identify four dimensions of IEM. The first is comprehensiveness, in order to consider all of the ecosystem components, all of the sectors or actors using those components, and the stakeholders – both private and public – with the capacity to influence the management approach. The second dimension is interconnectedness, which can be defined as the sum of all the physical, chemical and biological elements; its uses and its effects; and the actors comprising the community of interests. The third dimension is strategicness, which represents the need to look at the bigger picture to reduce the number of elements and interconnections identified above. This is a necessary step to make environmental management viable, identifying the key aspects and adapting to the political and institutional environment in which it takes place. Finally, the fourth dimension is interactiveness, which pertains to the applied aspects of IEM. Interaction is characterised by the strong interdependence between stakeholders and the need to share information in a context where information is scattered among different actors. It must lead to coordination, both to resolve conflicts of interests and to achieve cooperative decision-making.[119]

In the management of international watercourses, two approaches to IEM have a particular relevance, first because they have been developed consistently with the doctrine on the topic, but especially because they are considered by international watercourse operators and in the international agenda on sustainable development to represent the management paradigm. These approaches will be analysed below.

3.1 *Integrated Water Resources Management*

Efforts to manage water more holistically can be traced back several decades.[120] It was the 1992 Dublin Conference,[121] however, that opened the door to formalising the Integrated Water Resources Management (hereinafter, IWRM)

---

118 Lodhia, Sumit, Nigel Martin, and John Rice. 2018. "Appraising Offsets as a Tool for Integrated Environmental Planning and Management." *Journal of Cleaner Production* 178: 34–44.

119 Born, Stephen M., and William C. Sonzogni. 1995. "Integrated Environmental Management: Strengthening the Conceptualization." *Environmental Management* 19 (2): 167–81.

120 White, Gilbert F. 1998. "Reflections on the 50-Year International Search for Integrated Water Management." *Water Policy* 1 (1): 21–27.

121 International Conference on Water and the Environment, *Dublin Statement on Water and Sustainable Development*, 37.819/H/D/M1SC (1992), https://wedocs.unep.org/20.500.11822/30961.

paradigm and its inclusion in the international agenda on sustainable development through Agenda 21.[122] From this moment, IWRM gained wide acceptance among water practitioners and scholars, but also with international organisations and States.[123] The term also began to be capitalised in professional contexts and academic texts, being used to denote a specific approach to the 'integrated management of water resources'. In this sense, despite the wide dissemination of the concept and its status as the hegemonic paradigm, IWRM should not be identified automatically with the wider discussion on integrated management. Ten years after the Dublin Conference, the Plan of Implementation of the World Summit on Sustainable Development in 2002 advocated for this approach to achieve sustainable development in the water sector[124] and today, the SDG 6.5 targets the implementation of IWRM at all levels by 2030.[125]

The Guiding Principles announced at the Dublin Conference are commonly considered to provide some of the basic principles of IWRM. Those principles are: 1) "Fresh water is a finite and vulnerable resource, essential to sustain life, development and the environment"; 2) "Water development and management should be based on a participatory approach, involving users, planners and policy-makers at all levels"; 3) "Women play a central part in the provision, management and safeguarding of water"; and 4) "Water has an economic value in all its competing uses and should be recognized as an economic good."[126]

From this point, the concept of IWRM would be further developed by different actors in the water sector. One of the most well-known definitions is given by the GWP, which understands IWRM as "a process which promotes the coordinated development and management of water, land and related resources in order to maximize the resultant economic and social welfare in an equitable manner without compromising the sustainability of vital ecosystems."[127] Considering what "integration" entails in IWRM, there is a significant correspondence with the general definition of IEM set out above. The process of integration is also conceptually consistent with IEM, albeit much more detailed. The main particularities to be highlighted here are its focus on one resource, water, and

122 Agenda 21, *supra* note 15.

123 Allouche, Jeremy. 2016. "The Birth and Spread of IWRM – A Case Study of Global Policy Diffusion and Translation." *Water Alternatives* 9 (3): 412–33.

124 World Summit on Sustainable Development, *Plan of implementation of the World Summit on Sustainable Development*, in *Report of the World Summit on Sustainable Development*, A/CONF.199/20 (26 August-4 September 2002), undocs.org/en/A/CONF.199/20.

125 Agenda 21, *supra* note 15. Chapter 18.

126 Dublin Statement, *supra* note 121.

127 GWP. 2000. "Integrated Water Resources Management." *Technical Advisory Committee Background Papers*, no. 4.

its scale of application, the river-basin level. In fact, IWRM strongly promotes the establishment of IRBOs with the mandate to manage water and its related resources holistically.[128]

Thanks to the important endorsement by UN agencies[129] and other international actors,[130] IWRM has been adopted to some degree by a majority of the States, although usually in a merely discursive capacity rather than for practical application.[131] Some international watercourse agreements explicitly refer to IWRM[132] or make a generic reference to 'integrated management',[133] either as an objective of the treaty or as inspiration for their approach.

Here again, the Draft Water Charter for the Volta River Basin is the most comprehensive international watercourse agreement. The promotion of IWRM is positioned as one of the objectives of the Draft Charter[134] and is considered as one of the areas in which the States and the VBA must cooperate in order to achieve the sustainable development of the basin.[135] Furthermore, all stakeholders are given a specific role in establishing the IWRM approach: the VBA has the specific mandate to deliver technical, financial and material support for setting up the necessary consultation mechanisms and bodies; the States are responsible for the introduction of IWRM taxes and fees in their respective national territories; the national hydrographic basin water resource managing entities are given a general objective of promoting IWRM; and the water users must support national plans for IWRM and pay the taxes imposed for this purpose.[136]

---

128 GWP, and INBO. 2012. *The Handbook for Integrated Water Resources Management in Transboundary Basins of Rivers, Lakes and Aquifers*. Paris: GWP & INBO. 484–494.

129 See for instance the monitoring task undertaken by the UNEP on IWRM implementation: UNEP. 2021. *Progress on Integrated Water Resources Management. Tracking SDG 6 series: global indicator 6.5.1 updates and acceleration needs*. Nairobi: UNEP.

130 See, for instance, the "IWRM Action Hub" initiative launched by the Global Water Partnership with support of the Austrian Development Agency, which is meant to function as a support platform for the implementation of IWRM by facilitating the sharing of knowledge and expertise. In GWP. n.d. "About | GWP Toolbox." Accessed December 11, 2024. https://www.gwptoolbox.org/about.

131 Giordano, Mark, and Tushaar Shah. 2016. "From IWRM Back to Integrated Water Resources Management." In *Integrated Water Resources Management: From Concept to Implementation*, edited by Cecilia Tortajada, 364–76. Abingdon: Routledge.

132 See, for instance: Article 2 of the Water Charter of the Lake Chad Basin; Article 11.2° of the The Niger Basin Water Charter.

133 See, for instance: Article 5.2° of the Charter of Waters of the Senegal River; or Article 11 of the Framework Agreement on the Sava River Basin.

134 Draft Water Charter for the Volta River Basin, Article 1.

135 Ibid. Article 5.2.a).

136 Ibid. Articles 115.2.a), 116.2.g), 118.a), 121.a) and c).

The close relationship between international support and the actual adoption of IWRM is largely built on projects financed by international organisations and aid agencies.[137] However, despite this apparent political consensus for IWRM at both international and national level, this management approach contains inconsistencies that have been heavily criticised. One common argument concerns the inconsistency of a model that focuses on a single resource yet calls for an holistic approach.[138] Others accuse IWRM of masking the politics underlying all decisions regarding water.[139] Another stream of criticism focuses on the politics behind the popularity of this approach and the effects of its ubiquitous presence in the water sector. Giordano and Shah argue, for example, that the adoption and implementation of IWRM has become a goal in itself, rather than the management of problems that it was initially designed to solve. They also argue that IWRM stands in the way of other alternatives to water management that could be better moulded to particular situations and which are sometimes grounded in traditional systems.[140]

The use of the term 'integrated' in IWRM and its ubiquity in international water discourse may be misleading in considering its nature. There are other examples of IEM approaches focusing on particular resources and with particular objectives, such as Integrated Natural Resources Management[141]

137 See, for instance, the NB/ITTAS project financed by the GEF and the UNDP among others, with the aim of "Improving IWRM, knowledge-based management and governance of the Niger Basin and the Iullemeden-Taoudeni/Tanezrouft Aquifer System (ITTAS)" (NBA. n.d. "NB-ITTAS Project: « Improving IWRM, Knowledge-Based Management and Governance of the Niger Basin and the Iullemeden-Taoudeni/Tanezrouft Aquifer System (ITTAS)»." Accessed February 15, 2023. http://www.abn.ne/images/documents/ITTAS/presentation_nb-ittas_eng.pdf), and the IWRM-FERGANA project, financed by the Swiss Agency for International Development and Cooperation and implemented by the Interstate Commission for Water Coordination of Central Asia and the International Water Management Institute (Scientific-Information Center ICWC. n.d. "IWRM-FERGANA Integrated Water Resources Management in Fergana Valley." Accessed December 11, 2024. http://iwrm.icwc-aral.uz/index_en.htm).

138 Medema, Wietske, Brian S. McIntosh, and Paul J. Jeffrey. 2008. "From Premise to Practice: A Critical Assessment of Integrated Water Resources Management and Adaptive Management Approaches in the Water Sector." *Ecology and Society* 13 (2).

139 Jensen, Kurt Mørck. 2013. "Viewpoint-Swimming against the Current: Questioning Development Policy and Practice." *Water Alternatives* 6 (2): 276–83.

140 Giordano, Mark, and Tushaar Shah. 2016. "From IWRM Back to Integrated Water Resources Management." In *Integrated Water Resources Management: From Concept to Implementation*, edited by Cecilia Tortajada, 364–76. Abingdon: Routledge.

141 Roidt, Mario, and Tamara Avellán. 2019. "Learning from Integrated Management Approaches to Implement the Nexus." *Journal of Environmental Management* 237 (March): 609–16.

and Integrated Solid Waste Management.[142] While the former is concerned with increasing agricultural production in a sustainable manner by managing the implied resources in a more integrated and sustainable way,[143] the latter seeks to offer integrated solutions to the management of waste for urban areas to achieve environmental sustainability and economic efficiency objectives.[144] The partiality of these approaches, including IWRM, usually reflects the interests of the professional sector in which they have been designed and promoted. While Integrated Natural Resources Management was fostered by the Consortium of International Agricultural Research Centres, IWRM is a widespread practice among water professionals, agencies and international organisations dealing with water and watercourses (e.g. GWP, UNECE).

In any case, IWRM should not be confused with the principle of integration or with the application of the principle of integration to the management of international watercourses.[145] IWRM is a particular approach to the management of water, which may be useful from the point of view of the principle of integration, but is not necessarily the only option, nor is it sufficient to achieve effective integration. Complementarities can be found with other approaches,[146] and there is no obstacle to their simultaneous application, depending on the varying conditions of a given basin.

---

142 Marshall, Rachael E., and Khosrow Farahbakhsh. 2013. "Systems Approaches to Integrated Solid Waste Management in Developing Countries." *Waste Management* 33 (4): 988–1003.

143 Izac, A. M.N., and P. A. Sanchez. 2001. "Towards a Natural Resource Management Paradigm for International Agriculture: The Example of Agroforestry Research." *Agricultural Systems* 69 (1–2): 5–25.

144 Marshall, Rachael E., and Khosrow Farahbakhsh. 2013. "Systems Approaches to Integrated Solid Waste Management in Developing Countries." *Waste Management* 33 (4): 988–1003.

145 Although it must be said that there are differing opinions in this regard. Giupponi et al. consider that "IWRM can be regarded as the vehicle that makes the general concept of sustainable development operational for the management of freshwater resources". Giupponi, Carlo, Anita Fassio, Jacobo Feás Vàzquez, and Jaroslav Mysiak. 2006. "Sustainable Water Management and Decision Making." In *Sustainable Management of Water Resources: An Integrated Approach*, edited by Carlo Giupponi, Anthony J. Jakeman, Derek Karssenberg, and Matt P. Hare, 71–97. Cheltenham: Edward Elgar. 74.

146 For a discussion on complementarities between IWRM, Adaptive Management and Ecosystem-Based Approach see Schoeman, Jes, Catherine Allan, and C. Max Finlayson. 2016. "A New Paradigm for Water? A Comparative Review of Integrated, Adaptive and Ecosystem-Based Water Management in the Anthropocene." In *Integrated Water Resources Management: From Concept to Implementation*, edited by Cecilia Tortajada, 17–30. Abingdon: Routledge.

3.2 *Adaptive Governance and Management*

Adaptive governance is relevant to integration because it is clearly linked to the governance of interactions between humans and the environment. It has appeared to date as a predominantly scholarly discussion, with few attempts at application.[147] Nevertheless, it is worth taking adaptive governance into account for the purpose of this study since it is one of the most representative approaches with a clear focus on environmental management and sustainable development deriving from the field of governance. In fact, it is an approach to management that emerged from the wider debate on network governance[148] and reflexive governance,[149] on the one hand, but which is also closely related to the debate on resilience, since it relates governance action to the capacity of social-ecological systems to maintain their structure and functions.[150]

The concept of adaptive governance "rests on the assumption that landscapes and seascapes need to be understood and governed as complex social-ecological systems rather than as ecosystems alone."[151] This complexity must be understood in terms of complex systems theory, meaning that social-ecological systems are emergent and, hence, not predictable.

> What makes the interactions complex is how these rules, when set in motion among the diverse components a system, produce nonlinear relationships including reinforcing and stabilizing feedbacks. Because of the nonlinearity, local interactions give rise to larger-scale behavior that is not implicit in the parts of the system. This property of complex systems is called emergence.[152]

---

147 For a compilation of empirical examples that resemble adaptive governance see: Chaffin, Brian C., Hannah Gosnell, and Barbara A. Cosens. 2014. "A Decade of Adaptive Governance Scholarship: Synthesis and Future Directions." *Ecology and Society* 19 (3): 56. 8.

148 Meuleman, Louis. 2008. *Public Management and the Metagovernance of Hierarchies, Networks and Markets*. Contributions to Management Science. Heidelberg: Physica-Verlag HD. 36–37.

149 Voß, Jan-Peter, Dierk Bauknecht, and René Kemp, eds. 2006. *Reflexive Governance for Sustainable Development*. Cheltenham: Edward Elgar. 7.

150 Chaffin, Brian C., Hannah Gosnell, and Barbara A. Cosens. 2014. "A Decade of Adaptive Governance Scholarship: Synthesis and Future Directions." *Ecology and Society* 19 (3): 56.

151 Schultz, Lisen, Carl Folke, Henrik Österblom, and Per Olsson. 2015. "Adaptive Governance, Ecosystem Management, and Natural Capital." *Proceedings of the National Academy of Sciences* 112 (24): 7369–74.

152 Kim, Rakhyun E., and Brendan Mackey. 2014. "International Environmental Law as a Complex Adaptive System." *International Environmental Agreements: Politics, Law and Economics* 14 (1): 5–24. 7.

This poses an epistemological problem to governance. It is in this context that adaptive governance aims to address uncertainty,[153] which is considered inevitable to some extent, and which is driven by at least four factors: environmental variation, which is possibly the most prevalent source of uncertainty; partial observability, deriving from technical difficulties of monitoring; partial controllability of the actual effects of management measures on natural resources as compared to the intended purpose; and structural or process uncertainty regarding the "biological and ecological relationships that drive resource dynamics."[154]

While the prior assumptions on social-ecological systems are the same, adaptive management refers to the process in which adaptive governance is applied. It is built on a science-based monitoring cycle that allows for a constant reformulation of the policy in place. In this sense, the learning process is a key aspect of adaptive management since it "can more generally be defined as a systematic process for improving management policies and practices by learning from the outcomes of management strategies that have already been implemented."[155] According to the conceptualisation of adaptive management, the development and implementation of a policy could consist of five cyclical stages: problem definition; policy formulation; policy implementation; monitoring and evaluation; and assessment, feedback and re-planning and reprogramming based on the results of monitoring.[156] From this point of view, adaptive management can be considered the core aspect of adaptive governance: "[adaptive governance] can be thought of simply as the social conditions that enable ecosystem management through the implementation of adaptive management."[157]

It is argued that the main challenge for adaptive management is institutional rather than technical, since institutions are established with the purpose of maintaining a stable framework for thinking and decision-making, while adaptive management requires flexibility, openness to alternatives and

153 Folke, Carl, Thomas Hahn, Per Olsson, and Jon Norberg. 2005. "Adaptive Governance of Social-Ecological Systems." *Annual Review of Environment and Resources* 30: 441–73. 443.

154 Williams, Byron K. 2011. "Adaptive Management of Natural Resources-Framework and Issues." *Journal of Environmental Management* 92 (5): 1346–53. 1348.

155 Pahl-Wostl, Claudia, Jan Sendzimir, Paul Jeffrey, Jeroen Aerts, Ger Berkamp, and Katharine Cross. 2007. "Managing Change toward Adaptive Water Management through Social Learning." *Ecology and Society* 12 (2): 30. 4.

156 Ibid. 5–7.

157 Chaffin, Brian C., Hannah Gosnell, and Barbara A. Cosens. 2014. "A Decade of Adaptive Governance Scholarship: Synthesis and Future Directions." *Ecology and Society* 19 (3): 56. 7.

participatory decision-making.[158] This is especially true for legal regimes, where stability is prioritised over flexibility. In order to overcome the problems that traditional law poses for adaptive management, McIntyre affirms that "robust joint institutions, enjoying adequate mandates and resources, are needed."[159] Hence, in the case of international watercourse management, the mandate and resources given to IRBOs will be decisive in the actual application of adaptive management.

The US-Ca IJC is the most noteworthy adoption of adaptive management in the context of an international watercourse. The International Watersheds Initiative (IWI), which is the framework established by the US-Ca IJC to approve management projects for the watercourses shared by the two countries, enshrines adaptive management as one of its principles. According to the US-Ca IJC, the main purpose of this approach is to promote actions that adapt to the changing character of ecosystems and the evolution of stakeholders' needs and concerns.[160] In practice, the principle of adaptive management serves as the main basis for the several monitoring projects implemented by the basin boards of the US-Ca IJC, the main objective of which is to review water quality objectives and alert levels.[161]

---

158 Williams, "Adaptive Management of Natural Resources-Framework and Issues," 1352.

159 McIntyre, "The Legal Role and Context of River Basin Organizations," 36.

160 IJC. n.d. "History | International Joint Commission." Accessed December 11, 2024. https://ijc.org/en/what/iwi/history.

161 IJC. 2020. "Fifth Report to Governments on the International Watersheds Initiative". https://www.ijc.org/sites/default/files/2020-12/IWI-5th_Report_to_Governments_2020.pdf.

CHAPTER 12

Institutional Integration in the Planning of Projects Affecting International Watercourses: Project-Specific Integration

A project is probably the most basic action in which integration can take place. It is the level at which integration is most often carried out by institutions, since it does not challenge their internal functioning and can be implemented on a more *ad hoc* basis.[1] The most common instrument through which integration is applied at project level is the EIA, but there are similar methodologies with a different focus, such as social impact assessments and health impact assessments.

As noted by the ILA, the relative success in achieving integration at project level is probably due to the fact that project-specific integration "does not challenge the internal structure and processes of the institution itself, focusing as it does on specific schemes rather than systematic features, and certainly historically, EIAs were often not given the prominence necessary to ensure the development of a fully integrative and mainstreamed decision-making process."[2] In fact, a project is a very specific action, which in many cases may be the last step in a process that includes the drafting of a policy and the existence of organisations in charge of its design and finance, while in other cases may constitute an isolated action. That may explain why project-level integration is more limited in scope than integration in earlier stages.

Chapter 4 established the dependence of the substantive principles of international watercourses law on procedural rules. Cooperation between the riparian States of the international watercourse is essential in order to give specific content to the substantive principles in general, as well as to facilitate application of the principle of integration. While the uses of shared water resource are determined in the negotiation of the general policy, at project level the main issue at stake is the prevention of cross-border damage through the mechanisms of notification and consultation. It is therefore necessary to consider how the procedural rules contribute to ensuring that the decision-making

1 ILA. Committee on International Law on Sustainable Development. 2006. "Report of the Toronto Conference." https://www.ila-hq.org/en_GB/documents/conference-report-toronto-2006-14. 10.

2 Ibid.

 | DOI:10.1163/9789004736757_017

process for the proposed project allows for the integration of economic, social and environmental dimensions.

The purpose of this Chapter is to identify what methods the States sharing an international watercourse use in order to ensure that decision-making regarding the planning and execution of a project integrate the three sustainable development dimensions. Hence, the focus of the present analysis is not the domestic regulations on approval of projects (i.e. domestic regulation of EIA), but rather the international regulation of EIAs applicable to international watercourses and the eventual existence of a regulated process at basin level (i.e. guidelines for conducting a transboundary EIA drawn up by an IRBO).

1 Methods for Informed Decision-Making at Project Level

States and IRBOs have several methods at their disposal for the application of the principle of integration when a project affecting an international watercourse can potentially have transboundary effects. The most common tools are impact assessments, as covered in the first Subsection, of which EIAs are the most widely applied. However, Social Impact Assessments (hereinafter, SIAs), Health Impact Assessments and Human Rights Impact Assessments will also be considered in Subsection two. These are less known and less widely applied in the context of international watercourses, but they are important for their potential complementarity with EIAs in terms of ensuring integration. The third Subsection deals with nexus assessments, whose cross-sectoral character is significantly different to that of impact assessments.

1.1 *Environmental Impact Assessments*

Environmental Impact Assessments are the most widely applied type of impact assessment. They are a structured process designed to provide decision-makers with the means to make informed decisions on the effects of a project on the environment. They generally comprise: ways of determining the applicability of the process; the methods for the assessment itself; the dissemination of results; a participatory process; and post-project monitoring arrangements.[3] Although originally applied in the United States of America in the 1960s, they have integrated into the national legislation of many countries and

3 Craik, *International Law of Environmental Impact Assessment.* 3–22.

are the subject of significant regulation in regional[4] and sectoral[5] treaties. In this regard, they are more widely applied than SEAs, which have been analysed earlier in relation to policy integration.

The obligation to conduct an EIA for activities potentially having a transboundary effect has been recognised by several international instruments.[6] From a soft law perspective, Principle 17 of the Rio Declaration[7] identifies EIA as an obligation of national authorities for activities likely to have a significant effect on the environment. Despite its non-binding nature and the lack of reference to transboundary damage, the inclusion of EIAs in the Rio Declaration is indicative of their importance for sustainable development.

Binding international instruments do link the need to conduct an EIA to the possibility of transboundary impact.[8] Of these, special mention should be made of the UN Convention on International Watercourses, Article 12 of which states that the notification of the planned measure "shall be accompanied by available technical data and information, including the results of any EIA, in order to enable the notified States to evaluate the possible effects of the planned measures."[9]

At the level of the UNECE, two instruments make reference to this form of assessment. Firstly, the preamble of the 1991 Espoo Convention clearly

4 See: Protocol on Strategic Environmental Assessment to the Convention on Environmental Impact Assessment in a Transboundary Context, May 21, 2003, 2685 U.N.T.S. 140.; or the EU SEA Directive (Directive 2001/42/EC of the European Parliament and of the Council of 27 June 2001 on the assessment of the effects of certain plans and programmes on the environment, 2001 O.J. (L 197) 30, 37).

5 See, for instance, Article 14.1(a).

6 For a general introduction to Environmental Impact Assessments see, for instance: Craik, *International Law of Environmental Impact Assessment*; Hundloe, *Environmental Impact Assessment*; or Elias, "Environmental Impact Assessment."

7 United Nations Conference on Environment and Development, *Rio Declaration on Environment and Development*, in Report of the United Nations Conference on Environment and Development, A/CONF.151/26 (Vol. I) (12 August 1992), undocs.org/en/A/CONF.151/26/Rev.1(vol. I). Principle 17.

8 See Convention on Biological Diversity, June 5, 1992, 1760 U.N.T.S. 79. Article 14; United Nations Framework Convention on Climate Change, May 9, 1992, 1771 U.N.T.S. 107. Article 4.1(f); ILC, *Draft Articles on Prevention of Transboundary Harm from Hazardous Activities*, A/56/10 (2001), https://legal.un.org/ilc/texts/instruments/english/commentaries/9_7_2001.pdf. Article 7; ILC, *Draft Articles on the Law of Transboundary Aquifers with Commentaries*, A/63/10 (2008), https://legal.un.org/ilc/texts/instruments/english/commentaries/8_5_2008.pdf. Article 15.2.

9 Convention on the Law of the Non-Navigational Uses of International Watercourses, May 21, 1997, 2999 U.N.T.S. Article 12.

identifies the principle of integration as one of its underlying principles,[10] along with sustainable development.[11] The Espoo Convention is the most advanced international instrument to regulate EIAs, although it is not a universal instrument. Secondly, the UNECE Water Convention is even more stringent than the UN Watercourses Convention regarding EIAs,[12] as it obliges the Parties to the Convention sharing a watercourse to undertake the necessary measures to conduct an EIA under certain circumstances.[13]

The requirement to conduct EIAs is widespread among countries sharing a watercourse. Especially in the most recent African international watercourse agreements, EIAs are foreseen explicitly, usually in statements to the effect that they must accompany the prior notification of planned measures.[14] In other cases, such as in the US-Ca IJC regime, EIAs are regulated in non-binding documents under the name of guidelines or recommendations,[15] while in the case of several European international watercourses in which the EU regulation is applicable, EIAs are mandatory for the planning of projects.[16]

Generally, the States are in charge of carrying out the EIAs, while the IRBO is merely required to receive and transmit the assessment to the other Parties as part of the notification.[17] However, some international watercourse agreements grant the IRBO powers to conduct EIAs. In the case of the agreement regulating cooperation on the River Pilcomayo, for instance, the Comisión Trinacional para el Desarrollo de la Cuenca del Río Pilcomayo is competent in the matter of EIAs in relation to joint projects but not projects planned by

10 Convention on Environmental Impact Assessment in a Transboundary Context, February 25, 1991, 1989 U.N.T.S. 309. Preamble, first paragraph.

11 Ibid. Preamble, second paragraph.

12 Convention on the Protection and Use of Transboundary Watercourses and International Lakes, March 17, 1992, 1936 U.N.T.S. 269. Article 3.1(h).

13 The complementarity between those two norms can be noticed in the explicit reference to the Espoo Convention in international watercourse agreements inspired in the UNECE Water Convention. See, for instance, Article 17 of the Dniester River Basin Treaty.

14 See, for instance: Article 24 of the Charter of Waters of the Senegal River; Article 20 of The Niger Basin Water Charter; Article 45 and 54 Water Charter of the Lake Chad Basin.

15 IJC. 2012. "Guidance in Seeking Approval for Uses, Obstructions, or Diversions of Waters Under the Boundary Waters Treaty of 1909." https://ijc.org/sites/default/files/2018-07/Guidance-in-Seeking-Approval-for-Uses.pdf

16 For instance, for the rivers Danube, Rhine and Sava it is applicable the EU EIA Directive (Directive 2014/52/EU of the European Parliament and of the Council of 16 April 2014 amending Directive 2011/92/EU on the assessment of the effects of certain public and private projects on the environment, 2014 O.J. (L124) 1, 18), although some of the members of the watercourse agreements are not EU members.

17 See, for instance: Article 7.5.f of the Danube River Protection Convention; Article 20 of The Niger Basin Water Charter; Article 54 of the Water Charter of the Lake Chad Basin.

each individual State that have a potential impact on the shared watercourse.[18] The VBA, meanwhile, is foreseen to have a general mandate to cooperate with Member States in the process of conducting EIAs, with the aim of ensuring their quality[19] and guaranteeing that the interests of all riparian countries are duly considered.[20] Since most international watercourse agreements do not explicitly state whether it is sufficient to consider impact at the national level or if transboundary impact must also be assessed, the scope of EIAs is a rather undefined question.[21]

EIAs are seen as a necessary tool to prevent transboundary harm and, by extension, as a practical application of sustainable development and the precautionary principle, as much as a necessary step to comply with the principle of 'good faith negotiations' in a transboundary context.[22]

The obligation to conduct EIAs has also been recognised as an obligation of international law by the International Court of Justice in the *Pulp Mills on the River Uruguay (Argentina v. Uruguay)*.[23] Neither Argentina nor Uruguay questioned the obligation to assess environmental impact, but they disagreed on the content and the scope of such an assessment,[24] since neither aspect is defined by the 1975 Statute[25] or in general international law.[26] The Espoo Convention, to which Argentina alluded before the tribunal,[27] provides in its first and second annexes a list of the activities for which an EIA is required and a list of the elements that an assessment should include.[28]

---

18 Acuerdo Constitutivo de la Comisión Trinacional para el Desarrollo de la Cuenca del Rio Pilcomayo [Agreement constituting the National Commission for the Development of the Riverbed Rio Pilcomayo], February 9, 1995, ECOLEX TRE-001235. Article IV(d).

19 Draft Water Charter for the Volta River Basin, Article 79. In that case, the IRBO has a mandate to assuring the quality of the terms of reference for the transboundary EIAs, the final reports, and the following implementation of the environmental management plans.

20 Ibid. Article 84.

21 In fact, only the Water Charter of the Lake Chad Basin makes reference to both kinds, while Article 79 of the Draft Water Charter for the Volta River Basin refers to 'transboundary environmental and social assessments'.

22 McIntyre, *Environmental Protection of International Watercourses*, 369–370.

23 Pulp Mills on the River Uruguay (Argentina v. Uruguay), 2010 Judgment, I.C.J. Rep. 14 (April 20). Para. 204.

24 Ibid. Para. 203.

25 Statute Of The Uruguay River, 1975.

26 Ibid. Para. 205.

27 Pulp Mills on the River Uruguay (Argentina v. Uruguay), 2010 Judgment, I.C.J. Rep. 14 (April 20). Para. 203.

28 "(a) A description of the proposed activity and its purpose, (b) A description, where appropriate, of reasonable alternatives (for example, locational or technological) to the proposed activity and also the no-action alternative, (c) A description of the environment

Nevertheless, the Court noted that neither Argentina nor Uruguay are part of this Convention, hence it is the States that must determine the "specific content of the EIA required in each case, having regard to the nature and magnitude of the proposed development and its likely adverse impact on the environment as well as to the need to exercise due diligence in conducting such an assessment."[29]

Though recent, there is evidence to suggest a certain minimum standard content of EIAs at the international level. On the one hand, it must be taken into account the similarity between the list provided by the Espoo Convention and the UNEP Goals and Principles of Environmental Impact Assessment,[30] especially considering the general character of the aspects included in the

---

likely to be significantly affected by the proposed activity and its alternatives, (d) A description of the potential environmental impact of the proposed activity and its alternatives and an estimation of its significance, (e) A description of mitigation measures to keep adverse environmental impact to a minimum, (f) An explicit indication of predictive methods and underlying assumptions as well as the relevant environmental data used, (g) An identification of gaps in knowledge and uncertainties encountered in compiling the required information, (h) Where appropriate, an outline for monitoring and management programmes and any plans for post-project analysis, and (i) A non-technical summary including a visual presentation as appropriate (maps, graphs, etc.)." (Espoo Convention, *supra* note 10. Annex II).

29 Pulp Mills on the River Uruguay (Argentina v. Uruguay), 2010 Judgment, I.C.J. Rep. 14 (April 20). Para. 205.
This ruling was recalled in Certain Activities Carried Out by Nicaragua in the Border Area (Costa Rica v. Nicaragua) and Construction of a Road in Costa Rica along the San Juan River (Nicaragua v. Costa Rica), Judgment, 2015 I.C.J. Rep. 665 (December 15). Para. 157.

30 "UNEP's instrument provides the following list of minimum aspects that an EIA should include:
(a) A description of the proposed activity; (b) A description of the potentially affected environment, including specific information necessary for identifying and assessing the environmental effects of the proposed activity; (c) A description of practical alternatives, as appropriate; (d) An assessment of the likely or potential environmental impacts of the proposed activity and alternatives, including the direct, indirect, cumulative, short-term and long-term effects; (e) An identification and description of measures available to mitigate adverse environmental impacts of the proposed activity and alternatives, and an assessment of those measures; (f) An indication of gaps in knowledge and uncertainties which may be encountered in compiling the required information; (g) An indication of whether the environment of any other State or areas beyond national jurisdiction is likely to be affected by the proposed activity or alternatives; (h) A brief, non-technical summary of the information provided under the above headings." (UNEP, Governing Council, *UNEP Goals and Principles of Environmental Impact Assessment*, UNEP/GC/DEC/14/25 (16 January 1987), https://elaw.org/system/files/unep.EIA_.guidelines.and_.principles.pdf. Principle 4).

lists. Also relevant are the guidelines drawn up by international development banks[31] or by international expert groups.[32]

On the other hand, significant considerations were made by the arbitral court in *Indus Waters Kishenganga Arbitration* (*Pakistan vs. India*), where the two Parties in the dispute applied different standards in conducting the EIA. The Court did not rule on the content of the EIA itself, but on the adequacy of its comprehensiveness to the "existing state of the river, the magnitude of anticipated changes, the importance of the proposed project, and the availability of time, funding, and local expertise."[33] It deemed the assessment conducted by Pakistan much more suitable than the one conducted by India, which only took into account a single indicator: the water depth available for fish. In any case, despite their general acceptance, and as acknowledged by the ICJ, there is not a universal instrument establishing a unified standard on the content of EIAs. This may explain the diversity in the regulation and practice of EIAs across international watercourse regimes, which will be discussed next.

An EIA is a process rather than a one-time action on the way to the approval of a project. Moreover, this process may include several stages ranging from preliminary screening and scoping to follow-up studies and evaluation of performance.[34] From the point of view of the principle of integration, the scoping stage is crucial. The outputs of this stage should be: the involvement of relevant stakeholders; the definition of important issues and impacts requiring further study (beyond the initial screening process); identification of alternatives to the proposed action; and the establishment of Terms of Reference (ToR) for the EIA.[35] Hence, the focus will mostly be on the capacity of EIAs to facilitate integrated decision-making through the scoping stage.

---

31 European Bank for Reconstruction and Development. 2003. *Environmental Policy*. European Bank for Reconstruction and Development. https://www.ebrd.com/downloads/research/policies/policy.pdf.

32 See, for instance, the WMO/GWP Associated Programme on Flood Management. 2007. "Applying Environmental Assessment for Flood Management – A Tool for Integrated Flood Management." APFM Technical Document No. 8, Flood Management Tools Series. WMO. Accessed December 11, 2024. https://www.gwp.org/globalassets/global/toolbox/references/applying-environmental-assessment-for-flood-management-apfm-wmogwp-2007.pdf.

33 Indus Waters Kishenganga Arbitration (Pakistan vs. India). Final award, 31 R.I.A.A (Perm. Ct. Arb. 2013). Para. 99.

34 For a detailed explanation of the process of EIA see: Abaza, Bisset and Sadler, *Environmental and Strategic Environmental Assessment*, 39–62; or Craik, *International Law of Environmental Impact Assessment*. 132–174.

35 Abaza, Bisset and Sadler, *Environmental and Strategic Environmental Assessment*, 48.

Beyond general references to the need to conduct EIAs in some international watercourse agreements,[36] the only detailed binding regulation on EIAs that could be found at the level of international watercourses is the Appendix 3 to the Draft Water Charter for the Volta River Basin, which specifies the content of EIAs.[37] This may be because EIAs are usually conducted by the Sates in whose territory the project is planned to be carried out. In these cases, EIAs must abide by national regulations on the matter. When EIAs are conducted by the IRBO, their structure is rather *ad hoc*. For instance, the EIA conducted by the Organisation pour la Mise en Valeur du fleuve Gambie (OMVG) in relation to the planning of "Projet Energie" – which includes two hydroelectric power stations and their interconnection – was carried out in accordance with the regulations of the five actors involved: the four States belonging to the OMVG and the African Development Bank.[38] This is also the case of the EIA conducted by the OMVS in relation to the project "Système Intégré de Transport Multimodal."[39]

The lack of harmonisation at basin level can be overcome by applying non-binding guidelines drawn up by the IRBO. This is the case of the MRC, which in 2018 published the Guidelines for Transboundary Environmental Impact Assessment in the Lower Mekong Basin.[40] This document consists merely of recommendations to be applied by the members of the Commission when conducting EIAs of planned projects affecting the basin. Nonetheless, its

36 The Water Charter of the Niger Basin establishes that the Parties will "resort systematically to environmental assessments". In Article 12, paragraph 5, of the The Niger Basin Water Charter.

37 More concretely, this Appendix provides a list of elements to be submitted with the notification in case that they were not included in the EIA (VBA, Appendix 3 to the Water Charter for the Volta Basin on the Prior Notification of Planned Measures (August 2019), https://abv.int/wp-content/uploads/2022/02/Annex3_Notification_Planned_Measures_Water_Charter_VBA_Eng.pdf. Article 1).

38 Mission d'Appui Conseil a l'OMVG pour la realisation de son projet energie. 2014. "Étude d'impact Environnemental et Social Du Projet Energie (Revue Du Rapport COTECO 2008) Projet de Rapport Final." https://knowledge.uclga.org/IMG/pdf/etudedimpactenvironnementaletsocialduprojetenergie.pdf.

39 OMVS – Société de gestion et d'Explotaition de la Navigation sur le Fleuve Sénégal. 2014. "Etude d'Impact Environnemental et Social Des Travaux de Dragage et de Deroctage Des Chenaux d'Acces et Des Aires d'Accostage Des Quais Existants Du Fleuve Sénégal a Rosso En Mauritanie, Podor Au Sénégal et Ambidedi Au Mali." 2014. https://cda-omvs.org/wp-content/uploads/2017/02/14427_EIES_Dragage_Quais-existants_Feuve-Senegal_Resume-non-technique.pdf.

40 MRC. 2023. *Guidelines for Transboundary Environmental Impact Assessment in the Lower Mekong River Basin* (*TbEIA*). Vientiane: MRC Secretariat. https://doi.org/10.52107/mrc.aqrsbk.

utility is obvious: not only can it help to make the EIAs accompanying notifications more mutually understandable but, more importantly, it establishes a minimum standard to be adhered to.

1.2 *Impact Assessments Focusing on Non-Environmental Issues*

Social Impact Assessments (SIAs) are a newer tool than EIAs and a less widespread practice, although their relevance has been growing. They can be defined as "the processes of analysing, monitoring and managing the intended and unintended social consequences, both positive and negative, of planned interventions."[41] Social concerns are usually included in EIAs, which is why the distinction between the two tools is not always clear and the Social Impact Assessment community usually calls for Social Impact Assessments to be integrated into EIAs.[42] Nonetheless, it is also possible to conduct independent Social Impact Assessments, either in parallel with an EIA or as standalone assessments. However, given the close relationship between environmental and social impacts, it is not advisable to consider either in isolation. Indeed, the best practice would be to conduct both assessments in an integrated manner. According to Abaza *et al.*, two reasons justify the need for this integrated approach.

On the one hand, individuals and social groups are part of their environment, so they are affected by the impacts the project has on this environment but can also be the cause of these impacts. On the other hand, local populations do not usually benefit from the planned project. A good understanding of the relationship between environmental and social impacts is therefore crucial in adapting projects to include social development objectives such as equity or gender.[43] Alongside these reasons, it might also be considered that an integrated assessment of the environmental and social dimensions is a prerequisite for ensuring that the final decision on the project and the subsequent monitoring are sustainable.

Far less provision is made for Social Impact Assessments than for EIAs in binding and non-binding international instruments. In its definition of 'impact', the Espoo Convention considers the potential effect on some social elements, such as historical monuments, cultural heritage, or socio-economic

41 Vanclay, Frank. 2003. "International Principles for Social Impact Assessment." *Impact Assessment and Project Appraisal* 21 (1): 5–12. 6.

42 Ibid.

43 Abaza, Bisset and Sadler, *Environmental and Strategic Environmental Assessment*, 138–139.

conditions,[44] but it is rather vague regarding the weight that these aspects should have in the overall assessment or how they should be assessed.

Among the international watercourse agreements analysed here, only three mention explicitly the need to conduct a Social Impact Assessment: the Niger Basin Water Charter provides that the notification of a planned measure must include the results of *any* environmental and social impact assessment;[45] the same provision is made in the Water Charter of the Lake Chad Basin[46] and the Charter for the Volta River Basin,[47] although in these cases the compulsory character of the norm is stressed.[48] The latter two agreements refer to 'environmental and social impact assessment', implying that the environmental and social impacts form part of the same assessment and are not independent processes. The Charter of Waters of the Senegal River makes an undefined reference to "les études d'impact."[49] Again, the Draft Water Charter for the Volta River Basin is the only international watercourse agreement which specifies to any extent the required content of Social Impact Assessments, although it focuses mostly on health-related aspects.[50] Despite the lack of regulation, it is still possible to find international watercourses where Social Impact Assessments have been conducted independently of the parallel EIA without any explicit provision to this effect.[51]

Health Impact Assessments are a much rarer element in projects affecting an international watercourse. The World Health Organisation (WHO) defines them as follows:

> [A] practical approach used to judge the potential health effects of a policy, programme or project on a population, particularly on vulnerable or disadvantaged groups. Recommendations are produced for decision-makers and stakeholders, with the aim of maximizing the proposal's positive health effects and minimizing its negative health effects. The

44 Espoo Convention, *supra* note 10. Article 1(vii).
45 The Niger Basin Water Charter, Article 20.
46 Water Charter of the Lake Chad Basin, Article 45.
47 Draft Water Charter for the Volta River Basin, Article 89.
48 Ibid. Article 79.
49 Charter of Waters of the Senegal River, Article 24.
50 VBA, Appendix 3 to the Water Charter for the Volta Basin on the Prior Notification of Planned Measures (August 2019), https://abv.int/wp-content/uploads/2022/02/Annex3_Notification_Planned_Measures_Water_Charter_VBA_Eng.pdf. Article 1.
51 See, for instance, the Social Impact Assessments conducted in the framework of several dam projects in the Mekong river basin since 2010. List of projects available at: MRC. n.d. "PNPCA Prior Consultations." Accessed December 11, 2024. https://www.mrcmekong.org/news_and_events_cat/pnpca-prior-consultations/.

approach can be applied in diverse economic sectors and uses quantitative, qualitative and participatory techniques.[52]

There is no international instrument to regulate Health Impact Assessments in this particular context, nor are they foreseen in any international watercourse agreement. However, they are an existing practice in other contexts and there is no apparent reason for them not to be applied in planned measures affecting an international watercourse.[53] In fact, since health is a key aspect of sustainable development, impacts on the health of the basin population should be considered in the management of any development project in an international watercourse carried out with an integrated approach. If health is considered in the broadest sense, encompassing not only biophysical impacts but also socio-economic inequalities as drivers of health, the nexus between environmental, social, economic and health impacts becomes undeniable. Bad health induced by the socio-economic impact of a project could derive, for instance, from a degraded resource base as a result of a pollution by the planned project, which in turn could cause poorer nutrition.

Although Health Impact Assessments are not specifically referred to in global conventions on international watercourses, a concern for health is clearly present and the UN Watercourses Convention mentions human health as one of the parameters for considering harm deriving from pollution,[54] while the UNECE Water Convention includes it as one of the elements which define transboundary impact.[55]

Similar references can also be found in some international watercourse agreements,[56] in particular the Charter of Waters of the Senegal River and the Draft Water Charter for the Volta River Basin, which link the requirement of conducting an EIA (or 'environmental and social impact assessment' in the latter) to the project's potential effects on human health. In the first case, the treaty establishes dangers to public health as one of the aspects which may

52 WHO. n.d. "Health Impact Assessments." Accessed December 11, 2024. https://www.who.int/tools/health-impact-assessments.

53 For a complete explanation of HIA see, for instance: Kemm, John. 2012. *Health Impact Assessment: Past Achievement, Current Understanding, and Future Progress*. Oxford: OUP.

54 Convention on the Law of the Non-Navigational Uses of International Watercourses, May 21, 1997, 2999 U.N.T.S. Article 21(2).

55 Convention on the Protection and Use of Transboundary Watercourses and International Lakes, March 17, 1992, 1936 U.N.T.S. 269. Article 1(2).

56 See for instance Article IV of the Boundary Waters Treaty; articles 1(5), 2 and 10 of The Niger Basin Water Charter; or articles 7(b°), 21(a) of the Water Charter of the Lake Chad Basin.

require the previous authorisation of a project, and which in turn requires to be notified with the inclusion of an EIA according to Article 24 of the same treaty.[57] In the case of the Draft Water Charter for the Volta River Basin, in addition to being a chriteria to require a previous authorisation,[58] impacts on health are identified as a reason to conduct an environmental and social impact assessment[59] and are a formal requirement of the content assessment.[60]

Another type of impact assessment that is relevant from the point of view of integration is the Human Rights Impact Assessments. This instrument assesses the impact of a given project on human rights, whether or not this is the intended aim of the project. In the first case, the assessment determines the effectiveness of the project actions, while in the second case, the purpose is to identify the potential undesired impact on human rights.

Although Human Rights Impact Assessments constitute an evolution of EIAs and, especially, Social Impact Assessments, they differ in some important aspects. First and foremost, the benchmark against which impacts are analysed is the normative framework of binding international human rights law. This legal framework gives Human Rights Impact Assessments two important comparative advantages over other forms of impact assessment: on the one hand, the recommendations deriving from Human Rights Impact Assessments have greater moral legitimacy and legal accountability, which in turn may limit the extent to which trade-offs are acceptable;[61] on the other, since human rights come with specific obligations, impacts on these rights are more easily measurable.[62]

Secondly, Human Rights Impact Assessments are more comprehensive than the other impact assessments considered above. In fact, they are almost as comprehensive as human rights themselves, encompassing civil, political, economic, social and cultural rights, what fosters a cross-sectoral approach in the assessment process. In practice, environmental protection is not usually

57 Charter of Waters of the Senegal River, Article 10.

58 Draft Water Charter for the Volta River Basin, Article 79(1).

59 "Environmental and social impact assessment: a process to examine the beneficial and adverse effects of a proposed development project on the environment and human health and to ensure that such effects are duly taken into account in project design". In Ibid. Article 3(21).

60 In VBA, Appendix 3 to the Water Charter for the Volta Basin on the Prior Notification of Planned Measures (August 2019), https://abv.int/wp-content/uploads/2022/02/Annex3_Notification_Planned_Measures_Water_Charter_VBA_Eng.pdf. Article 1.

61 The Nordic Trust Fund, and The World Bank. 2013. *Study on Human Rights Impact Assessments*. Washington, D.C.: The World Bank. 7.

62 Bürgi, *Sustainable Development in International Law Making and Trade*. 88–89.

included in Human Rights Impact Assessments unless it overlaps directly with these types of rights,[63] but this type of assessment could be useful for evaluating projects affecting an international watercourse in a more integrated manner, if it is conducted as a complement to an EIA. This said, no examples of the application of a Human Rights Impact Assessments in this context were found, nor have them been found mentioned in any binding or non-binding instrument.

1.3 *Nexus Assessments*

As seen earlier in Chapter 10,[64] the WEF Nexus approach is intended to safeguard water, energy and food security, avoiding sectoral trade-offs and promoting synergies by coordinating the sectors involved in a more holistic way. Recent developments have made it possible to consider WEF Nexus linkages at the level of more specific activities, such as the planning of projects, by translating the WEF Nexus approach into an assessment method. The NBA adopted in 2022 the *Guidelines for the integration of the Water, Energy, Food Security, and Environmental Sustainability Nexus approach in the development of sustainable development programs and projects in the Niger Basin,*[65] marking the first occasion on which an IRBO has formally adopted a document based on the WEF Nexus approach.[66]

This instrument is the outcome of a project led and co-financed by the GIZ,[67] which started in 2018. The process was open to actors from the nine members of the NBA, who were invited to participate in three-day national workshops. These actors were representatives of several ministries, civil society and the private sector from both the water, energy and food sectors, although with a clear predominance of the water sector.[68]

63 The Nordic Trust Fund, and The World Bank. 2013. *Study on Human Rights Impact Assessments*. Washington, D.C.: The World Bank. 8.

64 See Subsection c(i) of Chapter 10 above.

65 NBA. 2022. "41st Ordinary Session of the Council of Ministers of the Niger Basin Authority." http://www.abn.ne/images/documents/Conseil_Ministres/CM2022/rapport_41_cm_final_eng.pdf.

66 On the role of IRBOs in the application of the nexus approach see Dombrowsky, Ines, and Oliver Hensengerth. 2018. "Governing the Water-Energy-Food Nexus Related to Hydropower on Shared Rivers – The Role of Regional Organizations." *Frontiers in Environmental Science* 6 (153): 1–16.

67 NBA, and GIZ. 2022. "Factsheet: Nexus Regional Dialogue in the Niger Basin." http://www.abn.ne/images/documents/FME2022/fiche_nexus_en.pdf.

68 Information provided by the Regional Nexus Coordinator of the Niger Basin from the GIZ at the webinar "The Water-Energy-Food-Ecosystem Nexus: how to improve governance and accountability", organized by the Bonn Water Network and the Water Integrity Network, 4th November 2022.

The first proposal was presented as a Directive,[69] but it was deprived of binding force by the representatives of the NBA Member States at a later stage. In any case, being the first document of their kind, the Guidelines contain innovative elements that are relevant to the subject of this thesis. Firstly, they are applicable to any type of project or programme affecting the basin, regardless of the implementing actor.[70] This is one of the most noticeable differences between the proposal and the adopted instrument, since the draft Directive was applicable only to NBA investments.[71]

Secondly, the Guidelines contain a comprehensive list of general and specific principles. The general principles illustrate the integrative approach adopted in the creation of this instrument, as several of the principles clearly go beyond the specific purpose of the WEF Nexus approach. See, for instance, the polluter-pays principle or the principle of social equity, this last one defined as "whereby the interests and concerns of women, men, and vulnerable segments of society are taken into account in the formulation of capacity development policies and planning of programs and projects."[72]

It is the specific principles, however, that embody the integrative aim of the WEF Nexus approach itself. The *principle of the systematic multisector effects* establishes that any intervention in the basin is presumed to produce effects in all three sectors as well as the environment and that it is up to the Member States of the NBA to demonstrate that the negative effects are negligible, where this is the case. In fact, this can be considered the core principle of the Guidelines, since it expresses the idea that the effects on each sector must be considered jointly.[73] The *principle of the cumulative effect* is also integrative

69 NBA. 2022. "Directive nexus sur le renforcement des synergies intersectorielles et la réduction des antagonismes des investissements et projets dans le bassin du Niger." [preparatory unpublished document elaborated on the 22 May 2022].

70 NBA, *Resolution No. 7: on the adoption of the Guideline for the integration of Nexus (Water-Energy-Food Security, and Environmental sustainability) in developing NBA Projects and Programmes, adopted in the 41st Ordinary Session of the Council of Ministers of the Niger Basin Authority* (8 December 2022), http://www.abn.ne/images/documents/NEXUS/guidelines_resolution_nba_nexus_en.pdf. Article 3.

71 NBA. 2022. "Directive nexus sur le renforcement des synergies intersectorielles et la réduction des antagonismes des investissements et projets dans le bassin du Niger." [preparatory unpublished document elaborated on the 22 May 2022]. Article 2.

72 NBA, *Resolution No. 7: on the adoption of the Guideline for the integration of Nexus (Water-Energy-Food Security, and Environmental sustainability) in developing NBA Projects and Programmes, adopted in the 41st Ordinary Session of the Council of Ministers of the Niger Basin Authority* (8 December 2022), http://www.abn.ne/images/documents/NEXUS/guidelines_resolution_nba_nexus_en.pdf. Article 4, paragraphs iii) and vii).

73 Ibid. Article 4.i).

since it is intended to ensure that each activity in the basin is considered in relation to the other activities already in place.[74] Finally, the *principle of promoting intersectoral efficiency* translates the purpose of creating sectoral synergies embedded in the WEF Nexus approach by prioritising those programmes and activities that contribute to resource efficiency in all sectors, together with social and environmental concerns.[75]

The Guidelines also establish a method for conducting nexus assessments,[76] distinguishing between a simplified evaluation for any kind of project or programme, and a detailed evaluation for those cases in which the simplified evaluation reveals a likelihood of significant adverse effects.[77] They also contain a comprehensive list of the information relevant to determining what kind of evaluation should be conducted, and a methodology for simplified evaluation based on a scoring scale.[78] In the final version, it is not clear at what stage the States must notify the other Member States or the NBA of the results of the nexus assessments. In the proposal submitted to the Council of Ministers, the nexus assessments were to be included in the prior notification process.[79] The removal of that provision leaves a vacuum that should be filled in the practical implementation of assessment process.

However, the nexus assessments conducted according to these Guidelines cannot be considered to substitute any other impact assessment that might be compulsory under international law. Indeed, these assessments are general in character and are to be applied in the initial stages of the planning of a project or programme in order to detect inter-sectoral impacts, but an EIA or Social Impact Assessment may still have to be conducted at a later stage.[80]

74 Ibid. Article 4.ii).

75 Ibid. Article 4.iii).

76 This method was developed with the collaboration of the UNECE Water Convention Secretariat and the Southern Africa Development Community (SADC).

77 NBA, *Resolution No. 7: on the adoption of the Guideline for the integration of Nexus (Water-Energy-Food Security, and Environmental sustainability) in developing NBA Projects and Programmes, adopted in the 41st Ordinary Session of the Council of Ministers of the Niger Basin Authority* (8 December 2022), http://www.abn.ne/images/documents/NEXUS/guidelines_resolution_nba_nexus_en.pdf. Articles 16 and 17.

78 Ibid. Annexs I and II.

79 NBA, Committee of Regional Experts, *Guidelines for the integration of the Water, Energy, Food Security, and Environmental Sustainability Nexus approach in the development of sustainable development programs and projects in the Niger Basin* (2 September 2022) [preparatory unpublished document].

80 Insights provided by the Regional Nexus Coordinator of the Niger Basin from the GIZ in the course of an interview conducted on the 4th November 2022.

2 Involvement of Stakeholder in Project Planning and Implementation

Public involvement has several beneficial effects in the management of international watercourses. On the one hand, it creates awareness of foreseen specific activities. On the other hand, it supports the decision-making process by helping to monitor, inspect or enforce measures and, more importantly for this study, by improving the quality of decisions through public input that States can otherwise have difficulty in obtaining due to scarce resources.[81] The planning of a sustainable project affecting an international watercourse requires accurate information to foresee the potential effects on the basin. As such, it is unlikely that a planning effort of this kind could be successful without the information provided by the many stakeholders involved in the watercourse, either as users, managers, or with any other legitimate interest.

The previous Section established that the application of the principle of integration at project level depends on the capacity to collect and analyse this information in a truly integrated manner. At the same time, as it is the local population that will be most directly affected, the application of the principle of integration would be questioned if they were not given a meaningful say in the decision-making process. EIAs are the most common mechanism to convey public participation in relation to the planning of projects, although there are also other mechanisms for that purpose.[82] This Section analyses both.

2.1 *Public Participation in the Framework of Environmental Impact Assessments*

Today, there is no doubt about the customary nature of the obligation to carry out an EIA whenever a project is likely to have significant transboundary effects, especially since the ICJ so considered it,[83] but there is much uncertainty about the structure that EIAs must have according to international law.[84] As seen above, due to the wide adoption of EIAs without any globally applicable

81 Bruch, Carl. 2005. "Evolution of Public Involvement in International Watercourse Management." In *Public Participation in the Governance of International Freshwater Resources*, edited by Carl Bruch, Libor Jansky, Mikiyasu Nakayama, and Kazimierz A. Salewicz. New York: United Nations University Press. 23.

82 On this topic see Tignino, Mara. 2010. "Les Contours Du Principe de La Participation Publique et La Protection Des Ressources En Eau Transfrontières." *VertigO – La Revue Électronique En Sciences de l'environnement* 7: 1–11. 4–8.

83 Pulp Mills on the River Uruguay (Argentina v. Uruguay), 2010 Judgment, I.C.J. Rep. 14 (April 20). Para. 204.

84 In this regard, Boyle suggests that the 1987 UNEP Goals and Principles of Environmental Impact Assessment (*supra* note 30) should be amended to adapt them to the international practice.

convention on the topic, the process might diverge significantly across different regulations, with some parts given less weight or not considered relevant at all. This is the case of public participation in the context of EIAs, which is the focus of interest here.

The ICJ ruled in *Pulp Mills on the River Uruguay* (*Argentina v. Uruguay*) that, although conducting an EIA is an obligation of international law, consultation of the public as part of the process is not.[85] The Court also clarified that: "it is for each State to determine in its domestic legislation or in the authorization process for the project, the specific content of the environmental impact assessment required in each case, having regard to the nature and magnitude of the proposed development and its likely adverse impact on the environment."[86] However, the EIA concerning the planned pulp mills on the River Uruguay included a public consultation legal obligation, as Uruguay organised public hearings both in Uruguay and in Argentina.[87] It has recently been noted that the growing tendency to frame EIA regulation in human rights discourse is gradually making public participation an inherent part of the assessment process, especially where indigenous groups are concerned.[88] However, according to the current state of international law, public participation in EIAs remains subject to regional variations in conventional regulation.[89]

---

85 The ICJ rejected the applicability of the Espoo Convention invoked by Argentina along with the non-binding instruments of the 1978 UNEP Goals and Principles of Environmental Impact Assessment and the 2001 International Law Commission Draft Articles on Prevention of Transboundary Harm from Hazardous Activities. In Pulp Mills on the River Uruguay (Argentina v. Uruguay), 2010 Judgment, I.C.J. Rep. 14 (April 20). Paras. 215–219.

86 Ibid. Para. 105.

87 Ibid. Para. 217. Judge Vinuesa, in his dissenting opinion, argued against the court as he considered that Uruguay did have such obligation of consulting the affected local population. In addition, the consultation process had been conducted when the project had been already approved. Therefore, according to him, Uruguay "has not complied with its due diligence obligation to consult the affected populations prior to the issue of the authorization to build the Orion (Botnia) mill." Pulp Mills on the River Uruguay (Argentina v. Uruguay), 2010 Judgment, I.C.J. Rep. 14 (April 20) (Vinuesa, R., dissenting opinion). Para. 65.

88 See Craik, Neil. 2018. "Environmental Impact Assessment." In *Principles of Environmental Law*, edited by Ludwig Krämer and Emanuela Orlando. Edward Elgar. 203–205.

89 The ICJ has been very reluctant to determine the content of EIAs, but in *Certain Activities Carried Out by Nicaragua in the Border Area* (*Costa Rica v. Nicaragua*) and *Construction of a Road in Costa Rica along the San Juan River* (*Nicaragua v. Costa Rica*) the Court established that no national regulation can preclude the obligation under general international law to conduct an EIA. See Certain Activities Carried Out by Nicaragua in the Border Area (Costa Rica v. Nicaragua) and Construction of a Road in Costa Rica along the San Juan River (Nicaragua v. Costa Rica), Judgment, 2015 I.C.J. Rep. 665 (December 15). Para. 157.

In any case, not only is it quite an extended practice to conduct consultations as part of an EIA,[90] it is also considered to be a good practice.[91] The Espoo Convention gives the public an important role in these processes,[92] and there are many examples of EIAs of international watercourse projects that have included the consultation of the local population and non-governmental actors where there was no legal obligation to do so. Abaza *et al.* lists several benefits of this approach, three of which are especially relevant from the point of view of the principle of integration: "allowing the public to express its view on the scope and content of an EIA (and the proposed development action); obtaining local and traditional knowledge (corrective and creative) before decision-making; allowing more sensitive consideration of alternatives, mitigation measures and trade-offs; ensuring that important impacts are not overlooked and benefits are maximized."[93]

Another example of public consultations in the context of an impact assessment are the EIA[94] and the Social Impact Assessment[95] of the Xayabury dam project[96] carried out by Laos in 2010, which were not compulsory and were conducted prior to the publication in 2018 of the Guidelines for Transboundary Environmental Impact Assessment in the Lower Mekong Basin. These

90 The decision of the ICJ has been severely criticised by many commentators, arguing that public consultation in the context of EIAs is a necessary aspect of EIA. See, for instance, Boyle, Alan. 2010. "Pulp Mills Case: A Commentary." https://www.biicl.org/files/5167_pulp_mills_case.pdf.

91 See, generally, Troell et al. "Transboundary Environmental Impact Assessment," 175.

92 See Espoo Convention, *supra* note 10, Articles 2.6 and 3.8.

93 Abaza, Bisset and Sadler, *Environmental and Strategic Environmental Assessment*, 66.

94 MRC. 2010. "Final Report. Environmental and Impact Assessment of Xayabury Hydroelectric Power Project, Lao PDR." https://www.mrcmekong.org/assets/Consultations/2010-Xayaburi/Xayaburi-EIA-August-2010.pdf.

95 MRC. 2010. "Final Report. Environmental Impact Assessment of Xayabury Hydroelectric Power Project." 2010. Accessed June 15, 2023. https://www.mrcmekong.org/assets/Consultations/2010-Xayaburi/Xayaburi-SIA-August-2010.pdf.

96 The Xayabury dam is located in northern Laos and its main purpose is hydropower generation. The station is in functioning from 2019 and is currently operated by a Thai company. However, the construction started in 2012 and was stopped shortly after due to complaints from Vietnam and Cambodia. As the EIA and the Social Impact Assessment showed, there are strong concerns on the impacts of this infrastructure on households, the biodiversity and the fisheries. This also motived the lawsuit by the NGO Thai Mekong People's Network from Eight Provinces against the agreement of the Electricity Generating Authority of Thailand to buy electricity from the Xayaburi Dam. In 2022, the Thailand's Supreme Administrative Court ruled in favour of the defendant arguing that the agreement did not by itself had any environmental or social impact.

guidelines recommend public participation, dissemination of information and consultation within the potentially affected country.[97]

Moreover, the submission by Laos of the EIA and Social Impact Assessment to the MRC as part of the prior notification stage was followed by stakeholder consultations as part of the prior consultation process, which is not foreseen in the 1995 Mekong Agreement[98] or in the 2003 Procedures for Notification, Prior Consultation and Agreement.[99]

The process allowed stakeholders in the four countries affected by the project to contribute very detailed feedback concerning a wide spectrum of topics,[100] something that would have not been possible with a top-down analysis. Although this first public consultation was severely hampered by disagreements between Laos and the other MRC members regarding the period available to conduct them,[101] it marked the start of a tendency to include public consultations in the prior consultation process, which has been replicated in subsequent projects.[102]

In the UNECE region, public consultation as part of EIAs is a more established mechanism as the Espoo Convention[103] has been signed by most European nations. Recent international watercourse agreements such as the 2012 Dniester Treaty even explicitly state that EIAs will abide by the Espoo Convention.[104] This means that the State of origin is obliged to give the affected population of other countries the opportunity to participate in the EIA in at least the same meaningful way as its own affected population.[105]

---

97 MRC. 2023. *Guidelines for Transboundary Environmental Impact Assessment in the Lower Mekong River Basin (TbEIA)*. Vientiane: MRC Secretariat. https://doi.org/10.52107/mrc.aqrsbk.

98 Mekong Agreement.

99 MRC, *Procedures for Notification, Prior Consultation and Agreement* (30 November 2003), https://www.mrcmekong.org/wp-content/uploads/2024/08/Procedures-Notification-Prior-Consultation-Agreement.pdf.

100 MRC Secretariat. 2011. "Prior Consultation for the Proposed Xayaburi Dam Project. Prior Consultation Project Review Report. Volume 2. Stakeholder Consultations Related to the Proposed Xayaburi Dam Project." https://www.mrcmekong.org/assets/Consultations/2010-Xayaburi/2011-03-24-Report-on-Stakeholder-Consultation-on-Xayaburi.pdf.

101 Rieu-Clarke, Alistair. 2014. "Notification and Consultation Procedures under the Mekong Agreement: Insights from the Xayaburi Controversy." *Asian Journal of International Law* 5 (1): 143–75. 10.

102 MRC. n.d. "PNPCA Prior Consultations." Accessed December 11, 2024. https://www.mrcmekong.org/news_and_events_cat/pnpca-prior-consultations/.

103 Espoo Convention, *supra* note 10.

104 Dniester River Basin Treaty, Article 17.

105 Espoo Convention, *supra* note 10. Articles 2.6 and 3.8.

2.2 *Public Participation in Relation to the Planning of Projects Outside Environmental Impact Assessments*

Although much rarer, public participation in relation to the planning of projects can also take place outside the EIA process. The US-Ca IJC, for instance, conducts public consultations every year on several topics. They commonly are organised in parallel with the elaboration of plans, but they can also be part of the process of projects affecting shared watercourses, such as the construction or the decommissioning of dams. In these cases, the public is invited to provide comments by mail or email.[106]

Mechanisms of public participation such as public consultations can play a role in controlling the planning and approval phases of projects. They are also important in ensuring that the principle of integration is effectively applied, since local populations and other stakeholders are especially sensitive to the environmental and socio-economic impacts on the basin. It is in the practice of IRBOs where the mechanisms that allow for the public participation regarding the implementation of projects can be found.

A good example is the recent institutionalisation of public participation in the OMVS. It is organised through national coordination units, which work with the *Comités locaux de coordination* (CLC). Their mandate can vary from country to country, but they serve as the main consultation framework between the OMVS and the local populations. The units have two functions: 1) to assist the OMVS in the preparation, coordination and monitoring of the implementation of its projects; and 2) to inform, raise awareness and organise the population with regard to OMVS projects.[107]

106 See, for instance, the public consultation regarding the decommissioning of the Milltown Generating Station on the St. Croix River, which was open to comments from June 2 of 2022 to June 15 of 2022. In IJC. n.d. "Public Comments – Decommissioning of the Milltown Generating Station, St. Croix River | International Joint Commission." Accessed December 11, 2024. https://ijc.org/en/public-comments-decommissioning-milltown-generating-station-st-croix-river.

107 Sangbana, "La Participation Du Public Dans Le Cadre de l'Organisation Pour La Mise En Valeur Du Fleuve Sénégal," 81–82.

CHAPTER 13

Final Conclusions

1 The Emergence, Content and Nature of the Principle of Integration

The integration of the economic, social and environmental dimensions has been construed as an ancillary principle of sustainable development, which in turn has been a prominent element of UN discourse and policy for decades. This evolution has been significantly led by the UN General Assembly throughout a series of international conferences held in relation to sustainable development since the pioneering 1972 United Nations Conference on the Human Environment in Stockholm. The analysis of the soft law instruments emanating from these events provides a preliminary identification of the general traits of the principle of integration, which has acquired an increasingly central role in both international environmental law and UN policy on sustainable development. The centrality of the principle of integration is particularly apparent in international environmental law, the context in which the integration of environmental concerns into developmental concerns first emerged as a necessity. The principle of integration also provides international law with the logic along which one of the primary concerns of the international community, sustainable development, must be pursued.

In relation to its legal nature, it can be affirmed in the first place that the principle of integration has become an emergent norm of customary law as a general and consistent practice can be ascertained, while there is an *opinio iuris* on the bindingness of its nature. However, this can only be ascertained insofar as it applies to the obligation to carry out an integrated decision-making process. Secondly, in addition to being a customary norm, the principle of integration can also be found in several treaties, mostly pertaining to the environmental domain, hence it has a significant conventional base.

The content of the principle of integration has developed along two dimensions, determined by the context in which it operates. A first dimension of the principle of integration is presented as a specific answer by the international community to a fragmented international legal order. Where the furthering of sustainable development is hampered by interactions between areas of international law that respond to different and opposing interests, an integrative solution based on legal integration is sought to provide a more coherent outcome.

 | DOI:10.1163/9789004736757_018

This legal integration is aimed at creating inter-systemic links and can operate in two stages. In the first stage it operates through the creation of integrated norms that allow for the consideration of environmental norms in the application of developmental norms and vice versa. For example, a treaty regulating international trade might make reference to another treaty protecting biodiversity, thus providing a tool to weigh the conflicting interests enshrined in each instrument. In the second stage it operates as a principle of integrated application and interpretation of norms in international law bearing on sustainable development. For instance, the evolutionary interpretation of certain concepts by an international court might reflect the evolution of international law in the sense of a better understanding of the interrelation between the environment and human life.

This aspect of the principle of integration is characterised by the generality of a legal principle; as such, and despite its insertion in several international treaties, the principle of integration is often not interpreted as a binding rule by international courts and arbitral tribunals, but it is certainly applied in a number of cases. This dimension of the principle of integration is synthesised through the concept of 'legal integration'.

Conversely, a second dimension of the principle of integration has certainly acquired the character of an emerging binding rule, where it is understood as a principle furthering the merging of economic, social and environmental concerns in the decision-making process. The overall purpose of this dimension is to provide a sense of the need to structure the processes leading to a decision affecting sustainable development in a manner consistent with its three-fold character. This rule has been developed as a substantive norm that encompasses an obligation of behaviour, which may be identified with the duty of due diligence that has to be implemented through specific instruments. The performance of an Environmental Impact Assessment as a prior step to any decision on the planning of an activity that might potentially affect the environment is the most widespread manifestation of such an obligation, but it is not the only one. This dimension of the principle of integration is synthesised through the concept of 'institutional integration'.

This does not preclude the acknowledgement that there are still significant obstacles to recognising the legally binding nature of the principle of integration. From the perspective of legal integration, and despite its inclusion in various international treaties or its identification as a customary norm, at least in an emerging sense, the violation of the principle of integration hardly triggers international responsibility. Indeed, given the uncertainty about the content of the principle (which is often formulated in an incomplete or overly general manner), it is challenging to determine exactly what international responsibility its breach can incur. However, as noted above, from the perspective of the mechanisms that should underlie or accompany the decision-making process, i.e. from the perspective of institutional integration, when the international rule clearly prescribes concrete behaviour, it is more feasible to construct a system of international responsibility, since violation of the procedures will trigger the legal responsibility of the violator.

2 Recognition of the Principle of Integration in the Context of International Watercourse Law

Sustainable development and international watercourse law have exerted a mutual influence for many years. This can be seen in the numerous references to international watercourses in the preparatory works of international conferences on sustainable development, such as the 1992 Dublin Statement on Water and Sustainable Development, but also in the near-ubiquitous presence of sustainable development in the global and regional treaties on international watercourses adopted over the last three decades. The UN Watercourses Convention, the 1994 Danube River Protection Convention or the 2002 Charter of Waters of the Senegal River, are just some examples.

This relationship has led, on the one hand, to the consideration of international watercourses as an essential field for sustainable development, thus helping to settle a growing concern over the need for cooperation on international watercourses. This has placed international watercourses high on the UN political agenda and led to the creation of UN organisms directly concerned with this topic, such as UN Water, as well as the emergence of myriad international NGOs and networks involved in political or academic advocacy in this area, such as Global Water Partnership or the International Network of Basin Organisations.

On the other hand, the principle of integration has laid the foundation for the adoption of sustainable development as a specific objective of international watercourse law, as both a customary and a conventional norm. The inclusion of mechanisms in international basin agreements for the protection of the environment in the context of river navigation or mechanisms to set a sufficient ecologic flow to secure ecosystem services are examples of integrative measures for the sustainable development of international watercourses. Although each international watercourse regime is adapted to the particular environmental and human conditions of the watercourse, they provide a varied bank of integration mechanisms for international watercourse law, which would otherwise be too general. The role of the International Court of Justice and some international arbitral awards have been key in this process, as sustainable development has become a significant legal issue through international disputes concerning international watercourses.

The second element conditioning the application of the principle of integration in the cooperation on an international watercourse is the scope of the cooperation regime. Considering the complexity of the eco-social system the principle of integration is intended to serve, it is to be assumed that the broader the definition of international watercourse adopted by the riparian States and the wider the scope of uses included in the cooperation framework, the greater the guarantee of integrated governance. On the one hand, if part of the water that belongs to the international watercourse system is excluded, it is more difficult to establish a coherent plan on the basis of the several factors that might affect the watercourse. This situation most typically arises when groundwater is deliberately excluded from the cooperation framework or when one or more of the riparian States is not party to an existing international basin agreement. On the other hand, the greater the number of uses that are included in the cooperation framework, the greater the capacity to integrate and to avoid trade-offs between economic, social and environmental factors.

The comparative analysis of cooperation regimes on international watercourses reveals that there is a correlation between the degree of development and capacity to apply the principle of integration and the scope of physical parameters and regulated uses encompassed by the regimes. Most of the analysed regimes are applicable to the whole of the basin, including groundwater, which can be considered the ideal scope for the application of the principle of integration in the area of international law. In relation to the uses of the watercourse, most of the international basin agreements analysed here provide non-exhaustive lists of uses, which seem to give the regimes sufficient flexibility to govern all the necessary aspects with a bearing on sustainable development.

The principle of equitable and reasonable utilisation, the no harm principle and the principle of protection of the watercourse form a highly interdependent set of substantive principles of international watercourse law. This relationship has been termed internal integration. The interests that these principles are intended to protect are the same that the principle of integration must accommodate. Although it can be debated whether the principle of protection of watercourses can be considered a substantive principle of equal standing to the other two principles, it clearly coincides with the environmental dimension of sustainable development. The economic and social dimensions, meanwhile, are reflected in the principle of equitable and reasonable utilisation and the no harm principle, as they are the most long-standing interest regulated by this area of international law. While unequitable use or significant harm might take the form of environmental damage, the environment plays a secondary role to the other two substantive principles.

In any case, provided that the watercourse environment is protected to a sufficient extent, equitable and reasonable utilisation and no harm principles form a suitable legal basis for the principle of integration in the context of an international watercourse. They are intended to provide the framework for mutual respect of economic and social interests between riparian States. Internal integration, therefore, provides the basis for legal integration in the context of international watercourse law. As long as a balance is found between substantive principles, the principle of integration can be effectively applied.

The application of the substantive principles of international watercourse law relies on the existence of an effective machinery of procedural rules, which the riparian States apply as a manifestation of their cooperation. This relationship has been called the external integration of the norms of international watercourse law. These procedural obligations – the obligation of prior notification, the obligation to conduct an Environmental Impact Assessment, the obligation to consult with other riparian States, and the obligation to exchange data and information – are key to complying with the substantive principles as they provide the mechanisms for joint decision-making on issues affecting the watercourse. Therefore, they are also the basis for an integrated decision-making process in the application of the principle of integration; in other words, external integration of substantive principles and procedural rules of international watercourse law is the basis for institutional integration in this are of international law.

3 The Legal Integration of the Economic, Social and Environmental Dimensions in the Context of International Watercourse Law

Several techniques contribute to integrating the economic, social and environmental dimensions of sustainable development in the regulation of cooperation on international watercourses. They differ significantly in terms of the margin of discretion granted to the subject responsible for applying the norm, but also in the extent to which they are effectively used in practice. They can be grouped in three blocks.

First, the mandate for integration might be included in a treaty, as in most of the international basin agreements analysed here. The majority of them include sustainable development as an objective or a principle of the treaty, thus containing an indirect mandate for integration; but some international basin agreements lay down the principle explicitly, most commonly with varying formulations establishing that riparian States must adopt protection or management plans that give due consideration to economic, social and environmental concerns. However, these are general clauses whose effective application is difficult to assess.

Second, legal integration through inter-disciplinary integration techniques – albeit rarely used – results in norms with quite straightforward content. One of the rare cases in which these techniques can be found is the Great Lakes Water Quality Agreement, the annex to which contains a reference to the International Convention for the Prevention of Pollution from Ships and the International Convention on Liability and Compensation for Damage in Connection with the Carriage of Hazardous and Noxious Substances by Sea. More often, these international basin agreements refer to general regimes, such as the regulations of the International Maritime Organization referenced in the Great Lakes Water Quality Agreement. These mechanisms could be used more widely in the international basin agreements analysed here, which contain very few of them. These legal integration mechanisms could provide fertile ground for the application of the principle of integration if the international basin agreements are revised and recast.

Third, legal integration might be carried out through the application of international instruments that produce intentional integration. It operates through a series of techniques that can generate the integrating effect indirectly at the time these international instruments are implemented. Intentional integration, therefore, operates through norms that produce integration as a secondary effect when integration is not the main purpose of their inclusion in a given treaty. Such instruments are widely used and are the core mechanism of legal integration in international basin cooperation frameworks.

They can be divided into three types. The first type, intra-treaty integration, consists of the inclusion of economic, social (e.g. access to water of population; health) and environmental (e.g. pollution prevention; protection of ecosystems) values in an international watercourse agreement, with the consequence that the application of the treaty implies the consideration of these values.

The second type is the inclusion of guiding principles of the application of the treaty that are not primarily intended to convey the principle of integration but which do so indirectly. In international watercourse agreements, this is particularly the case of some environmental principles such as the principle of prevention, the principle of precaution and the principle of participation. Principles implying the integration of social concerns are much rarer.

The third type of intentional integration is the inclusion in international basin agreements of integrative concepts developed in soft law instruments. In a variety of cases, the development of these concepts in instruments external to the international basin agreement reflects the development of science and policy in such a manner that the interrelations between the economic, social and environmental dimensions are better understood, thus promoting integration when utilised in a binding treaty. This is the case of the concepts of ecosystem services, environmental flows, food security and energy security. In sum, institutional integration mechanisms are much more widely used than interdisciplinary integration mechanisms. While this may reflect their lower reliability and less specific nature in terms of the legal outcome they are intended to produce, the range of options they offer is enormous and can be expected to continue to evolve rapidly.

Legal integration through interpretation is a scarcely used recourse in the resolution of disputes concerning the utilisation of international watercourses. Only a few examples could be found in the case law of the International Court of Justice and international arbitral tribunals, while no cases were found of disputes resolved through the jurisdictional mechanisms provided by International River Basin Organisations. It is striking that the growing presence of new concepts and principles – especially those deriving from environmental law and policy – embedded in international basin agreements has not given ground to more differences of opinion between States sharing a watercourse. These concepts are developed outside the legal instruments, either because they are the result of political processes or because they reflect scientific evolution. As such, their interpretation in the application of binding instruments could be expected to lead to differing interpretations. However, these differences do not transcend into international disputes resolved by a jurisdictional or arbitral body.

The tendency of international tribunals to make integrative interpretations of the provisions set in international basin agreements remains limited, as very few examples of it could be found. This is consistent with the preference of States to resort to diplomatic means of resolving disputes over water use, to the detriment of more formal mechanisms, or mechanisms leading to a binding decision, but it contributes little to the development of the principle of integration of sustainable development through what the International Law Association has defined as integration as a judicial reasoning tool.

In any case, the few examples of integrative interpretation operate through three different interpretative mechanisms. First, in some cases, the teleological interpretation of treaties might lead to integration when the treaty in question promotes environmental protection in addition to developmental interests. Second, the interpretation of open-textured obligations might also result in an integrative interpretation, either because it leads the court or tribunal to apply the principle of systemic integration of Article 31 of the Vienna Convention on the Law of the Treaties, or because it provides for consideration of the evolution of international law. The interpretation of evolutionary terms, the third interpretatitive mechanism, certainly has the potential to produce integrative interpretations, as it has done in other domains of international law such as the law of the sea, but this has yet to be seen in international watercourse law.

4 The Institutional Integration of the Economic, Social and Environmental Dimensions in the Context of International Watercourse Law

Institutional integration is the second dimension of the principle of integration. Its purpose is to provide the means to account for greater complexity in the decision-making process. It has therefore been defined as the array of mechanisms that allow economic, social and environmental considerations to be taken into account in decision-making for the achievement of sustainable development. Since the environment is traditionally left out of this process, applying the principle of integration most commonly translates into implementing mechanisms to ensure that the environmental dimension is given due consideration in the decision-making process. This is certainly the case of cooperation on international watercourses, where the instruments the analysed International River Basin Organisations use to ensure institutional integration tend to focus on environmental issues.

From an organisational point of view, institutional integration in international watercourse cooperation requires the establishment of IRBOs. However, these organisations do not always have a sufficient mandate to achieve integrated governance and are not necessarily endowed with enough or the appropriate human and material resources. That is why many international cooperation projects financed by donors such as the World Bank, the World Meteorological Organization and national aid agencies have focused precisely on the capacity of International River Basin Organisations in the Global South.

The analysis of the selected International River Basin Organisations has revealed that they play an essential role in the monitoring and analysis of data, often through the establishment of observatories, such as the *Observatoire de l'Environnement* of the *Organisation pour la mise en valeur du fleuve Sénégal*. They also facilitate the exchange of necessary information through online platforms that are increasingly accessible to the Parties and, to a greater or lesser extent, to other stakeholders. Likewise, International River Basin Organisations are central to providing spaces for public participation, whether in central decision-making or advisory bodies (e.g. the Water Resources Advisory Committee of the Lake Chad Basin Commission) or through geographically decentralised bodies that are more accessible to local stakeholders (e.g. the Niger Basin Authority's *Coordination Nationale des Usagers*).

Institutional integration relies on the capacity of the institution in charge of conveying it to ensure an informed and participatory decision-making process. In other words, information and participation are two pillars of institutional integration. Mechanisms for informed decision-making are key to institutional integration because the relationship between development and the environment is necessarily complex, and assessing how any activity will affect or is affected by those dimensions requires a large amount of information and data.

For a similar reason, mechanisms to facilitate public participation in the decision-making process are necessary for the principle of integration. It is unlikely that the governance of an eco-social system such as an international watercourse could achieve sustainable development without a significant degree of involvement by relevant non-State actors. Since in the context of international watercourses both the gathering and processing of information and the processes of public participation require cooperation between the riparian States, International River Basin Organisations provide the framework to convey institutional integration, while their success in doing so will depend largely on the extent to which they are provided with sufficient resources, an adequate mandate and a suitable institutional set-up.

At the same time, the mechanisms used by International River Basin Organisations in the application of the principle of integration vary depending on the level at which they are applied, whether for the development of an international basin policy, the management of shared water resources, or the planning of a project. In the present book, these aspects have been approached from a multiscale perspective considering the three different levels of action: basin policy, watercourse management planning, and specific projects carried out in the international watercourse.

Firstly, at the level of basin policy, the comparative analysis of International River Basin Organisations in this study reveals that Strategic Environmental Assessments are the most common instrument to inform the policy elaboration process. They are not foreseen in either of the global conventions on international watercourses and are provided for in only one international basin agreement in force, the Water Charter of the Lake Chad Basin, so the performance of Strategic Environmental Assessments remains a largely *ad hoc* practice. The structure of Strategic Environmental Assessments varies greatly from basin to basin, but the expansion of this instrument is positive in terms of the principle of integration, since they achieve wider acknowledgement of the impacts and issues that the policy in preparation must take into account.

Sustainability Impact Assessments are another instrument that could inform policy-level integration, but unlike Strategic Environmental Assessments, no cases of their application have been found in the regimes of the International River Basin Organisations analysed in this study. Since Sustainability Impact Assessments have a wider focus than Strategic Environmental Assessments, they are *a priori* more suited to integrating economic, social and environmental concerns. However, their complete lack of adoption in the context of cooperation on international watercourses might suggest that riparian States believe economic and social interests are already well protected under the current state of regimes.

The analysis conducted in this book confirms that stakeholder participation in the design of international basin policies is a very rare event. Only a small number of examples could be identified in the Niger and Dniester basin cooperation frameworks. This participation could take place in the framework of a Strategic Environmental Assessment in the context of the Mekong River Commission, so this type of instrument is well-suited to conveying the principle of integration at this level of international watercourse governance. In any case, as a general rule, riparian States clearly prefer policy design to remain an inter-State process and only allow the public to participate once the cooperation framework has been established. This is therefore an area in which the principle of integration must be reinforced.

At this level of basin policy, international practice comprises different specific approaches to conducting and operationalising the integration of the economic, social and environmental dimensions through the decision-making process. The choice of one approach over another might be due to its greater suitability to the particular characteristics of each basin. The ecosystems approach is adopted far more often than the Policy Coherence for Sustainable Development, which, although useful in theory, is not considered in any of the international watercourse cooperation regimes analysed here. Basins under more hydric stress due to a lack of water or structural unsustainable use of water resources are more likely to adopt the Water-Energy-Food Nexus approach.

These are useful frameworks for policy design and international watercourse planning, harmonising economic, social and environmental interests and thus contributing to the application of the principle of integration at the institutional level. Opting for one approach might also reflect the specific cooperation objective pursued. While the ecosystem approach is better suited to understanding the international watercourse as a living organism that must be allowed to function as such in order to provide ecosystem services, the Water-Energy-Food Nexus approach focuses on the possible utilisation of the water resources flowing along the watercourse to satisfy certain human needs: water consumption, energy provision and food production. The latter, then, is not only more utilitarian but also maximalist in terms of the use of the watercourse.

Secondly, with regard to the management of international watercourses, the core element is the planning process. As such, institutional integration requires the instruments employed for this purpose to be informed and participatory, successfully leading to the adoption of a management plan. In the area of the informed decision-making process, a specific good practice has been identified: the performance of a Transboundary Diagnostic Analysis to evaluate the current state of the watercourse. Although this practice is not widespread, it is recommended in the context of the UNECE and provides relevant information for subsequent integrated planning.

The planning process should lead to the adoption of an information system according to the information necessities identified by planners (e.g. sediments, floods, pollution), in keeping with the obligation to exchange information and data clearly expressed in international watercourse law. Information systems are becoming increasingly powerful due, in part, to the growing use of new technologies that make data collection more affordable and accessible, but also to the growing capacity to consider more factors, providing for more integrated analyses and better predictions. A good example of an instrument for enhanced exchange of information and data is the Mekong River Commission Data and Information Service Portal.

However, there remains a tendency to share information and data primarily concerning the bio-physical state of the international watercourse, with socio-economic information largely disregarded. This has been identified as a major impediment to integrated management as most agreements on the exchange of information with international watercourse management bodies do not make reference to socio-economic aspects and cannot be considered in the planning process. Once the information to be shared has been clearly defined, monitoring systems are necessary to maintain a permanent and reliable flow of information. Observatories are commonly created to oversee this task, such as the Niger Basin Observatory and the *Observatoire de l'Environnement* of the *Organisation pour la mise en valeur du fleuve Sénégal.*

Public participation at this level of watercourse management is more effective; stakeholders have a much greater capacity to exert influence at this stage of action than at basin-policy level, both in terms of full participation mechanisms and through simple consultation. Although organic participation gives the public a more stable role in management decisions, consultation processes are widespread in the management international watercourses and therefore provide a valuable opportunity for stakeholder contributions to influence management decisions.

Public participation is channelled through well-established mechanisms, especially the granting of observer status to stakeholders in decision-making bodies, but also through participation in advisory bodies, expert groups and working groups. The role of stakeholders in these bodies is particularly important for providing insights on the international watercourse that would otherwise be inaccessible to the International River Basin Organisation but it is also relevant to the subsequent implementation of decisions. A paradigmatic International River Basin Organisation in this regard is the International Joint Commission between the United States and Canada, where the Advisory Boards foresee the participation of a wide variety of stakeholders. The advantage of consultation mechanisms over such participatory mechanisms is their capacity to gather the widest array of insights from a larger number and more diverse group of stakeholders, although this is to the detriment of their capacity to influence decisions and only confers a rather passive role.

Consultation mechanisms usually consist of broad stakeholder forums organised on a more or less regular basis or as *ad hoc* public consultations on specific issues. Since they are an assembly-like mechanism, stakeholder forums provide a dynamic and flexible means of consultation. Public consultations are conducted in particular cases, either generally in the planning process or in relation to more specific decisions. Consultation mechanisms by themselves are probably insufficient to fulfil the participation requirements of integrated management, but if used as a complement to other mechanisms, they may be useful for gathering key information that only a broad group of stakeholders can provide.

Also at this level, different specific approaches allow the integration of the economic, social and environmental dimensions to be conducted and operationalised through the decision-making process. A widely accepted and – to a varying extent – broadly applied paradigm has emerged: the Integrated Water Resources Management. This is endorsed by the UN and explicitly adopted by most of the analysed International River Basin Organisations. The fact that it has been developed in direct relation to the main instruments on sustainable development, particularly from the Guiding Principles announced at the International Conference on Water and the Environment (the Dublin Conference), makes Integrated Water Resources Management the most common management paradigm in cooperation on international watercourses.

However, there are other approaches that serve similar purposes in this context (e.g. Integrated Natural Resources Management). In fact, adaptive management plays an important role in the work of some International River Basin Organisations. The different approaches reflect the distinct challenges arising from inter-sectoral integration and, far from being incompatible, often share several principles and are adopted simultaneously by the same International River Basin Organisations. In particular, the International Joint Commission between the United States and Canada applies both Integrated Water Resources Management and Adaptive Management.

Thirdly, institutional integration is applied with particular success at the specific project level. Informed decision-making processes at this level are based on the use of a widely employed instrument, the Environmental Impact Assessment, which is well established in international law. However, there is a mismatch between the instruments available for this purpose as identified in the literature and the instruments that are effectively applied. Analysis of the International River Basin Organisations considered in this book reveals that although Environmental Impact Assessments are widely applied (e.g. their inclusion in west-African international basin agreements or the elaboration of guidelines for their performance in the context of the MRC or the US-Ca IJC), other types of impact assessment that could provide highly relevant information for project planning are used rarely or not at all. Social Impact Assessments, Health Impact Assessments and Human Rights Impact Assessments, in addition to inter-sectoral instruments such as nexus assessments, are mostly absent from the international watercourse regimes analysed here. Three international basin agreements provide for the performance of Social Impact Assessments, and only the Niger Basin Authority has developed guidelines for conducting water, energy and food nexus assessments, while Health Impact Assessments and Human Rights Impact Assessments have yet be given a role in these cooperation regimes.

Public participation at the specific project level takes place mainly in the context of Environmental Impact Assessments, which, despite the varying ways in which they might be conducted, foresee the consultation of stakeholders to some extent. The guidelines on Environmental Impact Assessments adopted by the Mekong River Commission are a good example of this role of Environmental Impact Assessments. However, it is also true that these mechanisms continue to prioritise a consultation model that does not generally guarantee stakeholders a high degree of influence over the decision-making process.

Beyond Environmental Impact Assessments, the only other form of stakeholder involvement in specific projects is public consultations, which are rarely carried out. The only notable examples are the consultations performed annually in the framework of the International Joint Commission between the United States and Canada, which usually include questions in relation to projects. Therefore, there is considerable scope for improving institutional integration through the creation of public participation mechanisms.

5 The Contribution of the Principle of Integration to International Environmental Law within the Context of International Watercourse Law

Despite the wide availability of instruments for the recognition and application of the principle of integration, the analysis of the international watercourse cooperation mechanisms carried out in this book reveals that they are insufficiently utilised. On the one hand, this can be observed internally; in current practice, the principle of integration depends to a much greater extent on the institutional dimension than on legal integration instruments. While the mechanisms for legal integration are widely underused, the analysis of International River Basin Organisations show considerable flexibility in the adoption of institutional integration mechanisms that are not foreseen in international basin agreements or even in other binding instruments. In this sense, legal integration is the main area of international watercourse law in which further progress is required for the effective recognition and application of the principle of integration.

On the other hand, with the exception of well-established instruments such as the Environmental Impact Assessment, there is a great diversity in the measures adopted for each international watercourse cooperation regime, due to the highly fragmented application of the institutional dimension of the principle of integration. It is therefore difficult to delimit this dimension, which appears to be evolving rapidly and continuously acquiring new materialisations.

It is paradoxical that the instruments which should contribute to greater unity between the legal values represented in the different dimensions of sustainable development – both legal and institutional – also reflect the fragmentation of international law. A legal regime committed to sustainable development should ideally include all of these instruments that, according to the characteristics of each international watercourse, allow for the integration of the economic, social and environmental dimensions. The fact that this is not the case suggests that States are unwilling to reverse the traditional use of international watercourses, and that although the principle of integration is widely adopted in the discourse, in terms of practical measures there is still much ground to cover in the vast majority of international watercourses.

If this trend is not reversed, water stress in international watercourses can only increase, posing a threat to the environment, to human life and, ultimately, to international peace. The urgency of ensuring effective implementation of the principle of integration cannot be overstated in the face of the environmental and human disaster to which the global ecological crisis and climate change are leading.

Bibliography

Books

Abaza, Hussein, Ron Bisset, and Barry Sadler. 2004. *Environmental and Strategic Environmental Assessment: Towards an Integrated Approach*. Geneva: UNEP.

Amerasinghe, C. F. 2005. *Principles of the Institutional Law of International Organizations*. 2nd ed. Cambridge: Cambridge University Press.

Asselt, Harro van. 2014. *The Fragmentation of Global Climate Governance*. Cheltenham: Edward Elgar.

Aura y Larios de Medrano, Adela M. 2008. *La Regulación Internacional Del Agua Dulce. Practica Española*. Navarra: Editorial Aranzadi.

Birnie, P, A Boyle, and C Redgwell. 2009. *International Law and the Environment*. 3rd ed. Oxford: OUP.

Boisson de Chazournes, Laurence. 2021. *Fresh Water in International Law*. Second Edition. Oxford: OUP.

Bonet, Jordi. 2019. *La Internormatividad Entre Las Dimensiones Económica y Social Del Ordenamiento Jurídico Internacional. ¿Un Espacio Jurídico Para La Efectividad de Los Derechos Económicos, Sociales y Culturales?* Barcelona: Huygens Editorial.

Bréthaut, Christian, and Géraldine Pflieger. 2020. *Governance of a Transboundary River: The Rhône*. Cham: Palgrave Macmillan.

Bürgi Bonanomi, Elisabeth. 2015. *Sustainable Development in International Law Making and Trade*. Cheltenham: Edward Elgar.

Campins Eritja, Mar, and Aurèlia Mañé Estrada, eds. 2014. *Building a Regional Framework in Central Asia. Between Cooperation and Conflict*. Barcelona: Institut Català Internacional per la Pau.

Cordonier Segger, Marie-Claire, and Ashfaq Khalfan. 2004. *Sustainable Development Law: Principles, Practices, & Prospects*. New York: OUP.

Craik, Neil. 2008. *The International Law of Environmental Impact Assessment*. Cambridge: Cambridge University Press.

Dhondt, Nele. 2003. *Integration of Environmental Protection into Other EC Policies. Legal Theory and Practice*. Groningen: Europa Law Publishing.

Díez de Velasco Vallejo, Manuel. 2010. *Las Organizaciones Internacionales*. 16th ed. Madrid: Tecnos.

Díez de Velasco Vallejo, Manuel. 2013. *Instituciones de Derecho Internacional Público*. 18th ed. Madrid: Tecnos.

Fernández de Casadevante Romani, Carlos. 2007. *Sovereignty and Interpretation of International Norms*. Berlin Heidelberg: Springer.

Fernández Liesa, Carlos R., and Ana Manero Salvador, eds. 2017. *Análisis y Comentarios de Los Objetivos de Desarrollo Sostenible de Las Nacionaes Unidas*. Navarra: Aranzadi Thomson Reuters.

Fernández Pons, Xavier. 2006. *La OMC y El Derecho Internacional*. Madrid: Marcial Pons.

Freestone, David, and Ellen Hey, eds. 1996. *The Precautionary Principle and International Law: The Challenge of Implementation*. The Hague: Kluwer Law International.

French, Duncan. 2005. *International Law and Policy of Sustainable Development*. New York: Juris Publisher.

García, Luis; Rodríguez, Juan Diego; Wijnen, Marcus; Pakulski, Inge. 2016. *Earth Observation for Water Resources Management: Current Use and Future Opportunities for the Water Sector*. Washington, DC: World Bank.

Gardiner, Richard. 2008. *Treaty Interpretation*. New York: OUP.

Grigg, Neil S. 2011. *Governance and Management for Sustainable Water Systems*. London: IWA Publishing.

Grigg, Neil S. 2016. *Integrated Water Resource Management: An Interdisciplinary Approach*. Cham: Palgrave Macmillan.

Hoff, Holger. 2011. *Understanding the Nexus. Background Paper for the Bonn2011 Nexus Conference*. Stockholm: Stockholm Environment Institute.

Huck, Winfried. 2022. *Sustainable Development Goals. Article-by-Article Commentary*. Baden-Baden, Germany: Nomos.

Hundloe, Tor. 2021. *Environmental Impact Assessment*. Cham: Springer.

Islam, Nahid. 2010. *The Law of Non-Navigational Uses of International Watercourses. Options for Regional Regime-Building in Asia*. Alphen aan den Rijn: Wolters Kluwer.

Jaria-Manzano, Jordi. 2020. *La Constitución Del Antropoceno*. Valencia: Tirant Humanidades.

Jordan, Andrew, and Andrea Lenschow. 2008. *Innovation in Environmental Policy? Integrating the Environment for Sustainability*. Cheltenham: Edward Elgar.

Juste Ruiz, José, and Mireya Castillo Daudí. 2014. *La Protección Del Medio Ambiente En El Ámbito Internacional y En La Unión Europea*. Valencia: Tirant lo Blanch.

Kemm, John. 2012. *Health Impact Assessment: Past Achievement, Current Understanding, and Future Progress*. Oxford: OUP.

Kiss, Alexander, and Dinah Shelton. 2004. *International Environmental Law*. Third Edit. Ardsley, NY: Transnational Publishers.

Lammers, Johan G. 1984. *Pollution of International Watercourses: A Search for Substantive Rules and Principles of Law*. Boston: Martinus Nijhoff.

Leb, Christina. 2013. *Cooperation in the Law of Transboundary Water Resources*. Cambridge: Cambridge University Press.

Leb, Christina. 2020. *Data Innovations for Transboundary Freshwater Resources Management. International Water Law*. Leiden: Brill.

Linderfalk, Ulf. 2007. *On the Interpreation of Treaties*. Dordrecht: Springer.

Marsden, Simon. 2008. *Strategic Environmental Assessment. International & European Law*. Sterling: Earthscan.

Martin-Nagle, Renée. 2020. *Governance of Offshore Freshwater Resources. Legal Aspects of Sustainable Development*. Leiden: Brill Nijhoff.

McCaffrey, Stephen C. 2019. *The Law of International Watercourses*. 3d ed. Oxford: OUP.

McIntyre, Owen. 2007. *Environmental Protection of International Watercourses under International Law*. Aldershot: Ashgate.

Meadows, Donella H, Dennis L Meadows, Jorgen Randers, and William W. Behrens III. 1972. *The Limits to Growth*. New York: Universe Books.

Meuleman, Louis. 2008. *Public Management and the Metagovernance of Hierarchies, Networks and Markets*. Heidelberg: Physica-Verlag HD.

Movilla Pateiro, Laura. 2014. *El Derecho Internacional Del Agua: Los Acuíferos Transfronterizos*. Barcelona: J.M. Bosch.

Movilla Pateiro, Laura. 2021. *La Dimensión Normativa de La Gobernanza Internacional Del Agua Dulce*. Valencia: Tirant lo Blanch.

Petersmann, Ernst-Ulrich. 1995. *International and European Trade and Environmental Law after the Uruguay Round*. London: Kluwer Law International.

Rieu-Clarke, Alistair, Ruby Moynihan, and Bjørn-Oliver Magsig. 2012. *UN Watercourses Convention: User's Guide*. Dundee: IHP-HELP Centre for Water Law, Policy and Science.

Rodrigo Hernández, Ángel J. 2015. *El Desafío Del Desarrollo Sostenible*. Madrid: Marcial Pons.

Sadeleer, Nicolas De. 2002. *Environmental Principles: From Political Slogans to Legal Rules*. Oxford: OUP.

Sands, Philippe, Jacqueline Peel, Adriana Fabra Aguilar, and Ruth MacKenzie. 2012. *Principles of International Environmental Law*. 3rd ed. Cambridge: Cambridge University Press.

Sangbana, Komlan. 2017. *La Protection Des Eaux Douces Transfrontières Contre La Pollution: Dimensions Normatives et Institutionnelles*. Geneva: Schulthess.

Schmeier, Susanne. 2013. *Governing International Watercourses: River Basin Organizations and the Sustainable Governance of Internationally Shared Rivers and Lakes*. Abingdon: Routledge.

Sindico, Francesco. 2020. *International Law and Transboundary Aquifers*. Cheltenham: Edward Elgar.

Tanzi, Attila, and Maurizio Arcari. 2001. *The United Nations Convention on the Law of International Watercourses*. The Hague: Kluwer Law International.

Voigt, Christina. 2009. *Sustainable Development as a Principle of International Law*. Leiden: Martinus Nijhoff.

Voß, Jan-Peter, Dierk Bauknecht, and René Kemp, eds. 2006. *Reflexive Governance for Sustainable Development*. Cheltenham: Edward Elgar.

Weiss, Edith Brown. 1999. *Un Mundo Justo Para Las Futuras Generaciones : Derecho Internacional, Patrimonio Común y Equidad Intergeneracional.* Madrid: Mundi-Prensa.

Yihdego, Zeray, and Julie Gibson. 2020. *Implementing International Watercourses Law through the WEF Nexus and SDGs: An Integrated Approach Illustrated in the Zambezi River Basin.* Leiden: Brill.

Young E., Margaret. 2011. *Trading Fish, Saving Fish: The Interaction between Regimes in International Law.* Cambridge University Press.

Book Chapters

Barral, Virginie, and Pierre-Marie Dupuy. 2016. "Principle 4: Sustainable Development through Integration." In *The Rio Declaration on Environment and Development: A Commentary*, edited by Jorge E. Viñuales, 157–79. Oxford: OUP.

Barral, Virginie. 2018. "The Principle of Sustainable Development." In *Principles of Environmental Law*, edited by Ludwig Krämer and Emanuela Orlando, 103–14. Cheltenham: Edward Elgar.

Boer, Ben. 1995. "Implementation of International Sustainability Imperatives at a National Level." In *Sustainable Development and Good Governance*, edited by Konrad Ginther and Erik Denters, 111–36. Dordrecht: Martinus Nijhoff.

Boisson de Chazournes, Laurence. 2013. "Organismes et Commissions de Bassin: Aspect de Cooperation Régionale et de Règlement de Différends." In *Liber Amicorum Raymond Ranjeva : L'Afrique et Le Droit International : Variations Sur l'organisation Internationale = Africa and International Law : Reflections on the International Organization*, 435–44. Paris: Editions A. Pedone.

Bonzi, Christopher, Janina Onigkeit, Holger Hoff, Brian Joyce and Katja Tielbörger. 2016. "Analysing Stakeholder Driven Scenarios with a Transboundary Water Planning Tool for IWRM in the Jordan River Basin". In *Integrated Water Resources Management: Concept, Research and Implementation*, edited by Borchardt, Dietrich, Janos J. Bogardi, and Ralf B. Ibisch, 413–434. Cham: Springer.

Bruch, Carl. 2005. "Evolution of Public Involvement in International Watercourse Management." In *Public Participation in the Governance of International Freshwater Resources*, edited by Carl Bruch, Libor Jansky, Mikiyasu Nakayama, and Kazimierz A. Salewicz, 21–73. New York: United Nations University Press.

Caflisch, Lucius. 2018. "Equitable and Reasonable Utilization and Factors Relevant to Determining Such Utilization (Articles 5 and 6)." In *The UN Convention on the Law of the Non-Navigational Uses of International Watercourses: A Commentary*, edited by Laurence Boisson de Chazournes, Makane Moïse Mbengue, Mara Tignino, Komlan Sangbana, and Jason Rudall, 77–94. Oxford: OUP.

Caflisch, Lucius. 2019. "Prior Notice and Related Issues." In *Research Handbook on International Water Law*, edited by Stephen C. McAffrey and Riley T. Denoon, 109–25. Cheltenham: Edward Elgar.

Campins Eritja, Mar. 2021. "The Arctic Ocean: Ecosystem Approach in a Context of Extreme Vulnerability." In *Biological Diversity and International Law*, edited by Mar Campins Eritja and Teresa Fajardo del Castillo. Cham, Switzerland: Springer.

Casanovas y la Rosa, Oriol. 2011. "Aproximación a Una Teoría de Los Regímenes En Derecho Internacional Público." In *Unidad y Pluralismo En El Derecho Internacional Público y En La Comunidad Internacional*, edited by Ángel J. Rodrigo and Caterina García, 41–60. Madrid: Tecnos.

Cazala, Julien. 2009. "Le Rôle de l'interprétation Des Traités à La Lumière de Toute Autre « règle Pertinente de Droit International Applicable Entre Les Parties » En Tant Que « passerelle » Jetée Entre Systèmes Juridiques Différents." In *La Circulation Des Concepts Juridiques : Le Droit International de l'environnement Entre Mondialisation et Fragmentation*, edited by Hélène Ruiz Fabri and Lorenzo Gradoni, 95–136. Paris: Société de législation comparée.

Dessouassi, Robert. 2015. "État Du Processus de Gestion Intégrée Des Ressources En Eau Dans Le Bassin Du Niger : Expériences de l'implication Des Acteurs Non Étatiques et de La Prévention Des Conflits Entre Usagers de Ressources." In *Public Participation and Water Resources Management: Where Do We Stand in International Law?*, edited by Mara Tignino and Komlan Sangbana, 69–76. Paris: UNESCO.

Doelle, Meinhard. 2009. "Integration among Global Environmental Regimes: Lessons Learned from the Climate Change Mitigation." In *The Future of Ocean Regime -Buidling : Essays in Tribute to Douglas M. Johnston*, edited by Aldo Chircop, Ted McDorman, and Susan Rolston, 63–85. Leiden: Koninklijke Brill NV.

Dubin, Laurence. 2009. "Fonction Intersystémique Du Concept de Développement Durable." In *La Circulation Des Concepts Juridiques : Le Droit International de l'environnement Entre Mondialisation et Fragmentation*, edited by Hélène Ruiz Fabri and Lorenzo Gradoni, 175–98. Paris: Société de législation comparée.

Duvic-Paoli, Leslie-Anne. 2018. "Principle of Prevention." In *Principles of Environmental Law*, edited by Ludwig Krämer and Emanuela Orlando, 161–73. Cheltenham: Edward Elgar.

Duvic-Paoli, Leslie-Anne, and Pierre-Marie Dupuy. 2015. "The Polluter-Pays Principle in the 1992 UNECE Convention on the Protection and Use of Transboundary Watercourses and International Lakes." In *The UNECE Convention on the Protection and Use of Transboundary Watercourses and International Lakes*, edited by Attila Tanzi, Owen McIntyre, Alexandros Kolliopoulos, Alistair Rieu-Clarke, and Rémy Kinna, 176–94. Leiden: Brill Nijhoff.

Elias, Olufemi, and Meagan Wong. 2021. "Environmental Impact Assessment." In *Research Handbook on International Environmental Law*, edited by Malgosia Fitzmaurice, Marcel Brus, and Panos Merkouris, 188–208. Cheltenham: Edward Elgar.

Ellis, Jaye. 2010. "Sustainable Development and Fragmentation in International Society." In *Global Justice and Sustainable Development*, edited by Duncan French, 57–74. Leiden: Martinus Nijhoff.

Fajardo del Castillo, Teresa. 2018. "Environmental Law Principles and General Principles of International Law." In *Principles of Environmental Law*, edited by Ludwig Krämer and Emanuela Orlando, 38–51. Cheltenham: Edward Elgar.

Fajardo del Castillo, Teresa. 2021. "Principles and Approaches in the Convention on Biological Diversity and Other Biodiversity-Related Conventions in the Post-2020 Scenario." In *Biological Diversity and International Law*, edited by Mar Campins Eritja and Teresa Fajardo del Castillo, 15–34. Cham: Springer.

Farrajota, M. M. 2005. "Notification and Consultation in the Law Applicable to International Law". In *Les Ressources En Eau et Le Droit International = Water Resources and International Law*, edited by Laurence Boisson de Chazournes and Salman M.A. Salman, 281–339. Leiden: Martinus Nijhoff.

Fernández Pons, Xavier. 2021. "Conservation and Sustainable Use of Biodiversity in the International Regulation of Trade in Goods." In *Biological Diversity and International Law: Challenges for the Post 2020 Scenario*, edited by Mar Campins Eritja and Teresa Fajardo del Castillo, 79–99. Cham: Springer.

Fitzmaurice, Malgosia, and Panos Merkouris. 2015. "Scope of the UNECE Water Convention." In *The UNECE Convention on the Protection and Use of Transboundary Watercourses and International Lakes*, edited by Attila Tanzi, Owen McIntyre, Alexandros Kolliopoulos, Alistair Rieu-Clarke, and Rémy Kinna, 103–15. Leiden: Brill Nijhoff.

Fitzmaurice, Malgosia, and Virginie Barral. 2021. "The Relationship between the Law of International Watercourses and Sustainable Development." In *Research Handbook on International Environmental Law*, edited by Malgosia Fitzmaurice, Marcel Brus, and Panos Merkouris, 413–40. Cheltenham: Edward Elgar.

Fleming, Ruven C. 2021. "The Energy Trilemma." In *Energy Law, Climate Change and the Environment*, edited by Martha M. Roggenkamp, Kars J. de Graaf, and Ruven C. Fleming, 31–40. Cheltenham: Edward Elgar.

George, Clive, and Colin Kirkpatrick. 2009. "Have Sustainability Impact Assessments of Trade Agreements Delivered on Development Issues: A Reflexive Analysis of the Emergence and Main Contributions of Trade SIAs." In *Trade, Globalization and Sustainability Impact Assessment: A Critical Look at Methods and Outcomes*, edited by Paul Ekins and Tancrède Voituriez, 63–84. London: Earthscan.

Giordano, Mark, and Tushaar Shah. 2016. "From IWRM Back to Integrated Water Resources Management." In *Integrated Water Resources Management: From Concept to Implementation*, edited by Cecilia Tortajada, 364–76. Abingdon: Routledge.

Giupponi, Carlo, Anita Fassio, Jacobo Feás Vàzquez, and Jaroslav Mysiak. 2006. "Sustainable Water Management and Decision Making." In *Sustainable Management of Water Resources: An Integrated Approach*, edited by Carlo Giupponi, Anthony J. Jakeman, Derek Karssenberg, and Matt P. Hare, 71–97. Cheltenham: Edward Elgar.

Gradoni, Lorenzo. 2009. "Systèmes Juridiques Internationaux : Une Esquisse." In *La Circulation Des Concepts Juridiques : Le Droit International de l'environnement Entre Mondialisation et Fragmentation*, edited by Hélène Ruiz Fabri and Lorenzo Gradoni, 27–52. Paris: Société de législation comparée.

Haas, Peter M., and Casey Stevens. 2017. "Ideas, Beliefs, and Policy Linkages." In *Governing through Goals. Sustainable Development Goals as a Governance Innovation*, edited by Norichika Kanie and Frank Biermann, 137–64. Massachusetts: MIT.

Hare, Matt P., Olivier Barreteau, Beck M. Bruce, Rebecca A. Letcher, Erik Mostert, J. David Tàbara, Dagmar Ridder, Valerie Cogan, and Claudia Pahl-Wostl. 2006. "Methods for Stakeholder Participation in Water Management." In *Sustainable Management of Water Resources: An Integrated Approach*, edited by Carlo Giupponi, Anthony J. Jakeman, Derek Karssenberg, and Matt P. Hare, 177–231. Cheltenham: Edward Elgar.

Huici Sancho, Laura. 2018. "Water and International Security: The Conceptual Framework." In *Agua, Recurso Natural Limitado. Entre El Desarrollo Sostenible y La Seguridad Internacional*, edited by Ana M. Badia Martí and Laura Huici Sancho, 173–84. Madrid: Marcial Pons.

Koester, Veit. 2018. "Environmental Principles and Concepts in Biodiversity Treaties." In *Principles of Environmental Law*, edited by Ludwig Krämer and Emanuela Orlando, 538–56. Cheltenham: Edward Elgar.

Lammers, Johan G. 2018. "The Interplay between the UN Watercourses Convention and the UNECE Convention on the Protection and Use of Transboundary Watercourses and International Lakes." In *The UN Convention on the Law of the Non-Navigational Uses of International Watercourses: A Commentary*, edited by Laurence Boisson de Chazournes, Makane Moïse Mbengue, Mara Tignino, Komlan Sangbana, and Jason Rudall, 409–27. Oxford: OUP.

Leb, Christina. 2019. "Implementation of the General Duty to Cooperate." In *Research Handbook on International Water Law*, edited by Stephen C. McAffrey and Riley T. Denoon, 95–108. Cheltenham: Edward Elgar.

Lipponen, Annukka, and Lea Kauppi. 2015. "Monitoring and Assessment and the Duty of Cooperation under the Water Convention: Exchange of Information Among the Riparian Parties." In *The UNECE Convention on the Protection and Use of Transboundary Watercourses and International Lakes*, edited by Attila Tanzi, Owen McIntyre, Alexandros Kolliopoulos, Alistair Rieu-Clarke, and Rémy Kinna, 251–67. Leiden: Brill Nijhoff.

Lowe, Vaughan. 1999. "Sustainable Development and Unsustainable Arguments." In *International Law and Sustainable Development. Past Achievements and Future Challanges*, edited by A. Boyle and D. Freestone, 19–37. Oxford: OUP.

Lowe, Vaughan. 2000. "The Politics of Law-Making: Are the Method and Character of Norm Creation Changing?" In *The Role of Law in International Politics*, edited by Michel Byers, 207–26. New York: OUP.

Mbengue, Makane Moïse. 2013. "Les Chartes de l'eau: Vers Une Nouvelle Conception de La Gestion Des Ressources En Eau Partagees En Afrique ?" In *Liber Amicorum Raymond Ranjeva : L'Afrique et Le Droit International : Variations Sur l'organisation Internationale*, edited by M Kamga and M. M. Mbengue, 201–13. Paris: Pedone.

Mbengue, Makane M, and Mara Tignino. 2005. *Transparency, Public Participation, and Amicus Curiae in Water Disputes*. Edited by Edith Brown Weiss, Laurence Boisson de Chazournes, and Nathalie Bernasconi-Osterwalder. *Fresh Water and International Economic Law*. Oxford: OUP.

McCaffrey, Stephen C. 2019. "Interwined General Principles." In *Research Handbook on International Water Law*, edited by Stephen C. McAffrey and Riley T. Denoon, 83–94. Cheltenham: Edward Elgar.

McIntyre, Owen. 2013. "Procedural Rules and Protection of Transboundary Rivers." In *International Law and Freshwater. The Multiple Challenges*, edited by Laurence Boisson de Chazournes, Christina Leb, and Mara Tignino, 239–65. Cheltenham: Edward Elgar.

McIntyre, Owen. 2015. "The Principle of Equitable and Reasonable Utilisation." In *The UNECE Convention on the Protection and Use of Transboundary Watercourses and International Lakes*, edited by Tanzi, Attila, Owen McIntyre, Alexandros Kolliopoulos, Alistair Rieu-Clarke, and Rémy Kinna. Leiden, The Netherlands: Brill Nijhoff.

McIntyre, Owen. 2015. "The Water Convention Other UNECE Environmental Treaties." In *The UNECE Convention on the Protection and Use of Transboundary Watercourses and International Lakes*, edited by Attila Tanzi, Owen McIntyre, Alexandros Kolliopoulos, Alistair Rieu-Clarke, and Rémy Kinna, 73–87. Leiden: Brill Nijhoff.

McIntyre, O. 2017. "Substantive Rules of International Water Law." In *Routledge Handbook of Water Law and Policy*, edited by Alistair Rieu-Clarke, Andrew Allan, and Sarah Hendry. Abingdon: Routledge.

McIntyre, Owen. 2019. "Environmental Protection and the Ecosystem Approach." In *Research Handbook on International Water Law*, edited by Stephen C. McAffrey and Riley T. Denoon, 126–46. Cheltenham: Edward Elgar.

McIntyre, Owen. 2020. "The Legal Role and Context of River Basin Organizations." In *River Basin Organizations in Water Diplomacy*, edited by Anoulak Kittikhoun and Susanne Schmeier, 25–48. Abingdon: Routledge.

Nikiforova, Nataliya. 2017. "Strengthening the Implementation of Transboundary Water Agreements: Insights from the UNECE Water Convention Implementation

Committee." In *Routledge Handbook of Water Law and Policy*, edited by Alistair Rieu-Clarke, Andrew Allan, and Sarah Hendry, 275–86. Abingdon: Routledge.

Nollkaemper, André. 2002. "Three Conceptions of the Integration Principle in International Environmental Law." In *Environmental Policy Integration: Greening Sectoral Policies in Europe*, edited by A. Lenschow, 22–32. London: Earthscan.

Pallàs Secall, Pol. 2023. "Contribuciones Del Enfoque Del Nexo Agua-Energía- Alimentación Al Derecho de Los Cursos de Agua Internacionales." In *Derecho y Agua En El Horizonte 2030*, edited by Marta Fernández Prieto, 459–80. Pamplona: Aranzadi.

Pérez de Armiño, Karlos. 2013. "La Gobernanza Global de La Seguridad Alimentaria: Debilidades, Disparidades e Iniciativas de Reforma." In *Alimentación y Derecho Internacional. Normas, Instituciones y Procesos*, edited by Xavier Pons Ràfols, 83–117. Madrid: Marcial Pons.

Pigrau Soler, Antoni, and Susana Borràs Pentinat. 2008. "Diez Años Del Convenio de Aarhus Sobre El Acceso a La Información, La Participación y El Acceso a La Justicia En Materia de Medio Ambiente." In *Acceso a La Información, Participación Pública y Acceso a La Justicia En Materia de Medio Ambiente: Diez Años Del Convenio de Aarhus*, edited by Antoni Pigrau Soler, 21–84. Barcelona: Atelier.

Ponte Iglesias, María Teresa. 2012. "El Derecho de Los Usos de Los Cursos de Agua Internacionales Para Fines Distintos de La Navegación." In *La Politica Comunitaria de Aguas: Marco de La Acción Estatal y Autonómica*, edited by Adela M. Aura y Larios de Medrano, 218–33. Madrid: Dykinson.

Pons Ràfols, Xavier. 2013. "La Seguridad Alimentaria Mundial: La Acción Política e Institucional de La FAO." In *Alimentación y Derecho Internacional. Normas, Instituciones y Procesos*, edited by Xavier Pons Ràfols, 28–81. Madrid: Marcial Pons.

Redgwell, Catherine. 2018. "Sustainable Use of Natural Resources." In *Principles of Environmental Law*, edited by L. Krämer and E. Orlando, 115–24. Cheltenham: Edward Elgar.

Remiro Brotons, Antonio. 2011. "La Noción de Regímenes Internacionales En El Derecho Internacional Público." In *Unidad y Pluralismo En El Derecho Internacional Público y En La Comunidad Internacional*, edited by Ángel J Rodrigo Hernández and Caterina García, 167–76. Madrid: Tecnos.

Rieu-Clarke, Alistair. 2015. "The Sustainability Principle." In *The UNECE Convention on the Protection and Use of Transboundary Watercourses and International Lakes*, edited by Attila Tanzi, Owen McIntyre, Alexandros Kolliopoulos, Alistair Rieu-Clarke, and Rémy Kinna, 195–210. Leiden: Brill Nijhoff.

Rieu-Clarke, Alistair, 2019. "Remarks on the Drafting history of the convention." In *The UNECE Convention on the Protection and Use of Transboundary Watercourses and International Lakes*, edited by Attila Tanzi, Owen McIntyre, Alexandros Kolliopoulos, Alistair Rieu-Clarke, and Rémy Kinna, 3–14. Leiden: Brill Nijhoff.

Rieu-Clarke, Alistair. 2019. "From Treaty Practice to the UN Watercourses Convention." In *Research Handbook on International Water Law*, edited by Stephen C. McAffrey and Riley T. Denoon, 11–25. Cheltenham: Edward Elgar.

Rodrigo Hernández, Ángel J. 2011. "La Integración Normativa y La Unidad Del Derecho Internacional Público." In *Unidad y Pluralismo En El Derecho Internacional Público y En La Comunidad Internacional*, edited by Ángel J Rodrigo Hernández and Caterina García, 321–55. Madrid: Tecnos.

Sadeleer, Nicolas De. 2021. "The Principles of Prevention and Precaution in International Law: Two Sides of the Same Coin?" In *Research Handbook on International Environmental Law*, 151–87. Cheltenham: Edward Elgar.

Salman, Salman M.A. 2015. "The Notification Process." In *International Water Law*, edited by Laurence Boisson de Chazournes and Mara Tignino, 105–60. Cheltenham: Edward Elgar.

Salman, Salman M.A. 2018. "The Obligation Not to Cause Significant Harm (Article 7)." In *The UN Convention on the Law of the Non-Navigational Uses of International Watercourses: A Commentary*, edited by Laurence Boisson de Chazournes, Makane Moïse Mbengue, Mara Tignino, Komlan Sangbana, and Jason Rudall, 95–122. Oxford: OUP.

Sands, Philippe. 1995. "International Law in the Field of Sustainable Development: Emerging Legal Principles." In *Sustainable Development and International Law*, edited by Winfried Lang, 53–66. London: Graham & Trotman / Martinus Nihjoff.

Sands, Philippe. 1999. "Sustainable Development: Treaty, Custom, and the Cross-Fertilization of International Law." In *International Law and Sustainable Development. Past Achievements and Future Challanges*, edited by A. Boyle and D. Freestone, 39–60. Oxford: OUP.

Sangbana, Komlan. 2015. "La Participation Du Public Dans Le Cadre de l'Organisation Pour La Mise En Valeur Du Fleuve Sénégal." In *Public Participation and Water Resources Management: Where Do We Stand in International Law?*, edited by Mara Tignino and Komlan Sangbana, 77–83. Paris: UNESCO.

Sangbana, Komlan. 2017. "The Role of Non-State Actors in the Development and Implementation of International Water Law." In *Routledge Handbook of Water Law and Policy*, edited by Alistair Rieu-Clarke, Andrew Allan, and Sarah Hendry, 287–96. Abingdon: Routledge.

Sangbana, Komlan. 2018. "Notification and Consultation Concerning Planned Measures (Articles 11–19)." In *The UN Convention on the Law of the Non-Navigational Uses of International Watercourses: A Commentary*, edited by Laurence Boisson de Chazournes, Makane Moïse Mbengue, Mara Tignino, Komlan Sangbana, and Jason Rudall, 159–90. Oxford: OUP.

Schmeier, Susanne, and Ivan Zavadsky. 2020. "Managing Disagreements in European Basins What Role for River Basin Organizations in Water Diplomacy?" In *River Basin*

Organizations in Water Diplomacy, edited by Anoulak Kittikhoun and Susanne Schmeier, 275–92. Abingdon: Routledge.

Schoeman, Jes, Catherine Allan, and C. Max Finlayson. 2016. "A New Paradigm for Water? A Comparative Review of Integrated, Adaptive and Ecosystem-Based Water Management in the Anthropocene." In *Integrated Water Resources Management: From Concept to Implementation*, edited by Cecilia Tortajada, 17–30. Abingdon: Routledge.

Schwartz, Priscilla. 2018. "The Polluter-Pays Principle." In *Principles of Environmental Law*, edited by Ludwig Krämer and Emanuela Orlando, 260–72. Cheltenham: Edward Elgar.

Sindico, Francesco, and Laura Movilla. 2018. "The Interplay between the UN Watercourses Convention and the Law on Transboundary Aquifers (Article 2)." In *The UN Convention on the Law of the Non-Navigational Uses of International Watercourses: A Commentary*, edited by Laurence Boisson de Chazournes, Makane Moise Mbengue, Mara Tignino, Komlan Sangbana, and Jason Rudall, 383–408. Oxford: OUP.

Spijkers, Otto. 2021. "Participation of Non-State Actors and Global Civil Society in International Environmental Law-Making and Governance." In *Research Handbook on International Environmental Law*, edited by Malgosia Fitzmaurice, Marcel Brus, and Panos Merkouris, 45–61. Cheltenham: Edward Elgar.

Szabó, Marcel. 2017. "Sustainable Development in the Judgments of the International Court of Justice." In *Sustainable Development Principles in the Decisions of International Courts and Tribunals: 1992–2012*, edited by Marie Claire Cordonier Segger and C. G. Weeramantry, 266–80. Abingdon: Routledge.

Tanzi, Attila. 2019. "The Global Water Treaties and Their Relationship." In *Research Handbook on International Water Law*, edited by Stephen C. McAffrey and Riley T. Denoon, 44–58. Cheltenham: Edward Elgar.

Tanzi, Attila. 2021. "Substantialising the Procedural Obligations of International Water Law between Compensatory and Distributive Justice." In *A Bridge Over Troubled Waters: Dispute Resolution in the Law of International Watercourses and the Law of the Sea*, edited by Hélène Ruiz Fabri, Erik Franckx, Marco Benatar, and Tamar Meshel, 351–76. Boston: Brill Nijhoff.

Tanzi, Attila, and Cristina Contartese. 2015. "Establishment of an Implementation Mechanism under the Water Convention." In *The UNECE Convention on the Protection and Use of Transboundary Watercourses and International Lakes*, edited by Attila Tanzi, Owen McIntyre, Alexandros Kolliopoulos, Alistair Rieu-Clarke, and Rémy Kinna, 319–29. Leiden: Brill Nijhoff.

Tanzi, Attila and Alexandros Kolliopoulos. 2015. "The No-Harm Rule". In *The UNECE Convention on the Protection and Use of Transboundary Watercourses and International Lakes*, edited by Attila Tanzi, Owen McIntyre, Alexandros Kolliopoulos, Alistair Rieu-Clarke, and Rémy Kinna, 133–145. Leiden: Brill Nijhoff.

Timoshenko, Alexandre S. 1995. "From Stockholm to Rio: The Institutionalization of Sustainable Development." In *Sustainable Development and Interantional Law*, edited by Winfried Lang, 143–60. London: Graham & Trotman / Martinus Nihjoff.

Tomkiewicz, Vincent. 2009. "L'interprétation Téléologique Au Sein de l'OMC." In *La Circulation Des Concepts Juridiques : Le Droit International de l'environnement Entre Mondialisation et Fragmentation*, edited by Hélène Ruiz Fabri and Lorenzo Gradoni, 243–66. Paris: Société de législation comparée.

Trevisanut, Seline. 2009. "La Convention Des Nations Unies Sur Le Droit de La Mer et Le Droit de l'Environnement : Développement Intrasystémique et Renvoi Intersystémique." In *La Circulation Des Concepts Juridiques : Le Droit International de l'environnement Entre Mondialisation et Fragmentation*, edited by Hélène Ruiz Fabri and Lorenzo Gradoni, 397–426. Paris: Société de législation comparée.

Trevisanut, Seline, Nikolaos Giannopoulos, and Rozemarijn Roland Holst. 2020. "Introduction: Regime Interaction in Ocean Governance." In *Regime Interaction in Ocean Governance*, edited by Seline Trevisanut, Nikolaos Giannopoulos, and Rozemarijn Roland Holst, 1–21. Leiden: Brill Nijhoff.

Troell, Jessica, Carl Bruch, Angela Cassar, and Scott Schang. 2005. "Transboundary Environmental Impact Assessment as a Tool for Promoting Public Participation in International Watercourse Management." In *Enhancing Public Participation and Governance in Water Resources Management*, edited by Libor Jansky and Juha I. Uitto, 53–82. Tokyo: United Nations University Press.

Tsioumani, Elsa. 2018. "Public Participation in Environmental Decision-Making." In *Principles of Environmental Law*, edited by L. Krämer and E. Orlando, 366–78. Cheltenham: Edward Elgar.

Vykhryst, Serhiy. 2015. "Public Information and Participation under the Water." In *The UNECE Convention on the Protection and Use of Transboundary Watercourses and International Lakes*, edited by Attila Tanzi, Owen McIntyre, Alexandros Kolliopoulos, Alistair Rieu-Clarke, and Rémy Kinna, 268–284. Leiden: Brill Nijhoff.

Wouters, Patricia, and Christina Leb. 2015. "The Duty to Cooperation in International Water Law – Examining the Contribution of the UN Water Conventions to Facilitating Transboundary Water Cooperation." In *The UNECE Convention on the Protection and Use of Transboundary Watercourses and International Lakes*, edited by Attila Tanzi, Owen McIntyre, Alexandros Kolliopoulos, Alistair Rieu-Clarke, and Rémy Kinna, 285–295. Leiden: Brill Nijhoff.

Zarbiev, Fouad. 2009. "L'interprétation Téléologique Des Traités." In *La Circulation Des Concepts Juridiques : Le Droit International de l'environnement Entre Mondialisation et Fragmentation*, edited by Hélène Ruiz Fabri and Lorenzo Gradoni, 199–242. Paris: Société de législation comparée.

Ziganshina, Dinara R. 2018. "Protection, Preservation, and Management, Ch. 11 Management (Article 24)." In *The UN Convention on the Law of the Non-Navigational*

Uses of International Watercourses: A Commentary, edited by Laurence Boisson De Chazournes, Makane Moïse Mbengue, Mara Tignino, Komlan Sangbana, and Jason Rudall, 214–37. Oxford: OUP.

Journal Articles

Alland, Denis. 2012. "L'interprétation Du Droit International Public." *Collected Courses of the Hague Academy of International Law* 362: 41–394.

Allouche, Jeremy. 2016. "The Birth and Spread of IWRM – A Case Study of Global Policy Diffusion and Translation." *Water Alternatives* 9 (3): 412–33.

Al-Saidi, Mohammad, and Nadir Ahmed Elagib. 2016. "Towards Understanding the Integrative Approach of the Water, Energy and Food Nexus." *Science of the Total Environment* 574 (2017): 1131–39.

Arif, Abdullah Al. 2017. "Legal Status of Maximum Sustainable Yield Concept in International Fisheries Law and Its Adoption in the Marine Fisheries Regime of Bangladesh: A Critical Analysis." *International Journal of Marine and Coastal Law* 32 (3): 544–69.

Arnstein, Sherry R. 1969. "A Ladder Of Citizen Participation." *Journal of the American Planning Association* 35 (4): 216–24.

Atapattu, Sumudu. 2012. "International Environmental Law and Soft Law: A New Direction or a Contradiction?" *Non-State Actors, Soft Law and Protective Regimes* 12 (1991): 200–226.

Bazilian, Morgan, Holger Rogner, Mark Howells, Sebastian Hermann, Douglas Arent, Dolf Gielen, Pasquale Steduto, et al. 2011. "Considering the Energy, Water and Food Nexus: Towards an Integrated Modelling Approach." *Energy Policy* 39 (12): 7896–7906.

Belinskij, Antti. 2015. "Water-Energy-Food Nexus within the Framework of International Water Law." *Water (Switzerland)* 7 (10): 5396–5415.

Benson, David, Animesh K. Gain, and Josselin J. Rouillard. 2015. "Water Governance in a Comparative Perspective: From IWRM to a 'nexus' Approach?" *Water Alternatives* 8 (1): 756–73.

Benvenisti, Eyal, and George W. Downs. 2007. "The Empire's New Clothes: Political Economy and the Fragmentation of International Law." *Stanford Law Review* 60 (2): 595–631.

Berbés-Blázquez, Marta, José A. González, and Unai Pascual. 2016. "Towards an Ecosystem Services Approach That Addresses Social Power Relations." *Current Opinion in Environmental Sustainability* 19: 134–43.

Bogers, Maya, Frank Biermann, Agni Kalfagianni, and Rakhyun E Kim. 2022. "Sustainable Development Goals Fail to Advance Policy Integration: A Large-n Text Analysis of 159 International Organizations." *Environmental Science and Policy* 138 (2022): 134–45.

Born, Stephen M., and William C. Sonzogni. 1995. "Integrated Environmental Management: Strengthening the Conceptualization." *Environmental Management* 19 (2): 167–81.

Bourne, C. B. 1997. "The Primacy of the Principle of Equitable Utilization in the 1997 Watercourses Convention." *Canadian Yearbook of International Law* 35: 215–32.

Bourne, Charles B. 1997. "The Case Concerning the Gabčíkovo-Nagymaros Project: An Important Milestone in International Water Law." *Yearbook of International Environmental Law* 8 (1): 6–12.

Boyle, Alan. 2012. "Human Rights and the Environment: Where Next?" *European Journal of International Law* 23 (3): 613–42.

Boyle, Alan. 2022. "International Lawmaking in an Environmental Context." *Collected Courses of the Hague Academy of International Law* 427: 51–108.

Brunnée, Jutta. 2019. "Procedure and Substance in International Environmental Law." *Collected Courses of the Hague Academy of International Law* 405: 75–240.

Brunnée, Jutta, and Stephen J. Toope. 1997. "Environmental Security and Freshwater Resources: Ecosystem Regime Building." *American Journal of International Law* 91 (1): 26–59.

Burke-White, William W. 2004. "International Legal Pluralism." *Michigan Journal of International Law* 25 (4): 963–79.

Caflisch, Lucius. 1989. "Règles Générales Du Droit Des Cours d'eau Internationaux." *Collected Courses of the Hague Academy of International Law* 219 (VII): 9–225.

Campins Eritja, Mar. 2011. "Un Nuevo Paso En La Dirección Correcta: La Gestión Integrada de Las Zonas Costeras Mediterráneas." *Revista General de Derecho Europeo* 24.

Campins Eritja, Mar, Jaume Saura Estapá, and Xavier Pons Ráfols. 2015. "Towards Improved Regional Co-Operation over Water Uses in Central Asia: The Case of Hydroelectric Energy and Inland Fisheries." *Asian Journal of International Law* 6 (1): 119–58.

Cardesa-Saltzmann, Antonio, and Antoni Pigrau Soler. 2017. "La Agenda 2030 y Los Objetivos Para El Desarrollo Sostenible. Una Mirada Crítica Sobre Su Aportación a La Gobernanza Global En Términos de Justicia Distributiva y Sostenibilidad Ambiental." *Revista Española de Derecho Internacional* 69 (1): 279–85.

Chaffin, Brian C., Hannah Gosnell, and Barbara A. Cosens. 2014. "A Decade of Adaptive Governance Scholarship: Synthesis and Future Directions." *Ecology and Society* 19 (3): 56.

Colliard, Claude-Albert. 1968. "Régime Des Fleuves Internationaux." *Collected Courses of the Hague Academy of International Law* 125: 337–442.

Dargin, Jennifer, Bassel Daher, and Rabi H. Mohtar. 2019. "Complexity versus Simplicity in Water Energy Food Nexus (WEF) Assessment Tools." *Science of the Total Environment* 650 (2019): 1566–75.

De Lucia, Vito. 2015. "Competing Narratives and Complex Genealogies: The Ecosystem Approach in International Environmental Law." *Journal of Environmental Law* 27 (1): 91–117.

De Lucia, Vito. 2018. "A Critical Interrogation of the Relation between the Ecosystem Approach and Ecosystem Services." *Review of European, Comparative and International Environmental Law* 27 (2): 104–14.

Dernbach, John C. 2003. "Achieving Sustainable Development: The Centrality and Multiple Facets of Integrated Decisionmaking." *Indiana Journal of Global Legal Studies* 10 (1): 247–85.

Díaz-Galán, Elena. 2022. "The 2030 Agenda for Sustainable Development's Legal Value: A New Regulatory Trend?" *Iberoamerican Journal of Development Studies* 11 (2): 30–52.

Dinstein, Yoram. 2006. "Customary International Law and Treaties." *Collected Courses of the Hague Academy of International Law* 322: 423–27.

Dombrowsky, Ines, and Oliver Hensengerth. 2018. "Governing the Water-Energy-Food Nexus Related to Hydropower on Shared Rivers – The Role of Regional Organizations." *Frontiers in Environmental Science* 6 (153): 1–16.

Dupuy, Pierre-Marie. 1999. "The Danger of Fragmentation or Unification of the International Legal System and the International Court of Justice." *New York University Journal of International Law* 31: 791–807.

Eckstein, Gabriel. 2020. "The Status of the UN Watercourses Convention: Does It Still Hold Water?" *International Journal of Water Resources Development* 36 (2–3): 429–61.

Eckstein, Yoram, and Gabriel E Eckstein. 2005. "Transboundary Aquifers: Conceptual Models for Development of International Law." *Groundwater* 43 (5): 679–90.

Fitzmaurice, Malgosia. 2001. "International Protection of the Environment." *Collected Courses of the Hague Academy of International Law* 293: 9–488.

Folke, Carl, Thomas Hahn, Per Olsson, and Jon Norberg. 2005. "Adaptive Governance of Social-Ecological Systems." *Annual Review of Environment and Resources* 30: 441–73.

Forteau, Mathias. 2003. "Les Renvois Inter-Conventionnels." *Annuaire Français de Droit International* 49 (1): 71–104.

Friedmann, W. 1969. "General Course in Public International Law." *Collected Courses of the Hague Academy of International Law* 127: 39–246.

Fuentes, Ximena. 1999. "Sustainable Development and the Equitable Utilization of International Watercourses." *British Yearbook of International Law* 69 (1): 119–200.

Funtowicz, Silvio.O., and J.R. Ravetz. 1999. "Information Tools for Environmental Policy under Conditions of Complexity." *Environmental Issues Series – European Environment Agency*, no. 9: 1–34.

Futhazar, Guillaume. 2021. "The Normative Nature of the Ecosystem Approach: A Mediterranean Case Study." *Transnational Environmental Law* 10 (1): 109–33.

Gerlak, Andrea K., Jonathan Lautze, and Mark Giordano. 2011. "Water Resources Data and Information Exchange in Transboundary Water Treaties." *International Environmental Agreements: Politics, Law and Economics* 11 (2): 179–99.

Hey, Ellen. 2000. "International Water Law Placed in a Contemporary Environmental Context: The Gabcikovo-Nagymaros Case." *Physics and Chemistry of the Earth, Part B: Hydrology, Oceans and Atmosphere* 25 (3): 303–8.

Hey, Ellen. 2012. "The Persistence of a Concept: Maximum Sustainable Yield." *International Journal of Marine and Coastal Law* 27 (4): 763–71.

Hoekman, Bernard, and Hugo Rojas-Romagosa. 2022. "EU Trade Sustainability Impact Assessments: Revisiting the Consultation Process." *Journal of International Economic Law* 25 (1): 45–60.

Izac, A. M.N., and P. A. Sanchez. 2001. "Towards a Natural Resource Management Paradigm for International Agriculture: The Example of Agroforestry Research." *Agricultural Systems* 69 (1–2): 5–25.

Jennings, R. Y. 1967. "General Course on Principles of International Law." *Collected Courses of the Hague Academy of International Law* 121 (II): 323–619.

Jensen, Kurt Mørck. 2013. "Viewpoint-Swimming against the Current: Questioning Development Policy and Practice." *Water Alternatives* 6 (2): 276–83.

Jong, Eileen de, and Marjanneke J. Vijge. 2021. "From Millennium to Sustainable Development Goals: Evolving Discourses and Their Reflection in Policy Coherence for Development." *Earth System Governance* 7 (100087): 1–12.

Karabulut, Armağan Aloe, Eleonora Crenna, Serenella Sala, and Angel Udias. 2017. "A Proposal for Integration of the Ecosystem-Water-Food-Land-Energy (EWFLE) Nexus Concept into Life Cycle Assessment: A Synthesis Matrix System for Food Security." *Journal of Cleaner Production* 172 (2018): 3874–89.

Kearns, Thomas R. 1972. "Open Texture and Judicial Law-Making." *Social Theory and Practice* 2 (2): 177–87.

Kim, Rakhyun E., and Brendan Mackey. 2014. "International Environmental Law as a Complex Adaptive System." *International Environmental Agreements: Politics, Law and Economics* 14 (1): 5–24.

Kirkpatrick, Colin, and Clive George. 2006. "Methodological Issues in the Impact Assessment of Trade Policy: Experience from the European Commission's Sustainability Impact Assessment (SIA) Programme." *Impact Assessment and Project Appraisal* 24 (4): 325–34.

Kivimaa, Paula, and Per Mickwitz. 2006. "The Challenge of Greening Technologies-Environmental Policy Integration in Finnish Technology Policies." *Research Policy* 35 (5): 729–44.

Lafferty, William M., and Eivind Hovden. 2003. "Environmental Policy Integration: Towards an Analytical Framework." *Environmental Politics* 12 (3): 1–22.

Lautze, Jonathan, Kai Wegerich, Jusipbek Kazbekov, and Murat Yakubov. 2013. "International River Basin Organizations: Variation, Options and Insights." *Water International* 38 (1): 30–42.

Leese, Matthias, and Simon Meisch. 2015. "Securitising Sustainability? Questioning the 'Water, Energy and Food-Security Nexus.'" *Water Alternatives* 8 (1): 695–709.

Lewald, Hans. 1929. "La Théorie Du Renvoi." *Collected Courses of the Hague Academy of International Law* 29: 515–620.

Lodhia, Sumit, Nigel Martin, and John Rice. 2018. "Appraising Offsets as a Tool for Integrated Environmental Planning and Management." *Journal of Cleaner Production* 178 (2018): 34–44.

Lostal, Marina. 2013. "The Role of Specific Discipline Principles in International Law: A Parallel Analysis between Environmental and Cultural Heritage Law." *Nordic Journal of International Law* 82 (3): 391–415.

Margerum, Richard D., and Stephen M. Born. 1995. "Integrated Environmental Management: Moving from Theory to Practice." *Journal of Environmental Planning and Management* 38 (3): 371–92.

Märker, Carolin, Sandra Venghaus, and Jürgen Friedrich Hake. 2018. "Integrated Governance for the Food – Energy – Water Nexus – The Scope of Action for Institutional Change." *Renewable and Sustainable Energy Reviews* 97 (2018): 290–300.

Marshall, Rachael E., and Khosrow Farahbakhsh. 2013. "Systems Approaches to Integrated Solid Waste Management in Developing Countries." *Waste Management* 33 (4): 988–1003.

McArthur, John W. 2014. "The Origins of the Millennium Development Goals." *SAIS Review of International Affairs* 34 (5): 5–24.

McGrane, Scott J., Michele Acuto, Francesca Artioli, Po-Yu Chen, Robert Comber, Julian Cottee, Geremy Farr-Wharton, et al. 2019. "Scaling the Nexus: Towards Integrated Frameworks for Analysing Water, Energy and Food." *The Geographical Journal* 185 (4): 419–31.

McIntyre, Owen. 2013. "Utilization of Shared International Freshwater Resources – the Meaning and Role of 'Equity' in International Water Law." *Water International* 38 (2): 112–29.

McIntyre, Owen. 2014. "The Protection of Freshwater Ecosystems Revisited: Towards a Common Understanding of the 'ecosystems Approach' to the Protection of Transboundary Water Resources." *Review of European, Comparative and International Environmental Law* 23 (1): 88–95.

Medema, Wietske, Brian S. McIntosh, and Paul J. Jeffrey. 2008. "From Premise to Practice: A Critical Assessment of Integrated Water Resources Management and Adaptive Management Approaches in the Water Sector." *Ecology and Society* 13 (2): 29.

Médici Colombo, Gastón. 2018. "El Acuerdo Escazú: La Implementación Del Principio 10 de Río En América Latina y El Caribe." *Revista Catalana de Dret Ambiental* IX (1): 1–66.

Meijerink, Sander, and Dave Huitema. 2017. "The Institutional Design, Politics, and Effects of a Bioregional Approach: Observations and Lessons from 11 Case Studies of River Basin Organizations." *Ecology and Society* 22 (2): 41.

Mendelson, Maurice H. 1998. "Formation of Customary International Law." *Collected Courses of the Hague Academy of International Law* 272: 155–410.

Milman, Anita, and Andrea K. Gerlak. 2020. "International River Basin Organizations, Science, and Hydrodiplomacy." *Environmental Science and Policy* 107 (2020): 137–49.

Monaco, Riccardo. 1968. "Cours Général de Droit International Public." *Collected Courses of the Hague Academy of International Law* 125 (III): 93–335.

Morgera, Elisa. 2005. "An Update on the Aarhus Convention and Its Continued Global Relevance." *Review of European Community and International Environmental Law* 14 (2): 138–47.

Movilla Pateiro, Laura. 2022. "La Progresiva Ecologización Del Derecho Internacional de Los Cursos de Agua. Manifestaciones Convencionales, Jurisprudenciales y Consuetudinarias." *Revista Catalana de Dret Ambiental* XIII (2): 1–42.

Mucklow, Fiona. 2000. "The Integration of Environmental Principles into the World Bank." *Review of European Community and International Environmental Law* 9 (2): 100–111.

Muradian, R., M. Arsel, L. Pellegrini, F. Adaman, B. Aguilar, B. Agarwal, E. Corbera, et al. 2013. "Payments for Ecosystem Services and the Fatal Attraction of Win-Win Solutions." *Conservation Letters* 6 (4): 274–79.

Newman, Edward. 2011. "A Human Security Peace-Building Agenda." *Third World Quarterly* 32 (10): 1737–56.

Nielson, Daniel L., and Michael J. Tieraey. 2003. "Delegation to International Organizations: Agency Theory and World Bank Environmental Reform." *International Organization* 57 (2): 241–76.

Oberthür, Sebastian. 2009. "Interplay Management: Enhancing Environmental Policy Integration among International Institutions." *International Environmental Agreements: Politics, Law and Economics* 9 (4): 371–91.

Olawuyi, Damilola. 2019. "Sustainable Development and the Water-Energy-Food Nexus: Legal Challenges and Emerging Solutions." *Environmental Science and Policy* 103 (2020): 1–9.

Pahl-Wostl, Claudia, Jan Sendzimir, Paul Jeffrey, Jeroen Aerts, Ger Berkamp, and Katharine Cross. 2007. "Managing Change toward Adaptive Water Management through Social Learning." *Ecology and Society* 12 (2): 30.

Pallemaerts, Marc. 1992. "International Environmental Law from Stockholm to Rio: Back to the Future?" *Review of European Community & International Environmental Law* 1 (3): 254–66.

Pascual, Unai, Jacob Phelps, Eneko Garmendia, Katrina Brown, Esteve Corbera, Adrian Martin, Erik Gomez-Baggethun, and Roldan Muradian. 2014. "Social Equity Matters in Payments for Ecosystem Services." *BioScience* 64 (11): 1027–36.

Peñalver i Cabré, Alexandre. 2014. "El Derecho Humano Al Medio Ambiente y Su Protección Efectiva." *Revista Vasca de Administración Pública / Herri-Arduralaritzarako Euskal Aldizkaria* 99–100 (Special Issue): 2333–57.

Peters, Anne. 2017. "The Refinement of International Law: From Fragmentation to Regime Interaction and Politicization." *International Journal of Constitutional Law* 15 (3): 671–704.

Prieur, Michel. 2022. "Revisión de Los Cincuenta Años Del Derecho Internacional Ambiental: La Definición de Los Principios." *Revista Catalana de Dret Ambiental* 13 (2): 1–10.

Rieu-Clarke, Alistair. 2014. "Notification and Consultation Procedures under the Mekong Agreement: Insights from the Xayaburi Controversy." *Asian Journal of International Law* 5 (1): 143–75.

Rodrigo Hernández, Ángel J. 1998. "La Aportación Del Asunto Gabcikovo-Nagymaros Al Derecho Internacional Del Medio Ambiente." *Anuario Español de Derecho Internacional* XIV (August): 769–807.

Rodrigo Hernández, Ángel J. 2012. "El Principio de Integración de Los Aspectos Económicos, Sociales y Medioambientales Del Desarrollo Sostenible." *Revista Española de Derecho Internacional* 64 (2): 133–61.

Roidt, Mario, and Tamara Avellán. 2019. "Learning from Integrated Management Approaches to Implement the Nexus." *Journal of Environmental Management* 237 (2019): 609–16.

Rowe, Gene, and Lynn J Frewer. 2000. "Public Participation Methods: A Framework for Evaluation." *Science, Technology, & Human Values* 25 (1): 3–29.

Rowe, Gene, and Lynn J. Frewer. 2004. "Evaluating Public-Participation Exercises: A Research Agenda." *Science, Technology, & Human Values* 29 (4): 512–57.

Šahović, Milan. 1972. "Codification Des Principes Du Droit International Des Relations Amicales et de La Coopération Entre Les Etats." *Collected Courses of the Hague Academy of International Law* 137: 243–310.

Salman, Salman M.A. 2010. "Downstream Riparians Can Also Harm Upstream Riparians: The Concept of Foreclosure of Future Uses." *Water International* 35 (4): 350–64.

Sands, Philippe. 1994. "International Law in the Field of Sustainable Development." *British Yearbook of International Law* 65 (1): 303–381.

Schmeier, Susanne. 2015. "The Institutional Design of River Basin Organizations – Empirical Findings from around the World." *International Journal of River Basin Management* 13 (1): 51–72.

Schoenbaum, Thomas J. 1992. "Free International Trade and Protection of the Environment: Irreconcilable Conflict?" *American Journal of International Law* 86 (4): 700–727.

Schrijver, N. J. 2007. "The Evolution of Sustainable Development." *Collected Courses of the Hague Academy of International Law* 329: 217–412.

Schultz, Lisen, Carl Folke, Henrik Österblom, and Per Olsson. 2015. "Adaptive Governance, Ecosystem Management, and Natural Capital." *Proceedings of the National Academy of Sciences* 112 (24): 7369–74.

Schulze, Sabine. 2012. "Public Participation in the Governance of Transboundary Water Resources? Mechanisms Provided by River Basin Organizations." *L'Europe En Formation* 3 (365): 49–68.

Schulze, Sabine, and Susanne Schmeier. 2012. "Governing Environmental Change in International River Basins: The Role of River Basin Organizations." *International Journal of River Basin Management* 10 (3): 229–44.

Scott, Karen N. 2011. "International Environmental: Managing Fragmentation Through Institutional Connection." *Melbourne Journal of International Law* 12: 177–216.

Sixt, Gregory N., Claudia Strambo, Jingjing Zhang, Nicholas Chow, Jie Liu, and Guoyi Han. 2020. "Assessing the Level of Inter-Sectoral Policy Integration for Governance in the Water-Energy Nexus: A Comparative Study of Los Angeles and Beijing." *Sustainability (Switzerland)* 12 (17): 1–19.

Sohn, Louis B. 1973. "Stockholm Declaration on the Human Environment." *Harvard International Law Journal* 14 (3): 422–515.

Spijkers, Otto. 2016. "The Cross-Fertilization between the Sustainable Development Goals and International Water Law." *Review of European, Comparative and International Environmental Law* 25 (1): 39–49.

Stafford-Smith, Mark, David Griggs, Owen Gaffney, Farooq Ullah, Belinda Reyers, Norichika Kanie, Bjorn Stigson, Paul Shrivastava, Melissa Leach, and Deborah O'Connell. 2017. "Integration: The Key to Implementing the Sustainable Development Goals." *Sustainability Science* 12 (6): 911–19.

Steele, J. 2001. "Participation and Deliberation in Environmental Law: Exploring a Problem-Solving Approach." *Oxford Journal of Legal Studies* 21 (3): 415–42.

Stefano, Lucia de, James Duncan, Shlomi Dinar, Kerstin Stahl, Kenneth M. Strzepek, and Aaron T. Wolf. 2012. "Climate Change and the Institutional Resilience of International River Basins." *Journal of Peace Research* 49 (1): 193–209.

Strasser, Lucia De, Annukka Lipponen, Mark Howells, Stephen Stec, and Christian Bréthaut. 2016. "A Methodology to Assess the Water Energy Food Ecosystems Nexus in Transboundary River Basins." *Water (Switzerland)* 8 (59): 1–28.

Sušnik, Janez, Chengzi Chew, Xavier Domingo, Simone Mereu, Antonio Trabucco, Barry Evans, Lydia Vamvakeridou-Lyroudia, Dragan A. Savić, Chrysi Laspidou, and Floor Brouwer. 2018. "Multi-Stakeholder Development of a Serious Game to Explore the Water-Energy-Food-Land-Climate Nexus: The SIM4NEXUS Approach." *Water (Switzerland)* 10 (139): 1–21.

Tignino, Mara. 2010. "Water, International Peace, and Security." *International Review of the Red Cross* 92 (879): 647–74.

Tignino, Mara. 2010. "Les Contours Du Principe de La Participation Publique et La Protection Des Ressources En Eau Transfrontières." *VertigO – La Revue Électronique En Sciences de l'environnement* 7: 1–11.

Timmerman, Jos G., and Sindre Langaas. 2005. "Water Information: What Is It Good for? The Use of Information in Transboundary Water Management." *Regional Environmental Change* 5 (4): 177–87.

Torres Cazorla, María Isabel. 2000. "Otra Vuelta de Tuerca Del Derecho Internacional Para Regular Los Cursos de Agua Internacionales: El Convenio de Helsinki de 17 de Marzo de 1992." *Anuario Español de Derecho Internacional* XVI: 225–62.

Trevisanut, Seline, and Nikolaos Giannopoulos. 2018. "Investment Protection in Offshore Energy Production: Bright Sides of Regime Interaction." *Journal of World Investment and Trade* 19 (5–6): 789–827.

Underdal, Arild. 1980. "Integrated Marine Policy. What? Why? How?" *Marine Policy* 4 (3): 159–69.

Utton, Albert E. 1996. "Which Rule Should Prevail in International Water Disputes: That of Reasonableness or That of No Harm?" *Natural Resources Journal* 36 (3): 635–41.

Viñuales, Jorge E. 2013. "The Rise and Fall of Sustainable Development." *Review of European, Comparative and International Environmental Law* 22 (1): 3–13.

Virally, Michel. 1983. "Cours Générale de Droit International Public." *Collected Courses of the Hague Academy of International Law* 183 (V): 9–382.

Virally, Michel. 1985. "La Distinction Entre Textes Internationaux de Portée Juridique et Textes Internationaux Dépourvus de Portée Juridique." *Yearbook of the Institute of International Law* 60 (I): 328–57.

Visscher, Paul De. 1972. "Cours Général de Droit International Public." *Collected Courses of the Hague Academy of International Law* 136: 7–202.

Weitz, Nina, Måns Nilsson, and Marion Davis. 2014. "A Nexus Approach to the Post-2015 Agenda: Formulating Integrated Water, Energy, and Food SDGs." *SAIS Review of International Affairs* 34 (2): 37–50.

Weitz, Nina, Claudia Strambo, Eric Kemp-Benedict, and Måns Nilsson. 2017. "Closing the Governance Gaps in the Water-Energy-Food Nexus: Insights from Integrative Governance." *Global Environmental Change* 45 (2017): 165–73.

White, Gilbert F. 1998. "Reflections on the 50-Year International Search for Integrated Water Management." *Water Policy* 1 (1): 21–27.

Wiegleb, Viviana, and Antje Bruns. 2018. "What Is Driving the Water-Energy-Food Nexus? Discourses, Knowledge, and Politics of an Emerging Resource Governance Concept." *Frontiers in Environmental Science* 6 (128): 1–15.

Williams, Byron K. 2011. "Adaptive Management of Natural Resources-Framework and Issues." *Journal of Environmental Management* 92 (5): 1346–53.

Wolf, Francis. 1967. "L'interdépendence Des Conventions Internationales Du Travail." *Collected Courses of the Hague Academy of International Law* 121 (II): 2–217.

Wouters, Patricia K., and Alistair S. Rieu-Clarke. 2001. "The Role of International Water Law in Promoting Sustainable Development." *Journal of Water Law* 12 (5): 281–83.

Conference Proceedings

Bauer, A., and E. Rametsteiner. 2007. "Policy Integration and Co-Ordination: Theoretical, Methodical and Conceptual Aspects." In *Proceeding of the 1st COST Action E51 Joint MC and WG Meeting*, edited by Ewald Rametsteiner, 31–48. Vienna: University of Natural Resources and Applied Life Sciences.

Briassoulis, Helen. 2004. "Policy Integration for Complex Policy Problems: What, Why and How." In *Berlin Conference on the Human Dimensions of Global Environmental Change: Greening Greening of Policies – Interlinkages and Policy Integration*, 1–30. Berlin.

Meijers, Evert, and Dominic Stead. 2004. "Policy Integration: What Does It Mean and How Can It Be Achieved? A Multi-Disciplinary Review." In *Berlin Conference on the Human Dimensions of Global Environment Change: Greening of Policies – Interlinkages and Policy Integration, Berlin*, 1–15. Berlin.

Doctoral Theses

Elizalde Carranza, Miguel Ángel. 2006. "Las Medidas Comerciales Multilaterales Para La Protección Del Medio Ambiente y El Sistema Multilateral Del Comercio." Universitat Pompeu Fabra.

Schellekens-Gaiffe, Marie-Ange. 2017. "La Sécurité Environnementale Dans Les Relations Extérieures de l'Union Européenne." Université La Rochelle.

Treaties

International Basin Agreements

Treaty relating to the boundary waters and questions arising along the boundary between the United States and Canada, United States of America-Canada, January 11, 1909, 36 U.S.T. 2448.

Convention regarding the regime of navigation on the Danube, August 18, 1948, 33 U.N.T.S. 181.

Statute of the Committee for Co-ordination of Investigations of the Lower Mekong Basin, October 31, 1957, 12 U.N.L.S. 267.

Convention and Statutes Relating to the Development of the Chad Basin, May 22, 1964, LEX-FAOC001076.

Agreement concerning the Niger River Commission and the navigation and transport on the River Niger, November 25, 1964, 587 U.N.T.S. 19.

El Tratado de la Cuenca del Plata [Treaty on the Rio de la Plata Basin], April 23, 1969, ECOLEX TRE-001020.

Convention relative au Statut du fleuve Sénégal [Convention relating to the statute of the Senegal river], March 11, 1972, LEX-FAOC016004.

Convention creating organization for the development of the Senegal River, May 11, 1972, LEX-FAOC091150.

Statutes of the River Uruguay, February 26, 1975, 1295 U.N.T.S. 331.

Treaty for Amazonian Cooperation, July 3, 1978, ECOLEX TRE-000515.

Convention on Cooperation for the Protection and Sustainable use of the Danube River, June 29, 1994, 342 O.J. 19.

Agreement between the Government of Ukraine and the Government of Moldova on joint boundary waters management and protection, November 23, 1994, LEX-FAOC065455.

Acuerdo Constitutivo de la Comisión Trinacional para el Desarrollo de la Cuenca del Rio Pilcomayo [Agreement constituting the National Commission for the Development of the Riverbed Rio Pilcomayo], February 9, 1995, ECOLEX TRE-001235.

Agreement on the Cooperation for the Sustainable Development of the Mekong River Basin, April 5, 1995, 2069 U.N.T.S. 3.

Agreement between the Governments of Angola, the Republic of Botswana and the Republic of Namibia on the establishment of a Permanent Okavango River Basin Water Commission (OKACOM), September 15, 1995, LEX-FAOC017435.

Convention on the Protection of the Rhine, April 12, 1999, 289 O.J. 31.

Revised Protocol on Shared Watercourses in the Southern African Development Community (SADC), August 7, 2000, 3370 U.N.T.S.

Charte des eaux du fleuve Sénégal [Charter of Waters of the Senegal River], May 28, 2002, ECOLEX TRE-153511.

Framework Agreement on the Sava River Basin, December 3, 2002, 2366 U.N.T.S. 479.

Agreement on the establishment of the Zambezi Watercourse Commission, July 13, 2004, 3369 U.N.T.S.

Convention portant Statut du fleuve Volta et création de l'Autorité du Bassin de la Volta [Convention establishing the Volta River Statute and the Volta Basin Authority], January 19, 2007, LEX-FAOC180705.

Statuts de l'Autorité du Bassin de la Volta [Statutes of the Volta Basin Authority], November 16, 2007, FAOLEX LEX-FAOC180706.

La Charte de l'Eau du Bassin du Niger [The Niger Basin Water Charter], August 23, 2008, ECOLEX TRE-146761.

Water Charter of the Lake Chad Basin, January 1, 2011, FAOLEX LEX-FAOC203691.

Protocol amending the Agreement between Canada and the United States of America on Great Lakes water quality, 1978 as amended on October 16, 1983 and November 18, 1987, June 7, 2012, 3125 U.N.T.S.

Treaty between the Government of the Republic of Moldova and the Cabinet of Ministers of Ukraine on Cooperation in the Field of Protection and Sustainable Development of the Dniester River Basin, Moldova-Ukraine, November 29, 2012, ECOLEX TRE-160050.

Global Treaties

United Nations, Statute of the International Court of Justice, October 24, 1945, N/A. U.N.T.S.

Articles of Agreement of the International Monetary Fund, December 27, 1945, 2 U.N.T.S. 39.

General Agreement on Tariffs and Trade, October 30, 1947, 64 U.N.T.S. 187.

Vienna Convention on the Law of the Treaties, May 23, 1969, 1155 U.N.T.S. 331.

Convention on wetlands of international importance especially as waterfowl habitat, February 2, 1971, 996 U.N.T.S. 245.

Convention for the protection of the world cultural and natural heritage, November 16, 1972, 1037 U.N.T.S. 151.

Convention on International Trade in Endangered Species of Wild Fauna and Flora, March 3, 1973, 993 U.N.T.S. 243.

Protocol additional to the Geneva Conventions of 12 August 1949, and relating to the Protection of Victims of International Armed Conflicts (Protocol I), June 8, 1977, 1125 U.N.T.S. 3.

Protocol of 1978 relating to the International Convention for the prevention of pollution from ships, February 17, 1978, 1340, 1341 U.N.T.S. 61, 3.

Convention on Long-range Transboundary Air Pollution, November 13, 1979, 1302 U.N.T.S. 217.

Convention on the Conservation of Migratory Species of Wild Animals, June 23, 1979, 1651 U.N.T.S.

United Nations Convention on the Law of the Sea, December 10, 1982, 1833 U.N.T.S. 3.

Montreal Protocol on Substances that Deplete the Ozone Layer, September 16, 1987, 1522 U.N.T.S. 3.

Basel Convention on the Control of Transboundary Movements of Hazardous Wastes and their Disposal, March 22, 1989, 1673 U.N.T.S. 57.

Convention on the Protection and Use of Transboundary Watercourses and International Lakes, March 17, 1992, 1936 U.N.T.S. 269.

United Nations Framework Convention on Climate Change, May 9, 1992, 1771 U.N.T.S. 107.

Convention on Biological Diversity, June 5, 1992, 1760 U.N.T.S. 79.

United Nations Convention to Combat Desertification in those Countries Experiencing Serious Drought and/or Desertification, Particularly in Africa, October 14, 1994, 1954 U.N.T.S. 3.

Agreement establishing the World Trade Organization, April 15, 1995, 1867 U.N.T.S.

Agreement for the Implementation of the Provisions of the United Nations Convention on the Law of the Sea of 10 December 1982 relating to the Conservation and Management of Straddling Fish Stocks and Highly Migratory Fish Stocks, December 4, 1995, 2167 U.N.T.S. 3.

Convention on the Law of the Non-Navigational Uses of International Watercourses, May 21, 1997, 2999 U.N.T.S.

Kyoto Protocol to the United Nations Framework Convention on Climate Change, December 11, 1997, 2303 U.N.T.S. 162.

Rotterdam Convention on the Prior Informed Consent Procedure for Certain Hazardous Chemicals and Pesticides in International Trade, September 10, 1998, 2244 U.N.T.S. 337.

Stockholm Convention on Persistent Organic Pollutants, May 22, 2001, 2256 U.N.T.S. 119.

Nagoya Protocol on Access to Genetic Resources and the Fair and Equitable Sharing of Benefits Arising from their Utilization to the Convention on Biological Diversity, October 29, 2010, 3008 U.N.T.S.

Paris Agreement, December 15, 2015, 3156 U.N.T.S.

Agreement under the United Nations Convention on the Law of the Sea on the Conservation and Sustainable Use of Marine Biological Diversity of Areas beyond National Jurisdiction, June 19, 2023, N/A U.N.T.S.

Regional Treaties

Convention for the protection of the Mediterranean Sea against pollution (with annex and Protocols for the prevention of pollution of the Mediterranean Sea by dumping from ships and aircraft and Protocol concerning co-operation in combating pollution of the Mediterranean Sea by oil and other harmful substances in cases of emergency), February 16, 1976, 1102 U.N.T.S. 27.

Kuwait Regional Convention for co-operation on the protection of the marine environment from pollution, April 24, 1978, 1140 U.N.T.S. 133.

ASEAN Agreement on the Conservation of Nature and Natural Resources, July 9, 1985, 67 ASEAN Legal Instruments.

Single European Act, February 17, 1986, O.J. (L 169) 1, 28.

Convention on Environmental Impact Assessment in a Transboundary Context, February 25, 1991, 1989 U.N.T.S. 309.

Bamako Convention on the Ban of the Import into Africa and the Control of Transboundary Movement and Management of Hazardous Wastes within Africa, January 30, 1991, 2101 U.N.T.S. 177.

Convention on the Transboundary Effects of Industrial Accidents, March 17, 1992, 2105 U.N.T.S. 457.

Convention on the Protection of the Black Sea Against Pollution, April 21, 1992, 1764 U.N.T.S.

Convention for the Protection of the Marine Environment and the Coastal Region of the Mediterranean, February 16, 1995, 1102 U.N.T.S. 27.

Protocol concerning Specially Protected Areas and Biological Diversity in the Mediterranean, June 10, 1995, 2102 U.N.T.S. 181.

Convention on Access to Information, Public Participation in Decision-Making and Access to Justice in Environmental Matters, June 25, 1998, 2161 U.N.T.S. 447.

Protocol on Water and Health to the 1992 Convention on the Protection and Use of Transboundary Watercourses and international Lakes, June 17, 1999, 2331 U.N.T.S. 202.

Protocol on Strategic Environmental Assessment to the Convention on Environmental Impact Assessment in a Transboundary Context, May 21, 2003, 2685 U.N.T.S. 140.

Amendments to Articles 25 and 26 of the Convention on the Protection and Use of Transboundary Watercourses and International Lakes, November 28, 2003, 2897 U.N.T.S.

Protocol on Integrated Coastal Zone Management (ICZM) in the Mediterranean, January 21, 2008, 2742 U.N.T.S.

Consolidated Version of the Treaty on the Functioning of the European Union, May 9, 2008, 2008 O.J. (C 115) 47.

Regional Agreement on Access to Information, Public Participation and Justice in Environmental Matters in Latin America and the Caribbean, March 4, 2018, 3397 U.N.T.S.

Case Law

International Court of Justice

Corfu Channel case (United Kingdom v. Albania), Judgment, 1949 I.C.J. Rep. 4 (April 9).

North Sea Continental Shelf (Federal Republic of Germany/Denmark; Federal Republic of Germany/Netherlands), Judgment, 1969 I.C.J. Rep. 3 (February 20).

Fisheries Jurisdiction (United Kingdom v. Iceland), Judgment, 1974 I.C.J. Rep. 3 (25 July).

Military and Paramilitary Activities in and against Nicaragua (Nicaragua v. United States of America), Judgment, 1986 I.C.J. Rep. 14 (June 27).

Legality of the Threat or Use of Nuclear Weapons, Advisory Opinion, 1996 I.C.J. Rep. 226.

Gabčikovo-Nagymaros Project (Hungary/Slovakia), Judgment, 1997 I.C.J. Rep. 7 (September 25).

Gabčikovo-Nagymaros Project (Hungary/Slovakia), Judgment, 1997 I.C.J. Rep. 7 (September 25) (Weeramantry, C.G., separate opinion).

Gabčikovo-Nagymaros Project (Hungary/Slovakia), Judgment, 1997 I.C.J. Rep. 7 (September 25) (Bedjaoui, M., separate opinion).

Land and Maritime Boundary between Cameroon and Nigeria (Cameroon v. Nigeria), Preliminary Objections, Judgement, 1998 I.C.J. Rep. 275 (June 11).

Pulp Mills on the River Uruguay (Argentina v. Uruguay), 2010 Judgment, I.C.J. Rep. 14 (April 20).

Pulp Mills on the River Uruguay (Argentina v. Uruguay), 2010 Judgment, I.C.J. Rep. 14 (April 20) (Vinuesa, R., dissenting opinion).

Pulp Mills on the River Uruguay (Argentina v. Uruguay), 2010 Judgment, I.C.J. Rep. 14 (April 20) (Al-Khasawneh, A.S. and Simma, B., joint dissenting opinion).

Certain Activities Carried Out by Nicaragua in the Border Area (Costa Rica v. Nicaragua) and Construction of a Road in Costa Rica along the San Juan River (Nicaragua v. Costa Rica), Judgment, 2015 I.C.J. Rep. 665 (December 15).

Dispute over the status and use of the waters of the Silala (Chile v. Bolivia), Judgement, 2022 I.C.J. Rep. 614 (December 1).

International Tribunal for the Law of the Sea

Request for Advisory Opinion (Sub-Regional Fisheries Commission), Case No. 21, Advisory Opinion of April 2, 2015, 19 ITLOS Rep. 4.

World Trade Organisation Appellate Body

Appellate Body Report, *United States – Import Prohibition of Certain Shrimp and Shrimp Products*, WTO Doc. WT/DS58/AB/R (adopted October 12, 1998).

Court of Justice of the European Communities

Case 41/74, Yvonne van Duyn v. Home Office, 1974 E.C.R. 133.

Inter-State Arbitration

Trail smelter case (United States/Canada), 3 R.I.A.A (Perm. Ct. Arb. 1941).
Lac Lanoux (Espagne/France), 12 R.I.A.A (Perm. Ct. Arb. 1957).
Arbitration Regarding the Iron Rhine ("Ijzeren Rijn") Railway (Belgium/Netherlands), 27 R.I.A.A (Perm. Ct. Arb. 2005).
Indus Waters Kishenganga Arbitration (Pakistan vs. India). Final award, 31 R.I.A.A (Perm. Ct. Arb. 2013).
The South China Sea Arbitration (The Republic of Philippines v. The People's Republic of China). Final award, 33 R.I.A.A (Perm. Ct. Arb. 2016).

Index

www.ingramcontent.com/pod-product-compliance
Lightning Source LLC
Chambersburg PA
CBHW071248230926
51849CB00001B/271
* 9 7 8 9 0 0 4 7 3 6 7 4 0 *